CHICAGO STUDIES IN THE
HISTORY OF AMERICAN RELIGION

Editors

JERALD C. BRAUER

AND MARTIN E. MARTY

A CARLSON PUBLISHING SERIES

For a complete listing of the titles in this series,
please see the back of this book.

Souls or the Social Order

THE TWO-PARTY SYSTEM
IN AMERICAN PROTESTANTISM

Jean Miller Schmidt

PREFACE BY MARTIN E. MARTY

CARLSON
Publishing Inc

BROOKLYN, NEW YORK, 1991

Please see the end of this volume for a listing of all the titles in the Carlson Publishing Series *Chicago Studies in the History of American Religion*, edited by Jerald C. Brauer and Martin E. Marty, of which this is Volume 18.

Library of Congress Cataloging-in-Publication Data

Schmidt, Jean Miller.
    Souls or the social order : the two-party system in American
Protestantism / Jean Miller Schmidt ; preface by Martin E. Marty.
        p. cm. — (Chicago studies in the history of American
religion ; 18)
    Includes bibliographical references and index.
    ISBN 0-926019-54-6 (alk. paper)
    1. Protestant churches—United States—History—19th century.
2. United States—Church history—19th century. 3. Fundamentalism-
-History of doctrines—19th century. 4. Social gospel—History of
doctrines—19th century. 5. Federal Council of the Churches of
Christ in America. 6. Church controversies—History—19th century.
I. Title. II. Series.
BR525.S334 1991
280'.4'0973—dc20   91-26848

Typographic design: Julian Waters

Typeface: Bitstream ITC Galliard

Case design: Alison Lew

Index prepared by Scholars Editorial Services, Inc., Madison, Wisconsin, using NL Cindex, a scholarly indexing program from the Newberry Library.

Printed on acid-free, 250-year-life paper.

Manufactured in the United States of America.

Contents

Part One
Reforming the Nation by Reforming the Individual

Part Two
Christianizing the Social Order

Part Three
Two Types of Christianity: The Individualistic and the Social

An Introduction
to the Series

The *Chicago Studies in the History of American Religion* is a series of books that deal with topics ranging from the time of Jonathan Edwards to the 1970s. Three or four deal with colonial topics and three or four treat the very recent past. About half of them focus on the decades just before and after 1900. One deals with blacks; two concentrate on women. Revivalists, fundamentalists, theologians, life in the suburbs and life in heaven and hell, the Beecher family of old and a monk of new times, Catholics adapting to America and Protestants fighting one another—all these subjects assure that the series has scope. People of every kind of taste and curiosity about American religion will find some books to suit them. Does anything serve to characterize the series as a whole? What does the stamp of "Chicago studies" mean?

Yale historian Sydney Ahlstrom in *A Religious History of the American People*, as influential as any twentieth-century work in its field, pays respect to the "Chicago School" of American religious historians. William Warren Sweet, the pioneer in such studies (beginning in 1927) at Chicago and, in many ways, in America at large represented the culmination of "the Protestant synthesis" in this field. Ahlstrom went on to name two later generations of Chicagoans, including the seminal Sidney E. Mead and major figures like Robert T. Handy and Winthrop Hudson and ending with the two editors of this series. He saw them as often "openly rebellious" in respect to Sweet and his synthesis.

If, as Ahlstrom says, "a disproportionate number" of historians have some connection with the Chicago School, it must be said that the new generation represented in these twenty-one books carries on both the lineage of Sweet and something of the "openly rebellious" character that scholars at Chicago are encouraged to pursue. This means, for one thing, that the "Protestant synthesis" does not characterize their work. These historians question the canon of historical writing produced in the Protestant era even as many of them continue to pursue themes shaped in a Protestant culture. Few of them concentrate on the old "frontier thesis" that marked the early years of the school. The shift for most has been toward the urban and pluralist scene. They call into question, not in devastating rage but in steady patterns of inquiry, the received wisdom about who matters, and why, in American religion.

So it is that this series of books focuses on blacks, women, dispensationalists, suburbanites, members of "marginal" denominations, "ethnics" and immigrants as readily as it does on white men of progressive urban bent in mainstream denominations and of long standing in America. The authors relish religious diversity and enjoy discovering the power of people once considered weak, the centrality to the American plot of those once regarded as peripheral, and the potency of losers who were once disdained by winners. Thus this series enhances an understanding of an America overlooked by the people of Sweet's era two-thirds of a century ago when it all, or most of it, began.

Rebellion for its own sake would not long hold interest; it might tell more about the psychology of rebels and revisers than about their subject matter. Revision, better than rebellion, characterizes the scholars. Re+vision: that's it. There was an original vision that characterized the Chicago School. This was the contention that in secular America and its universities religion mattered, as a theme in the national past and as a presence in the present. Second, it argued that the study of religious history belonged not only in the seminaries and archives of denominations, but also in the rough-and-tumble of the secular university, where no religious meanings were privileged and where each historian had to make a case for the value of his or her story.

Other assumptions from the earliest days pervade the books in this series. They are uncommonly alert to the environment in which expressions of faith occur. That is, they do not take for granted that religion comes protected in self-evidently important and hermetically sealed packages. Churches and denominations are porous, even when they would be sealed off; they cannot be understood apart from the ways the social environs effect them, but their power to effect change in the environment demands equal and truly unapologetic treatment. These writers do not shuffle and mumble and make excuses for their existence or for the choice of apparently arcane subject matter. They try to present their narrative in such ways that they compel attention.

A fourth characteristic that colors these works is a refusal in most cases to be typed in a fashionable slot labeled, variously, "intellectual" or "institutional" history, "cultural" or "social" history, or whatever. While those which concentrate on magisterial thinkers such as Jonathan Edwards are necessarily busy with and devoted to his intellectual achievement, most of the books deal with figures who cannot be understood only as exemplars in a sequence of studies of "the life of the mind." Instead, their biographies and circumstances come very much into play. On the other hand, none of these writers is a reductionist who sees religion as "nothing but" this or that—"nothing but" the working out of believers' Oedipal urges or expressing the economic and class interests of the subjects. Social history becomes in its way intellectual history, even if the intellects are focused on something other than the theologians in the traditions might like to see.

Some years ago *Look* magazine interviewed leaders in various denominations. One was asked if his fellow believers considered that theirs was the only true faith. Yes, he said, but they did not believe that they were the only ones who held it. The editors of this series of studies and the contributors to it do not believe that the "Chicago School," whenever and whatever it was, is the only true approach to American religious history. And, if they did, they would not hold that Chicagoans alone held it. To do so would imply a strange solipsistic or narcissistic impulse that would be the death of collegiality in the historical field. They have welcomed the chance to be in a climate where their inquiries are given such encouragement, where they find a company of fellow scholars in the Divinity School, the History Department, and the Committee on the History of Culture, whence these studies first emerged, and elsewhere in a university that provides a congenial home for massed and massive concentration of a special sort on American religious history.

While the undersigned have been consistently involved, most often together, in all twenty-one books, we want to single out a third person mentioned in so many acknowledgment sections, historian Arthur Mann. He has been a partner in two or three dozen religious history dissertation projects through the years and has been an influential and decisive contributor to the results. We stand in his debt.

Jerald C. Brauer
Martin E. Marty

Editor's Preface

Unfortunately for Protestantism but perhaps fortunately for the country as a whole, the majority religious *Gestalt* of America has for the better part of a century been divided by a profound schism. On the one hand are the moderate-to-liberal churches and forces that make up the "mainstream" or "mainline" counterparts to mainstream Catholicism and Judaism. These are believers who are quite ready to make adaptations and concessions to the presence of each other, other religions, and many kinds of secularists. On the other is that cluster of forces code-named variously "fundamentalist," "conservative," "pentecostal," and, most important, "evangelical," who are thoroughly at home in the modern world but are suspicious of versions of Christianity or religion other than their own. They draw sharper boundaries, build thicker walls, and create greater distances between their meaning-systems or patterns of action and all others.

Jean Miller Schmidt documents, as no previous historian has with such consistency, how that split between these two camps developed. As late as 1858, during a revival, there seemed to be only "evangelical" Protestantism. It was, of course, denominationally divided and there were significant internal differences to keep editors of theological journals and passers of pamphlets busy. But with the spinning off of Unitarians and Universalists into their separate camps, most others were content to be thought of as "evangelical," which meant Protestant, concerned with evangelizing others in the name of the Christian evangel, ready to talk about personal experience, and eager to reshape society, chiefly by reforming individuals and sending them forth as citizens.

Then something happened. Modernity came along, with its corrosive and erosive as well as alluring forces. One party greeted the changes as inevitable, demanding interpretation and adaptation. It would make sense of evolution as "God's way of doing things," biblical criticism as a new opening on God's word in a scientific age, and the city and industry, the factory and corporate life, as arenas for new challenge to bearers of the evangel or Gospel. The other party greeted the changes as partly unnecessary assaults on a world that was being lost, a world Protestants had run and should continue to dominate. Evolution undercut the Bible and morality; biblical criticism was the devil's instrument. The new human city was beguiling but often demonic, and demanded rejection. Believers should remain unspotted by the world, uncompromising. They could serve it best by "saving souls," to use the term Schmidt prefers; they would rescue people from the world.

Both parties had humane individuals in them. The second party thought that one met society's ills and problems by transforming individuals and calling them to serve. The first party, the social Christians or Social Gospellers, did not disdain the role of the individual. But they believed that the structures of society themselves were in need of redemption and that people who professed and worked for the coming Kingdom of God could make the difference.

By 1912 a split had taken place. In that year, the Federal Council of Churches, formed in 1908 as the product of and organ for united social action of the churches, had to yield to conservative pressure and create a Commission on Evangelism to balance its Commission on the Church and Social Service, thus institutionalizing the split. How to get a handle on this complicated story? Schmidt has found an effective and ingenious way: she concentrates on the polemics, the rhetoric of anger and dismissal used by both parties. By patiently listening and registering what each said about the other she helps deduce what they meant by way of self-understanding.

It goes without saying that the outcome of this struggle is relevant to contemporary social thought, politics, and day-to-day existence. How Americans vote on issues like abortion, nuclear weapons, saluting the flag, prayer in schools, and other priorities is determined in no small measure by the way these Protestant parties line up. Schmidt's is a revealing and even exciting story of how they first lined each other up, getting them into their figurative gunsights, to start a spiritual warfare about the temporal order, a set of battles that continue without much abatement today.

Martin E. Marty

Acknowledgments

It is a privilege to be able to acknowledge indebtedness not only at the completion of the dissertation process, but in retrospect, after more than twenty years.

In 1969, I thanked dissertation adviser, Martin E. Marty, for his wealth of ideas, his unfailing interest, and his consistent thoughtfulness. I still thank him for these. I admire his willingness to leave monographic works to others while boldly aiming to describe and interpret the larger picture. My own work has attempted to do the same.

The contributions made by Arthur Mann and former Divinity School Dean Jerald C. Brauer to my doctoral studies were of enduring value. I remain grateful to them for their own scholarly example as well as interest in and support of me.

Since becoming a faculty member at the Iliff School of Theology in 1975, I have incurred new debts: to Presidents S. Jameson Jones and Donald E. Messer; Deans H. Edward Everding, Delwin Brown, and especially Jane I. Smith; and to both faculty and students with whom I have worked over the years.

My own scholarly and personal commitments have been shaped particularly by colleagues in the doctoral area of Religion and Social Change. Vincent Harding and Will Gravely helped me see American religious history with new eyes. Together they have taught me more than they realize about the histories of the black freedom struggle, the black church, abolitionism, and southern religion and culture. Will Gravely probably understands my work best. I thank him for his generosity and commitment to my growth as a scholar; having him here has been one of the joys of my being in Denver.

My husband Stephen, although neither a historian nor an academic but a film maker, understands and respects the creative process and is the best story teller I know. Without his encouragement I might have despaired of finishing this project. He and my stepchildren Erik and Jennifer have immeasurably complicated and enriched my life since 1972. They will rejoice in the publication of this book.

A final word of thanks goes to Ralph Carlson, of Carlson Publishing, for his patience and helpfulness in bringing this work to completion.

Since I wrote Acknowledgments in 1969, three of the people I thanked then, my parents and friend Tom Green, have died. From Iliff, Jameson Jones and beloved colleague Barbara Hargrove are also gone. This book is dedicated to their memory.

Introduction: A Twenty Years' Retrospective

In coming back to this dissertation twenty years later, I was tempted to think of rewriting parts of it. With Ralph Carlson's encouragement, I have managed to resist that temptation. I have abbreviated some of the longer quotations, tried as unobtrusively as possible to use inclusive language, and updated the most pertinent literature in the notes. In other words, I have tried to make the original dissertation more useful to the contemporary reader without changing its basic nature. It remains a dissertation published twenty years after it was written, and in that sense in itself a historical document. For this reason I have also included the original Introduction.

This Introduction, however, is entirely new. In the genre of the *Christian Century*'s ongoing series, "How My Mind Has Changed/Remained the Same," it attempts to do three things: 1) to talk about the gaps in the original dissertation; that is, with the wisdom of hindsight and the perspective of twenty years of my own scholarly, as well as larger religious and cultural, developments, how would I now approach the same topic, 2) to review both the literature and developments of the last twenty years on the issue, and 3) to say how my mind has remained the same; what in the original dissertation has stood the test of time, and what would I now conclude about these matters?

When the Invisible Becomes Visible: How My Mind Has Changed

I have been interested in evangelical/liberal tensions since college days when, as a Religion major, I wrote a paper on the Fundamentalist movement and an honors thesis on the rise and development of the Pentecostal movement. Like many other graduate students in the late 1960s, I found it necessary to justify to myself the luxury of the academic enterprise in such turbulent times by writing a "relevant" dissertation. Concerned by the painful and often bitter division in those years between social activist and conservative evangelical Christians, I tried to discover how two parties that obviously laid claim to the same mid-nineteenth-century evangelical Protestant tradition could have arrived at such different convictions about the appropriate role of the church in relation to society. Because my research indicated that the same evangelical Protestants were likely to be involved in saving souls *and* social reform in the 1830s to 1850s, I surveyed the period from 1857 to the 1920s in order to discover how and why a split of such consequence had occurred.

It was a strange and frankly embarrassing experience for me to reread my dissertation twenty years after its original writing. I was struck by the northern, white, almost male tone to the original work, and appalled by my blindness with regard to blacks, women, and even my own Methodist tradition. In part, of course, this points to the excitement of the historical enterprise in the last twenty years: the hearing of new voices, the quality of personal and social experience, the impact of social historical studies on the way historians now interpret the American past. It has been an incredible time to be a historian, and I can mark off for myself the distance we have come by the gaps between my original dissertation and the way I now see the past. In Anne Firor Scott's words, things previously invisible have come to be visible, and nothing remains the same![1]

When I came to Iliff in 1975, I was often asked to speak on evangelical versus social Christianity. The first of these lectures was part of a Colorado Endowment for the Humanities Bicentennial Lecture Series on Religion in America; I entitled it "The Rift in the Righteous Empire: Liberals versus Evangelicals in American Protestantism." Several years later my colleague in Religious Studies at the University of Denver, Will Gravely, got me intrigued with the possibilities of religion and modernization as an interpretive framework for historians. We taught a Lilly Foundation seminar for college history professors on the subject, and I found it suggestive and useful for further reflection on the relation between one's private faith and the public order. Also helpful were courses team-taught in the late 1970s on American Civil Religion and on Faith and Ethics in Religious Biography.

Most important for my maturing historical perspective was the launching in 1981 of a Joint Doctoral Program in Religious and Theological Studies by the Iliff School of Theology and the University of Denver. I became a core faculty member of one of the four areas of that program, American Religion and

Culture (later to become Religion and Social Change). Other core faculty members of this interdisciplinary area were American historians Will Gravely and Vincent Harding (fellow Chicago graduate who came to Iliff in 1981 as Professor of Religion and Social Transformation), sociologist of religion Barbara Hargrove, and ethicist Dana Wilbanks. One of the course requirements for Ph.D. students was participation in the doctoral colloquium offered annually by the area faculty. In 1982 we decided that each of the faculty would take a session to present his or her most important scholarly work, and accordingly I talked about my dissertation and my current thinking about it.

Vincent Harding's response was typically appreciative but critical. In his gentle but probing way, he asked how I could write a dissertation about a split in American Protestantism and omit *black* Protestants, in whose church experience the evangelical and the social were not separate. He suggested that my research agenda (or at least my vision) ought to include the experience of free folk who were black, the black churches trying to change social structures from Reconstruction on, and the social gospel in the black church. He and Barbara Hargrove also pushed me to think about both race and gender in relation to the theoretical paradigm of modernization. In the last chapter of my dissertation I had referred to Billy Graham and Martin Luther King, Jr. as examples of the deep division in Protestantism in the 1960s. Yet I never made the connection between King and the black church experience that should have forced me to explore black religious history in light of my question. Needless to say, the colloquium experience was one of those painful but grace-filled dislocations.[2]

I gradually came to a new awareness of women and religion and an increased knowledge of Methodist history as a result of my own teaching, research, and professional involvements in the 1980s. Moreover, the fields themselves of women's history and Methodist history matured significantly in these same years. Since the field of women's history as we know it was only in its infancy in the latter years of the 1960s, scholars trained when I was have largely had to educate themselves in this field.[3] My efforts in this regard were stimulated by the national women's history project launched by the United Methodist Church following its 1976 General Conference. In February 1980, I attended the groundbreaking Women in New Worlds Conference on the history of women in the United Methodist tradition, and subsequently became involved with the work of successive project coordinators Hilah F. Thomas, Carolyn DeSwarte Gifford, and later, Susan Eltscher.

All of this became focused in an important way for me in 1983, when I was invited to give one of the keynote addresses at the Methodist Bicentennial Historical Consultation at Drew University that spring. I spent a two-quarter sabbatical leave from Iliff preparing for that lecture, "Reforming the Continent and Spreading Scriptural Holiness: Reexamining the Public/Private Split."[4] I read widely not only in Methodist history and women's history, but also with specific attention to Methodist involvement in movements for social reform, especially abolitionism and the social gospel. I also used the occasion as an opportunity to review over a decade of literature and developments with regard to the public/private split, including the possibilities of modernization as an interpretive framework.

From both reading and ongoing conversations with Will Gravely, I sharpened my knowledge of the unsuccessful Methodist struggle to establish an antislavery norm; of Bishop Gilbert Haven, Methodism's outstanding nineteenth-century opponent of "caste" (racism) in all its forms;[5] of the rise of independent black Methodist churches; of abolitionism, of things southern, and of the foremost social gospel leader of the African Methodist Episcopal Church, Bishop Reverdy Ransom.[6] As part of the preparation, I also explored in depth the whole area of Wesleyan and Methodist teaching on holiness and perfection and its relation to social concern.[7]

Since 1969, then, both my knowledge and my perspective have been enormously enriched and significantly changed by these and related developments. Let me try to illustrate what a difference that makes when I return to my dissertation twenty years later.

There was at Chicago when I was there (perhaps as a legacy from the years when William Warren Sweet envisioned American religion as fundamentally Methodist in style and shape) a strong inclination to steer clear of denominational history, thereby avoiding its attendant dangers of parochialism and triumphalism. Curiously therefore I paid little attention in my dissertation to the Methodists, concentrating on those who were first to develop a social gospel (Congregationalists and Episcopalians) and those who were most involved in the Fundamentalist-Modernist struggle of the 1920s (Presbyterians and Baptists). This resulted in some strange quirks; for example, talking about mid-nineteenth-century evangelicalism as the Methodist age in American religious history while saying little about the Methodists! Even more striking in retrospect was my tendency to interpret Methodism through the lenses of the then-dominant Calvinist-Puritan paradigm. It was not until my Methodist bicentennial lecture in 1983, for example, that I became convinced of the existence within Methodism from its beginnings of a liberationist tradition whose representatives sought to overcome the public/private split, to relate private faith to public order in ways not typical for their time.

I now believe that disillusionment over the failure to enforce an antislavery norm, and the consequent shift in early American Methodism from attacking the institution of slavery to a religious concern for slaves *within* the system, helped to establish the Methodist pattern of overcoming social evils by reforming individuals. (In the dissertation I discerned this pattern in Bishop William McKendree's famous statement to the 1816 General Conference that Methodist preachers were to "reform the continent *by* spreading scriptural holiness over these lands.")

Twenty years ago, the connections and continuities across Reconstruction between abolitionism and the social gospel were largely obscured for me. Because I saw slavery primarily as a *southern* problem, I tended to interpret the abolitionist denunciation of the sin of slavery as not really an attack upon systemic evil. The *real* problems in northern society I thought lay elsewhere. From the perspective of evangelical Protestantism, I viewed the period from 1837 to 1877 largely in terms of continuity rather than discontinuity. My focus was on the failure of Protestant churches in those years to criticize the economic status quo, rather than on the significance of the failure of Reconstruction for what Vincent Harding calls "the other American revolution."[8] In other words, I was for the most part blind to the issue of race, while attending pretty consistently to the economic issues I understood to be the major concerns of the developing social gospel. (To give one further illustration of this: when I discussed the opposition of Southern Methodist Bishop Warren A. Candler to Methodist reunion in the 1920s, I assumed the divisive issue was the northern social gospel rather than the issue of race.)

Almost no one saw women in American religious history in those years. It would have greatly enriched and complicated the story I was trying to tell to have had women in the picture, not only as individual contributors, or even as group participants, but most important for the light their presence would have shed on public/private issues.

My dissertation began by characterizing the evangelical Protestant mainstream of the mid-nineteenth century. The Protestant split that ensued was seen as growing out of this mainstream, and I suggested that it is impossible to understand either of the parties that resulted without first comprehending the Protestant Evangelicalism that was their common ancestor.

Much has been written in the last two decades about women and evangelical religion.[9] Even in the colonial era, women were the majority of church members and, in the great awakenings, female converts often outnumbered men three to two. By the decade of the 1830s, there was widespread agreement in American culture on a new standard of womanhood, the segregated woman's sphere prescribed by the cult of domesticity. According to this view of gender complementarity, men were to be active in the public sphere of work and politics, while women's peculiarly religious and moral nature suited them to reign in the private sphere of the home. From this base it was assumed that women would influence the character not only of their husbands and children, but also of society itself.[10]

While offering severe limits to women, evangelical religion also offered them enlarged possibilities. Evangelical religion gave women a new sense of identity and esteem within a supportive community, as well as a socially approved outlet through women's societies (such as women's prayer groups and moral reform and maternal associations) for their considerable energies and abilities.[11] Religious experience and belief, the appeal to an authority "beyond the world of men,"[12] could be of crucial importance to women who dared to step beyond the accepted bounds of society. In the egalitarian spirit of the revivals, women were encouraged to pray, testify, and exhort in mixed congregations. By the early years of the nineteenth century, women in a number of denominations were experiencing a call from God to preach the gospel and answering that call by becoming unordained traveling evangelists.

More commonly, women gained access to public roles by working through their own separate sphere. In an important article with the intriguing title "On Seeing and Not Seeing," Anne Firor Scott described women's voluntary associations in the nineteenth century as a classic case of "historical invisibility." Since women were barred from almost all public roles, they created among themselves organizations through which to shape social values and develop their own skills. As Scott aptly put it, "what business and public life were to aspiring nineteenth-century men, the voluntary association was to aspiring women."[13] By the 1830s and 1840s, women were participating in a whole array of organizations concerned with temperance, moral reform, education, the needs of women and children, and even antislavery. When the Civil War broke out, Scott claims, women were better equipped for their part than men were for theirs. Soldier's aid societies all over the North did the basic work of the U.S. Sanitary Commission. Local soldier's aid societies also multiplied in the South. Having engaged in this "larger sphere of usefulness," women after

1865 were ready to create their own women's foreign and home missionary societies to do women's work for women and children, eventually taking the whole world into their purview. Most historians of women agree that the role of women during the Civil War had a permanent effect on the expansion of woman's sphere.

All of this is important background for understanding what I now see when I read my dissertation twenty years later. Revivalism and social reform through voluntary associations were central to my depiction of Protestant evangelicalism, but there are essentially no women in the picture I have drawn. I saw the "laymen's revival" of 1857-58 as an important indication of the domestication and institutionalization of revivalistic evangelical piety, but none of the lay women evangelists (foremost of whom was probably Methodist holiness proponent Phoebe Palmer) whose work had helped to shape this popular piety are there.[14] There is no indication that some exceptional women like the Grimké sisters lectured in public in the 1830s on the evil of slavery, nor that black and white women organized the national Female Anti-Slavery Association in 1837 to fight both for the abolition of slavery and for equal rights for women, nor that women played a crucial part in transforming public opinion on slavery through antislavery petition campaigns in the 1830s to 1840s.[15] In *Modern Revivalism*, William McLoughlin listed a number of well known evangelists who were active in the 1850s and 1860s.[16] He included in this list the widow Maggie Van Cott (the first woman to receive a preacher's license from the Methodist Episcopal Church, in 1869); in referring to his list I omitted her, I assume because she did not seem important.

Also absent are women aiding the soldiers in the Civil War, Frances Willard and the Woman's Christian Temperance Union (Willard herself has only passing mention), the women's foreign and home missionary societies, women's training schools, and women's role in the social gospel, first as deaconesses and then in racial reform through the women's missionary societies (north and south!).[17] As I suggested earlier in discussing my blindness to the issue of race, it is astonishing what happens to the history we write when (to paraphrase Scott) some hitherto unseen part of past reality is brought into visibility.

The implications of this remarkable association-forming activity of women are also suggestive for any further consideration of the so-called public/private split. Women were moving the values of "woman's sphere," that is, their homes, into the public realm and trying to institutionalize them. As Beverly Harrison pointed out in the early 1970s, these women were responding to the subtly encroaching split between the interpersonal and the public sphere that industrialism (modernity) was effecting. They wanted to "feminize" the ever more remote public world.[18]

A recent contribution to the literature on fundamentalism helps to sharpen this picture even more. Betty A. DeBerg's 1990 book *Ungodly Women: Gender and the First Wave of American Fundamentalism* argues persuasively that fundamentalism in the period 1880-1930 must be seen as a response to the drastic and threatening changes in gender ideology and behavior in those years. She describes the demise after 1880 of the rigid Victorian gender ideology of separate male and female spheres, as the "New Woman" moved into leadership in the public realm through higher education, separate women's organizations, the church, and finally women's suffrage. She urges that the rise and fall of Victorian gender ideology constituted a major cultural crisis in the lives of the late-Victorian middle class, and that an analysis of popular fundamentalist rhetoric reveals how central gender issues were to this movement.[19]

In a fascinating chapter entitled "Reclaiming the Church for Men," DeBerg demonstrates that fundamentalist ministers were working on two fronts: they called in question the legitimacy of women's speaking and holding positions of authority over men in the church, and they replaced "feminized Christianity" with aggressive language and military rhetoric. She suggests that this exaggerated attention to masculinity explains much of the attraction of Billy Sunday's revivalism.[20]

The implications of DeBerg's work are striking. Once we see the fundamentalist agenda from 1880 to 1930 as attempting to salvage traditional gender ideology and behavior by defending exclusive male access to the public sphere, supporting male domination in the home, and reclaiming the church for men, the continuities with the pro-family orientation of recent fundamentalism become clear. Furthermore, we begin to suspect the importance of gender issues for both Protestant parties. Relevant here is the earlier work of Janet Forsythe Fishburn, who suggested that the social gospel in its defense of the middle-class family and emphasis on Christian manhood was a response to these changes in gender roles and ideology. Perhaps the male social gospelers by reasserting the church's role in the public sphere were in their own way attempting to counter the feminization of religion.[21]

To put the northern, white, male temper of my dissertation in perspective for myself, I reviewed the historiography of the social gospel over the last twenty years, and found it to be characterized by the same social location, and therefore myopia, until very recently. Works that attempted to offer a corrective were few and noteworthy. Ronald C. White, Jr., and C. Howard Hopkins, *The Social Gospel: Religion and Reform in Changing America* was suggestive rather than conclusive.[22] At least it included chapters on Christian abolitionism (by Will Gravely), the New South, the impact of W. E. B. DuBois on Washington Gladden in 1903, and the involvement of Christian women in the temperance movement. With the appearance of *Liberty and Justice for All: Racial Reform and the Social Gospel* by Ronald C. White, Jr., in 1990, it is clear that much of this earlier, more tentative exploration has now come to fruition.[23]

In this most recent work, White focuses on the interconnections between the social gospel and racial reform. He broadens the understanding of the social gospel by showing how well known leaders of the movement later came to be more involved in issues of racial reform. Even more important, by looking at racial issues, his cast of social gospel characters has been expanded to include names missing from most social gospel histories: black and white religious leaders in *both North and South* committed to education of the freed people after the Civil War and working through a whole host of organizations such as the American Missionary Association and the Commission on Interracial Cooperation. The possible ramifications of this study are both exciting and promising for future social gospel scholarship.

Also suggestive for this line of interpretation is William McGuire King's work on social gospel radicalism.[24] According to King, it was the social reconstructionist position, explicit by about 1912, that provided the basis for social gospel radicalism after World War I. Combining commitment to a cooperative society with greater institutional realism and keener intellectual rigor, it engaged in a comprehensive and penetrating critique of American society. Christian reconstructionists understood "how interrelated were the issues of anti-capitalism, racial justice, civil liberties, and anti-militarism." (Issues of gender and imperialism might well be added to this list.)[25]

In short, because so much that was invisible has become visible in the last twenty years, my mind has changed significantly in the direction of a larger and more encompassing vision.

The Two-Party Thesis Since 1970: Literature and Developments

Chapter 17 of Martin E. Marty's prize-winning historical essay *Righteous Empire: The Protestant Experience in America*[26] was entitled "The Two-Party System: A Division within Protestantism." The Acknowledgments section at the back paid tribute to Marty's graduate students who had contributed to his work on the themes of the book. My name (then Jean Miller) was listed for Section VI, along with the admission, "I believe that only Jean Miller can legitimately complain that I plagiarized (in chapter 17) but almost all will find occasional plundered ideas on these my pages."[27] The footnotes for section VI began as follows: "Jean Miller's unpublished doctoral dissertation at the University of Chicago provided both quotations and plot for the first chapter in this section."[28]

"My chapter" might well be claimed to be pivotal for the interpretive scheme of this book. For example, in reviewing the historiography of American religion, Henry Warner Bowden referred to Marty's *Righteous Empire* in this way:

> The search for new organizing principles or integrative techniques elicited two more significant contributions. Martin E. Marty has published extensively in American religious history, producing books and articles in such profusion that readers hardly know how to assimilate all of them. Standing out from the rest of Marty's work, however, was his *Righteous Empire: The Protestant Experience in America* (1970) wherein he crystallized an interpretive theme adumbrated in some of his earlier writings. There Marty boldly asserted that denominational classifications in modern America were less important than differences between members of the same church. He saw liberal and conservative clusters of adherents who resembled each other across denominational lines. This "two-party system" was, he suggested, more helpful than the old organizational labels for understanding religious patterns in contemporary times.[29]

There has been then, between Marty and me, a kind of common ownership of this idea (although the name "two-party system" was Marty's). It has been interesting to me to follow Marty's use and development of the idea in later work.

Marty's *A Nation of Behavers*[30] was a helpful effort to describe the new religious landscape in America resulting from changes in the 1960s and 1970s, particularly the resurgence of Evangelicalism and setbacks experienced by the Mainline churches. (Dean Kelley captured the sense of these changes in his important 1972 book *Why Conservative Churches Are Growing*.)[31] This new map of religious America concentrated on social behavior rather than theological, institutional, or political distinctions. On this basis, Marty discerned six major clusters: Mainline Religion, Evangelicalism and Fundamentalism, Pentecostal-Charismatic Religion, the New Religions, Ethnic Religion, and Civil Religion.[32]

The usefulness of this mapping of group identity in terms of social behavior, what religious people *do*, was evident in Marty's careful distinctions between Evangelicalism and Fundamentalism. As he put it, "the two orthodoxies have different orthopraxises"; that is, they practice their shared beliefs in different ways. According to Marty, Evangelicals were more ecumenical in style than Fundamentalists, more responsive to social concerns, more open to intellectual and cultural matters, and more embracing of worldliness. Evangelicals themselves agreed that the differences were a matter of mood, temperament, attitudes.[33]

By the early 1980s, Marty was working with modernity as a conceptual framework for illuminating conflict and division in the religious realm. This was evident in *The Public Church* (1981), where he described the chopping up of life that occurred in modernity and the resulting struggle all religious traditions had to relate private faith to the public order. He saw the public church as a "communion of communions," a convergence of constituencies from within mainline Protestantism, evangelicalism, and Roman Catholicism that together could address the crisis of public and social morale and common weal. With the turn to the new decade, Marty discerned that believers were being called to "reconnect the inward journey of the seventies to the inward/outward course" of the public church.[34]

Modernity was also crucial to Marty's characterization of fundamentalism as "resurgent antimodern religion" in an important *Daedalus* article published in 1982.[35] Finally, in volume 1 of *Modern American Religion*, entitled *The Irony of It All: 1893-1919* (1986), the shaping of twentieth-century religion by its encounter with modernity became the central organizing framework. Accordingly, the various figures and movements of American religion were located along a spectrum of responses, from embracing to rejecting modernity.[36]

Some of the themes found in chapter 17 of *Righteous Empire* appeared again, greatly enlarged, in chapter 11 of *Irony*, "The Carapaces of Reactive Protestantism," where Marty treated Moody's revivals and premillennialist views, Samuel P. Jones, Billy Sunday, A. C. Dixon, and B. Fay Mills as part of the "countermodern reaction." In a concluding section on "Transmodernism," he creatively explored several major attempts, including Social Christianity, to go beyond the extreme differentiations of the modern toward a recovered wholeness.[37]

Also in 1986, a second edition of *Righteous Empire* was published with the new title *Protestantism in the United States: Righteous Empire*. This new edition contained two new chapters (11 and 27) on the struggles of women in Protestantism and on power shifts in the 1970s and 1980s. With regard to the "classic 'two-party' situation," Marty admitted that the old "private" Protestantism appeared to have turned "public" with New Christian Right leaders like Jerry Falwell and others. But he cautioned that great numbers of evangelicals, fundamentalists, and pentecostals still wanted to keep a distance between religious leadership and politics, and that even where religious leadership was no longer private, but had clearly become political, it was not necessarily public in the proper sense of the term.[38]

Has Martin E. Marty changed *his* mind about the two-party system over the past two decades? From his published works, I would conclude that he is still convinced of the validity of the basic interpretation, while having refined and enlarged his view of it by experiencing and interpreting the religious and cultural developments of the past twenty years.[39]

Since 1970, the two-party thesis has been subjected by sociologists to empirical research, and a number of writers have explored possible approaches toward overcoming the split.[40] Evangelical scholars like George Marsden and Donald Dayton have questioned the adequacy of the label "private" as a description of their own tradition, reminding us of the social concern of evangelicals and holiness groups prior to the "Great Reversal" which began about 1900.[41] There has also been much more sophisticated reflection on the meaning of the term "public."[42]

In the literature dealing with this split in Protestantism, two historical works published in the 1980s are of particular importance: George Marsden's *Fundamentalism and American Culture* (1980) and Ferenc Szasz's *The Divided Mind of Protestant America* (1982).[43] I want briefly to look at the approach taken by these two works.

George Marsden's interpretation of fundamentalism as "militantly anti-modernist Protestant evangelicalism" differed from that of Ernest Sandeen a decade earlier primarily in viewing it as a broader cultural phenomenon.[44] An important key to understanding the fundamentalism of the 1920s, according to Marsden, was its ambivalent relationship to American culture (what

Marsden referred to as the establishment-or-outsider paradox). He also detected an ambivalence about social reform growing out of its roots in both the individualistic revivalist-pietist tradition exemplified by Dwight L. Moody and an older Puritan-Calvinist heritage.

Most interesting to me was chapter ten, "The Great Reversal," in which Marsden specifically addressed the question of what happened to the evangelicals' interest in social concerns in the early years of the twentieth century. Marsden was critical of the public party/private party thesis of non-evangelical interpreters Miller [Schmidt] and Marty, on what seem to be basically three grounds: 1) it failed to distinguish clearly between types of social concern, particularly with regard to political action; 2) it did not sufficiently acknowledge the evangelical social concern arising out of holiness teachings in the last half of the twentieth century; and 3) it did not recognize the "two quite distinct stages" of the disappearance of evangelical social concerns: the lessening of interest in political action from 1865 to 1900, and the "Great Reversal" itself, from 1900 to 1930, when (in reaction to the liberal social gospel) "all progressive social concern became suspect." Having said this, Marsden did recognize the significance of instituting a commission on evangelism in the Federal Council of Churches in 1912 to balance its social activism, and admitted that, by this time, the issue of evangelism versus social service was central.[45]

Ferenc Szasz's book was the only major historical work besides my own (and Marty's) to focus on the Protestant split. His title, *The Divided Mind of Protestant America, 1880-1930*, [emphasis mine] accurately conveys his approach. Where I concentrated on the issue of evangelism versus social reform, he dealt primarily with ideas, with the theological and more broadly intellectual issues at stake in the schism, particularly the intellectual traumas of evolution, comparative religion, and the higher criticism of the Scriptures. Although Szasz's book covered the years of the Fundamentalist-Modernist controversy in the 1920s, over half of it was devoted to the period from 1901 to 1917, which he saw as crucial for sowing the "seeds of conflict." Szasz suggested that the fifty years from 1880 to 1930 should be called the "Age of Division" for mainstream Protestantism. He called the "two distinct points of view" that emerged during those years "liberal" and "conservative," and insisted that this division had replaced denominational distinctions in significance and that the resulting realignment persisted to the present.[46]

One chapter of Szasz's work addressed the issue of social concerns, especially in relation to the Progressive reform movement. He claimed that historians' "traditional separation of the clergy between those concerned with the Social Gospel and those concerned only with individual salvation" was not accurate for the period from 1901 to 1917, when "both liberal and conservative Protestant groups worked to alleviate social ills, each in its own way."[47] He cited as examples conservative urban pastors who later became Fundamentalists, evangelical slum workers, and southern evangelicals. Highlighting the contribution of the clergy to Progressive reforms, he concluded: "Never again would the social question have the undivided church support of the years before World War I. In large measure it declined when liberal and conservative pastors began to see each other as more dangerous enemies than the social evils around them."[48] That had already begun to happen, I would contend, by 1912.

What has been the fate of this two-party concept in recent historical scholarship? Leonard Sweet's introductory historiographical essay in *The Evangelical Tradition in America* has a section on the shattering of the evangelical consensus that occurred between 1855 and 1915.[49] Referring to it (without quotation marks) as the Great Split, Sweet suggested that we still do not know adequately *why* Evangelicalism splintered into these competing segments, nor do we know exactly what to call the contending parties ("Public Christians" versus "Private Christians" [Marty], modernists versus fundamentalists, liberals versus conservatives, and social gospelers versus personal gospelers all being mentioned in the literature).[50] Sweet pointed to the evangelical roots of the progressive and social gospel movements and insisted that the late Victorian era of 1880 to 1920 remains understudied.

Recent works on liberal Protestantism in America have accepted without much qualification the fact of a fundamental split in the late nineteenth century.[51] There has been much discussion of "the fragmented mainline," which is usually seen as a continuation of the earlier division.[52] Probably the most significant recent work to deal extensively with issues of cross-denominational division in American religion is that of Princeton sociologist Robert Wuthnow. It has attracted well deserved attention.[53]

In *The Struggle for America's Soul*, Wuthnow depicts a major restructuring of American religion since World War II, involving both the declining significance of denominations and the heightened importance of liberal/conservative polarization, especially since the 1960s. He describes a "deep cultural divide between conservative or evangelical Christians, on one side, and religious liberals and secular humanists, on the other side." Two "clearly identifiable groups" he claims, have "lined up to wage spiritual warfare with each other." This cleavage "divides the nation into two opposing camps that are approximately equal in numbers, and it cuts directly through most of the nation's major denominational families and faith traditions."[54]

One of the strengths of Wuthnow's work is his examination of the larger social context in which this religious restructuring has taken place. He is deeply concerned about religion's role in the third, or voluntary, sector in American life. Consisting of those activities and organizations not subsumed within the government or the economic sector, this third sector, according to Wuthnow, is the locus of public discourse about the collective values of society. He sees a very real danger that the third sector will be squeezed out by the expansion of the other two, and that religion's public role may be weakened by unhealthy polarization between evangelicals and liberals. To guard against this, he urges the need for dialogue and for developing a stronger middle position as an alternative to the two extremes.[55]

How and why have the two sides lined up against each other? Wuthnow argues that the "chasm dividing American religion into separate communities has emerged largely from the struggle between these two communities," especially through the growth of "special purpose groups" since the 1960s.[56] His work sheds interesting light on some of the issues that have emerged regarding the two-party system in the last two decades. He finds a basic division in strategies since the 1960s between evangelism (to shape individual convictions) and social action (direct action aimed at changing the social structure to bring about social justice); the one directed to values, the other primarily to behavior. He sees the issues of feminism and the ordination of women as having a powerful role in fueling conservative/liberal tensions, in part because of the prominent role traditionally played by women churchgoers. Finally he recognizes that the polarization is fundamentally about two contrasting civil religions, the conservative and the liberal version, summed up roughly in the phrases "one nation under God" and "with liberty and justice for all."[57]

Wuthnow sees the heritage of fundamentalism and modernism as providing "only a starting point" for the present division. Because he regards fundamentalism as having largely ceased to exist as an organized movement by the end of World War II, he views the divisions of those years as largely between Protestants and Catholics, Christians and Jews, and members of different denominations.[58] Therefore he can claim that the present restructuring involves the replacement of Herberg's tripartite system

(Protestant-Catholic-Jew) by "what some have called a 'two-party system.' "[59] Where Wuthnow sees discontinuity, I see continuity, as I hope the final chapter of this book (covering the period from 1912 through the late 1960s) demonstrates. What he suggests about a widening gap since the 1960s, however, is intriguing for all who are concerned about these matters.

What do I see as the sum of two decades of reflection on the two-party system in American Protestantism? Two Protestant parties had emerged by 1912 out of the earlier evangelical Protestant consensus. They represented different understandings of how to make America Christian. Contrary to some interpretations, one party was not modern and the other traditional. Both parties were responding to the compartmentalization of individual and social spheres that modernity had effected. Neither side could be immune to modernity; thus innovation was involved in the differing responses of both parties. Both sides knew that the social order was changing. In their greater openness to modernity what I have called the public party at its best sought to go beyond the differentiations of modernity toward a greater wholeness by bringing religion into the public sphere. The so-called private party with its premillennialist views knew well that *a* world was ending, that Protestant America was yielding to a multicultural society. It lamented that passing and tried to reassert the old Protestant cultural hegemony.

After Twenty Years: How My Mind Remains the Same

The reader may well wonder at this point whether my mind remains the same in any important respects. The answer is yes; there are still some things I find exciting in coming back to my own dissertation after these many years. In this section, I want to indicate how I would sum up the contribution of my dissertation. What has proved to be of enduring value?

It now takes an exercise of the imagination to recall that when I wrote the dissertation in 1969, there were *no* scholarly works focusing on the split itself.[60] No one had as yet explored the historic roots of the Protestant division so painfully evident in the 1960s, or attempted in a single study to pay attention to both sides of the conversation.

More than twenty years later, I would sum up the most important contributions of my 1969 dissertation as follows: 1) I recognized then that this schism within mainline Protestantism not only cut across denominational lines but also had replaced denominational divisions in significance. That is, the factors involved in this split had become the *basic* cause of division among Protestants. 2) By attending to the developing polemic itself and listening to the rhetoric of the proponents as they lined up against each other, I was able to document *when* and *how* the split developed. (For this reason I regard Chapters Four, Five, and Six as the most original part of my dissertation.) Subsequent studies (as well as my own later work) have questioned whether my *interpretation* in 1969 was adequate, but I have seen nothing to dispute these conclusions. 3) How I understood the nature of the split was deeply affected by the shape of the division in the 1960s. I was looking for a usable past to help me, and others who shared my concern, to understand the present in order to chart a useful course for the future. Because the issues in the 1960s seemed polarized in terms of evangelism versus social reform, I tended to see the historical division in the same terms. While I now think there was more to it than that, as well as more to be said for those who struggled to hold the two together, I still believe that the basic interpretation was sound and continues to be useful, even critical, for understanding American Protestantism in the late twentieth century.

J.M.S.
Iliff School of Theology
Denver, Colorado
August 1991

Introduction, 1969

Contemporary American Protestantism is split into two camps, the lines of which are roughly indicated by the National Council of Churches, the *Christian Century*, and *Christianity and Crisis* on the one hand, and the National Association of Evangelicals, *Christianity Today*, and the *Christian Herald* on the other. While other factors are involved, one of the basic sources of disagreement is the issue of the church's role in the world. Essentially the division is between those who see the church's task as the transformation of society, and those who see its mission as individual salvation; in brief, between the advocates of social Christianity and the spokespersons for individualistic evangelicalism.

The question is, when did this split occur? How, when, and why did Protestants come to such different assessments of the purpose of Christianity and the relation between the church and the culture? It is easily demonstrated that there were not always two such parties in American Protestantism. At the time of the so-called laymen's revival of 1857-58, American Protestants were very nearly of one mind on the role of the church and its ministry. However, by 1912, a split had clearly taken place between the two sides. In that year, the Federal Council of Churches, formed in 1908 as the product of and organ for united social action of the churches, had to yield to conservative pressure and create a Commission on Evangelism to balance its Commission on the Church and Social Service, thus institutionalizing the split between social Christianity and individual evangelism.

In order to discover when Protestants lined up initially on one or the other side of this issue, I examined the period between these two end points, taking "depth soundings" of the major encounters between the two parties. It soon became evident which years were crucial for the sides being taken. Accordingly, this study is divided into three basic parts: before 1880; from 1880, when the evangelical ranks began to divide, to 1912, when the split was institutionalized in the Federal Council; and from 1912 to the late 1960s, in which the two sides have become virtually two Protestantisms.

The distinction between social Christianity and individual evangelism might be described in a number of ways. For example, by 1837, evangelicalism had become the characteristic pattern of American Protestantism. Protestant evangelicals in the mid-nineteenth century were generally agreed that the way to change society was to save individual souls. There is no question that the revivalism of Charles G. Finney in the 1830s, with its stress on sin as selfishness and on salvation as the beginning of a life of benevolent activity, was a powerful impulse toward social reform. But the voluntary societies through which the Protestant churches attempted to "fashion a Protestant America"[1] were largely concerned with individual salvation and personal moral issues like temperance and Sabbath observance. While some societies were devoted to charitable causes like the care of orphans, schooling for the needy, and the spiritual rescue of sailors and "females who have deviated from the paths of virtue,"[2] most of these enterprises were efforts to ameliorate conditions within the given social order. With the possible exception of antislavery, they did not call in question the social fabric itself.

By the 1890s, on the other hand, spokespersons for the social gospel were talking in terms of a transformation of society itself. Charles Worcester Clark made the distinction clear in an article published posthumously in 1893. "Charity," he explained, "whether public or private, mainly deals with results, to mitigate effects; public action must be applied to the industrial system itself, in order to prevent a continuation of their causes. Our philanthropy must concern itself not only with private helpfulness, but with public reform and economic reorganization."[3] The classic statement of this view was Walter Rauschenbusch's *Christianizing the Social Order* (1912), in which he called for the Christianizing of the great unredeemed portion of the social order, the economic system. The social gospelers[4] were no longer content with amelioration; they wanted to attack social evils by getting at their causes in the social system itself.

The problem with defining the difference between social Christianity and individual evangelism in terms of transformation versus amelioration, however, is that the distinction is not sufficiently refined. While it is helpful for indicating the general approach of each side, it does not make clear where the dividing line might be. That is, when does amelioration cease to be amelioration and become transformation, and vice versa?

Neither is it adequate to define social Christianity as the attempt to apply Christian precepts to every area of human life, including political, social, and economic institutions. Again, Christians primarily concerned with otherworldly matters would not relate that way to the affairs of this life, but there were many Christians preaching gospels vastly different from the social gospel—the gospel of wealth, for instance—who did seek to apply Christianity to every realm of life.

Closer to the heart of the issue would seem to be the understanding of sin, and more broadly, of the relationship between the individual and society, held by both sides. The evangelicals talked about sin as a matter of vice, that is, personal moral failure. They earnestly believed that the only way to change society was by changing the individual, after which the desired improvements in society would follow. The spokespersons for social Christianity, on the other hand, recognized that individuals could be powerless to effect changes in society without basic reforms of the social institutions themselves. That is, they recognized sin in its objective, social manifestations as well as in its personal forms. They acknowledged the influence of the environment on the individual, and actually believed that individuals might be changed by changing the society. While not overlooking the need for individual salvation, they were developing a social ethic as something distinct from individual morality.

I am interested in telling the history of a polemic in American Protestantism. While part of the task involves retracing steps in the history of social Christianity already chronicled by historians like Henry May, Charles H. Hopkins, and Aaron Abell,[5] my emphasis is different from theirs. I observe the occasions for and ways in which the more articulate exponents of social Christianity found it necessary to attack or criticize the soul-savers, and vice versa.

In a study of this nature, the historian must depend on the labors of others who have done the pioneering work in particular areas. I wish here to acknowledge a special debt to historians William G. McLoughlin, Jr., Ernest R. Sandeen, and James F. Findlay, Jr., who helped open up for me the history and significance of modern revivalism, premillennialism, and the career of Dwight L. Moody, respectively. The extent of my debt is evident throughout this work.

University of Chicago
August 1969

Souls or the Social Order

PART ONE

Reforming the Nation by Reforming the Individual

ONE

Evangelicalism at Mid-Century

By mid-century, evangelicalism had triumphed over other Protestant traditions in America and achieved a position of cultural dominance. As Timothy L. Smith has demonstrated, the denominations of popular evangelicalism, the Methodists and Baptists, accounted for nearly 70 percent of the total membership of the Protestant churches in 1855. The older lines of distinction between them and the Presbyterians and Congregationalists had been largely obliterated, and even the Episcopalian and Lutheran denominations had strong evangelical parties in the 1840s and 50s. The goal of the evangelicals was to shape a Protestant America, and by mid-century they had attained a remarkable influence. Protestant church membership had increased from an estimated one out of every fifteen persons in 1800, to one out of every seven in 1850, and church attendance among several denominations was often three times the membership. Philip Schaff reported to his former colleagues in Berlin in 1854 that the United States was "by far the most religious and Christian country in the world."[1]

In order to understand this popular evangelicalism, it is necessary to look briefly at developments in the first half of the century. By 1837, all the formative factors were present. From 1837 to 1877, vast changes were taking place in American society, but these did not immediately effect obvious adjustments in American Protestantism. Thus the 1857-58 revival with which Chapter II begins should be seen as occurring in the middle of a span of years having its own integrity rather than as beginning or ending an era. As disruptive and critical as the Civil War was in American life, it did not significantly change the pattern of evangelical Protestantism that was formed by 1837 and developed in the 1840s and 1850s. It is with these formative years that this chapter deals.

By 1837, American Protestantism had developed the organizational form, the theological understanding, the means of recruiting members, and the pattern of moral and social reform that were to dominate until the closing decades of the century. In many ways these developments represented drastic departures from the overwhelmingly Puritan pattern that prevailed throughout the colonial era. These years are crucial because they were formative of the evangelical norm to which many twentieth-century Protestants have looked back wistfully. It is usually not recognized that this normative pattern was of no more ancient origin than the early years of the nineteenth century.

Disestablishment and its Consequences

Basic to all other developments was the change so well elucidated by Sidney E. Mead, from the original intent to enforce uniformity of religious belief and control over both individuals and the civil order, to acceptance of disestablishment.[2] Foremost among the consequences of separation of church and state were the development of the denomination as the characteristic organizational form and the principle of voluntaryism—dependence on persuasion and free, uncoerced consent—as the pattern of the church's activity.

Not that the established churches took this step willingly. The rationale for religious freedom was best articulated in the Virginia debates on church and state by Thomas Jefferson and James Madison. There religion was defined as a matter of "opinion"[3] and the church described as a voluntary society whose laws extend to its own members only. The legal basis for separation of church and state was written into the Constitution (Article VI) and the First Amendment, effective in 1791. However, in the states the established churches were often forced into this position by a coalition of rationalists who agreed with Jefferson and Madison, and pietistic sectarians struggling for religious freedom. When the Federalists lost the fight to save the Standing Order in Connecticut, Lyman Beecher viewed the Congregational disestablishment in 1818 as bringing "irreparable injury" to the church. But he later regarded disestablishment as "the best thing that ever happened to the State of Connecticut."[4] How the Protestant churches successfully adjusted to this new state of affairs is to a considerable extent the theme of this entire period.

The Methodist Age in America

The shift from establishment to voluntaryism was accompanied by a theological realignment that might broadly be described as the shift from Neo-Calvinism to Arminianism, or the end of the Puritan and the beginning of the Pietist-Methodist age of American church history.[5] Central to this second development were a new emphasis on soul winning as the primary role and purpose of the church and its ministry, and the forging of a new revivalism as the principal weapon of the churches in their fight to Christianize America. This shift took place in three fairly distinct stages: (1) Timothy Dwight's battle against the infidels at Yale College and, in the West and South, camp meeting revivals on the frontier (both usually referred to as the Second Great Awakening), roughly 1795-1810; (2) the New Haven revivalistic theology of Lyman Beecher and Nathaniel William Taylor, 1810-1825; and (3) the New Measures revivalism of Charles G. Finney, 1825-1835.[6]

Historians generally agree that the years following the American Revolution were a low ebb of religious vitality for American Christianity. Deistic influence was strong in the East, and on the frontier many were without religious ties of any kind. This situation served to strengthen the evangelical emphasis on the necessity for conversion and to reinforce the churches' reliance on revivalism.

Common to both the northern and southern phases of the Second Great Awakening was a new stress on persuasion and consent, a direct appeal to human minds in an effort to get them to make a definite commitment.[7] The earliest colonial revivals had been largely unsought and uncalculated. They were generally regarded as the outpouring of God's blessing and there was little consciousness of human agency in them. This new revivalism, on the other hand, stressed increasingly human "measures" or "means." When President Dwight took it upon himself to battle infidelity at Yale, he was so skillful in depicting the dangers of infidelity and provoking a conscious decision on the part of the students between Christianity and infidelity that a religious revival took place on the campus in 1801-2. The frontier camp meetings competed for the attention of the common people. As in New England, the revivalist preachers operated on the conviction that if presented with alternatives, persons could make a reasonable decision in favor of Christianity and their own salvation.

5

This stress on human agency was fostered within Calvinism itself by Nathaniel W. Taylor and Lyman Beecher, both former pupils of Dwight's.[8] After graduation from Yale and four years of further study with Dwight, Taylor was called in 1812 to First Church (known as Center Church), New Haven, where there were revivals under his preaching in 1815 and 1816, 1820 and 1821. In 1822 he was made professor of didactic theology at the new Theological Department at Yale. His lifelong friend Lyman Beecher was called to Litchfield, Connecticut, in 1810. As outstanding in political and organizational activities as Taylor was in theology, Beecher led the campaign in 1810-18 to save the Standing Order, using revivals as one of his principal weapons. By the 1820s, New Haven served as headquarters for Beecher too.

These "New Haven theologians" were fighting a war on a number of fronts. Besides attempting to save the establishment, they were trying to defend orthodoxy against Unitarian charges, to defend themselves against the accusations of conservatives that they were departing from Calvinism, and to preserve some kind of evangelical unity. To do all these things was an impossible task.

Unlike the "Consistent Calvinists" (men like Jedidiah Morse and Leonard Woods of Andover, who saw themselves as faithful to the tradition of Jonathan Edwards), Taylor and Beecher began not with God's sovereignty but with sinners and common sense. They argued that if humans are punished for their sin they must have been free to choose between good and evil, otherwise they could not be held accountable by a just God. Therefore they must have free agency.[9] Conservatives and Unitarians alike pressed these men to reconcile their evangelical doctrine of free agency with the traditional Calvinist doctrines of foreknowledge and election. Taylor's explanation of the nature of sin as "certainty with power to the contrary"[10] failed to satisfy either. Before long it was generally recognized that Taylorism meant the forsaking of the old Calvinism.

The revivalistic religion of Beecher and Taylor was further discredited by reports of revivals in Presbyterian churches of western New York State under Charles G. Finney and his imitators, in which disruptive New Measures were being used. Among the measures that offended those who belonged to the older revival tradition were vehement preaching, praying for individuals by name, allowing women to pray in public meetings, permitting evangelists to invade local parishes without invitation and denounce the pastors for their coldness and opposition to the revivals, and general encouragement of emotional excesses in the services. In an effort to preserve unity within the church, Beecher and Taylor met with Finney and his colleagues at New Lebanon, New York, in 1827, but they were unable to persuade the western men to cease being "disturbers of the churches."[11]

The immediate result was to consolidate the conservative opposition to the New Haven men. In his famous address to the Connecticut clergy in 1828, Taylor expounded the position he had been defending for about a decade, that depravity is a human's own act. Soon thereafter the conservatives established their own theological institute and drew up their own articles of agreement. From then on they were in close league with the Old School Presbyterians, And since both Yale and Andover trained men for the Presbyterian as well as the Congregational ministry, Connecticut men infiltrated the Presbyterian ministry, where they formed the nucleus of the "New School."[12] Taylor remained at Yale until 1857, a year before his death. Sidney Mead suggests that his thought constituted the main bridge from the inherited orthodoxy of the eighteenth century to the liberal theology of the nineteenth.[13]

Revivalism and Social Reform

The man who was really responsible for knocking "the last props from under the old Calvinist system"[14] was Charles G. Finney. In the years 1825-1835, he provided the new "worked-up" revivalism with a coherent rationale and succeeded in institutionalizing it.[15] Born in Connecticut in 1792, Finney was brought up in western New York. In 1818, he began a law career which, although promising, was abruptly abandoned on his conversion experience in 1821. In 1824, he was ordained by the Oneida Presbytery and shortly thereafter began itinerant preaching in western New York. He became nationally known after conducting successful revivals in Western, Rome, Utica, Auburn, and Troy, New York, in 1825-27.[16] After the fruitless debates at New Lebanon in 1827, Finney made the decision to go east. Beginning with Wilmington, Delaware, he moved on to Philadelphia in 1828, and finally to New York City in 1829. There he preached for nearly a year. When he left in midsummer of 1830, he left behind a church devoted to his principles (the First Free Presbyterian Church), the *New York Evangelist*, a newspaper friendly to Finneyism, and the firm friendship of the Tappan brothers, Lewis and Arthur, wealthy New York merchants already influential in the various charitable and benevolent societies in the city.

The most successful and widely publicized of Finney's campaigns was the Rochester revival of 1830-31. When it was over, Finney was a man of such repute that Lyman Beecher himself, who had remarked to Finney at the close of the New Lebanon convention that he would fight him "every inch of the way to Boston and then I'll fight you there,"[17] wrote to invite Finney to Boston. He stayed there for seven months, from August 1831 to April 1832. Beecher could no longer successfully dissociate his and Taylor's views from those of Finney. Finney's sermon preached in late October on "Sinners Bound to Change Their Own Hearts" was attacked by conservatives as of a piece with the New Haven theology. By mid-century, the evangelical views of Finney, Beecher, and Taylor had practically become America's national religion.[18]

The essence of Finney's New Heart sermon was that men and women must be able to make themselves a new heart since it was unreasonable to think that God would require them to do what they could not do. Humans still retained the power of choice, and although they were prejudiced toward evil, they could be persuaded to prefer the glory of God and God's kingdom to their own selfish interests. Here was where the preacher came in. The Spirit of God often worked through the agency of the preacher to awaken sinners and convince them of the truth.[19]

All of this left ample room for the use of "means" in conversion, and in 1835, Finney published the fruits of his experience with revivalism in his *Lectures on Revivals of Religion*, essentially a handbook on the means of promoting revivals. If humans could change their own hearts, they could also promote revivals. Finney believed that all ministers should be revival ministers, and that revival preaching had to be exciting and in the language of the common people in order to attract their attention. Once listeners were "awakened," the revivalist must persuade them to decide to serve God by arguing reasonably, much like a lawyer addressing a jury.

In order to force a definite commitment, such measures as protracted meetings, the anxious bench, inquiry rooms, and appropriate music were helpful and should be used. The anxious bench was a front pew to which those anxious about their salvation could be brought forward during a revival service to be addressed particularly and made the object of special prayers. The point of the anxious bench was to force an immediate decision on the part of the awakened sinner. Anxious meetings or inquiry meetings were also held outside the main meeting place for those who needed more prolonged conversations.

Protracted or extended meetings were an adaptation of the frontier camp meetings for use in towns and cities. Originally in Finney's revivals in western New York State, they consisted of a continuous series of meetings for preaching, prayer, and inquiry sessions from sunrise to midnight, usually lasting for four days. During this time all other business in the town was to cease while the townspeople concentrated on the state of their souls. Finney had to modify this practice for the larger cities, where it was impractical to expect business to stop for several days. Consequently, revival meetings began to be held every evening for a period of several weeks. These measures were to become standard procedure for modern revivalism.[20]

Several aspects of Finney's thought were to have a significant influence on social reform in his day, namely his view that conversion is a change from selfishness to benevolence, and his beliefs in perfectionism and millennialism. The idea that all sin is selfishness and that holiness or virtue consists in disinterested benevolence came from Samuel Hopkins (1721-1803), the great disciple of Jonathan Edwards. Although the Hopkinsians in Finney's day were among the chief opponents of the New Haven liberalizing party within Congregationalism, Hopkins's stress on "the greatest good of mankind" or "the greatest good of the whole" as the purpose of the divine decrees and the goal of human benevolence had actually helped to modify the stern Calvinistic emphasis on divine sovereignty. Finney's doctrine of perfectionism reinforced his doctrine of benevolence, for persons who were perfect in holiness could hope consistently to prefer the glory of God and God's kingdom to their own selfish interest.[21] The doctrine of millennialism constituted the social equivalent of individual benevolence and perfection. Finney and most of his contemporaries held the postmillennial view of the return of Christ that Jonathan Edwards and Samuel Hopkins had taught in the eighteenth century. That is, they believed that Christ would return to earth *after* His millennial reign. His kingdom was thus made continuous with the present Christian agencies at work in the world. According to this optimistic view, the world was gradually working toward a state of perfection through the spread of Christianity, and eventually there would be a thousand-year period of universal peace and plenty, followed by Christ's return. Most evangelical ministers in the 1830s and 40s believed that the millennium might well begin in America in the very near future.

By contrast, the premillennial view was that Christ would return to earth *before* the millennium. His kingdom on earth would then be the result of His personal intervention rather than the climax of forces already at work. Those who held this more pessimistic view tended to think of social reform as useless and to concentrate on saving souls in the time remaining before Christ's return. In the 1830s and 40s, few held this view in America. But after the Civil War, almost every evangelist held the premillennial view. The postmillennialists of the post-Civil War era were the social gospelers.[22]

Finney's views could give a powerful impetus to reforming activities. Because true Christians "supremely value the highest good of Being," he said, "they will and must take a deep interest in whatever is promotive of that end. Hence their spirit is necessarily that of the reformer. To the universal reformation of the world they stand committed."[23] However, for Finney himself, the most important reform, to which all others must be secondary, was that of the individual soul. Therefore, as he saw it, benevolence should lead all Christians to soul winning and all reforms should be appendages to revivals. Because Finney thought of sin primarily in terms of individual morality, he really believed that once individuals were regenerated, the necessary economic, political, and social reforms would follow naturally. This confidence in the harmony of converted individuals he shared with most of his Protestant contemporaries.

Evangelical reforms have been subject to widely differing historical assessments. Henry May's *Protestant Churches and Industrial America* (1949) criticized the evangelical benevolent activity as an expression of religious conservatism and reserved most of its praise for humanitarianism in the prewar period for the liberal denominations—Unitarianism and Universalism.[24] Charles I. Foster's generally derogatory study of British and American evangelicalism, *An Errand of Mercy* (1960), also stressed the conservatism of the evangelical aims, while deploring the subtle coercion by which the evangelical united front tried to secure conformity to Victorian standards of conduct and attitude.[25] On the other hand, Timothy L. Smith, in his important *Revivalism and Social Reform* (1957), attempted to balance the account. Smith argued that not only did the new revival measures go hand in hand with progressive theology and humanitarian concern, but also the pre-Civil War evangelists, in their concern for reform, helped prepare the way for the later social gospel.[26] Any consideration of these varying claims must begin with the so-called benevolent empire, the network of societies that arose as part of the adjustment of the evangelicals to disestablishment.

The Benevolent Empire

Although these societies were nonsectarian and sought the cooperation on an individual basis of all evangelical Protestants, they tended to be dominated by Congregationalists and Presbyterians who, as heirs of the Calvinistic stewardship tradition, had "never lost their strong sense of the church's direct responsibility for the being and well-being of the commonwealth."[27] In his study of the benevolent societies, *Their Brothers' Keepers* (1960), Clifford S. Griffin made clear the centrality of the idea of stewardship combined with the idea of benevolence as the rationale for the societies. New England Calvinists had believed that the elect were to be responsible for the lives of others as well as their own. When this idea was combined with disinterested benevolence, working to make others moral came to be seen as a perfect expression of benevolence. Basic to the Federalist position had been the conviction that moral men should govern. Federalism had been the political means by which the rule of the righteous had been maintained. By 1810, as we have seen, the trustees were hard-pressed to maintain this rule. When disestablishment finally came in Connecticut in 1818, Lyman Beecher became one of the chief architects of this new system of moral reform through the voluntary societies. They were an attempt through moral suasion rather than coercion to fulfill the responsibility these men felt as stewards or trustees for the welfare of society.[28]

The leaders of these benevolent societies, centered mainly in New York City, Philadelphia, and Boston, were prominent clergy and wealthy laymen— merchants like Arthur and Lewis Tappan, bankers and financiers, businessmen like Anson Phelps and William E. Dodge, publishers and lawyers. As Griffin has pointed out, the societies were at the same time an expression of genuine concern for the souls and deeds of others, and an instrument for molding the country to conform to God's—and the stewards'—ideas. Thus these trustees sought to make others "sober, righteous, and godly"—like themselves. Because they were Protestants they denounced Catholics as a threat, because they were teetotalers themselves they denounced drinking,[29] because they were northerners who held no slaves they condemned southern slaveholders as sinners. And obviously those becoming wealthy through business, finance, and law would have some views on political, social, and economic questions.[30]

After 1815, peace with England opened the Mississippi Valley to settlers and if it had not seemed clear before, the election of Jackson to the presidency in 1829 left no question about the crucial need to win the West and thus save the nation. There were basically three types of benevolent societies: the more purely religious societies, those concerned primarily with personal moral reform, and those involved in great humanitarian crusades on a national scale. There were five "religious societies": the American Education Society (1815), the American Bible Society (1816), the American Sunday School Union (1824), the American Tract Society (1825), and the American Home Missionary Society (organized nationally in 1826, but building on the efforts of two earlier societies, the Missionary Society of Connecticut, 1798, and the Massachusetts Missionary Society, 1799, both of which were concerned with emigrants from their states). All of these societies were engaged after 1829 in a "general offensive"[31] in the Mississippi Valley,

Together with the various moral reform societies, their leaders tended to be more conservative, concerning themselves primarily with saving souls and personal morality. Typical of the latter were crusades against dueling, theaters, cardplaying, and dancing, and, in particular, efforts to elevate the morals of the neglected—the poor, the sailors, and the "degraded females." Among the more prominent societies of this kind were the American Seamen's Friend Society (1828) and the American Female Moral Reform Society (1834).

There were three more broadly "humanitarian" societies that were efforts to end the country's most alarming national evils: the American Society for the Promotion of Temperance (1826), the American Peace Society (1828), and the American Anti-Slavery Society (1833).[32]

All of these societies were controlled by small executive committees and boards of managers made up of prosperous laypeople and ministers. Most of them were run by the founders themselves or their successors and there was much overlapping of these officers. It is with justification then that Gilbert H. Barnes referred to this network of societies as "the benevolent empire" and Charles I. Foster called it "the evangelical united front." Most of the societies held their annual meeting in New York City during the second week of May, which was appropriately dubbed "Anniversary Week."[33] Much of the real work of the societies, however, was done on the local level by the auxiliaries and agents. By 1837, for example, the Bible Society had some 900 auxiliaries, the Tract Society claimed over 3,000, and the Anti-Slavery Society about 1,000.[34]

In the first great battle of the Protestant churches and infidelity at the turn of the century, orthodoxy under the command of fighters like Timothy Dwight was the decisive victor. Popular free thought died out in the great revivals, and intellectual deism was confined to the Unitarian minority in New England.[35] The second struggle between the churches and radicalism took place during the period of Jacksonian democracy. The chief culprits among the new generation of infidels were Frances Wright, Robert Dale Owen, and their skeptical and anticlerical supporters. This time the leading defender of orthodoxy was Lyman Beecher himself and the benevolent societies were part of the campaign.[36]

At stake in this battle of the 1820s as the evangelicals saw it, was the Christian character of the Republic and the churches' right to moral supervision.[37] On hand to challenge the Protestant vision for America were various freethinkers, reformers, and communitarian socialists—most of them immigrants, many of them atheistic or at least violently anticlerical—with their own "plans for society in their waistcoat pockets."[38] To orthodox Protestants like Beecher it was clear that Christianity was the only sure foundation of morals and government for the country. In sermons and lectures beginning in 1829, he did everything in his power to make clear the evil tendencies of atheism. Revealed religion, the family, private property, the state—all would be destroyed. Morality would be in a fearful state. Where "infidels preoccupy the soil," he urged, "there the convocation on the Sabbath is at the tavern, instead of the sanctuary, and hunting, and gambling, and horse-racing, and drunkenness, and fighting, and blasphemies prevail, till the Bible and Christian institutions overtake them."[39] And so Beecher pioneered in the organization of voluntary associations for the promotion of revivals, education, moral reform, and temperance.[40] The West, the cities, and education had to be saved for evangelicalism.

Theologically, men like Beecher and Taylor were liberals within evangelicalism. They stressed human agency rather than divine sovereignty, accepted the consequences of disestablishment and turned them toward the churches' advantage, pioneered in revivalism and benevolent societies. But they were unable to view the American republic apart from the old Federalist sense of their responsibility as trustees for the welfare of society.

In terms of the battle with radicalism, two incidents impinging on the political realm were highly revealing of evangelical goals and tactics. In 1827, Ezra Stiles Ely issued a call for a "Christian Party in Politics." In his Fourth of July sermon, Ely declared that Christians should elect and support as public officers "sincere friends of Christianity." The five chief Protestant sects, he asserted, "could govern every public election in the country."[41] Not surprisingly, freethinkers and radicals found this proposal proof of a conspiracy to unite church and state, while to the evangelical reformers, radical resentment of their political efforts seemed proof of the radicals' designs against all religion.[42]

Perhaps the greatest pitched battle between the radicals and the Protestant trustees, indicating the degree to which the latter had lost political power to those with different ideas and traditions, was the Sunday mail campaign of 1829-30. In 1828, concerned Protestants formed the General Union for Promoting Observance of the Christian Sabbath, and in 1829 they began an all-out petition campaign to persuade Congress to end Sunday mail service. The proposed reform was strongly opposed in both the Senate (1829) and the House (1830) by Richard M. Johnson of Kentucky. His committee's report insisted that Congress should never recognize one religion as superior to another, and accused the stewards of trying to establish an "ecclesiastical hierarchy."[43] Consequently, the reform was voted down, to the joy of the radicals and the dejection of the Sabbatarians.

The Popular Denominations

The radicals were not the only ones to object to the adjustments of the once-established churches to voluntaryism. Throughout the nation the configuration of denominations was rapidly changing as a result of immigration and the success of some of the smaller or newer churches on the frontier. By mid-century, the Methodists, Baptists, and Disciples had upset the old hegemony of the Congregationalists, Presbyterians, and Episcopalians. Before disestablishment was accomplished, Baptists and Methodists had frequently allied with rationalist forces to secure religious freedom. Although Beecher exulted that with establishment ended in Connecticut "the occasion of animosity" between Congregationalism and the "minor sects" was ended and the basis was laid for cooperation against the common enemy, infidelity,[44] it was not that simple. It was true that infidelity was effectively defeated by the combined forces of "traditionalism and sectarian-pietism"[45] in the new revivalism of the nineteenth century, but the vision of America held by the frontier preachers was often significantly different from that of the "heirs of theocracy."[46]

This difference is perhaps most strikingly seen in the Methodists. At the Christmas Conference in Baltimore in 1784, when the Methodist Episcopal Church in America was organized, the question was asked, "What may we reasonably believe to be God's Design in raising up the Preachers called Methodists?" The answer recorded was, "To reform the Continent, and to spread scriptural Holiness over these Lands." Whatever was meant by these two phrases, there seems to have been some distinction intended between them. But in his address to the General Conference of 1816, Bishop William McKendree affirmed that "God's design in raising up the preachers called Methodists in America, was to reform the continent by spreading scriptural holiness over these lands." By that time, Methodist preachers had taken literally Wesley's injunction, "You have nothing to do but to save Souls." They were confident that "if the man's soul was saved fundamental social change would inevitably follow."[47] As Sidney Mead pointed out, those of the Reformed or Puritan tradition never assumed so much. But since they assumed that Christianity was the only sound basis of morality and that the Christian life began with a conversion experience, their sense of Christian responsibility for society itself tended to reinforce the evangelical emphasis on revivals.[48]

The Methodist circuit riders labored among the poor on the frontier and did not hesitate to share their humble existence, but they made no attack on the causes for their misery in the economic order. They were above all concerned for the welfare of souls, regardless of their station in this life, and to this end they stressed conversion and personal morality. Similar in their respect for the common people were the Baptist farmer preachers. Both of these groups were far more sympathetic toward Jacksonian democracy than the northern trustees. Peter Cartwright, for example, the Methodist circuit rider who so perfectly embodied the "muscular Christianity"[49] of the frontier, served as a Jacksonian Democrat in the Illinois legislature, and was even defeated in the 1846 congressional race by Abraham Lincoln.[50]

Methodists and Baptists did not find it congenial to participate unreservedly in the benevolent societies. Resentful of the stress on an educated ministry by men like Lyman Beecher, and strongly sectarian in spirit, denominational leaders like the Methodist Nathan Bangs resisted cooperation in the American Temperance Society and promoted their own publishing ventures like the Methodist Book Concern. In 1824, the Baptists organized their own General Tract Society and in 1832, the American Baptist Home Missionary Society. The American Home Missionary Society, although giving the impression of national and interdenominational solidarity, was actually supported largely by Presbyterians and Congregationalists.

In many ways Charles G. Finney represented the process by which the distinctions between the two forces of the Protestant counteroffensive—the coalition of denominations with a Calvinistic heritage and the popular evangelicalism of the southern frontier—were gradually obliterated. As we have seen in Beecher and Taylor, the Calvinistic denominations moved in the

15

direction of a greater stress on human agency and free will, and Finney even adopted a Wesleyan view of Christian perfection after 1835. At first Finney's revivalism was closely related to the social ferment of the rising tide of Jacksonian democracy. But after 1827, he began to dissociate himself from the more extreme western revivalists. Although the reform aspect of his preaching was democratic in temper compared with Beecher's theocratic social outlook,[51] his insistence on the primacy of soul saving tended to make him cautious with regard to social action. He was one of the principal agents by which revivalism was "tamed and harnessed to the institutional structure of the churches."[52] Between 1830 and 1850, evangelical Protestantism came to be defined "almost wholly in Methodist terms."[53]

The Antislavery Struggle

It is revealing to compare how the various churches lined up on the issue of slavery, for as Henry May noted, opposition to slavery, far more than any other movement, strained the comfortable adjustment of Protestants to society.[54] In 1832, immediately following his campaign in Boston, Finney returned to New York to become pastor of the Second Free Presbyterian Church, housed in a remodeled theater and financed almost entirely by Lewis Tappan.[55] A few months later, Lyman Beecher also left Boston to become president and professor of theology at Lane Seminary in Cincinnati.

Inspired by the example of the British antislavery movement, the Tappans, Joshua Leavitt, and Theodore Weld, a young convert of Finney's, had since 1831 envisaged an American antislavery society. During the same year, William Lloyd Garrison began publishing a Boston weekly, called the *Liberator*, and was instrumental in organizing the New England Antislavery Society. Once convinced of the need to work for immediate emancipation, the Tappans, Leavitt, and Weld urged Finney to join them. The four were among the signers of a letter that appeared in the *Emancipator* on June 25, 1833, attacking the program of the American Colonization Society. Immediately after a bill for the emancipation of West Indian slaves had become law in late August 1833, the four organized the New York Antislavery Society. Finally, in December of that year, the national society was formed at a convention in Philadelphia, and Arthur Tappan was elected president.[56]

The opposition to the agitations of the antislavery society in 1834 was violent. Finney began to fear that a "censorious spirit" on both sides would

16

have ill effects on the church's main business of saving souls.[57] Meanwhile, at Lane Seminary in February 1834, the students had concluded nine days of consideration of the slavery question by voting unanimously for immediate abolition, and nine additional evenings by voting down colonization and organizing an antislavery society.[58] Beecher, as ever the believer in unity, advocated a plan for the assimilation of abolitionists and colonizationists, but promised to preserve the right of free discussion at the seminary. However, in New York to attend the May anniversary meetings, he must have become alarmed at the spread of antislavery discussions in other colleges. At any rate, he did nothing to prevent a conference of college presidents and officials from agreeing to suppress antislavery agitation and his own Lane trustees from passing rules that would end all such efforts there. Remaining away from the seminary until after the fall term had begun, Beecher returned to find an empty school. The "Lane rebels" had voted to move to Oberlin College, and to save this "cream of the revival crop"[59] led by Weld, none other than Finney was persuaded to go to Oberlin as professor of theology (and later president).

Finney's motives in going to Oberlin were clear. In accepting the offer, he explained to two of the Lane rebels, "I see and have seen that without a new race of ministers we can not possibly go much further."[60] In spite of the open disappointment of the Tappans with Finney's lack of participation in antislavery activities, he continued to insist that only as an appendage to a general revival would abolition save both the country and the freedom and souls of the slaves. He anxiously urged the Lane rebels "that we would accomplish the abolition work much sooner by promoting revivals."[61] Finney's increasingly militant outlook in the 1850s and 1860s was typical of the change in attitude throughout most of the North as the nation was swept on toward the "irrepressible conflict."

In 1836-37, according to Barnes, the doctrine of the Lane rebels—that slavery was not only an evil, but a sin—became part of the official gospel of abolitionism.[62] That winter, the American Anti-Slavery Society sent out a band of seventy, composed mainly of the Lane rebels and seminary students and ministers, and trained by Weld, to convert congregations among the state auxiliaries in the North to the duty of testimony against the slaveholders of the South.[63] Antislavery was certainly the most radical criticism of society undertaken by the evangelical reformers. Yet it still dealt with slaveholding as a personal moral evil—as a sin. And its criticism was directed primarily at the South rather than at its own social fabric. This is not to belittle the abolitionists' contribution; it took considerable courage to attack a fundamental vested interest like slavery, South or North. But the evangelical antislavery party largely ignored the real problems in its own society, like poverty, woman and child labor, the workers, incipient industrialism, women's rights, and the accumulation of wealth.

By 1837, this formative era was at an end. For one thing, success had loosened the bonds of alliance between the churches.[64] Infidelity had been vanquished and the churches had seen a rapid growth in membership as the result of the revivals. Furthermore, the four great national churches, the Baptists, Methodists, Episcopalians, and Presbyterians, were internally divided over revivalism and support of the united front. In 1832, the Baptists split into Old and New School parties, and in 1837, the Old School party within Presbyterianism exscinded five New School synods and established its own mission board. The panic of 1837 severely damaged all the benevolent societies because in it men like the Tappans, who had been their chief source of financial support, went bankrupt. Finally, the revivals of the 1820s-30s had burned themselves out. William McLoughlin described the situation well:

> The second great awakening was at an end by the time Finney left New York City for Oberlin in 1835. The reorientation in theology and ecclesiasticism was complete and the age of Jackson was shortly to give way to the reaction of 1840. The Presbyterian schism of 1837 was a last resort of the Old School but in the end it went for naught. Calvinism was dead and evangelical Protestantism was oiled and geared to coast complacently for a generation or more.[65]

1837-1877

Between 1837 and 1877, there were few new religious developments within evangelicalism. Although American society itself was changing very rapidly, and new forces were rising that would challenge the evangelical empire's adjustment to society, it was not until 1877 that the evangelicals began to feel the need for new ways of responding to these new forces. During this forty-year period, the implications of what had been achieved by 1837 were played out, and what had been disruptive and heretical in the 1830s was domesticated and orthodox by the 1870s.

Between 1840 and 1860, for example, itinerant evangelism became a respected profession whose task was to maintain a steady rate of church growth.[66] Books and lectures on the promotion of revivals indicated the degree to which revivals had been made "a subject of study, and an object of systematic effort."[67] Indeed, the "revival machinery"[68] was so well-oiled that it functioned automatically in the revival of 1857-58, without the leadership of any clergy at all. In the Baptist denomination, the careers of Jabez Swan and Jacob Knapp spanned this entire period from the 1830s to the 1870s, which saw the institutionalization of professional evangelism. Swan imparted a friendly, folksy tone that was to become fairly typical; Knapp added some of the commercialism and notoriety that would serve to discredit later revivalism. Finney himself continued to conduct revivals throughout the 1840s and 1850s and indeed held revivals annually at Oberlin until his death in 1875. Others who bridged the generation of Finney and the generation of Moody in the last quarter of the century were A. B. Earle, Edward Payson Hammond, and the British evangelists Henry Varley, Henry Moorhouse, and George C. Needham.[69]

In *Revivalism and Social Reform*, Timothy Smith dealt with just these years, and attempted to show that in spite of the decline of revivalism of the Finney type, revivalistic religion and the quest for Christian perfection continued to provide the impetus for social reform. Smith's study shows, if anything, the degree to which revivalism was accepted and institutionalized by the churches in this period. It is an important work in many ways. Smith makes it clear that revivalism flourished increasingly in the cities, and he is no doubt correct that some of the consequences of revivalism—lay leadership, the drive toward interdenominational fellowship, the primacy of ethics over dogma, and the democratization of Calvinism—were important in preparing the ground for the social gospel. However, it would seem more accurate to view these changes as part of the reorientation that took place in American Protestantism by 1837, producing evangelicalism—out of which, or better, in reaction to which, the social gospel arose in the last quarter of the century.

Smith cites the Christian perfectionism and postmillennialism of many evangelicals, particularly Methodists in this period, as having kinship with transcendental strivings and providing the impetus for social reform. Here he would seem to be on solid ground, as in the first great age of reform (1820s to 1840s) it was those with an optimistic vision striving to bring in the millennium who cared enough to reform the things of this world. There is little evidence that either before or after the Civil War, the liberal denominations like the Unitarians had any closer connection with the early social gospel than did the mainline evangelicals. However, the men Smith gives as examples—William E. Boardman, A. B. Earle, William Arthur—closely resembled Finney not only in their perfectionism and postmillennialism, but also in the part that social reform played with regard to soul saving. Always the latter was primary because only as individuals were reformed would basic changes follow in the social order. And as with Finney, this conviction had the inevitable result of limiting social action. Basic to their view was an understanding of sin, of morality, and of the relationship between the individual and society that made sense in the early nineteenth century but was rapidly being made inadequate by a host of forces changing society during these middle years. It is significant that the social gospelers were still the optimists and postmillennialists, but their conception of the relationship of the individual to society had changed drastically by the end of the century. It is on these grounds that they must be distinguished from the people about whom Smith writes.

After 1837, the trustees in control of the benevolent societies turned more and more toward political action to secure their goals. The earliest effort to "legislate morality"[70] was the Sunday mail campaign of 1829-30. In 1837, the three major humanitarian societies all launched petition campaigns to secure favorable legislation. The American Peace Society petitioned congressmen to support a Congress of Nations, but the campaign failed, partly because the petitions were regarded in the House as abolition memorials. In 1837 also, the American Anti-Slavery Society extended the abolition campaign in Congress, John Quincy Adams championing the right to petition in the face of the "Pinckney gag" that would have tabled all antislavery petitions. After 1837, a wave of petitions was sent to state legislatures demanding action with regard to the liquor traffic. These resulted in a number of local option laws in the 1840s but they were often repealed.

In the 1840s and 1850s, the leaders of the benevolent societies continued to demand that national and state governments act to make people moral. These were years when nonevangelicals began to intrude on the American scene—Irish Catholic immigrants (in 1831 and 1832, over 65,000 entered the country),[71] urban Jews, Mormons. After 1837, the Bible Society tried to arouse its local auxiliaries and sympathizers to secure Bible reading in the public schools. Depending on the numerical strength of Catholics and the amount of anti-Catholic sentiment, local contests were often lively and Protestants were by no means always successful.

In 1846, the efforts of the American Peace Society were powerless to prevent a war with Mexico. In 1837, however, the Maine Temperance Union was formed, based on the pledge of abstinence, and in 1851, the teetotaling mayor of Portland, Neal Dow, succeeded in getting a state prohibition law passed by the legislature. Passage of the Maine law was followed by a movement to secure similar legislation in other states. Temperance agitation often led to breaking of old party lines, and such confusion was greatly increased by political abolitionism.

Between the 1830s and the 1850s, many changes occurred in the antislavery crusade. One of the greatest was the split in the abolitionist ranks that took place in 1840, partly on the issue of political action. On April 1 of that year, the New York abolitionists met to form a political third party, the Liberty Party. Convinced that political action would ruin what was basically a moral crusade, Garrison attacked the new Liberty Party and, packing the annual meeting of the American Anti-Slavery Society in May with his New England supporters, gained control of it. The New Yorkers then formed the American and Foreign Anti-Slavery Society and from then on the abolition crusade as carried on through the voluntary societies was divided.[72]

During the same decade, two of the largest Protestant denominations, the Methodists and the Baptists, split on the issue of slavery. In 1844, the Methodist General Conference spent much of its time considering the question of slavery, and when the antislavery temper of the majority became clear, a Plan of Separation was drawn up that would permit the southern churches to withdraw. Consequently, in 1845, the Methodist Episcopal Church, South was formed. That same year a convention of Baptists representing eight slaveholding states voted to separate from their northern brethren and organized the Southern Baptist Convention. Both Old and New School Presbyterians were also internally divided, southern New School delegates forming a United Synod of the South in 1857.

Although not proslavery in sentiment, the leaders of the benevolent societies were by no means all in favor of abolitionism. Most of the officers of the five "religious societies" had supported the American Colonization Society and objected to abolitionism. Many of them had economic ties with southerners and realized that the welfare of their organizations depended partly on southern donations.[73] Although the abolitionists, led by the Tappans, tried to gain the cooperation of the Bible, Tract, and Home Missionary societies, they were only partially successful. The Bible Society refused to make any special efforts to supply the slaves with Scriptures. The Tract Society was split over abolitionism in 1859, and only in 1856 did the Home Missionary Society agree to refuse subsidies to churches admitting slaveholders.

By 1850, the main antislavery impulse had passed into politics. Through first the Liberty Party and then the Free Soil Party, abolitionists attempted to secure political action against slavery. When most voters endorsed the Compromise of 1850, third-party antislaveryism declined, but in 1856 a national Republican Party was formed that turned all its fury against slavery. Although the trustees of the benevolent societies had deprecated sectional hatred and tried to preserve good will, they were soon forced into the Republican Party and the crusade to preserve the nation.

Clerical Laissez-Faire

One vast area remains to be considered. From the 1830s to the 1870s, American society was being rapidly transformed from a commercial to an industrial nation. What was the relationship of the Protestant evangelicals to the economic order and, in time, to industrialization?

Finney's ethic was based on the face-to-face commercial system with which America was still familiar in the 1830s. He attacked the credit system and economic theory that a businessman "might justly charge what the traffic will bear."[74] He urged Christian businessmen not to follow the practices of the world, but to do business on Christian principles and to seek to exemplify the self-denial and benevolent spirit of Christ. Finney's solution as always was the personal reformation of the individual. Because business was to his mind still a matter of personal relationship, it made more sense to talk about brotherly love and honesty in one's dealings.

Yet Finney was, like many of his fellow Protestants, guilty of certain assumptions and attitudes that would put the church in a more and more ambiguous position as the nation industrialized. First was his attitude toward the poor. If persons were poor, this was simply the station in life to which they had been ordained by providence. Therefore they should be submissive and content with their lot. Furthermore, Finney was blind to some of the broader dangers of incipient industrialism. He often was invited to hold revivals in factories and he tended to assume that if employers were concerned for the spiritual welfare of their employees, they would not be guilty of treating them with less than brotherly love. Finally, he allowed for the possibility that the accumulation of capital might be justified in terms of stewardship, a possibility that was fully exploited later in the century.

The eastern heirs of theocracy were, if anything, more guilty of adopting the social and economic doctrines of the privileged classes. Most of the lay officers of the benevolent societies were wealthy merchants, businessmen, lawyers, and financiers. Joseph Dorfman would seem to be justified in characterizing their economic views as paternalistic, in terms of their regard for private property, their advocacy of the interests of the merchant class, and an uneasy attitude toward the working and underprivileged classes.[75]

In the years from 1837 to 1877, Protestant evangelicals generally accepted the given social contract. By and large they set their stamp of approval on the burgeoning middle-class, acquisitive society. Many of the Protestant clergy wrote the college textbooks for the laissez-faire political economy that dominated the American scene from the 1820s until well into the 1880s. Among the best known of the clerical texts were John McVickar's *Outlines of Political Economy*, published in 1825, and especially Francis Wayland's *The Elements of Political Economy*, first published in 1837 and in its fourth edition by 1852.[76]

According to this "clerical laissez faire"[77] the laws of economics were part of natural law and, as established by God, were not to be tampered with. Wages were paid from a fixed wage-fund and could not be altered by labor action. Trade unions were therefore a positive evil. The unequal distribution of wealth was accepted as the natural order of things. Consequently, poverty, like wealth, was regarded as divinely ordained. It could be interpreted, according to circumstances, as an expression of Divine disfavor or simply as the schooling of Providence. In either case, the poor were advised to be content with their lot, and charity and philanthropy were directed toward relief of their misery. Moral rather than economic solutions were recommended for the ills of the working classes, while respectability was given to the activities of the upper classes.

The Jacksonian era was truly the era of individualism in American life. However, it was generally a healthy kind of individualism in which the emphasis was on equal opportunity and self-realization. In the Jacksonian era, laissez-faire as an economic doctrine was genuinely liberal, in the sense that it eliminated special privilege and opened competition. The economy was expanding, men were "on the make," and it was desired that government should afford no monopoly privileges, but rather equal protection to all.

The "take off" years for American industrialization were the 1840s to 1860s. Long after the nation had passed the "hump of transition" to industrialization it still retained this individualistic ideology.[78] In the post-Civil War years, the concepts of individualism, progress, and laissez-faire were still dominant, but their significance had changed. Individualism then meant self-interest, often as opposed to the general welfare; progress was seen as automatic; and laissez-

23

faire was used to preserve the status quo for those who "had it made."[79] Even in the prewar years, of course, the doctrine of laissez-faire left some behind in the race, but the consequences of this doctrine grew more disastrous as American society industrialized.

A notable exception to the dominant laissez-faire was Stephen Colwell, a well-known Presbyterian industrialist and economist, who in *New Themes for the Protestant Clergy* (1851) strongly criticized American Protestantism for accepting the existing social order. He attacked the conventional political economy as unchristian, acknowledged Christianity's debt to socialism for exposing "this hideous skeleton of selfishness,"[80] and called on Christians to develop a social economy in keeping with the teachings of Jesus. In terms of economic views, Colwell belonged to the school represented by Henry Carey, which rejected much of the classical political economy and favored a protective tariff. It may well be that even in terms of economics, Colwell was acting in the interests of social justice by supporting tariffs in the 1850s, since because of British competition, the interests of labor were probably more bound up with the welfare of manufacturers than with commerce. However, the real novelty and significance of Colwell's work lay in its criticism of the social teachings of American Protestantism.

C. H. Hopkins called Colwell's *New Themes* "the earliest statement of a social gospel in the modern sense."[81] In many ways such a case could be made. Certain of the presuppositions distinguishing social Christianity were also characteristic of Colwell's thinking. For example, he criticized the otherworldliness of orthodox Christianity, emphasized the need for sociological studies to aid in carrying out the second great commandment of charity to one's neighbors, called for Christian ethics based on the teachings of Jesus, and called on the church to lead the social crusade. Like the later social gospelers, Colwell criticized Protestantism for exalting theology above practical Christianity and for stressing the atonement and vicarious sacrifice of Christ rather than his precepts and example. Furthermore, he spoke as later reformers would of the Fatherhood of God and brotherhood of man.

Colwell recognized, as few men of his day did, that many were being brought into the churches whose "business morality" was little disturbed by their Christian profession and whose wealth was becoming a ruling element in the church machinery. He further saw the dangers of a system of "systematic benevolence,"[82] whereby the duty of charity was regarded as satisfied by contributing money.

24

Finally, he charged the maxims and requirements of business as being almost all opposed in spirit and results to Christ's precepts. Mentioned specifically were competition, the pursuit of wealth, considering human beings as mere machines for creating wealth, the inviolable nature of property, and free trade. He insisted that the social, political, and commercial institutions of the day constituted the great barriers to the progress of Christianity.[83] In terms of humanitarian and religious precepts, Colwell was perhaps as close to the views of the early social gospelers as he could be without the secular influences that were so important for them. If the social gospel is defined as the attempt to apply Christianity to all aspects of the social, economic, and political system, then Colwell was a precursor. In terms of the relationship between the individual and society, however, Colwell's ethic was still essentially individualistic. Although he offered few concrete proposals for social change beyond the tariff, the storm of protest that greeted his criticism demonstrated its rarity in the 1850s.

To sum up, evangelicalism based on voluntaryism, a theology compounded of Taylorism, Finneyism, and Methodism, and the institutionalization of revivalism had made a clean sweep in nearly all denominations by 1850. Among the challengers to the evangelical hegemony were other Protestants: the Unitarian liberals, those representing a churchly orientation like the Mercersburg school of theology among the Reformed, the German Evangelical Lutheran Synod of Missouri, Ohio and other States (later the Missouri Synod), and the Old Calvinist conservatives at Princeton. However, their protests were largely unheard in the evangelical age of American Protestantism and they failed to win any appreciable following. Far more threatening were the real intruders—German and Irish Catholics, urban Jews, and Mormons—who would soon turn America into a pluralistic society.

Generally speaking, the benevolent societies controlled by the Presbyterian and Congregational heirs of theocracy concentrated on soul saving and personal moral reform. Although Finney's stress on sin as selfishness and on salvation as the beginning of a life of benevolent activity was a powerful impulse to reform, Finney himself insisted that soul winning was still the primary task, and reforms like temperance and abolitionism must be appendages to revivals. Evangelicals of every stripe were agreed that the way to reform the nation was to reform the individual.

From 1837 to 1877, the rising forces of industrialization and nationalism were rapidly transforming American society. The kind of personal morality stressed by Finney as the solution for economic ills was more appropriate in the 1830s when business was carried on in terms of person-to-person relationships. It fast became inadequate as the country industrialized. Protestant evangelicals generally accepted the given social contract. They accepted the unequal distribution of wealth as divinely ordained and urged the poor to be content with their lot. By opposing the specific demands of labor, prescribing moral rather than economic solutions for the misery of the working classes, respecting private property and the right of the wealthy to accumulate capital for benevolent enterprises, and—with a few notable exceptions—failing to criticize the evils of laissez-faire, they set their stamp of approval on the burgeoning middle-class, acquisitive society.

By 1850, sectional hostility had greatly increased, three of the largest denominations had split over the issue of slavery, and the nation was fast heading toward a war that would be regarded by the North as a Christian crusade. In other respects, however, the evangelicals were still united, social reforms were not regarded as in opposition to soul saving, the split in Protestantism had not yet occurred. At this point the American nation was once again plunged into a financial panic, that of 1857.

TWO

Evangelical Blessing on Industrial America

The panic of 1857 ended two decades of unprecedented growth, prosperity, and change in American life. By 1845, the country had fully recovered from the depression of 1837 and had entered that crucial period in its economic development called by W. Rostow, the "take-off" into industrialization.[1] The symbol of American progress in these decades was the railroad. As early as 1844, Nathaniel Hawthorne had described in his notebook the "Sleepy Hollow episode," the paradigmatic event of the sudden appearance of the locomotive in the country. America's imaginative literature of the 1840s and 1850s was full of variations on the same theme, all of them stressing the "startling suddenness" with which the machine invaded the land.[2]

By the 1850s, the railroad was beginning to dominate American life. Although there were only some 1,000 miles of track laid in the 1840s, during the next decade this figure was increased by 21,000 miles, most of it in the new West. By 1860, the railroads had created a truly national market in America. "Rails" dominated also on the booming stock exchanges in the nation's major commercial and financial centers. Just before the 1857 panic, it was said that "the entire country was in stocks."[3] Since more than 25 percent of the total active capital in the country was invested in railroads, it was no wonder the financial structure collapsed when railroad profits proved smaller or slower than expected.[4] In 1857, the stock market—much of it built on fraudulent operations—collapsed, and with it the banks that had depended on railroad securities for their own collateral. It was this financial crash that appeared to touch off the religious awakening known as the "Laymen's Revival."

The "Laymen's Revival," 1857-58

In his history of two hundred years of evangelized America, Grover C. Loud devoted a chapter to this revival, entitling it "Post-Panic Repentance." His view that the revival was a response to the economic crisis is generally held by historians and indeed seems to have been recognized at the time. Loud quoted a Universalist pastor of Portsmouth, New Hampshire, Rev. A. J. Patterson, as saying:

> When men lose their fortunes and their hopes, when they see how insecure are things material and earthly, when their poor, disappointed hearts are bleeding and desolate, then they turn to religion for strength and consolation. The Gospel which in prosperity they neglected now claims their earnest attention in their hour of greatest need.[5]

James Waddell Alexander, pastor of New York's largest Old School Presbyterian church, thought the financial crisis proof that God had been pleased "by the ploughshare of his judgments to furrow the ground for the precious seed of salvation."[6] And ministers thought it appropriate that those losing treasure on earth should begin to think of laying up treasures in heaven.[7]

The revival was unusual in that it did not depend on the preaching of any prominent evangelists. The basic institution of the awakening was the noon prayer meeting, the first of which began on a daily basis on October 7, 1858, at the Old Dutch Church on Fulton Street, New York City, just a few days before the stock market crash. Its organizer was Jeremiah Lanphier, a neighborhood missionary. Soon many clerks and businessmen from the nearby financial district were unemployed because of the crash and the crowds grew until by midwinter they overflowed into the John Street Methodist Church around the corner.[8]

Similar noonday prayer meetings sprang up all over the city, the excitement and contagion greatly increased by two new means of communication, the daily "penny" newspapers, and the telegraph, which aided the spread of the revival to other cities. Outstanding among the secular newspapers were the *New York Herald*, edited by James Gordon Bennett, and Horace Greeley's *New York Tribune*, which gave full coverage to revival news. In April 1858, the *Tribune* devoted an entire issue to reports of the revivals. Telegraph companies allowing messages to be sent free of charge at certain hours made it possible for New York businessmen to send news of bankruptcy and prayer meetings to other cities and they too began prayer meetings. By April, according to Timothy Smith, twenty noonday prayer groups were in progress in New York alone.[9] A group met at Henry Ward Beecher's Plymouth Church in Brooklyn, and two famous meetings were held at Burton's Theater and the Music Hall.

Larger prayer meetings and numbers of conversions and reconsecrations were reported from Philadelphia, Boston, Cleveland, and Chicago. In Philadelphia, George H. Stuart and the young Dudley Tyng led a noonday prayer meeting in Jaynes Hall that was reportedly "thronged by three thousand a day for several months."[10] When Tyng died, George Duffield was inspired by his dying words to write the hymn "Stand Up for Jesus," which Loud called the hymn of the revival.[11] Dwight L. Moody, then a traveling salesman for a shoe company in Chicago, wrote home about his frequent attendance at prayer meetings in that rapidly growing city in 1857.[12] From the cities, the revival spread to small towns and rural communities.[13]

Two facts were noteworthy about these revival meetings: they were interdenominational and they were led by laypeople. Prominent in the organization of these prayer meetings were local units of the Young Men's Christian Association, the first American chapter of which was begun in Boston in 1851. Indeed, it is difficult to say which movement, the revival or the YMCA, was the motivating force, since in some cities they came into being together. In Philadelphia, John Wanamaker served the Philadelphia Association as corresponding secretary from 1857-60. His chief interest was the revivalistic noon prayer meeting there.[14] In Chicago, the YMCA came to life in the 1858 revival, its first meeting being called by several young men participating in the revival in March 1858. The YMCA in the 1850s was closely related to the evangelical Protestant churches. Its members had to be members in good standing in any evangelical church, and its general purposes were those of evangelicals elsewhere—evangelism and the expansion of evangelical influence, particularly in the cities. The prominence of these Christian associations reveals many of the characteristics of evangelical Protestantism in 1857-58: the considerable degree of lay participation and control, the close association of evangelicalism and the business community, the trend toward evangelical unity, the extent to which revivalism had become an accepted part of the life of the evangelical churches.

Few people in 1857-58 saw any reason to criticize the revival.[15] To those who interpreted the panic of 1857 as a divine judgment, it seemed to make sense to repent and return to religion. The 1857-58 revival was the last, perhaps the only, modern American revival to be so closely associated with an economic crisis. The people to whom it appealed were the small, independent businessmen, recently come to the city, for whom business decisions could still be made on the basis of person-to-person morality. In a few years the ongoing process of industrialization would make that kind of ethic inadequate.

Evangelicals and the Civil War

In 1858, then, the only split within the evangelical ranks was over the issue of slavery and by that time the split was sectional. When war broke out in 1861, it soon became both a war to save the Union and a "Christian crusade."[16] Of the prewar benevolent societies, the three most active in ministering to the northern servicemen were the Bible and Tract societies and the Temperance Union. By supplying New Testaments and cheap tracts, they did their best to see that the northern army was Christian and moral. However, the most efficient link between the evangelical churches and the northern armies was the United States Christian Commission, organized in the fall of 1861. The commission was the principal means by which the YMCA contributed to the war effort and it was built on the foundations of the prewar benevolent societies. As Clifford S. Griffin described it, "the Christian Commission was the benevolent societies geared for war."[17] Many of the leaders of these prewar societies were national officers of the commission. Its president and chairman of its executive committee was George H. Stuart, prominent in the 1858 revival in Philadelphia, and an officer of the Sunday School and Temperance unions. Its treasurer was Joseph Patterson, a bank president also from Philadelphia and manager of the Sunday School Union. Other officers and leaders included William E. Dodge, the prominent New York entrepreneur and financier and a member of the Bible Society and Temperance Union, and well-known evangelical ministers like Methodist bishop Charles P. McIlvaine, president of the Tract Society, and Russell S. Cook, secretary of the Tract Society.

The objects of the commission were both Christian and patriotic: "to promote the spiritual and temporal welfare of the men who are now in arms to put down a wicked rebellion."[18] Beginning in the spring of 1863, the commission systematically divided the northern armies into separate units, to each of which was assigned a paid field agent. It was their responsibility to direct the hundreds of volunteers who served in the army camps and hospitals. These delegates distributed Bibles and tracts, they comforted the sick, wounded, and dying, held revival and temperance meetings, and generally admonished the soldiers on issues of personal morality. Among the well-known evangelicals who served as volunteer delegates to the camps were revivalists like Dwight L. Moody,[19] C. C. McCabe, Edward N. Kirk, and Alfred Cookman.[20]

Evangelicals also aided the servicemen by participating in local branches of and contributing money to the United States Sanitary Commission, an organization as much concerned with the physical welfare of the Union soldiers as the Christian Commission was with their spiritual and moral well-being. Many leaders of the prewar benevolent societies participated in the local work of this commission.

With regard to abolition there was still division among evangelicals. Even after President Lincoln issued his Emancipation Proclamation, to take effect on January 1, 1863, the Bible Society remained silent and attempted to maintain friendly relations with the South. In 1863-64, for example, it actually managed to send some 218,000 volumes into the South, most of them to Confederate soldiers.[21] The Tract Society gradually affirmed its support of emancipation, while spokespersons for the Temperance, Home Missionary, and Education societies repeatedly urged the extinction of slavery.

As the war drew to a close in 1865, northerners began to make clear their ideas for the new South. Now freed from the evil of slavery, the South was ready for the "enterprise of the North."[22] And as the officers of the Home Missionary Society insisted, northern churches must go where northern enterprise went. The same ideas had been expressed even earlier by the celebrity preacher, Henry Ward Beecher. Addressing the annual meeting of the Home Missionary Society in Chicago in 1863, Beecher rejoiced that the North was growing rich by war, thus being prepared for the work ahead when the war ended. What this work would be, Beecher thought he saw quite clearly.

> We are to have the charge of this continent. The South has been proved, and has been found wanting. . . . This continent is to be from this time forth governed by Northern men, with Northern ideas, and with a Northern gospel.[23]

It was little wonder that the eventual victory of the North was widely interpreted as a vindication of northern society. The following exultation appeared in the *Congregationalist*, April 28, 1866:

> What cause have we for gratitude to God for his gift of such institutions to us, and of renewed confidence in them. . . . No other country . . . could have gone

through such a crisis, so much unmoved. . . . That only stands secure which stands broad and deep on the eternal foundations of human rights and the Divine law.[24]

Thus, although the issue of slavery more than any other strained the comfortable adjustment of Protestant evangelicals to society, the triumph of the Union cause made church spokesmen in the North less than ever inclined to question their basic institutions. As Henry May so aptly put it, the confidence of Protestantism in "the prevailing order and . . . in its own mandate were equally unimpaired."[25]

The Gilded Age

In the generation following the Civil War, the process of industrialization swept on at a giddy pace. Greatly stimulated by the demands of the war, the forces of industrial revolution within a generation completed the transformation of America into an industrial, urban nation. The recklessness with which the giants of railroads, industry, and finance scrambled to take possession of the country's resources earned for the age Vernon L. Parrington's disparaging epithet, the "Great Barbecue." This was the era dubbed by Mark Twain the "Gilded Age" for its poor taste, materialism, and extravagance. It was also a period of widespread corruption at every level of government. Historical studies have shown the need to reassess some of the overdrawn and oversimplified judgments of the age.[26] It was certainly a vigorous, exciting, and optimistic time, but the dislocations, readjustments, and new responses resulting from the rapid transition to the modern world were tremendous.

The peculiar lot of this generation that came of age between the Civil War and World War I has nowhere been more poignantly described than in the chapter of William Jewett Tucker's autobiography entitled "The Fortune of My Generation."[27] It was a generation that had to find its own way into the modern world, and as he put it, "it was not a time through which one could find his way clearly."[28] In attempting to specify what factors constituted the peculiar fortune of his generation, Tucker pointed to two: the intellectual detachment from the past brought about by the complete change of view that resulted from Darwin's theory of evolution, and the change from an individualistic to a socialistic conception of society brought about by industrialism. Although the impact of Darwinism and industrialism and its consequences was first felt in the Gilded Age, the effort to find "the way of knowledge" and "the way of duty" appropriate to this new era would occupy human lives on into the twentieth century.

Although the first American edition of Darwin's *Origin of Species* was widely reviewed in 1860, its real impact was delayed by the Civil War. By the early 1870s, Darwin's views on the transmutation of species and natural selection were accepted by all but a very few American scientists. Thereafter evolution penetrated the faculties and student bodies of colleges and universities with great rapidity. An impressive testimony to the new interest in scientific learning was the founding of Johns Hopkins University in 1876 as an institution devoted to research and free of ties to any religious denomination. Popular magazines like the *North American Review* moved from hostility to the new theories in the 1860s to forthright and enthusiastic approval by the early 1870s. One magazine that was to have long success, *Popular Science Monthly*, came into being in 1872 to satisfy the demand for scientific news.

The churches were more difficult to convince. The initial converts to evolution came from the intellectual leadership of the more liberal Protestant denominations in the 1870s. As twentieth-century Fundamentalism indicates, there were some areas where the concept of evolution never was accepted. To most churchpeople it seemed that evolution was irreconcilable with theism. It struck at the argument from design and thus at the existence of God. Human dignity and morality seemed threatened by Darwin's tracing of human ancestry to the monkey, particularly after the appearance of *The Descent of Man* in 1871. Charles Hodge's *What is Darwinism?* (1874) was typical of Protestant anti-Darwinian views. The first good omen for clerical acceptance of Darwinism was the acknowledgment by President James McCosh of Princeton University in his *Christianity and Positivism* (1871) that he accepted the hypothesis of the development of species. By 1880, the *Independent*, the most influential religious paper in the country, had gone over to evolutionary views. Finally, the most important pulpit was also won when Henry Ward Beecher became convinced of the truth of evolution by reading Darwin and Spencer. He and his successor at Plymouth Church in Brooklyn, Lyman Abbott, became the most significant popularizers of the compatibility of Christianity and evolution through their sermons and editorial responsibilities with the *Christian Union* and the *Outlook*, both well-known religious newspapers. Both men also wrote books on the subject. In *Evolution and Religion*, published in

1885, Beecher solved for himself the problem of the argument from design, claiming that "design by wholesale is grander than design by retail."[29] He frequently declared himself to be "a cordial Christian evolutionist." By the 1880s, most outstanding liberal theological figures had joined the ranks of the evolutionists, and evolution had been translated into divine purpose for those who were believers.

Social Darwinism

Darwin's theories were concerned with nature. It remained for others like Herbert Spencer to apply them to society and afford business America a philosophy fit for the Gilded Age. The Englishman's thought gained far greater vogue in America than it ever did in his own country. In the three decades following the Civil War, Spencerism was as much the reigning philosophy as Pragmatism was to be in the Progressive Era, or as Transcendentalism had been in the first great age of American reform. Even those who disagreed with him had to deal with him in his own terms. As V. L. Parrington put it, "Spencer laid out the broad highway over which American thought traveled in the later years of the century."[30]

Spencer's philosophy was well suited to the post-Civil War American society. It satisfied the popular desire for scientific learning. It was comprehensive, and embodied a theory of progress. In his *Synthetic Philosophy*, the first volume of which appeared in 1864, he joined in one system the findings of physics and biology, deducing from the principle of conservation of energy the key to universal evolution: the progress from homogeneity to heterogeneity. This supposition that a universal law of evolution could be formulated then led him to apply the biologic scheme of evolution to society. This was the fateful step. Influenced by Malthus's work on population, Spencer developed a theory of social selection (which preceded the first publication of Darwin's views) and actually coined the expression "survival of the fittest."[31] In his first book, *Social Statics*, Spencer used biological arguments to defend laissez-faire and the concept of the negative state. Since Spencer defined ethical progress in terms of the adaptation of human character to the conditions of life, he insisted that the state must not interfere with the natural development of society by which evil gradually disappears. Finally, in *The Study of Sociology*, published serially in *Popular Science Monthly* in 1872-73, he defined the task of sociology as charting this normal course of social evolution. Control was impossible, and any efforts to disturb this social progress would be harmful.

Spencer's system supplied the perfect scientific rationale for the competitive, laissez-faire society of the Gilded Age, itself "a vast human caricature of the Darwinian struggle for existence and survival of the fittest."[32] Businessmen and those who lauded them quickly seized on this justification for competition and the consolidation of industry. "The growth of a large business is merely a survival of the fittest," John D. Rockefeller told a Sunday school audience. He then used the analogy of the American beauty rose, which can be produced only by "sacrificing the early buds," to show that this was not an evil tendency, but "merely the working out of a law of nature and a law of God."[33] Spencer's doctrine that interference with the natural course of things would be harmful served to caution all would-be reformers and answer the demands of troublesome labor agitators. The system was a perfect rationalization of the status quo. What it meant for post-Civil War America was aptly summed up by Andrew Carnegie, who said that after reading Darwin and Spencer, his motto and "true source of comfort" was: "All is well since all grows better."[34]

This tendency to regard the millionaire as the product of natural selection received considerable support from the teaching and writings of "the most vigorous and influential social Darwinist in America,"[35] William Graham Sumner of Yale. Born and raised in Paterson, New Jersey, the son of a self-educated English laborer whose family industry had been disrupted by the growth of the English factory system, Sumner was brought up on the traditional Protestant economic virtues and the doctrines of classical political economy. To these he had only to add Darwinian natural selection and he had the major ingredients for his social thought.

Sumner's system was based on the Malthusian idea that the foundation of human society is the human-land ratio and that all of life therefore is a struggle against nature in which only the fittest survive. In his famous work of 1883, *What Social Classes Owe to Each Other*, Sumner argued that the hardships of life are incidents in this struggle against nature and that we cannot blame our fellow humans for succeeding in this struggle better than we have done. Granting that the person with capital has great advantage in the struggle, Sumner still insisted that capital is formed only by self-denial, and "if the possession of it did not secure advantages and superiorities of a high order men would never submit to what is necessary to get it."[36] As he put it, Nature "grants her rewards to the fittest." Believing that capital provided the necessary means for advancing civilization, Sumner regarded millionaires as a product of natural selection, their fortunes only the legitimate payment of society for their unique management abilities. Competition was a law of nature, and the progress of civilization depended on its unrestricted workings. Sumner did not hesitate to identify the "strong" with the "industrious" and the "frugal," the "weak" with the "idle" and the "extravagant." There was no point, then, in trying to aid the weak. The alternatives were simple: "liberty, inequality, survival of the fittest" or "not-liberty, equality, survival of the unfittest."[37] Like Spencer, Sumner was a social determinist. According to him, it was sheer folly to attempt to "make the world over."[38] The gradual process of societal evolution would continue regardless of human efforts. Poverty was an inevitable evil, part of the struggle for existence, and the only way to abolish it was to accumulate economic virtues. "Let every man be sober, industrious, prudent, and wise, and bring up his children to be likewise, and poverty will be abolished in a few generations."[39] As Richard Hofstadter said of Yale's professor of political and social science, "like some latter-day Calvin, he came to preach the predestination of the social order and the salvation of the economically elect through the survival of the fittest."[40]

To the tremendous weight of the social Darwinist argument for competition and inevitability in the decades after the Civil War were added economic and legal sanctions for laissez-faire. The orthodox political economists did not embrace social Darwinism; they already had their own rationale. As in the prewar years, classical political economy identified the economic process with the laws of God or with natural law, and declared the system of free competition beneficial for society. In a series of important decisions from the 1870s, the Supreme Court buttressed the economic arguments for laissez-faire by guaranteeing the protection of private property from government encroachment. The main guarantee of private rights was the due-process clause of the Fourteenth Amendment, passed in 1868, providing that liberty and property should not be subject to governmental interference without due process of law. In the case of *Santa Clara County vs. the Southern Pacific Railroad* in 1886, the court declared a corporation a "legal person," with all the rights to protection implied in such a designation. Finally, in a series of cases (the most famous of which was *Lochner vs. New York*, on the question of a ten-hour day in the baking industry in 1905), state attempts at labor legislation were set aside on the grounds that they interfered with "freedom of contract," the right of laborers to pursue their calling. Thus as Sidney Fine pointed out, laissez-faire became the law of the land in the three-and-a-half decades after the Civil War.[41]

Whereas the laissez-faire of the Jeffersonian-Jacksonian tradition had been genuinely liberal, protecting the freedom and equality of opportunity of the individual, laissez-faire in the industrialized America after 1865 was simply a defense of the status quo. Government action alone could restore some measure of justice and welfare to those left behind in the great competitive race for wealth. But before reform could become a possibility, the general complacency, approval of competition, and the "steel chain of ideas"[42] protecting the whole selfish system must be dissolved. Until the 1880s, few voices indeed would dispute the Spencerian contention that "nothing at all" could be done.[43]

In the Gilded Age, the American businessman was the dominating figure, and nowhere was there more enthusiastic endorsement of business success than in the Protestant churches.[44] Wealthy businessmen were becoming more and more prominent in the lives of the churches. Even the Baptists and Methodists, denominations that originally drew their greatest strength from the common people, were becoming wealthy and respectable.[45] Still armed with the laissez-faire political economy of the prewar years, and reinforced by their experience of the fruits of prosperity, Protestant clergy gave their support to the status quo. They justified the accumulation of wealth by preaching the duty of Christian stewardship to the rich. Poverty was often regarded as the result of drunkenness or laziness, and preachers extolled the virtue of hard work, still believing that there was room at the top for all those willing to be industrious and frugal.

A Gospel for the Upwardly Mobile

Typical of the attitude of evangelical churchmen was "that magnificent weathervane of respectable opinion,"[46] Rev. Henry Ward Beecher. Called to Plymouth Congregational Church in Brooklyn in 1847, Henry Ward Beecher was as much a giant in the years from 1837-77 as his father Lyman had been to his generation. In fact a comparison of the two men would reveal much about the changes that occurred in American Protestantism during the first three-quarters of the nineteenth century. From the pulpit of Plymouth Church, through speeches and addresses on all sorts of subjects, and from his editorial post on two widely read religious weeklies, the *Independent* and the

37

Christian Union, Beecher's views were well circulated and made him probably the most influential minister in America in these years.

Believing strongly that it was the duty of a Christian minister to preach on all moral issues concerned with everyday living, Beecher spoke out on practically every question, from emancipation and Reconstruction to immigration, the currency, and Republican politics. In the postwar years, as Henry May has pointed out, he was "a sturdy defender of freedom, prosperity and the status quo."[47] In the static society of his father's day, the poor had been advised to be content with their lot and to seek meaning in that station of life to which they had been ordained. Henry Ward Beecher's message was a gospel for an upwardly mobile society. Over and over again his congregations were told that poverty was unnecessary and sinful and that hard work and thrift could lead to prosperity.

Whether with regard to spiritual or worldly matters, the tone of Beecher's Christianity was dynamic, optimistic, active. In 1872, he urged the people of Plymouth Church:

> It is not for you to stand content on your present condition; it is not for you to reckon your whole life as treasured up in the past: it is for you, if you be a true man, touched by the Spirit of God, never to cease activity. . . .
> Open the furrows once more. Cast in the seed of new endeavors. . . .
> It is never too late to begin again. It is never too late to sow. It is never too late to reap. Go through life with the reaper's song in your mouth; and when you die carry your sheaves with you to heaven.[48]

To a large and well-to-do congregation, Beecher preached the value of hard work and adversity for the development of one's character. Everyone, no matter how well born, should earn a living, since the necessity of earning a livelihood was one of the principal means of developing such human virtues as patience, punctuality, honesty, and self-denial. Beecher did not caution his hearers against wealth. He perhaps explained his attitude best when he said:

> I have never cautioned you against it. I have rather exhorted you, if in the providence of God you had opened to you opportunities for acquiring wealth, to improve them. . . . I should as soon think of going into my barn-yard and saying "O Alderneys; be careful about giving too much milk," as I should think of saying to men, "Avoid getting rich." . . . I have never exhorted men not to seek wealth; but I have said to men, "Riches alone do not make manhood, nor produce happiness."[49]

At a time when the attractions of wealth were beginning to induce men and women to leave the farms and come to the cities to seek easier and more rapid ways to earn money, Beecher insisted that parents should teach their children how to earn a livelihood so that they would never be obliged to go without work. Only a few months before the depression of 1873 would result in large numbers of unemployed in the nation's cities, Beecher's advice was:

> "Eat the bread you earn, or else do not eat.". . . Be ashamed to be dependent. . . . Be willing to do that which you can do, down to the bottom, till you come to be a laborer on the road, or in the canal, rather than beg. Work, work, work out, not only your own salvation, but your own subsistence.[50]

In Beecher's eyes, poverty was unnecessary in post-Civil War America. "Nothing can be more certain in such a land as this," he said in 1875,

> under such a sky, and with such prodigal abundance, than that the ordinary wants of every man, woman, and child may be amply supplied. . . . There may be reasons of poverty which do not involve wrong, but looking comprehensively through city and town and village and country, the general truth will stand, that no man in this land suffers from poverty unless it be more than his fault——unless it be his *sin*.[51]

For Beecher, then, hard work and thrift were Christian virtues, and laziness was a sin. Like many of his fellow clergymen, he believed that success and morality usually could be found together. "Generally the proposition is true" he said, "that where you find the most religion there you will find the most worldly prosperity—in communities; I mean, not in single persons."[52]

In his optimistic approval of the individualism and competition of the burgeoning middle-class acquisitive society, Henry Ward Beecher was typical of evangelical Protestantism in the 1870s. The severest test of Protestant confidence in the soundness of American society was the depression following the panic of 1873. The economic crisis was severe and its consequences were felt throughout the nation. In New York City, about 25 percent of the workers, nearly 400,000 people, were unemployed in the winter months of 1873-74.[53] Strikes protesting wage cuts were widespread, and bands of unemployed laborers roamed from town to town seeking relief. Protestant churchpeople generally agreed with those of the middle and upper classes, particularly in the cities,[54] who insisted that recovery would come about through automatic processes and counseled the poor to be patient. "Be content with your wages, work for what you can get, but work" was typical of clerical advice.[55] Strikes were denounced as senseless and likely to prolong the depression.

There was much agitation in 1873-74 for public works for the unemployed. Street demonstrations by the unemployed occurred in November and December of 1873 in Boston, Cincinnati, Chicago, Detroit, Indianapolis, Louisville, Newark, New York, Paterson, Pittsburgh, and Philadelphia. Huge labor meetings were held in Chicago and Cincinnati. Everywhere the theme was the same: unemployment was widespread, charity was insufficient, and public aid and employment were necessary. The response to these demands from the middle classes, including the churches, was surprise, indignation, and refusal. Religious and secular newspapers agreed that the "government is not bound to find work for any man."[56] Like Henry Ward Beecher, many churchpeople and urban spokespersons reminded the unemployed that there was always plenty of land available in the country for earning a livelihood. The unemployed continued to be treated as paupers, and the only relief suggested was that of private charity.

Perhaps the earliest dissenting voices from the prevailing optimism of this postwar period came from those few ministers who had experienced firsthand the conditions in the urban slums. Even those with largely well-to-do congregations, however, were noticing in the 1870s the alarming fact that the city working classes were not attending the Protestant churches. In response to this situation, and out of genuine concern for the poor, Protestant evangelicals were beginning to develop city missions and philanthropic agencies.[57] In 1865, the leaders of the wartime United States Christian Commission decided to reorganize under the name American Christian Commission for peacetime service in the cities. Through surveys of conditions in a number of large cities, visitation, and the sponsoring of local, state, and national Christian conventions, this newly organized commission did much to spread knowledge of the problem of the city and compassion for responding to its needs. However, in this period, Protestant activity was still largely confined to evangelistic efforts among the urban poor.

Working People's Religion

Although the working classes in the cities were not attending the fashionable middle-class Protestant churches, they were not devoid of religious concerns and values. Particularly this first generation of industrial workers drew on the religious faith of preindustrial American Protestantism to justify labor organization and agitation and to criticize the prevailing absolutes of Gilded Age political economy and the conformist Christianity of respectable churchpeople.[58] They looked to Jesus, the carpenter, as the champion of the poor and working people, and found hope in the postmillennial Protestantism of the prewar years that looked for the establishment of the Kingdom of God on earth. Thus the urban poor called on Christians to champion their demands, and occasionally they were answered, as in the case of the Christian Labor Union of 1872. Begun by three men much in the spirit of prewar Christian perfectionism, Rev. Jesse H. Jones, a Congregational minister, Edward H. Rogers, a ship carpenter and Methodist layman, and T. Wharton Collens, a Roman Catholic lawyer, the Christian Labor Union was the first real attempt to join Christianity and the labor movement. It was supported by such labor reformers as Ira Steward and George McNeill and received the commendation of the Eight Hour League Convention of 1874 for its championing of labor demands. The union criticized the attitudes of the churches toward poverty and wealth and urged such organizations as the American Christian Commission to stress justice instead of charity.[59]

Such a response to working people was extremely rare in the 1870s. This Christian movement was either ignored or condemned by the main Protestant bodies. When a social gospel did develop in the churches, it drew on other sources, and only after genuine social criticism existed did these lonely figures receive tardy recognition. Just at the end of this period, Protestant clergy were beginning to become aware of the problems of working people. Washington Gladden's *Working People and their Employers* and R. Heber Newton's *Morals of Trade* were both published in 1876, but significant as they were for their genuine sympathy and concern, they still represented the individualistic middle-class outlook of most of their contemporaries. Henry May's judgment appears irrefutable, that as late as 1876, Protestantism still "presented a massive, almost unbroken front in its defense of the social status quo."[60]

Dwight L. Moody and Urban Revivalism

Perhaps the man whose own career best illuminates the dilemmas faced by evangelical Protestantism after 1870 was the famous American revivalist Dwight L. Moody. Fortunately, students of American religion have available not only the excellent shorter studies on Moody and modern revivalism done

41

by Bernard Weisberger and William McLoughlin, but also James F. Findlay's full-length biography of Moody that attempts to see him in the context of his times.[61]

The story of Moody's early life had many parallels in the Gilded Age. It was the story of a small-town boy who made good, of a rise from poverty to prosperity by dint of hard work, ingenuity, and boundless energy. Born in Northfield, Massachusetts, in 1837, Dwight L. Moody was the sixth of nine children in a family left fatherless when Edwin Moody died in 1841. Betsey Moody, Dwight's mother, was able to hold the family together and although they probably received some assistance from relatives in Northfield, the children had ample opportunity to learn the meaning of hard work, thrift, and self-help. Strangely enough considering Moody's later career, all the children were baptized as Unitarians. There was little education; Moody probably had no more than the equivalent of a seventh-grade education.

In 1854, Moody had his first taste of big city life and the business world when he went to Boston to work in his uncle's shoe store. There in 1855 he had something of a conversion experience and after once failing to satisfy the membership committee of the Congregational Church of which a New Measures man, Edward N. Kirk, was the pastor, was finally admitted to membership at the Mount Vernon Church in 1856. He remained in Boston only until the following fall, when he went west to the rapidly growing city of Chicago.

Moody thrived in that environment. Again working in a shoe store and eventually as a traveling salesman and collection agent for a shoe company, he was soon making a considerable amount of money[62] and throwing himself into the life of the evangelical churches in that city. In 1857, he joined the Plymouth Congregational Church. In 1858-59, he began a mission Sunday school for children of the poor, which was soon moved to satisfactory quarters in North Market Hall, and enlisted the services of John V. Farwell, a wealthy Chicago dry-goods merchant, as superintendent. He was active in the YMCA in Chicago, begun during the revival of 1858, and served as its president for four terms, from 1866 to 1870.

In 1860, Moody took the eventful step of giving up business altogether. Henceforth his only business would be serving the Lord, and he soon became as much a tycoon in the business of saving souls as a Rockefeller or a Vanderbilt in their secular businesses. When the Civil War broke out, he served as a volunteer agent of the U.S. Christian Commission in the army camps. In 1864, already a prominent member of the evangelical community in Chicago, he founded a nondenominational free church, the Illinois Street Church, which he pastored until 1866.

The last steps that led to the making of a full-time professional revivalist took place in the four years from 1868 to 1872. In 1868, Moody's preaching style was much influenced by his encounter with the Plymouth Brethren preacher Henry Moorhouse, on a visit to Chicago from England. Apparently Moorhouse's preaching for several consecutive nights on the text, "For God so loved the world . . ." (John 3:16), convinced Moody that this should be the central message of his own preaching.[63] In 1870, Moody met Ira D. Sankey at a YMCA convention in Indianapolis, and having heard him lead some hymn singing, persuaded him to become his singing partner for evangelistic meetings. Thus began a famous lifelong association. Finally, 1871 was a year of strain and spiritual uncertainty for Moody. In the great Chicago fire of that year were lost what must have seemed to Moody the fruits of all his labors there: his own home with all his family's possessions, the central building of the YMCA, which the members had financed under his leadership, and the Illinois Street Church. When in New York on a trip several months later, he experienced a second, and evidently much more profound conversion, the result of which was inner peace and a new resolve to leave Chicago and become a traveling evangelist. Thus it came about that in June 1873, Moody and Sankey set sail for England. After two years of headline-making revivals in Edinburgh, Glasgow, numerous cities throughout Britain, and finally five months in London, they came home famous men in August 1875.

On their return, their services were eagerly solicited by committees from the nation's largest cities. While Moody rested at his family home in Northfield he tried to devise a satisfactory revival itinerary. Having laid down two conditions for accepting an invitation to any city—united support and adequate facilities—Moody finally worked out a basic schedule. He and Sankey would begin in Brooklyn in October 1875, then move on to Philadelphia in November, New York City in February 1876, then Chicago, Boston, and eventually some of the smaller industrial centers of New England.

Moody did not invent professional revivalism; he adapted it to modern America and made it a suitable instrument for urban mass evangelism. As an editorial in *The Nation* said in describing the New York meetings in 1876, "The Moody and Sankey services are an old-fashioned revival with the modern improvements."[64] In many ways Moody's revivalism was typical of the Gilded Age. Observers most often commented on the similarity between Moody's methods and those of big business. After securing the support of the leading

43

evangelical clergy and citizens of a city, an executive committee was organized to take care of the preparations for the revival. It appointed heads of the various subcommittees, to handle finances, prayer meetings, home visitation, ushers, choir, publicity, and tickets. The expenses of the revivals were handled by prominent businessmen in the cities. In most cases a "guaranty fund" was subscribed in advance, at least to secure the cost of the hall or tabernacle, which was always the largest expense. The revivals were supported by the most successful entrepreneurs of the day: Jay Cooke and John Wanamaker in Philadelphia; Cyrus McCormick, George Armour, J. V. Farwell, and Charles P. Kellogg in Chicago; Cornelius Vanderbilt, J. P. Morgan, and William E. Dodge in New York. The Chicago meetings cost $70,000; the New York meetings, $42,000; the Philadelphia meetings, $50,000. In Philadelphia, John Wanamaker donated a former railroad freight depot, which he had renovated to seat 11,000 people, at a cost to himself of $20,000.[65]

All these advance preparations then were handled by ministers, prominent businesspeople, local church members, and YMCA staff. Once Moody arrived in a city, the pace of things increased considerably. He and Sankey usually allowed a day or so before the first scheduled meeting to give them time to check the hall, the seating, and the inquiry rooms to see that everything was in satisfactory order. The campaigns always included daily morning inspiration services and noon prayer meetings, but the main feature was the evening preaching services in the main tabernacle. These were well advertised on posters and in newspapers, usually on the amusement pages. All the meetings were conducted with briskness and businesslike efficiency. Things were always kept moving, both openings and adjournments were punctual, prayers and talks were short and songs frequent. Excesses of emotionalism were discouraged. Those who were concerned for their souls were asked to come forward at the close of the service, where they adjourned to more private inquiry rooms to talk with personal workers trained to answer their questions and doubts with appropriate Scriptural texts. It was no wonder businessmen supported Moody. As one of them said, "He is one of us."[66]

During the service itself, the singing was a special attraction, whether it was a solo by Sankey like "The Ninety and Nine," or gospel hymns sung by the choir, or congregational singing. Moody's preaching was simple; he much disliked "essay preaching."[67] His sermons consisted largely of biblical stories made vivid, real, and often quite contemporary, and rather sentimental anecdotes, superbly told, about those who were converted, or those long-suffering families, friends, loved ones who prayed for the conversion of a son or husband or dear friend. Yet there was nothing artificial about Moody. Audiences were moved by the genuine tenderness of the gruff and businesslike man. And his sense of humor and good taste saved his preaching from being too maudlin or offensive.

Moody's message was the simple gospel of the love of God. His theology was never systematic like Finney's, but repentance, conversion, and the gift of "power" through the Holy Spirit were recurrent themes. He spoke of faith in terms of a personal relationship with Jesus Christ. Repentance was "turning right about" and "a change of mind," and like Finney he insisted that God would not command repentance if people could not obey. For him individual salvation was always primary, and unlike Finney, he concentrated in his sermons primarily on the benefits of conversion for the individual believer.

Moody's views on success and poverty were typical of the evangelical Protestantism of his day. Noting how many prosperous businesspeople were devout church members, he frequently linked Christianity and success, "I never saw the man who put Christ first in his life that wasn't successful," he said.[68] Sincerely believing that the converted man or woman would develop those personal habits necessary for worldly success—hard work, thrift, temperance, self-reliance—he could urge soul winning among the poor as the way to cure their poverty. Poverty was thus the fault, even the sin, of the poor. During the depression, still resulting in some 50,000 unemployed in New York City when Moody was there in 1876, he could preach against laziness and idleness and urge the unemployed to work at any job they could find, whatever the wages. Speaking in Boston the following year to a group of the unemployed, Moody said: "Get something to do. . . . If you cannot earn more than a dollar a week, earn that. That is better than nothing and you can pray to God for more."[69] He still felt sure that there was room at the top in American society for those willing to work.

Moody was not a callous, uncaring man. His city mission work among the poor on Chicago's near north side indicated the sincerity of his concern. But his ethic was based on individualistic assumptions and, as Moody's biographer agreed, in spite of his earnestness, his response to the problems of late-nineteenth-century America was woefully inadequate.[70]

The Resurgence of Premillennialism

In spite of his seeming optimism about the possibilities for worldly success, Moody held what often strikes one as an incongruous belief in the imminent second coming of Christ. Here he departed radically from the optimistic postmillennialism of most American Protestants from Jonathan Edwards to Charles G. Finney. According to their view, the millennium—a thousand-year period of peace and plenty—would come first "usually as the fruit of the present Christian agencies at work in the world,"[71] and then would follow the return of Christ and the establishment of the kingdom of God on earth. Such a view in Finney's day left ample room for benevolence and perfectionism.

Moody's view, on the other hand, was basically pessimistic, the implication being that until Christ returned none of the basic problems of the world could be solved. This premillennial belief saw the world not as constantly improving, but as growing worse and worse, so that judgment was the only possible response to be expected from a just God. In a much-quoted sermon, Moody said, "I look upon this world as a wrecked vessel. God has given me a lifeboat and said to me, 'Moody, save all you can.' "[72]

Ernest R. Sandeen has demonstrated that both in England and the United States there was a resurgence of premillennialism in the years following the Civil War. Much of the impetus for this could be traced to the Plymouth Brethren, a pietistic sect begun in England by John Nelson Darby in 1830. Based on a literalistic view of the Bible, and emphasizing Christian unity and the absence of an organized ministry, the Brethren preached the imminent second coming of Christ. John Nelson Darby visited the United States and Canada seven times between 1862 and 1877, actually living or traveling there for nearly seven of the sixteen years. By the 1870s, the work of the Plymouth Brethren had begun to attract attention in the United States.[73]

It is certain that Moody was influenced to some extent by the Brethren. He met Darby himself when the Brethren leader was in Chicago in either 1868 or 1872. I have already noted the influence of Henry Moorhouse on Moody's preaching, and Moody himself acknowledged his indebtedness to C. H. Mackintosh, Darby's popularizer, for his commentaries on the Scriptures.[74] By the 1870s, Moody was preaching on the Second Coming at least once in each of his revival campaigns. Findlay seems to be right in his suggestion that at least initially, premillennialism served Moody primarily as a weapon for evangelism. It imparted the necessary note of urgency for winning souls and was a way of leading people away from preoccupation with the things of this

46

world to a concern for the things of the spirit.[75] When a man thinks that at any moment "Jesus Christ is coming back again to receive His friends to Himself," Moody said, "this world loses its hold upon him; gas-stocks and water-stocks, and stocks in banks and railroads, are of very much less consequence to him then. His heart is free, and he looks for the blessed appearing of his Lord."[76]

Most of Moody's prosperous supporters were no less firmly rooted in their optimistic endorsement of industrial society for hearing Moody's sermons on the imminent Second Coming. But there were some in Moody's revival audiences to whom this pessimistic view of the present life and offer of comfort and reward in the life to come appealed strongly. And their number was to increase along with the complexities of modern life in the next two decades as anxiety, perplexity, and disillusionment over the breakdown of traditional faith and values spread among evangelical Protestants, particularly in the cities. Here again, Moody was representative of the dilemmas faced by evangelical Protestantism in the Gilded Age, for the undertone of pessimism and the consequent emphasis on premillennialism in his preaching seems to have grown after 1878.

To the great disappointment of both British and American observers, it soon became apparent that Moody was unsuccessful in reaching the unchurched masses. The bulk of his revival audiences were not the poor, but the middle classes, and not the unsaved, but church members, many of them in need of reconsecration but still not without the influence of evangelical religion. Moody's revivals did fill a real need, however. They were part of the process by which thousands of rural-born or small-town Americans became acculturated to the stresses of urban life.

Moody's revivalism played a strange part in the ferment by which so much was profoundly altered in the last quarter of the nineteenth century. As William McLoughlin suggested, unlike Finney, who really helped to bring about the changes discussed in Chapter I as the "second great awakening," Moody represented the conservative aspect of what might be called America's third great awakening—namely, the tremendous "liberal" reorientation that took place on all levels of society, theological as well as social, between 1875 and 1915.[77] A true innovator in technique and management, Moody's faith was that of the past quarter-century of evangelical Protestantism. It was outdated for the world that was emerging in the 1870s. Thus it is true, as James Findlay says, that it was Moody who "enabled revivalism to survive in an urban mass society."[78] But with the wisdom available only in hindsight, we

47

can see that his very success made possible the schism between social Christianity and individual evangelism, by postponing the theological reexamination that might have tied the evangelical faith with the progressive trends of the late nineteenth century.

Thus Moody was a pivotal figure. It is interesting to note that during the 1870s, his revivals received endorsement across denominational lines, from men who later became social gospelers, like Lyman Abbott, Washington Gladden, and R. Heber Newton, conservatives like Charles Hodge, A. J. Gordon, and A. C. Dixon, and the celebrity preachers like Phillips Brooks, Henry Ward Beecher, and T. DeWitt Talmage.[79] As late as 1878, then, there was still no real schism within the Protestant ranks on the question of the church's mission in the world.

PART TWO

Christianizing
the Social Order

THREE

Beginnings of
Social Christianity

The social element in the Christian religion is deeply rooted in its Jewish heritage, in the teachings of Jesus, and in the account of the life of the early church. Throughout its subsequent history, the Christian Church has sought to exert its responsibility for society, to Christianize the whole of life. Its concern has been not only for the individual, but also for the Christian community, and beyond that, for the society itself. As we have seen, even early American Protestantism had this same social orientation. The Puritans hoped to establish a perfected society in the new world. It was only in the nineteenth century in America, by a series of changes traced in Chapter I, that Protestantism adopted an individualistic orientation according to which the principal role of the church and its ministry was to save individual souls. With the vast changes in social structures brought about by industrialization, the church became more and more identified with the private sphere—the family, leisure, one's private life—while the great public world of business, industry, and politics went on, largely independent of genuine Christian influence and judgment.

Even in the individualistic nineteenth century, there were sources that could later be drawn on in developing a social Christianity. Unitarianism and Transcendentalism shared a faith in the ideals of the Enlightenment and in human nature that led to an insistence on humanitarian service and concern for the affairs of this life. As we have seen, the evangelical tradition itself supplied important elements: a tradition of stewardship and responsibility for society stemming from Puritanism, a greater stress on human agency in the process of salvation and on benevolence as a fruit of regeneration, and the combination of lay influence, cooperative Christian effort, and the primacy of ethics over dogma that resulted from the voluntaryism and revivalism of mid-century evangelical Protestantism. The theological contributions of Horace

SOULS OR THE SOCIAL ORDER

Bushnell provided an important liberalizing link between the New England theology of Nathaniel William Taylor and Lyman Beecher and the "New Theology" of the last two decades of the nineteenth century. In his insistence on experience in theology, the inadequacy of language to contain theological truth, the continuity between nature and the supernatural, the centrality of Christ, and the organic nature of sin, Bushnell had a decisive influence on many of the pioneers of social Christianity.

One of the figures prominent in the social gospel movement in its peak years in the early twentieth century defined social Christianity as "the application of the teaching of Jesus and the total message of the Christian salvation to society, the economic life, and social institutions . . . as well as to individuals."[1] In general, the term "social Christianity" was used in the late nineteenth century to refer to all attempts to find Christian solutions to social problems. After 1900, the designation "social gospel" was common, referring primarily to the "moderately progressive" school[2] exemplified by men like Washington Gladden and Walter Rauschenbusch, which had important connections with the general middle-class reform movement known as Progressivism.

The question is, if the 1870s represented in some way the nadir of constructive criticism of the social order by the Protestant churches, why was it that as early as the following decade there were signs of a genuine social awakening? Although historians have stressed one or another factor as primary—whether it be labor crises or problems of the city—Charles H. Hopkins probably summed it up best when he indicated that the social gospel resulted from both liberalizing forces within the Christian community, and the stimulus of a new industrial, urban, and scientific environment.[3] The historian's task is to explain not only why something happened, but why *then*. The remainder of the chapter attempts to answer that question in terms of three developments in the 1880s: (1) an end to complacency; (2) new uses for Darwinian thought; and (3) the "New Theology."

The Resistless Intrusion of Social Crisis

It was the principal thesis of Henry May's major book, *Protestant Churches and Industrial America*, that the "immediate cause" of the important change from defense of the status quo to social criticism within the major Protestant churches was "the resistless intrusion of social crisis," particularly in the series

52

of "large-scale, violent labor conflicts" that occurred in 1877, 1886, and 1892-94.[4] As important as the other contributing factors were, it was these social upheavals that shocked the nation out of its complacency and made clear the need for new Christian social doctrine. As May put it, the other influences "could never have arisen" had not "the all-sufficient, optimistic formulae of Francis Wayland and Henry Ward Beecher been shattered by unanswerable events."[5]

In the phenomenal industrial expansion following the close of the Civil War, labor unionism, virtually nonexistent since 1837, revived. In 1866, the reformist and politically minded National Labor Union began to press for the eight-hour day in every state, consumers' and producers' cooperatives, immigration restriction, and currency reform. Under men of such stature as Ira Steward and the prototype of the universal reformer in the 1850s, George E. McNeill, the campaign for cooperative institutions and the eight-hour day was particularly vigorous in Massachusetts.[6]

Labor movements in the years before 1880 were characterized by a peculiar emphasis on broad demands for justice to all those prevented by the plutocracy from enjoying a life "enriched by industrialism, promised by democracy."[7] Thus the Noble and Holy Order of the Knights of Labor, begun in 1869 and organized nationally in 1878, welcomed all who worked for a living (both skilled and unskilled, so long as they were "producers"), and those with general reforming interests. Its basic aim was to make impossible the formation of a permanent laboring class by working toward a cooperative society in which workers would eventually become their own employers. The reduction of working hours without loss of wages was to be the first step in achieving cooperative institutions. The order was not a trade union; membership was on an individual basis and organization was on a geographical basis, in what were called "trade districts."

Early Protestant response to this postwar labor movement was negative. Labor demands were opposed by Protestant spokespersons as useless in the light of political economy and harmful to accepted values. It was widely believed that labor unions would drag ambitious workers down to the level of the lazy and shiftless, and the concept of an eight-hour day conflicted with commonly held views regarding the virtue of hard work and the danger of too much leisure.

Since the crash of 1873, labor conditions had been especially difficult. Striking labor unions were defeated in local contests of strength, and the roaming unemployed found little or no relief. Finally, in July 1877, a sudden

10 percent wage cut was announced on the majority of railroads east of the Mississippi. This precipitated a nationwide railroad strike that Henry May termed "the most destructive labor battle in American history."[8] At Baltimore and Pittsburgh, strikers fought with federal troops. Roundhouses and freight cars were set on fire and there was widespread looting.

The reaction of the religious press, surveyed by May, was one of shock, alarm, and fear. The *Independent* and the *Congregationalist* saw the rioting as an issue of law versus anarchy and recommended "bullets and bayonets" if necessary to stop it.[9] The *Christian Union* agreed that mercy would be a mistake.[10] Henry Ward Beecher preached two sermons condemning the strikes, in one of which he claimed that a man should be able to support a wife and family on wages of a dollar a day if he didn't smoke or drink beer. A man incapable of thus living within his means while the times required it was, according to Beecher, "not fit to live."[11]

Once the crisis was over, the Protestant consensus seemed to be that although laborers had the right to strike, such action was foolish, and coercion must never be allowed. As May made clear, the events of 1877 remained "a symbol of shock,"[12] even after the revival of prosperity. It was not until the mid-1880s, however, that a genuine social consciousness began to appear.

In 1879, Terence V. Powderly, a young man of only thirty years of age, became grand master of the Knights of Labor. In general, Protestants approved of him because he opposed strikes, preferring to work for the development of cooperatives. Some of his western subordinates were more militant than he, however, and after two labor victories against Jay Gould, owner of the entire southwest railway system, the total membership of the Knights rose in 1885-86 from 100,000 to over 700,000.[13] A third strike against Gould's railroad broke out in February 1886; it ended in utter defeat for the Knights. After 1886 their membership declined rapidly, and leadership in the labor movement was taken over by the new American Federation of Labor. Begun in 1886 under the presidency of Samuel Gompers, it abandoned the aim of labor solidarity and worked for practical goals like higher wages and shorter hours for the skilled workers of craft unions.

The southwestern railroad strike in 1886 was only one in a series of labor conflicts that year, most of them in favor of the eight-hour day. The religious press that spring was full of fear and foreboding. "In the darkest hours of the Civil War we never felt more sober than to-day,"[14] wrote the *Christian Advocate* in March. In a clash between strikers and strikebreakers in Chicago at the McCormick Harvester plant in May, several men were killed. A protest meeting was summoned the following day in Haymarket Square. Apparently it was a peaceful demonstration until nearly the end when a crowd of policemen arrived. Someone threw a bomb into the ranks of the police and, as a result, a number of policemen and workers were killed, and over one hundred people were injured.[15]

The Haymarket affair was the result of several months of conflict and increasing tension. Public opinion was merciless against the eight known anarchist leaders who were blamed for the bomb throwing. They were arrested and charged with murder, and with no evidence connecting them with the bombing, seven of them were sentenced to death. When Governor John P. Altgeld later pardoned two of the men and sentenced the third to life imprisonment, he was bitterly criticized throughout the country. The Protestant press fully shared the prevailing mood of hysteria. Anarchism must be destroyed and the violence of strikers was deplored. Many did distinguish between the anarchists and the majority of laborers, however, and by the end of the decade there was considerably more sympathy for working people. The labor crises in 1877 and 1886 were not the only cause of the development of social criticism in churches, but they brought about one major change: they ended the insistence that all was well.

The Storm Center: America's Cities

Protestants were also feeling the impact of urban problems in the 1880s. In that decade, the "rural exodus" and foreign immigration combined to produce extraordinary growth of the nation's cities. In 1870, a little over one-fifth of the population lived in cities. By 1890, the figure had risen to one-third.[16] In the ten years after 1880, Chicago became the second largest city in the nation, increasing in size over 100 percent. Midwestern cities like Minneapolis-St. Paul expanded at an extraordinary rate, and the Atlantic seaboard took on a generally urban character. These cities were faced with tremendous social problems: lawlessness and crime, poverty and slums, corrupt politics, inadequate sanitation and traffic provisions, and a host of other evils.[17]

Two books written in the mid-1880s, Josiah Strong's *Our Country* in 1885, and Samuel Lane Loomis' *Modern Cities and Their Religious Problems*, published the following year, called the attention of their fellow clergy and laypeople in the churches to the distressing conditions in the nation's cities. Both men were in a position to be well acquainted with urban problems;

Strong was pastor of a Congregational church in Cincinnati and Loomis was ministering in Brooklyn.

Strong's book in particular was effective in conveying a sense of immediate crisis. Published by the American Home Missionary Society, it was written for a practical purpose—to raise contributions for home missions to enable the crisis to be met. Presenting the alternatives of catastrophe or immediate action, Strong firmly believed it was in the hands of Christians in the United States in the next ten or fifteen years "to hasten or retard the coming of Christ's kingdom in the world by hundreds, and perhaps thousands, of years."[18] In all of this the American city played a crucial role, as both the "nerve center" and the "storm center" of civilization.[19] Here all the problems to be solved elsewhere in the nation were especially critical: immigration, Roman Catholicism, politics, extremes of wealth and poverty, and all the rest. And when free land in the West was exhausted and the frontier closed, the situation would become even more desperate. Then, said Strong, "*then* will come the real test of our institutions."[20] A long-lived best seller, *Our Country* was, as Henry May phrased it, "the *Uncle Tom's Cabin* of city reform."[21]

Monstrous Wealth and Debasing Want

Another evil to which Strong's book called attention and that was becoming more and more apparent to those exposed to urban conditions was the glaring discrepancy between the extremes of wealth and poverty. The 1880s were marked by the accumulation of vast new wealth, the consolidation of business, and the emergence of the corporation. Consolidation was taking place in all the major lines of economic endeavor, transportation, communication, and industry, and in agriculture and labor as well. From 1878 to 1890, no less than fifteen great new combinations organized on a national scale.[22] From 1860 to 1890, the national wealth increased from $16 to $78.5 billion, more than one-half of which was held by 40,000 families, or one-third of 1 percent of the population.[23] While Christians discussed and wrote on the problems of wealth and poverty, perhaps no one did more to awaken the social conscience of the nation to "the shocking contrast between monstrous wealth and debasing want" than Henry George.[24]

On a visit to New York City in 1868-69, George was shocked by these extremes of wealth and poverty and vowed to find an explanation for them. While living in California as a printer and newspaperman, he worked out his answer. It appeared in *Progress and Poverty* (1879), a work read by thousands who had never before read anything on economics. According to his son's estimate, more than two million copies had been printed by 1905.[25]

George's remedy for the poverty associated with progress was to substitute common ownership of land for individual ownership. His book called for a "single tax" on the increase in the value of land as communities grew up around it. This increase in value was created by society and thus totally unearned by the individuals who absorbed it. By taxing the unearned increment 100 percent, George felt that concentrated wealth would be smashed and the national wealth distributed more evenly. The revenues from the single tax would be used to benefit the community by providing medical, educational, cultural, and recreational facilities. George felt that the cooperative functions of the government should be extended and that public utilities should be government owned.

While heavy land taxes would appeal only to the urban poor and not to the farmers, and while few reformers could accept the "single tax" as in itself a sufficient remedy for complex problems, George's ideas served as a powerful stimulant to reform. In 1886, George ran for mayor of New York on the United Labor Party ticket and barely missed being elected. Although he lost to the Democratic candidate, Abram S. Hewitt, he ran ahead of the Republican candidate, Theodore Roosevelt. George had entered the campaign because he thought it would enable him to popularize discussion of the land question. In 1886, he was supported by single taxers, socialists, union members, and the discontented. Although he ran the following year for secretary of state of New York and was decisively defeated, he continued to devote his energies to propagating the single tax gospel. Both Progressives and later social gospelers acknowledged their heavy debt to Henry George. The official Knights of Labor journal testified in 1887 that "no man has exercised so great an influence upon the labor movement of today as Henry George."[26] And Walter Rauschenbusch said of him, "I owe my first awakening to the world of social problems to the agitation of Henry George in 1886, and wish here to record my life-long debt to this single-minded apostle of a great truth."[27]

To this suggestion of socialism in land was added in 1888 a native voice advocating complete socialism of production and distribution, to be peacefully achieved. The voice was Edward Bellamy's and the book was *Looking Backward*, a work whose popularity was comparable to that of *Progress and Poverty*. By the early 1890s one million copies were in active circulation, affording many Americans—including Protestant churchpeople—their first socialist reading of any kind.

According to Bellamy, there could be no middle ground between laissez-faire and the nationalization of the means of production and distribution. Bellamy denounced the existing system and proposed the establishment of a new economic order based on nationalized industry and economic equality. The state would be the employer of all labor, and all citizens would serve the state in an industrial or intellectual capacity from age twenty-one to age forty-five. Profits would be shared equally, and the state would guarantee "the nurture, education, and comfortable maintenance of every citizen, from the cradle to the grave."[28] Bellamy firmly believed that his program could be realized by a gradual process, beginning with the nationalization of a few basic industries like the railroads, communications, coal mines, liquor and insurance businesses, and the municipalization of local public utilities. These would constitute the nucleus for further nationalization.

Although Bellamy's proposals involved far too radical a change in existing institutions to appeal to the majority of Americans, their popularity was attested to by the formation of Nationalist clubs throughout the country. The first of these was begun in Boston in 1888, and by October 1890, there were 150 clubs in twenty-seven states.[29] Many Protestant ministers were affiliated with these clubs. Bellamy and his Nationalist supporters were highly influential in creating a public attitude favorable to social change.[30]

The combined effect of the labor crises of 1877 and 1886, the growing awareness of conditions in American cities, and the denunciations of inequality and injustice by native voices advocating some form of socialism was to put an end to the complacency so prevalent in the decade immediately following the Civil War. In addition, new uses for Darwinism and new socialistic trends in economics and sociology in the 1880s challenged the individualistic, laissez-faire theories that had supported the status quo.

New Uses for Darwinian Thought

In 1885, the American Economic Association was formed by young economists just back from German universities who, together with a considerable number of Protestant clergy, urged the united efforts of the church, the state, and science to solve the social problems of labor and capital. Influenced by the so-called historical school of political economy in Germany, these men recognized the relativity of economic truth and the consequent need for historical and inductive study. They also wanted to associate political economy more closely with ethical concerns and the possibilities of reform through government action.

The most influential of these young men, and the real founder of the American Economic Association, was Richard T. Ely. An Episcopalian and a young teacher at Johns Hopkins in the 1880s, Ely was for about a decade a conspicuous figure in the development of the social gospel.[31] He attacked the classical laissez-faire economics, welcomed the American labor movement, and urged that all attempts to solve social and economic problems be based on Christian principles. These he could summarize simply as love of God and love of one's neighbor. He believed it was the function of social science to teach how the second commandment might be fulfilled, and that it was the mission of Christianity to work for a kingdom of righteousness on earth. In an important book of 1889, *Social Aspects of Christianity*, he called on the theological seminaries to become chief intellectual centers for the study of sociology, and placed the blame for the alienation of the working classes squarely at the feet of the church leaders. He charged "the representative men and women in the church" with failing to love and understand working people, failing to "rebuke wickedness in high places"—that is, to criticize the methods by which the wealthy robbed the masses of their just due—and responding negatively to all proposals for reform.[32]

Ely's activities as a political economist and as a social Christian were thus perfectly complementary. Indeed, as Handy indicated, they were "rooted in the same ground."[33] In 1892, he was called to become professor of political economy and director of the School of Economics, Political Science, and History at the University of Wisconsin. He wrote both technical works and books and articles more directly concerned with the social gospel. Until the late 1890s, when he began to become disillusioned with the church as an agent for social reform, Ely was associated with most of the major social gospel organizations and programs.

In addition to the reaction from competition and laissez-faire that came from political economists in the 1880s, sociologists and philosophers were taking Darwinian thought in a different direction from that of Spencer, a direction that could provide an ideology for social reform. A key figure in this process was Lester Frank Ward, who probably ought to be considered the true founder of American sociology. Brought up in the frontier environment of Illinois in the 1840s and '50s, Ward was employed by the United States government for over forty years. He did not enter the academic world until 1906, when he became professor of sociology at Brown University. His monumental work, *Dynamic Sociology*, was completed in 1883 and gave to sociology a new orientation.

Ward's greatest contribution was to stress the discontinuity between progress in nature and progress in society. Where Spencer had rested his sociology on biology, Ward distinguished between genetic progress (the unconscious working of social forces that Spencer recognized as the only type of social progress) and what he called "telic" progress, which resulted from the application of the intellect to nature. Ward thought that the greater part of human evolution was of this type; his sociology thus rested on psychological foundations and called for intelligent social control. Having distinguished between the two kinds of progress, Ward went on to refute Spencer's central tenet of noninterference with the natural process by demonstrating the superiority of the telic method over the genetic. Whereas natural selection was wasteful, human interference with competition in nature resulted in true economy and the survival of the "fittest possible."[34] Thus far the telic method had been applied largely to physical and mechanical phenomena. Ward called on society as a whole to apply the dynamic, telic method to social phenomena in the interest of public welfare. For him the supreme purpose of sociology was "the betterment of society," and social planning and legislation were principal functions of government. Although Ward offered no concrete program of social reform, he provided the scientific basis for a planned society and undermined the Spencerian defense of laissez-faire.

Two other developments begun in the 1880s and more fully articulated in the 1890s contributed to the scientific sanction for social reform. One was the transition to solidarism within evolutionary thought itself. Men like John Fiske (*The Meaning of Infancy*, 1883), Henry Drummond (*The Ascent of Man*, 1894), and the Russian naturalist Peter Kropotkin (*Mutual Aid*, 1902) began to see the group as the unit of survival in nature and to regard solidarity, altruism, and cooperation as directly rooted in the evolutionary process. This trend seemed to knock another prop out from under individualistic competition.

Finally, Darwinian concepts were applied to human ideas themselves, with a very different result from the deterministic philosophy of Spencer. The pragmatic philosophy of William James stressed the active character of the human mind and left room for uncertainty and spontaneity in human life. John Dewey took his belief in the effectiveness of ideas and the possibility of novelties and made it the basis of a social philosophy. Agreeing with Ward's view of the mind as an organ of service for control of the environment in the interests of human betterment, he supplied Ward's social theory with an adequate psychology. As Richard Hofstadter has shown, pragmatism—with its emphasis on freedom and human control of the environment—became the dominant philosophy of the Progressive era just as Spencerism had reigned supreme in the Gilded Age. "Spencerianism had been the philosophy of inevitability; pragmatism became the philosophy of possibility."[35] It provided a satisfactory rationale for social reform.

One thing further was required for the development of a social Christianity. To the stimulus of external challenges and a climate of opinion favorable to reform must be added the intellectual framework for a social gospel. Such a framework was provided by the liberalizing movement within evangelical Protestantism known as the "new theology."

The "New Theology"

The "new theology" or "progressive orthodoxy" (as it was variously referred to by its adherents) was that Christocentric liberal tradition that replaced the modified Calvinism of the New England theology of Nathaniel William Taylor and Lyman Beecher in the last quarter of the nineteenth century. Although it attempted to come to terms with the modern world by accepting the implications of Darwinian evolution and the higher criticism of the Scriptures, it took its stand explicitly within the tradition and accepted as normative what it understood to be the essence of historic Christianity.[36] Its foremost representatives in the 1880s were a group of pastors, most of them in prominent New England pulpits, all of whom had been decisively influenced by Horace Bushnell. They included Newman Smyth, for twenty-five years the pastor at Center (Congregational) Church, New Haven, whose *Old Faiths in New Light*, published in 1879, dealt primarily with the implications of the evolutionary process. Also in New Haven, at United (Congregational) Church, was Theodore T. Munger. In the preface to his popular book of 1883, *The Freedom of Faith*, Munger referred to the new movement for the first time as the "new theology." At Old South Church in Boston was George A. Gordon, whose thought had been much influenced by German idealistic philosophy. Washington Gladden, pastor of the First Congregational Church in Columbus, Ohio, and Lyman Abbott, successor to Henry Ward Beecher at

Plymouth Church in Brooklyn, although not original or systematic theological thinkers, were well-known popularizers of the new theology.

The evangelical liberal tradition also had some important representatives in northeastern theological schools. During the 1880s, William Jewett Tucker and a number of professors at Andover Theological Seminary adopted liberal views that were circulated widely under the title "progressive orthodoxy" in the *Andover Review*, founded in 1884. The school was disrupted by a controversy on the issue of whether or not there was a "second probation" after death for those who had never heard of Christ in this life. Associated with the trial of Professor Egbert Smyth and involving the American Board of Commissioners for Foreign Missions because of its implications for missions, the controversy dragged on for six years. Actually, the real issue was that of universal salvation. The progressives generally talked of one probation for all persons, but without any bounds of time.

Two other well-known proponents of the new theology were William Newton Clarke, professor of Christian theology at Colgate from 1890, and William Adams Brown, professor of systematic theology at Union Theological Seminary in New York from 1892. Both these men were systematizers of the new theology. Brown's *Christian Theology in Outline* (1906), probably the best systematic presentation of evangelical liberalism, was largely a revision of Clarke's earlier *Outline of Christian Theology*, published in 1898.

In terms of its usefulness for the development of a social gospel, the new theology contributed essentially two things: it attempted to reconcile the Christian tradition with modern thought, particularly Darwinian evolution and biblical criticism, and as a direct consequence of this reconciliation, it imparted strong ethical influences on which a program of social action could be based. Crucial for its reinterpretation of traditional Christian teachings was evangelical liberalism's understanding of the Scriptures. It considered the biblical record as the history of a revelation, and accepted the principle of moral evolution or development, according to which the full meaning of God's revelation is always being evolved in history. For its strongly ethical tone it was much indebted to German theology, especially to the thought of Albrecht Ritschl (1822-1889), whose solidaristic view of sin and moral conception of the Kingdom of God were to have a profound influence on the social gospel in general, and on Walter Rauschenbusch in particular.

The central truth of liberal theology was the immanence of God, based on the evolutionary conception of a unified world. From this basic premise followed others, all of them stressing continuity between humans and God, between nature and the supernatural. God was understood not in terms of divine sovereignty, as in the old Calvinistic system, but in terms of fatherhood. Consequently, all men and women were brothers and sisters and human solidarity replaced the excessive individualism of earlier evangelical Protestantism.

The whole understanding of sin and redemption was transformed. Original sin became inherited evil tendencies, biologically and socially transmitted, which were then the occasion for actual sin. The substitutionary theory of the atonement whereby Christ dies to accept our punishment by a righteous judge was replaced by the moral influence theory, according to which the love of God as revealed in the life and death of Christ moves us to become transformed by the moral act of accepting this love in faith.

Finally, the idea of progress implied in the dynamic worldview basic to liberalism led to the belief in the amelioration of both the social organism and the environment, in short, belief in the possibility of the Kingdom of God on earth as the redemption of human society.

All of these doctrines had powerful implications for a social gospel. The fatherhood of God and brotherhood of man were inherently social concepts. The old separation between the religious and the secular was minimized, and all aspects of life were seen as in need of redemption. The continuity between the individual and society was such that personal salvation was seen to require social salvation as well, and social reforms were regarded as part of the progress toward the Kingdom.

Although both the new theology and the social gospel were practical and nondogmatic rather than metaphysical, this progressive tradition was able to supply the intellectual framework for a social understanding of Christianity. For most of the pioneers of social Christianity, liberal theology and the social gospel were inseparable, although it is not true that all theological liberals were interested in a social gospel. In the 1880s, the new theology contributed in many ways to an emphasis on the human, this-worldly, ethical side of the Christian faith.

During the 1880s, Protestant churchpeople began to see evils in the social order itself that could not be explained simply in terms of individualism. And they began to assert the responsibility of the church to be concerned as much with the fulfillment of the second great commandment as with the first. Often naive and overly optimistic, most of them retained a good deal of the individualism of the age and few of them knew much about sociology. But among this minority—and it was only a small minority—there was at least a genuine awakening of concern and an attempt to find Christian solutions to the pressing social problems.

Of these problems the most immediate and glaring was, of course, that of labor. The response of Protestant clergy to the labor crisis in this period can probably best be seen in Washington Gladden, who is typical of that moderately progressive movement later to be known as the social gospel. In fact, Gladden has often been described as "the father of the social gospel."[37] He was certainly one of the pioneers in the 1880s.

The Father of the Social Gospel

Born in Pottsgrove, Pennsylvania, in 1836 and raised on his uncle's farm near Oswego, New York, after his father's death when he was six, Washington Gladden graduated from Williams College in 1859 and ordained to the Congregational ministry the following year.[38] From 1866 to 1871, he served the North Adams Congregational Church, in North Adams, Massachusetts, and from 1871-75, he took the only break in what was to be a long pastoral career by serving as religion editor of the *Independent*, a nondenominational religious weekly published in New York.

During his pastorate at the North Congregational Church in Springfield, Massachusetts (1875-1882), he observed firsthand the unemployment and consequent suffering of the workers. Invited to address groups of both the unemployed workers and the employers, he began a pioneering series of lectures on the labor question, published in 1876 as *Working People and Their Employers*. Although he later recognized that he was not as sympathetic toward labor as he might have been, Gladden was pleased that at least he had maintained at that early date the right of labor to organize for its own protection. "Now that slavery is out of the way," Gladden had written in the preface to that book, "the questions that concern the welfare of our free laborers are coming forward; and no intelligent man needs to be admonished of their urgency."[39] The relations between labor and capital were always a central concern of the social gospel. From that first book on, Gladden was one of the foremost spokespersons on the problems of labor, discussing them in sermons and lectures (later published in books) that demonstrated an increasingly realistic appreciation of the situation and solutions appropriate to it.

In 1882, Gladden became pastor of the First Congregational Church in Columbus, Ohio, where he was to remain until his death in 1918. During the tense spring of 1886 when the bitter strike of the Knights of Labor against Jay Gould's railroad was only one of hundreds of strikes, Gladden was invited to speak to a mass meeting of working people and employers in Cleveland, where a severe strike was in progress. After underlining the fact that the workers were getting very little of the rapidly increasing wealth of the country, Gladden declared in words often quoted since, "If war is the order of the day, we must grant to labor belligerent rights."[40] The address was published in the *Century Magazine* in May 1886. As Robert Handy pointed out, it appeared at a very timely moment, for after the Haymarket riot of May 4, many people lost sight of the difference between strikes and anarchy.[41] The address became a chapter ("Is it Peace or War?") in *Applied Christianity*, published in 1886.

In this early period of social Christianity, the solutions suggested for the problem of labor tended to minimize economic causes and prescribe moral remedies. Employers and laborers were urged to apply the Christian law of love to industry and treat one another as brothers and sisters. However, on behalf of the workers, these pioneering voices refuted classical economics, insisting that labor was not a commodity. They maintained the right of labor to organize, but urged arbitration for the settlement of industrial conflicts. Finally, they looked for some form of industrial partnership to replace the purely competitive system, probably in the form of profit sharing. This principle, then being experimented with in Europe and Britain, was enthusiastically recommended by many of the early social Christians like Gladden, Ely, and Lyman Abbott. The most thorough investigation of it was Nicholas Paine Gilman's study, published in 1889. Thereafter his name was most commonly associated with the plan.

National Needs and Remedies

In 1885, Josiah Strong called attention to the impending crisis in the nation, particularly in the cities, in *Our Country*. With the publication of this book, Strong became a nationally prominent figure. Born in Naperville, Illinois, in 1847, he graduated from Western Reserve in Ohio in 1869 and attended Lane Seminary in Cincinnati. After a pastorate in Sandusky, Ohio, from 1876-1881, Strong became secretary of the Ohio Home Missionary Society and spent the next three years traveling through Ohio, Kentucky, West Virginia, and western

Pennsylvania. At the time of his writing of *Our Country*, he was pastor of the Vine Street (Congregational) Church in Cincinnati. In December 1885, he called an "Interdenominational Congress" in his church to discuss current problems such as the urban situation, socialism, and the indifference of the working classes toward the churches. Early social gospel leaders like Washington Gladden, Richard T. Ely, Lyman Abbott, and Amory Bradford attended. The session lasted five days and ended with the recommendation that religious surveys be made in as many cities as possible.

The following year Josiah Strong was called to be general secretary of the American branch of the Evangelical Alliance. Under his leadership, what C. H. Hopkins referred to as "the three most significant conferences ever held in the United States in the interest of social Christianity"[42] took place in 1887, 1889, and 1893. The first of these met in Washington, D. C., and attempted to rouse the Christian public to the "perils and opportunities" facing the church and the nation, and the need for denominational cooperation to meet these. The perils dealt with were most of the issues I have considered: labor and capital, the city, immigration, the misuse of wealth. The next national gathering took place in Boston in 1889. The report of this meeting, *National Needs and Remedies*, was in general concerned primarily with reporting the progress made on all fronts since the Washington meeting. The most significant of the three was the conference held in Chicago in connection with the World's Columbian Exposition in 1893. Its great object was to point out the social mission of the church; it is considered in greater detail in the following chapter.

As we shall see, Josiah Strong was involved in almost all the significant social gospel gatherings and organizations in the next two decades. Because the state of the manuscript materials is such that his biography has never been written, his importance for the social gospel movement has often been minimized. However, the work of Dorothea R. Muller has made clear the extent to which he was a pioneer "in recognizing the significance of the urban movement and . . . in devising methods of meeting the challenge the city presented."[43]

The Institutional Church

One of the more successful attempts to meet the physical as well as the spiritual needs of the cities was the so-called institutional church, which began in this decade. According to Josiah Strong, the term originated in a chance remark made by William Jewett Tucker.[44] The term was commonly used to describe churches that expanded their programs to minister to the whole of human life. Thus they commonly included recreational and educational facilities, special services like employment bureaus, loan associations and medical clinics, and, in general, programs designed to minister to the needs of rapidly changing neighborhoods. One of the earliest and most successful institutional churches was St. George's (Protestant Episcopal) Church, located on New York's East Side. Its rector, William S. Rainsford, inaugurated such a program shortly after his arrival there in 1882.[45] Other institutional churches begun in the 1880s included St. Bartholomew's Episcopal Church in Manhattan, whose rector was David H. Greer, and several Congregational churches: Fourth Church in Hartford under Graham Taylor, Plymouth Church in Indianapolis under Oscar C. McCulloch, and Berkeley Temple in Boston under Charles A. Dickinson. The Presbyterians, Baptists, and Unitarians each had one important institutional church in the 1880s. A. T. Pierson was minister of the Bethany Presbyterian Church in Philadelphia, Russell H. Conwell began at Grace Church (Baptist) in Philadelphia and later moved to the Baptist Temple (from the institutional program of which Temple University began), and the Unitarians had All Souls' Church in Chicago under Jenkin Lloyd Jones. Many well-known institutional churches were begun in the following decade, like S. Parkes Cadman's (Methodist) Metropolitan Temple in New York City.

Another major step forward at this time was the implementation of Richard T. Ely's suggestion that theological schools become major intellectual centers for the teaching of sociology. In the 1880s, three eastern divinity schools offered instruction in social ethics. Professor Francis Greenwood Peabody taught the first such course at Harvard, in 1880. By the end of the decade, Graham Taylor at Hartford and William Jewett Tucker at Andover were developing similar programs.

It may already be apparent that many of the early efforts in social Christianity were led by Congregationalists. There are several reasons for this. Congregationalists inherited the New England Puritan tradition of responsibility for society. Their clergy had always prided themselves on their educational leadership and were probably most immediately influenced by the liberalizing influences of the new theology. They tended to be situated in urban, industrial areas where they could see firsthand the problems of labor and the city. And Congregational policy was such that individual ministers and congregations had more freedom than in most other denominations.

Christian Socialism American Style

The other major denomination to develop a social gospel at an early date was the Protestant Episcopal Church. Here the influences were somewhat different, and I consider its contribution separately because many of its foremost exponents were more radical social Christians, adopting a form of Christian Socialism. Both Episcopalian progressives and radicals acknowledged the considerable influence of English Christian Socialism on their thinking. Long before Americans were shocked by the labor crises of 1877 and 1886, English Christian Socialists under the leadership of Frederick Denison Maurice and Charles Kingsley were attacking the effects of English industrialism, publishing tracts and founding cooperatives. (The movement was at its height from 1848-1854). After social Christianity began in America in the 1880s, Episcopalians especially were influenced by all phases of British social thought and action.[46] As Henry May pointed out, the "church" tendencies of responsibility for society and the high conception of priestly authority held by many of the social gospel leaders in Episcopalianism gave them power many clergy in other denominations lacked.[47]

During the 1880s there were two highly effective Episcopal organizations established for the propagation of social Christianity. The first was the Church Association for the Advancement of the Interests of Labor, founded in 1887 by a group of New York Episcopal clergy and laity, including Bishops Frederick Dan Huntington and Henry Codman Potter, J. O. S. Huntington, the radical son of Bishop Huntington, and for a time Richard T. Ely. More than any other major church organization, CAIL stressed solidarity with the labor movement.[48] Especially in the 1890s it campaigned against sweatshops and slums, celebrated one Sunday a year as Labor Sunday, and actively worked for arbitration of strikes, Bishop Potter serving as president of the Council of Conciliation and Arbitration, set up in 1893. J. O. S. Huntington was active in his support of Henry George's United Labor Party candidacy for mayor of New York in 1886, addressing several street meetings to advocate George's election. Men like J. O. S. Huntington and W. D. P. Bliss were members of the Knights of Labor.

The other major Episcopal organization founded in the 1880s was the Society of Christian Socialists, organized by William Dwight Porter Bliss in 1889.[49] Bliss was born in Constantinople in 1856, the son of an American missionary. He completed undergraduate work at Amherst College and attended Hartford Theological Seminary. Originally a Congregational minister, he became interested in socialism in 1885 after reading Henry George and observing the life of the working classes in Massachusetts, and decided he could have greater freedom to apply Christianity to social problems in the Episcopal Church. He entered that church the following year, and in 1888 was settled as minister of Grace Church in South Boston. Early in 1889 he took part in the formation of the first Nationalist club based on the thought of Edward Bellamy. Dissatisfied with the secular character of Nationalism, however, Bliss and a group of Boston clergymen formed the Society of Christian Socialists in the spring of 1889.

The basic principles of the society were that "the teachings of Jesus Christ lead directly to some specific form or forms of Socialism" and that the church must "in simple obedience to Christ, apply itself to the realization of the social principles of Christianity."[50] The society's function was seen to be primarily educational. Shortly after its organization it began to publish *The Dawn*, a monthly journal for propagating faith in the kind of evolutionary progress toward a cooperative society advocated by the Christian Socialists. Bliss was the paper's editor; its associate editors included Philo W. Sprague, R. Heber Newton, Edward Bellamy, and Hamlin Garland, and later also J. O. S. Huntington and Frances Willard. Bliss welcomed contributions from all the leading social thinkers of the day. The society also worked out study courses and reprinted useful articles. The most complete explication of the society's views was Philo Sprague's *Christian Socialism, What and Why?*, published in 1891. Although most American social Christians were not willing to demand the complete reconstruction of the social order along socialist lines, the Christian Socialists exerted an important influence even on the more moderate social gospelers.

For the Right

One last development of the 1880s was of great significance for the future of social Christianity. In 1886, a young man named Walter Rauschenbusch accepted the pastorate of the Second German Baptist Church in the area of

New York City known as Hell's Kitchen.[51] Only twenty-five years of age, he had recently completed a Bachelor of Divinity degree from Rochester Theological Seminary, after earlier education in Rochester and at the Evangelical Gymnasium in Gutersloh, Germany. He came from a long line of pietistic ministers, but his eleven-year ministry to the poverty-stricken New York congregation was to take his thought in new directions. In 1889, after being much influenced by Henry George's campaign three years before, Rauschenbusch and a few friends including Leighton Williams began publishing a monthly paper called *For the Right*, devoted to the interests of the working people in New York City. In the twentieth century, Walter Rauschenbusch would become the outstanding leader of the social gospel movement.

It would be very misleading to assume that the movement I have been describing was in any sense the dominant perspective in the mainline Protestant churches in the 1880s. In that decade, genuine social criticism arose as a response to the industrial crisis. But there were only a few proponents of social Christianity in this early period, most of them Congregationalists or Episcopalians. Much of Protestant Christianity was simply the persistence of the old: evangelicalism still tied to the status quo and justifying competition and the unequal distribution of wealth.

The Gospel of Wealth

Social Darwinism was still dominant, as was the older political economy. In 1878, Francis Wayland's text, "the epitome of prewar clerical laissez faire,"[52] was revised by Rev. Aaron L. Chapin, president of Beloit College. The revised text went through eight subsequent editions. In a sense the culmination of the laissez-faire philosophy of the businessman was Andrew Carnegie's "Gospel of Wealth," first set forth in an article in the *North American Review* in June 1889. Like Sumner, Carnegie insisted that the accumulation of wealth in the hands of the few was "essential for the future progress of the race." However, to the doctrine of self-interest, he added the concept of stewardship. The wealthy had an obligation to administer their wealth wisely, and Carnegie felt he should use his fortune during his lifetime for the benefit of the community. Thus he might donate funds to establish universities, hospitals, recreational and cultural facilities, and perhaps the wisest gift of all to a community, free public libraries. Carnegie actually regarded his Gospel of Wealth as a solution for the social problems of the day. Returning to older aristocratic views, he believed that millionaires would know better than the people's government how to expend funds for the general welfare.[53]

In the churches themselves, by no means all of even the theological liberals became advocates of the social gospel. Much of both conservative and liberal Protestantism remained attached to the older laissez-faire views. The new theology was too devoid of normative content to escape easy identification with whatever were conceived to be the highest goals of the existing culture.[54] Thus Gladden could use it as the intellectual framework for a social understanding of Christianity, while in the hands of other "princes of the pulpit"[55] it was compatible with endorsement of the existing order of things.

In the 1880s, Phillips Brooks was still at Trinity Church in Boston, preaching a cheerful and warmly humanitarian gospel basically untroubled by external events. Until his death in 1887, Henry Ward Beecher was telling his congregation at Plymouth Church in Brooklyn that hard work and frugality were likely to result in prosperity and that poverty in America was usually the result of sin. This middle-class aspirant gospel was given its clearest expression by Russell H. Conwell, minister of the Baptist Temple in Philadelphia. Like a clerical counterpart of Andrew Carnegie, Conwell preached the duty of getting rich. He toured the country with a lecture entitled "Acres of Diamonds," which he was said to have given some 6,000 times. "To secure wealth is an honorable ambition," he told his audiences over and over, and it is "one great test of a person's usefulness to others."[56] Like Beecher, Conwell felt that almost everyone should be able to accumulate wealth in this land of opportunity if they would only work hard and be alert to their opportunities. Obviously there were many Protestants whose complacency was still undisturbed in the 1880s.

Bible and Prophetic Conferences

Just as social Christianity was beginning to develop in this decade, so also were these years important for what was to be the conservative thrust. After 1880, Dwight L. Moody spent less time organizing mass revivals and more consolidating his efforts through various educational enterprises. In 1879, he founded the Northfield School for Girls, and in 1881, Mount Hermon School for Boys. One of the purposes of these secondary schools was to give an education to young men and women who lacked the money to secure it

71

elsewhere. However, Moody hoped that they would become schools for the training of lay evangelists. This hope was not to be realized, but the Northfield schools under competent academic leadership developed into private academies of high quality. Even during his lifetime, Moody's influence on the schools was primarily a personal one. Although he raised most of the money to finance the schools and preached and held prayer meetings there when in Northfield, Moody always left the actual administration to college-trained educators.[57]

Moody's hopes were more fully realized with the founding of Moody Bible Institute in Chicago later in the decade. From 1881 to 1884, Moody was out of the country on a return trip to England that apparently was considerably less successful than his earlier tour had been.[58] After his return he met with some of his Chicago supporters to consider opportunities for evangelism in their city. As a result of these contacts, he returned to Chicago early in 1886 to win support for a new plan, to establish a training school for Christian workers, chiefly for city missions. He asked local businessmen to raise $250,000 to guarantee the success of the project. As we have seen, the mid-1880s were a time of considerable industrial tension and frequent strikes throughout the nation. In the Chicago area, strikes took place at the Pullman Palace Car Company and at Cyrus McCormick's harvester works in 1884 and 1885 and again at the McCormick plant in 1886. In addition there was a small but flourishing anarchist movement among Chicago's lower classes, particularly German immigrants. It was this element that was blamed for the horrible Haymarket riot. Thus the task of urban evangelism seemed much more urgent to Moody's supporters in 1886. In March of that year Moody had warned them: "Either these people are to be evangelized or the leaven of communism and infidelity will assume such enormous proportions that it will break out in a reign of terror such as this country has never known."[59] Moody's answer to the question of what was to be done for working people was to save their souls and convert them into "peaceful helpful citizens."[60] To this end he proposed a new school to produce "gapmen"[61]—workers without seminary degrees but with some formal theological training—to go into city mission work in order to reach the urban masses. Consequently, the Chicago Evangelization Society was organized in 1887, and in 1889, Moody Bible Institute officially opened as a school for the training of urban lay revivalists. A similar enterprise established in Boston in 1889 was Adoniram Judson Gordon's Missionary Training School.

At the same time Moody was setting up the schools in Northfield, he began to conceive of a plan for a series of summer conferences at Northfield to provide education and spiritual renewal for the laity of the evangelical churches.[62] The first of these conferences was held in 1880 and there was one the following summer, but they began in earnest after Moody's return from Britain. Two of the most significant were the conferences of 1885 and 1886. The topic for 1885 was "Life and Service," and particularly stressed foreign missions. The conference the following year dealt with "Dispensational Truth," and as Ernest Sandeen and others have pointed out, speakers included almost all the prominent supporters of premillennial and dispensationalist thought, including A. J. Gordon, A. T. Pierson, and George Needham.[63]

In 1886, at the instigation of Luther Wishard and C. K. Ober, professional leaders of the youth division of the YMCA, the first student summer conference was held at Northfield. At this conference, speakers like A. T. Pierson and Robert Wilder, a student at Princeton active in the student YMCA and well known for his interest in missions, pressed the cause of foreign missions. Before the conference ended, 100 students had pledged themselves to work in the foreign mission field after finishing college. This was the beginning of the Student Volunteer Movement, whose motto was "the evangelization of the world in this generation." Both Findlay and Sandeen, noting that the movement originated in a conference completely dominated by premillennial views, have suggested that the feeling of urgency expressed in the movement and its motto was the result of premillennial beliefs about the imminent second coming of Christ.[64]

Ernest R. Sandeen has made a significant contribution to our understanding of the place of millenarian (that is, premillennial, as distinguished from postmillennial) views in late-nineteenth-century evangelicalism. As we saw in Chapter II, there was a resurgence of millenarianism in both Britain and America in the years following the Civil War. Moody himself adopted millenarian beliefs in the 1870s, and some of those who constituted his audiences in the famous revival campaigns shared this basically pessimistic view. According to Sandeen, American millenarianism after 1875 became a "proto-denominational fellowship"[65] with enlarged doctrinal concerns that were to attract the support of other conservatives in succeeding decades. The chief expressions of this fellowship in the 1870s and 1880s were the various Bible and prophetic conferences, of which the Niagara conferences were probably the best known.

Known during its first years as the Believers' Meeting for Bible Study,[66] the Niagara Bible Conference was organized informally by a group of Darbyite dispensationalists in New York City in 1868. Early in the 1870s several of these men died and the meetings were interrupted for several years, but the conference was refounded in Chicago in 1875. From 1883 to 1897, the conference met at Niagara-on-the-Lake, Ontario, thus giving it its name. The "founding father"[67] of the conference and its president from 1875 was a Presbyterian minister from St. Louis, Missouri, James Hall Brookes. It was Brookes who drew up the famous fourteen-point Niagara Creed in 1878, affirming the verbal inerrancy of the original autographs of the Scriptures, the premillennial second advent of Christ, and a very conservative, Calvinistically oriented group of articles on human depravity and salvation by faith in the blood of Christ. This creed was to become the touchstone of Fundamentalist beliefs in the twentieth century.[68] In the Niagara conferences the minister's chief role became that of Bible teacher, and Bible reading assumed a central place. Other leaders in these conferences were A. J. Gordon and A. T. Pierson, whose names we have encountered as speakers at Moody's Northfield conferences.

Of the Bible and prophetic conferences, the most significant was that held in 1878 in New York's Holy Trinity Episcopal Church. Sandeen referred to it as the "coming out party of millenarianism."[69] The call for the conference came from 122 millenarians from the northeastern United States. Among those signing the call, Presbyterians and Episcopalians were disproportionately represented. The conference was to present a common front of millenarian witness against postmillennial clergy and others. The gathering attracted sufficient attention for liberals to express some concern about the movement. In an article in the *New York Evangelist* after the 1878 conference, Presbyterian liberal Charles A. Briggs declared that if the millenarians persisted in their aggressive movement they might be forced to depart from the orthodox churches and form another heretical sect.[70]

Another conservative manifestation in the 1880s was the publication in the 1881 *Presbyterian Review* of an article by A. A. Hodge and Benjamin B. Warfield setting forth the doctrine of inspiration central to the so-called Princeton theology. As Ernest Sandeen pointed out, the Princeton professors insisted that they were merely defending the Westminster Confession, but actually they had created a new apologetic based ultimately on eighteenth-century standards of rationality. Thus where the confession insisted that only the witness of the Spirit could convince persons that the Scriptures are the Word of God, Hodge and Warfield argued that the Scriptures are the Word of God because they are inspired. The emphasis in the confession was on internal proofs, while the Princeton theologians tended to rely on external proofs. The epitome of their position was that the original autographs of Scripture were verbally inspired and inerrant. In their reliance on a literal and inerrant Bible, millenarians and Princeton conservatives were on common ground, and as Sandeen has shown, they were allied in many aspects of the pre-World War Fundamentalist movement.[71]

What was important about the 1880s was that the evangelical unity so evident at mid-century and still very much a reality in the early 1870s was beginning to break down. During that decade the Protestant churches in America had to cope with serious challenges to both their social program and their system of thought.[72] Under the impact of these challenges, the evangelical ranks began to divide, almost imperceptibly at first. Thus we have seen in this chapter the persistence of the older evangelicalism, enthusiastic in its endorsement of the burgeoning middle-class society, and the beginnings of the development out of this of a genuine social Christianity on the one hand, and an aggressive, millenarian conservatism on the other. Only the beginnings were evident in the 1880s, but they were the seed from which the later schism in Protestantism developed.

First Major Confrontations: The 1890s

In his history of the social gospel, Charles H. Hopkins referred to the decade 1890 to 1900 as the years of the social gospel's "coming of age."[1] As might be expected, it was in the 1890s that the first major confrontations between social Christianity and individual evangelism took place. In that decade, the problems of labor and the nation's cities that had stimulated the beginnings of a social Christianity in the 1880s grew even more serious, and the new solidaristic trends in philosophy, psychology, and sociology became more fully developed and articulated and more widely accepted.

Continued Social Upheavals

The period from 1892 to 1894 was the last and most alarming in the series of great social upheavals that shocked the nation out of its complacency. By the 1890s, the practical unionism of the American Federation of Labor was supplanting the general reformism of the Knights of Labor.

The third crisis began in the spring of 1892, when the Carnegie Steel Corporation announced new wage cuts to employees at its plant in Homestead, Pennsylvania. Skilled workers of the Amalgamated Association of Iron, Steel, and Tin Workers refused to accept the new contract and the plant's general manager, Henry Clay Frick, refused any further negotiations with the union and shut down the plant. Early in July, Frick sent in two barges of armed Pinkerton detectives to guard the mills. These were driven off by the strikers and company control was reestablished only with the help of the state militia. With militia protection the plant was reopened with nonunion labor and when the strike was officially called off in November, only some 800 of the original Homestead working force of nearly 4,000 were reinstated. Frick's plan to break the union had been a complete success.[2]

The People's Party

In addition to the labor unrest, the nation was troubled by deepening agricultural problems. For some time farmers had suffered from heavy debts, high commodity prices and shipping costs, and low prices for farm produce. Farmers' Alliances had been organized in the late 1870s and 1880s as a means of redressing grievances, but although they facilitated social contact, the exchange of information, and sometimes cooperative business ventures, they were ineffective politically. Finally in Omaha, Nebraska, in July 1892, a national political third party known as the People's (or Populist) Party was formed. Its platform called for the union of all the laboring elements in the nation, the return of the control of the country to the "plain people," and the expansion of the powers of government "to the end that oppression, injustice, and poverty shall eventually cease in the land."[3] As a demonstration of their sense of the common interests of rural and urban labor, the members of the convention expressed sympathy with the Knights of Labor in their strike against Rochester clothing manufacturers. In return, the Populist Party won support from the Knights of Labor, the followers of Henry George and Edward Bellamy, and Eugene Debs. In the elections of 1892, the Populists won some important victories. The number of Populist-minded U.S. senators rose to five, of representatives to ten. Populist governors were elected in Kansas, North Dakota, and Colorado, and the newly elected governor of Illinois, John P. Altgeld, although a Democrat, agreed substantially with virtually all of the Omaha platform. Many sympathetic state legislators and county officials were elected.[4]

In 1893, the nation was once again hit by a panic and depression, the third since the end of the Civil War (1873, 1884-85). According to Henry May, this crisis was in many respects "the most serious challenge to American political and economic institutions between the Civil War and the depression of 1929-37."[5] Once again no economic or political agency seemed able to take any measures to cure or relieve the slump. In 1894, when the depression was at its worst, ragged bands of unemployed, of which Jacob Coxey's "army" was the most famous, descended on the nation's capital demanding relief through public works and large issues of paper money. Most of the major churches condemned the movement.

That year was one of widespread strikes, as workers fought desperately to sustain falling wages. In most cases the large corporations were able to defeat the laborers. The climax of labor strife came with the Pullman strike of 1894. Pullman employees lived in a model town that was attractive to look at but whose owners actually exercised a petty tyranny, since rents, public utilities, supplies and services were all higher there than in surrounding communities, and employees had no choice about living there. With the depression of 1893, the Pullman Company laid off more than 3,000 of its 5,800 employees and reduced the wages of those remaining by 25 to 40 percent without any corresponding reduction in rent for the company houses.[6] When George Pullman refused to consider their grievances, the employees called a strike.

Having recently become affiliated with the year-old American Railway Union, led by Eugene V. Debs, the Pullman workers appealed to the national union for help. Although reluctant to involve the young union in such a full-scale encounter, Debs agreed to back up the strikers and declared a nationwide boycott against the Pullman Company and all railroads using its cars. Debs counseled restraint and nonviolence, but the conflict soon developed into a war between the union and the General Managers' Association, composed of executives of twenty-four railroads entering Chicago. Federal troops were sent to Chicago by President Cleveland over the protest of Governor Altgeld, and a blanket injunction resulted in the imprisonment of Debs and nearly all the leaders, thus crushing the strike.[7]

In spite of the growing sympathy for labor in the Protestant churches, opinions expressed in the major religious papers wholeheartedly approved the injunction and federal troops and deplored the idea of a sympathetic railway strike. Except for the Christian Socialists, who supported the strikers, the one dissenter from the majority point of view was William H. Carwardine, minister of the Methodist Church in Pullman. Carwardine blamed the strike on the company's tyrannical practices and destroyed the notion of satisfactory living conditions in the company town. He not only supported the strikers, but also evidently played an important part in persuading the A.R.U. to declare its sympathetic boycott.[8]

Combined with deepening agricultural distress, the labor unrest resulted in considerable foreboding among the middle class. For a time it seemed as if the Populist Party might succeed in its effort to build an effective union of the laboring elements of the country. In 1896, the Populists and the Democrats both named William Jennings Bryan as their presidential candidate. In the election against McKinley, however, he carried only the predominantly agricultural states.[9] The impetus for reform was to pass by the turn of the century to a more urban, more middle-class movement known as Progressivism. Part of the reason for the failure of Populism was the inherent instability of the coalition between farmers and urban laborers. Although the Knights of Labor had supported Populist goals, by the middle 1890s the American Federation of Labor had replaced the Knights as the advocate for labor. Concerned chiefly with securing specific and immediate gains for the skilled workers in terms of wages and hours, the A. F. of L. tended to avoid involvement with the Populists. Many of the Populist goals, however, were to be continued by the new progressive reforming movement.

The effect of the social upheavals of 1892-94 was to deepen the concern of many Protestants and to make undeniably clear the need for some solution to the very real problems posed by strikes and unemployment.

Urban conditions too continued to disturb and challenge the churches in the 1890s. Josiah Strong's popular book *Our Country* was issued in a revised edition in 1891, and two years later he wrote *The New Era* on the problems facing the nation as it approached a new century. In that book he outlined a plan for city evangelization by house-to-house visitation in the residential areas, and institutional churches and missions in the business and tenement districts. An integral part of his program was the federation of local churches in a community to deal with social problems and questions of municipal reform.[10]

One of the most widely read pleas for city reform in this decade was William T. Stead's *If Christ Came to Chicago!*, published in 1894. Stead was a British journalist who came to Chicago for the World's Columbian Exposition in 1893 and stayed long enough to collect information to expose the city's evils, largely because he believed that the Windy City might be the future world's capital.[11] One result of Stead's book was the organization of the Chicago Civic Federation, a reform pressure group.

New solidaristic trends beginning to be developed in sociology, philosophy, and psychology in the 1880s were expanded and more fully articulated in the following decade. In 1892, Albion W. Small, whose understanding of sociology was much influenced by the thought of Lester Frank Ward, was called to the University of Chicago to head the first department of its kind, in sociology.[12] William James's *Principles of Psychology* was published in 1890, and the Pragmatist movement was officially launched when James addressed the Philosophical Union of the University of California on "Philosophical Conceptions and Practical Results" in August 1898. The application Dewey was to make of James's pragmatism after 1900 was already evident in his writings in the field of ethics in the 1890s. And it was in the 1890s that the transition to solidarism became apparent with the publication of Henry Drummond's *The Ascent of Man* (1894), Benjamin Kidd's *Social Evolution* (1894), and, in preliminary form, Peter Kropotkin's *Mutual Aid*.[13] In 1894, Henry Demarest Lloyd's *Wealth Against Commonwealth* expressed the view common among Populist-minded reformers that all monopolies should be publicly owned.

Finally, the wholehearted acceptance of Darwinian evolution by progressive American theologians in this decade produced three basic ideas that constituted a logical frame of reference for social Christianity: the immanence of God, the organic view of society, and the hoped-for kingdom of God on earth.[14] In short, by 1895, all the causes for the rise of social Christianity were present, all the major resources for social criticism and remedies were available, and, as Henry May phrased it, "the movement was started . . . on all the paths it was to follow in later years."[15]

The Kingdom Ideal

In his working-class parish in New York City, Walter Rauschenbusch was confronted with all the urban social problems of his day—poverty, insecurity, unemployment, tenement housing, disease, crime. His individualistic evangelical background had not prepared him to deal with this situation. "When I had begun to apply my previous religious ideas to the conditions I found," he later explained, "I discovered that they didn't fit." His friends were urging him to give up his social work for "Christian work," but, deeply convinced that it was "Christ's work," he kept trying to find a basis for the Christian teaching of a social gospel.[16] Finally in 1891, on a year of study in England and Germany, he discovered the doctrine of the kingdom of God.

> So Christ's conception of the Kingdom of God came to me as a new revelation. Here was the idea and purpose that had dominated the mind of the Master himself. All his teachings center about it. His life was given to it, and death was suffered for it. . . .
>
> When the Kingdom of God dominated our landscape, the perspective of life shifted into a new alignment. . . . [This new conception of the purpose of Christianity] responded to all the old and all the new elements of my religious

81

life. The saving of the lost, the teaching of the young, the pastoral care of the poor and frail, the quickening of starved intellects, the study of the Bible, church union, political reform, the reorganization of the industrial system, international peace,—it was all covered by the one aim of the Reign of God on earth.[17]

The Brotherhood of the Kingdom

In the 1890s the new social Christianity was generally rationalized in terms of the kingdom ideal. Two of the major social gospel movements began in that decade, both of them based on a rediscovery of the idea of the kingdom. The first of these was the Brotherhood of the Kingdom, founded in 1892, in order to "reestablish this idea in the thought of the church, and to assist in its practical realization in the world."[18] The brotherhood originated with a small group of young Baptist ministers in and about the New York area: Walter Rauschenbusch and Leighton Williams; their close friend Nathaniel Schmidt, then teaching at Colgate University; and Samuel Zane Batten, pastor of the Baptist Church of Mayayunk near Philadelphia.[19] Among the earliest members of the fellowship were also George Dana Boardman and William Newton Clarke, the eminent theologian.

At a meeting in Philadelphia in December 1892, the group drew up a statement on the "Spirit and Aims of the Brotherhood of the Kingdom." In it, each member pledged to exemplify obedience to the ethics of Jesus in his personal life, to propagate the thoughts of Jesus to the limits of his ability, to "lay special stress on the social aims of Christianity" and endeavor to make operative Christ's teaching concerning wealth, to "take plans to keep in contact with the common people, and to infuse the religious spirit into the efforts for social amelioration."[20] Members of the brotherhood were to meet frequently for prayer and discussion, to correspond with one another and exchange articles they had written, and to support one another "in the public defense of the truth."[21]

In August 1893, the group met at the summer home of Leighton Williams's father at Marlboro-on-the-Hudson, New York, to read and discuss papers for a possible book of essays on the kingdom. The summer gathering thereafter became an annual affair; it was the one meeting of the brotherhood each year and lasted for a week. The membership was small, never more than fifty. Bound by their common purpose "to see the idea of the Kingdom of God on earth once more become the inspiration of Christian effort, the basis of

Christian union, the object of prayer, and the synthesis of thought,"[22] the members met for prayer, meditation, and discussion of papers on theological and social questions. Believing that the Kingdom of God embraced the whole of human life, they considered such practical issues as strikes and unions, monopolies, the ethics of business, socialism, the single tax, and social work. In order to make possible the kind of fellowship its members felt was so much the essence of the brotherhood, local chapters were founded in other cities. Rauschenbusch founded a Rochester chapter when he began teaching at the Theological Seminary there in 1897, and there was a very active chapter in Boston. Over the years the membership included more and more non-Baptists; many of the leaders of the religious social movement were brought to its occasional fellowship.[23] The brotherhood provided the context for Rauschenbusch's creative and monumental contributions to the social gospel. Some of the major ideas of the brotherhood were brought to the attention of English-speaking Protestantism with the publication in 1907 of Rauschenbusch's *Christianity and the Social Crisis*. The brotherhood was truly one of the most remarkable of all social gospel movements.[24]

Applied Christianity and the Kingdom Movement

The other movement begun in the 1890s was very different in spirit, but for a time, at least as significant. This was the Kingdom movement led by George Herron and based at Iowa College, where he had accepted the newly created Chair of Applied Christianity in 1893. Robert Handy has suggested that this movement was in fact "the single most important phase of social gospel history in the 1890s."[25]

It was one of the very few social gospel movements that can be seen meaningfully against the background of Populism in the mid-1890s. Various commentators have stressed the environment of religious fervor associated with Populism or the revivalistic nature of frontier Congregationalism in which Herron was raised, by way of explaining something of his mystical personality and crusading zeal. His radicalism exceeded that of most contemporary social Christians, but it was the radicalism of a social prophet. By 1896 most of the Protestant churches and religious journals had rejected Herron and his position, but in three years he had had considerable influence on the entire social gospel movement.[26]

Herron was born in Indiana in 1862 of deeply religious Scottish parents. According to his own testimony he was a mystic when still a child; he could not recall a time when he had been without the sense of God's presence. Already away from home at work in a print shop, he joined the church at age thirteen. The foreman of the shop befriended him and taught him to read Shakespeare and the Greek classics. For three years he attended the preparatory department of Ripon College, but most of his education was self-acquired. He read widely in economics, philosophy, and contemporary German theology, and was also much influenced by the works of Frederick Denison Maurice and Giuseppe Mazzini. In 1883 he entered the Congregational ministry.[27]

In 1890, Herron gave an address at the Minnesota Congregational Club in Minneapolis, entitled "The Message of Jesus to Men of Wealth." In it he pressed the concept of stewardship to self-sacrifice and urged the wealthy men in the churches to follow Christ by living sacrificially in the service of their fellow humans. Herron's address attracted wide attention and from the many calls he received as a result of it, he chose to go to the First Congregational Church of Burlington, Iowa. Josiah Strong preached the sermon at his installation there in December 1891.[28] Herron remained in the Burlington pastorate for seventeen months, during which time he became a nationally known figure. His sermons were published in several books (*The Larger Christ*, *A Plea for the Gospel*, and *The Call of the Cross*), he carried on a socialized church program, and gave a series of addresses on labor and capital, poverty and wealth that were well attended by working people and officially approved by union labor.[29] In the summer of 1892, he held the first of his ministers' retreats at Iowa College in Grinnell.

In 1893, he left Burlington to accept the Chair of Applied Christianity created for him at Iowa College by Mrs. Rand, one of his well-to-do parishioners. It was at Iowa College (later Grinnell College) that he was to have such an influence on the rising social gospel. In addition to his courses at the college, which were apparently very popular, he held evening meetings on Bible study and Christian discipleship. He gave lectures throughout the Midwest and at Union Seminary and Princeton University in the East. These addresses were published in 1893 as *The New Redemption* and *The Christian Society*. Some of his lectures the following year were published as *The Christian State*.

In the summer of 1893, Herron helped to found the American Institute of Christian Sociology at Chautauqua under the presidency of Richard T. Ely. (He was followed as president by Josiah Strong and then by Herron.) The aims of the organization were similar to those of the (Episcopalian) Christian Social Union founded in 1891: "To claim for the Christian law the ultimate authority to rule social practice, to study in common how to apply the principles of Christianity to the social and economic difficulties of the present time, and to present Christ as the Living Master and King of men, and His kingdom as a complete idea of human society, to be realized on earth."[30] The institute's methods were primarily educational. It sponsored the Summer School of Applied Christianity, which Herron had already organized at Iowa College. In 1894, Ely, Herron (principal of these "Schools of the Kingdom"), Josiah Strong, John R. Commons, George Gates (president of Iowa College), and B. Fay Mills served as leaders in the school's sessions. The following year a similar institute was held at Oberlin with Gladden as president.[31]

In 1894, a group of social Christians led by Gates and Herron took over the former *Northwest Congregationalist*, published in Minneapolis, and turned it into a journal of applied Christianity entitled *The Kingdom*. In its first issue, April 20, George Gates paid tribute to George Herron for inaugurating a new religious movement, "a Movement for the Kingdom," of which the new journal was to serve as a mouthpiece.[32] The editorial board of the journal was composed of Gates, Herron, Strong, Mills, John R. Commons, and several others. The journal was published weekly for just five years and was probably "the outstanding social gospel journal published prior to the first World War."[33] Its general position, though somewhat to the left of the major social gospel trends of the 1890s, was considerably less radical than that of Herron himself, but it was firm in its defense of him.

Herron's message was deeply religious: it was essentially a call to the church to reconstruct society according to the ethics of Jesus. More drastically than any of his colleagues, Herron broke with the still prevalent economics and sociology. In *The New Redemption*, he described the current state of unrest as the beginnings of a revolution, and he was quite certain that it would be a work of God.

> God honors our generation by bringing upon it the sorrow and trial of seeking a road to social order. . . . The idea of brotherhood, cooperation, unity, is both destroying and recreating the world. . . . The belief that sacrifice and not self-interest is the social foundation, that the Golden Rule is natural law, is everywhere gaining disciples and power. . . . The socialistic idea is leading the world. Whether the passion for oneness works the weal or woe of society depends entirely upon its reception or rejection by the Christian church.[34]

Herron then went on to damn the existing industrial order. Far from being based on natural law, the present system of competition was anarchy. Monopolies were its natural fruit, and the whole social question was "fast resolving itself into a question of whether or not capital can be brought into subjection to law."[35]

Like an Old Testament prophet, Herron also condemned the Protestant churches for their praise of the philanthropy of the rich.

> There is no harder resistance to the kingdom of God, no evil which more bitterly resents the redemption of society, than the so-called philanthropy which founds public institutions and enriches missionary funds out of wealth that has been gathered by extortion and social cruelty. . . . The priests who accompanied the pirate ships of the sixteenth century, to say mass and pray for the souls of the dead pirates for a share of the spoil, were not a whit more superstitious or guilty of human blood, according to the light of their teaching, than Protestant leaders who flatter the ghastly philanthropy of men who have heaped their colossal fortunes upon the bodies of their brothers.[36]

To approve of such a civilization was to reject Christ and all that he stood for. "The worst charge that can be made against a Christian," Herron said, "is that he attempts to justify the existing social order."[37]

Herron favored the reconstruction of society along socialist lines in order to achieve human justice. Yet in the early 1890s his message was basically religious. He did not deal so much with specific, practical remedies as with religious mandates. For him, the imperative of the hour was the assertion of the cross (sacrifice) as the eternal principle of all divine and human action.[38] Thus he called on the state to be "born again," to be delivered from "commercial and police conceptions of its functions" and to make its institutions "the organized expression of Christ's law of love."[39]

While recognizing the need for specific proposals to "adjust the inequalities of society," he reminded his hearers that no political legislation "has power, or ever can have power," to make people unselfish.[40] Like an evangelist, he called American society to repentance.

> Christ is disappointed in this nation. We are a fallen nation, an apostate people. We have done those material and political things we ought not to have done, and left undone the social and righteous things we ought to have done. . . .
> I see no other hope for our nation, no other redemption for society, than a religious revival such as the world has never known, that shall enthrone Christ

in our national ideals, and give men the common will and the power to put the Christ life into social practice.[41]

This yearning for a revival that would bring about social as well as individual regeneration seems to have been widespread among the supporters of the Kingdom movement. In an article written for the April 27, 1894 issue of *The Kingdom*, John P. Coyle commented on the reasons for the failure of a revival to appear after the depression of 1893.

> The real cause of its delay . . . is that the consciousness of the need for social regeneration is so strong and so widespread that it is impossible for a religious awakening to expend itself, as such movements have done in the recent past, in purely individualistic lines, leaving the social structure as pagan as it found it. . . . It will be to the infinite peril of the Church if a revival does not follow this financial crisis. It will be to her equal peril, if this revival be other than a quickening to social righteousness.[42]

Henry May suggested that "more fundamentally than he was ever a socialist, Herron was a social revivalist, the first preacher in America who was able to combine the method of Moody or Talmage with the doctrines of Christian radicalism.[43] Contemporaries also remarked on Herron's evangelistic appeal and drew comparisons between his movement at Iowa College and that of Finney at Oberlin. "Dr. Herron is hardly to be classed with professors of sociology," observed Rev. Joseph H. Chandler, "he is an evangelist of social Christianity to our time. . . . [His lectures] will make Iowa College the center of a religious movement as powerful in its way as the one centered at Oberlin in the person of Finney fifty years ago."[44]

Herron was not the only man in this decade to attempt to combine the technique and rhetoric of revivalism with a message of social Christianity. As I describe later in this chapter, one of Herron's converts to the social gospel in 1893, the revivalist B. Fay Mills, tried even more explicitly to bring together evangelism and social Christianity. The early social gospelers were evangelicals and as such they attempted in various ways to reconcile personal religion and social reform. It may well be that these efforts in the 1890s represented one last attempt to do what Moody, in adapting individualistic revivalism to urban America, failed to do: that is, to link evangelical Protestantism to progressive thought and the new solidaristic trends and thus make it a satisfactory form of faith for the modern world.

Unlike most Protestant spokespersons in the 1890s, who had little understanding of or sympathy for agrarian unrest, the Kingdom movement seems to have had some relationship to Populism. The ties between Populism and Protestantism in the Midwest still need to be further explored, but we do know that the Populists welcomed Herron's message and even wished to nominate him for a seat in the Iowa legislature.[45] However, he refused the Populist candidacy because he saw his vocation as primarily religious rather than political.

Herron probably influenced the moderate social Christians more than any other radical, especially in the peak years of the Kingdom movement, 1893-96. A contemporary observer thus described the leadership of the movement: "The scribe of this movement in America is the Rev. Josiah Strong, D.D.; its prophet is the Rev. George D. Herron, D.D.; its apostle is the Rev. B. Fay Mills; while President George A. Gates is by some regarded as its leader."[46] Josiah Strong wrote an introduction to one of Herron's early books and invited him to speak at the 1893 meeting of the Evangelical Alliance. However, the executive committee of the Evangelical Alliance finally induced Strong to resign as an editor of *The Kingdom* because they objected to any link with Herron's increasing radicalism.[47]

Herron eventually lost the support of more moderate social gospel leaders because of his repeated denunciations of institutions, particularly his negative attitude toward the church. By 1896 he had passed the peak of his influence in the churches.[48] From 1897 to 1899 he gradually moved left, both theologically and in terms of social and economic views. He was associated with progressive reformers of various stripes in the National Social Reform Union founded in 1899. Bliss was president of the union; among the vice presidents were Henry Demarest Lloyd, author of *Wealth Against Commonwealth*; Eugene Debs; Governor Altgeld; "Golden Rule" Jones, the reforming mayor of Toledo; Hazen Smith Pingree, the progressive governor of Michigan; B. Fay Mills; George Gates; Herron; and Benjamin Orange Flower, editor of the *Arena*.[49]

In the winter of 1899, Herron resigned from his teaching post at Iowa College. In 1901, he joined J. Stitt Wilson's Social Crusade, an attempt to infuse socialism with the religious spirit. Eventually he came to the point of advocating a social order free of all coercive institutions. In 1901, he and his wife were divorced, he was deposed from the ministry, and he and Carrie Rand, the daughter of his wealthy benefactress, were married in a liberal ceremony in which they simply said their vows to each other as husband and wife. Thus ended one of the most brilliant episodes in the history of the social gospel.[50]

Several other developments of this decade, while not as spectacular in themselves as the movements just described, were more typical of the broad mainstream of social Christianity. Two of them were attempts to deal creatively with the problems of the city. In 1894, some prominent leaders in institutional church work organized the Open and Institutional Church League to multiply institutional churches and provide a means of exchange of ideas and methodology. (Because this organization was an important forerunner of the Federal Council of Churches, I consider it at greater length in a later chapter.) Another significant effort was the establishment of social settlements. A number of these were founded with specifically religious objectives. While including the general purpose of all settlements—to provide opportunity for actual residence in working-class neighborhoods—some were intended to be laboratories in social Christianity. For example, the Chicago Commons settlement, founded in 1894 by Graham Taylor, the new (and first) professor of Christian sociology in the country at Chicago Theological Seminary, was such a laboratory for his classes. One of the most famous of the settlements was Andover House in Boston, sponsored by a group of Andover Seminary alumni and directed by Robert A. Woods, who served as its head resident. These settlements were conceived as practical ways of demonstrating Christian principles of brotherhood "along the lines of educational, social, civic, and religious well-being."[51]

"What Would Jesus Do?": The Social Gospel Novel

One indication of the growing social awakening was the popularity of the social gospel novel. By far the most successful was another product of midwestern Congregationalism, the sermon story *In His Steps: What Would Jesus Do?*, by Rev. Charles M. Sheldon of Topeka, Kansas. In 1889, Sheldon had accepted a call to the Central Congregational Church of Topeka. *In His Steps* was the most popular of several serial sermon stories that Sheldon wrote and read to his congregation. First published in the Chicago *Advance* in 1896, the story was soon printed in book form and, by 1933, Sheldon estimated that some 23 million copies had been sold in English, with translations into twenty-one foreign languages.[52] There was even a motion picture in 1936 based on *In His Steps*.

The story opened with a dramatic incident at the close of the Sunday service in a comfortable church. A poor young man, unemployed and hungry, asked the congregation what it meant to follow Jesus when Christians lived in luxury while people like him suffered and died. When he passed away in the pastor's home where he was being cared for, the deeply moved minister asked his congregation to join him in a pledge to live for a year on the basis of what they thought Jesus would do. The rest of the story was an account of the reforms that resulted. Although the book was sentimental and posed the simple solution of a change of heart for complex social and economic problems, its very simplicity was probably a good part of the reason for its wide appeal. Its success demonstrated the considerable public interest in the 1890s in Christian proposals for social reform.

The Social Gospel and Revivalism

It was not until the 1890s that two evangelists came into the national limelight earlier occupied by Dwight L. Moody. Samuel Porter Jones and Benjamin Fay Mills both reached the peak of their careers at this time. Because they emphasized what seemed to be social questions, they were often considered part of the social gospel movement. However, only Mills really departed significantly from the old tradition of evangelism.

Jones was born in Alabama in 1847. He studied law but eventually had to abandon his law practice because of heavy drinking. In 1872, he dramatically gave up drinking after promising his dying father that he would, and was converted under his grandfather's preaching. That same year, he was received as an itinerant preacher by the North Georgia Conference of the Methodist Episcopal Church, South. In 1880, he became a fund-raising agent for the North Georgia Orphans' Home in Decatur and was given permission to preach anywhere in the United States. Under these auspices he held revivals until 1893, when he severed his relationship to the home in order to devote full time to professional evangelism.[53]

In the New South of the 1880s, Jones was hailed as a social force because he talked about moral conduct rather than "heart religion" and seemed concerned with this world instead of preoccupied with the next. His first big revival was in Nashville, Tennessee, a city of about 50,000 people, in 1885. In his revivals he called for civic reform. As he saw it, the purpose of a revival was to draw the line on the moral issues of the day (by which he meant liquor traffic, gambling and fraud, Sabbath-breaking, and public morals) and to demand that Christians take a stand. Departing from the traditional southern position that the churches were not to meddle in politics (a pre-Civil War position with regard to the slavery question), Jones urged legislative action, especially with regard to prohibition.[54]

Sam Jones made such a name for himself in the South that he was asked to lead revival campaigns in the North as well. In 1885, he held a month's meeting at the Brooklyn Tabernacle with T. DeWitt Talmage, one of the celebrity preachers of the late nineteenth century. In 1886, he spent five weeks in Cincinnati, five weeks in Chicago, and four weeks in Baltimore. In 1887, he even took on the formidable city of Boston for four weeks of revival meetings. Jones's message in these revivals differed considerably from that of Moody. In his stress on law and good works he more closely resembled Finney. Instead of preaching about God's love, he preached about sin. As he told a gathering of ministers in Cincinnati in 1886: "It is well enough to preach Christ and Him crucified, Christ's love and Christ's mercy, but you want to stop that now and tell these wicked old sinners that they have got to repent, that they have got to reform."[55] For him conversion was a change in moral conduct. A newspaper account of his Nashville revival noted particularly his view that there was one broad road in the moral universe, at one end of which was heaven, at the other hell. He then pictured repentance as a stop, an about-face, and a movement in the opposite direction.[56] He often talked about repentance as "quitting your meanness."

Newspapers in the northern cities where he held revivals praised him for his moral courage. David Swing, the liberal Chicago Presbyterian minister, spoke favorably about his meetings in Chicago, praising him as a "most powerful exponent and advocate of the religion of action, the religion of character, as opposed to that of mere belief and mere melancholy sentiment." He thought Jones the most "intellectual" revivalist Chicago had yet seen, and said his converts would be enrolled on the basis of "solid sense" rather than "transient sentiment." Finally, he regarded the revivalist as a valuable Christian moral force because "his heaven is here to-day, as well as over yonder to-morrow."[57]

However, for Jones, sin was still an individual matter, a question of vice, or personal moral conduct. The revivalist revealed both his own true colors and the sympathies of many evangelical churchpeople of the day when he confronted the liberal mayor of Toledo, Samuel M. ("Golden Rule") Jones in a pre-election revival campaign in Toledo in 1899. Samuel M. Jones was elected mayor of Toledo in 1897. From 1887 to 1892, he had lived in Lima, Ohio, where he worked for the Ohio Oil Company and tinkered with oil drilling machinery. He was a prominent member of the Methodist Church and

91

president of the YMCA. In 1892, he moved to Toledo, where he came under Herron's influence. In 1893, he was shocked by the depression and moved by Herron's book *The New Redemption*. In that book Herron had said, "He who builds a mercantile establishment upon the basis of the Golden Rule is a greater and wiser philanthropist than he who founds hospitals for the poor out of the gains of selfishness."[58]

In 1894, Samuel M. Jones opened a factory in Toledo to manufacture a new type of sucker rod (used in the oil industry) that he had invented and perfected himself. In 1895, he announced that his factory would be run according to the Golden Rule. He proceeded to institute a system of employee relations that was years ahead of its time. It included an eight-hour day, minimum wages of $2 per day, a Christmas bonus (profit sharing), an employee insurance plan, an employee restaurant that sold hot meals at less than cost, shares of stock in the company, summer vacations with pay, a park on the grounds, and an annual company picnic. In 1899, Jones was able to report that the Golden Rule works![59]

When Golden Rule Jones became mayor of Toledo in 1897, the city had a population of 100,000, roughly one-fourth of whom were foreign-born, especially German. He had campaigned on a platform of "good government," by which he meant concern for the public welfare. A teetotaler himself, he was willing to follow public sentiment in the matter of drinking. Because he believed that saloons were the result of wrong social conditions and also served as a social club for the poor, he refused to enforce the state law for Sunday closing. For this stand he was denounced from Protestant pulpits by ministers demanding that he enforce the blue laws. They also disliked his "socialistic" views on the public ownership of utilities.[60]

The next mayoral election was to be April 3, 1899. In 1898, the Ministerial Association of Toledo, composed of sixty Protestant ministers, invited the evangelist Sam P. Jones to conduct a city-wide revival the following March. Since the evangelist's views on civic reform and prohibition were well known, it was apparent that the churches were going into politics.

For the first week of the revival, no mention was made of the election campaign. On March 9, Mayor Jones entered the mayoralty race as an Independent, since both major parties had bypassed him because of his public-ownership policies. On March 12, the revivalist denounced "the rule of love that keeps the saloons open,"[61] and for the remainder of his stay in Toledo he continued to attack the mayor. The city's ministers, with few exceptions, joined in the denunciations. Mayor Jones told a ministerial committee that he would not sign a pledge promising, if elected, to enforce the blue laws. He insisted that the moral question was a red herring and that vested interests had seized on the revival and the prohibition question to cover their real objective—the maintenance of monopolistic utility franchises. He campaigned on a platform of public ownership of utilities, a minimum wage of $1.50 per day for eight hours of common labor, and organized labor to be employed on all public works. He spoke not in terms of socialism, but of Christianity and brotherhood.

The final meeting of the revival was held March 22. The evangelist's parting shot was the subsequently much-quoted comment, "I am for the Golden Rule myself, up to a certain point, and then I want to take up the shotgun and the club."[62] He likened the owners of saloons, gambling houses, and brothels to mad dogs and asked, "would any man in this house attempt to use the Golden Rule on such an animal?"[63] In spite of all this opposition, Mayor Jones was reelected by a landslide, carrying every ward in the city except one.

After 1900, Sam Jones concentrated his revivals on the South, where the Law and Order Leagues, which often followed his campaigns, were important in effecting statewide prohibition amendments. He sincerely believed that prohibition offered the cure for most of the country's problems, from poverty and labor agitation to corrupt politics. Because the liquor traffic as a social evil was also a concern of many progressive reformers, Jones's espousal of prohibition made him appear a genuine reformer, thus blurring the distinction between individual evangelism and social Christianity. Yet in their understanding of the relationship between the individual and society, the two sides remained separate. Sam Jones was a representative of the traditional, individualistic view, as he revealed so clearly in his Toledo confrontation with Mayor Jones. As William McLoughlin pointed out, the Toledo revival indicated the path that professional evangelism was to take in the twentieth century.[64]

Yet there was one major attempt to bring together social Christianity and individual evangelism in this decade by preaching the social message from the revival platform; the evangelist who tried it was a follower of George Herron, Rev. B. Fay Mills. Mills was born in Rahway, New Jersey, in 1857. His father, Thornton A. Mills, was a prominent Old School Presbyterian minister. Ordained to the Congregational ministry in 1878, he graduated from Lake Forest College in Illinois the following year. After graduation he served pastorates in the Dutch Reformed Church of Greenwich, New York, and the West Parish Congregational Church in Outland, Vermont. In 1887, he decided to become a revivalist. His first revivals were in small towns like Montclair and Morristown, New Jersey; Andover and Newburyport, Massachusetts; Decatur and Jacksonville, Illinois. Although he conducted some meetings in larger cities like Brooklyn, Wilmington, Boston, and Philadelphia, they were not city-wide revivals but local meetings in which several churches joined.[65]

In Cleveland in 1891, he developed what he called a "District Combination Plan" of revivalism, which he tried out for the first time in meetings in Cincinnati the following year. The plan entailed an elaborate system of organization. The city was divided into districts, each with a complete set of committees to handle finances, advertising, canvassing, music, ushers, and devotional matters. Revival meetings held in each of the districts then culminated in a series of services in a central tabernacle. The Mills' Meetings Executive Committee was in charge of all the planning and organizational work. During the meetings the campaign took precedence over all ordinary church plans. Mills was director; his assistant for the Cincinnati meetings was a good friend and former classmate at Lake Forest, J. Wilbur Chapman.[66]

Before 1893, Mills had been a conventional revivalist with one aim, "salvation from sin through Christ."[67] During his Cincinnati campaign in 1892, he said, "The one reason for our being here in this life is that we may save souls."[68] Sometime in 1893, he heard Herron and became convinced of the necessity for a social gospel. From then on, although he remained a revivalist, there was a decisive change in the content of his message.

In 1893, he gave an address before the World's Parliament of Religions entitled "Christ, the Saviour of the World." In this, as in a volume of sermons published in 1894 called *God's World and Other Sermons*, he stressed the typical social gospel themes of human solidarity and the fatherhood of God and brotherhood of man. Christ's coming was not to save people out of the world (as Moody had said), but to save the world itself. In 1894, Mills became one of the associate editors of *The Kingdom*, and that summer he taught a series of biblical studies on "the Kingdom of Heaven upon the Earth" as part of the School for the Kingdom at Iowa College.[69] That same spring, Herron had apparently invited him to give a series of lectures in the Department of Applied Christianity at Iowa College. An article in the June 1, 1894, issue of *The Kingdom*, written by Truman O. Douglass, Jr., one of Herron's graduate students,[70] praised Mills in glowing terms.

Mr. Mills is a living proof both that the social gospel has in it the greatest inspiration to personal effort and hope, and that the social evangelist strikes deeper and truer and more heroic chords in the hearts of men than the evangelist of mere individual salvation. . . . Not since John Wesley has there appeared an evangelist with so distinctive a mission, with such combined sweetness and power of spirit.[71]

Mills's most effective attempt to combine the social gospel with personal evangelism was his Columbus revival of 1895. A city-wide campaign, this revival was organized much like Mills's earlier meetings. The city was divided into districts, and there were the usual committees. Meetings were held in the northern and western districts from November 19 to 26, and in the eastern, southern, and central districts from November 27 to December 4. The campaign concluded with meetings in a central location until December 16. Thirty-eight churches in the city cooperated in the campaign. This revival appears to have been the major effort of the one man who tried to combine professional soul-winning and the social gospel.[72]

When Mills came to Columbus, it was with the full support of the city's well-known social gospel leader, Washington Gladden, who had been pastor of the First Congregational Church there since 1882. Gladden presided over the meeting of pastors that voted to call Mills, he sat on the platform when Mills preached, he opened First Church for midday services, and he contributed the introduction to the memorial volume on the meetings. The secretary of the executive committee for the Mills's meetings and editor of the memorial volume was Henry Stauffer, Gladden's former assistant as pastor of the Mayflower Chapel, associated with First Church.[73]

Mills did not neglect a personal gospel. He held the normal preaching services, but when he gave the call to conversion it was a call to "come and be saviors."[74] He felt that the invitation to be saved in order to give all one's energy for the establishment of the Kingdom of God on earth was the most effective impulse to salvation.

The keynote of Mills's effort in Columbus, however, was his series of noonday sermons on "The Kingdom of Heaven on Earth." In these sermons he described his conversion to "the cleansing and inspiring conception of the Kingdom of God"[75] as equal in significance to his first conversion, the consciousness of personal forgiveness of sin. He presented the typical social gospel view of the church as instrumental to the establishment of the Kingdom. He quoted Gladden and the principal figures in the Kingdom movement based at Iowa College—Herron, George Gates, and Josiah Strong.

95

He even engaged in some muckraking, criticizing the churches for accepting "tainted money" and owning tenement houses. He blamed the indifference, selfishness, and cowardice of so-called Christians for "the security of the saloon and the distillery and the gambling house and the brothel." Under the "business of the Church" he included discovering and uprooting the sources of poverty, concern for the physical welfare of cities and their citizens, and providing the inspiration and moral courage for the enactment of more Christian laws, the purification of politics, and the promotion of a spirit of brotherhood between employer and employed. Finally, he urged the need for a Christian Socialism, going so far as to say, "If I had to choose between being a Socialist in the spirit of Christ, but without His name, or being an unsocial Christian, I would be more loyal to Him in the former choice than in the latter."[76]

Still another aspect of the revival that indicated its uniqueness was the Christian Convention held for four days toward the end of the meetings. Ministers were invited from the surrounding area. The topics to be discussed were arranged in such a way as to parallel the process of salvation for the individual. That is, they were to produce conviction and sorrow for social sins, and then a new and stronger faith in Christ as the only sufficient Savior of the individual and society: "The Sins of the City" (for example, "Evils in Material Conditions," "Business Sins," "Political Sins," "The Sins of the Church"), "The Redemption of the City" ("The Cleansing of the Slums," "The Christianization of Business," "The Regeneration of Politics" presented by Gladden, "The Purification of the Church"), "Entire Consecration," and "The Holy Spirit." Mills preached a sermon on "Power" and closed the meeting with a consecration service at which dozens of people gave testimonies.[77]

The immediate results of the Columbus revival were gratifying. Nearly 2,500 cards were signed during the meetings, but accessions to the churches were considered only one of the many fruits of Mills's meetings. Much more frequently mentioned, at least in the memorial volume, were a new understanding of the Kingdom of God, a new sense of the sacredness of every phase of life, and the discovery that Christians could be a real power for good in the community.[78]

Gladden spoke of Mills as a new type of evangelist,[79] and Stauffer hailed the appearance of a new evangelism, which differed from the old mainly in the fact "that to conviction of personal sins and effort to save men from them, is added conviction and sorrow for social sins and a practical effort to improve the material, political and social environment in which the individual lives."[80] He felt Mills's meetings had shown that the old-time revival, with its fervor and power, could be an interdenominational, all-inclusive religious movement quickening in all people whatever makes for personal and social righteousness.

In this Stauffer was mistaken: the results of such promising beginnings were in the end negligible. In an attempt to provide some means of continuing the effort begun by the revival, a Civic Federation was founded and Washington Gladden appointed head. The Roman Catholics and Jews of Columbus were invited to join. But the pastors of the city did little besides preach a sermon on law enforcement shortly after the revival ended, and attempt to persuade the mayor to close the gambling places in the city. As McLoughlin pointed out, what Mills had hoped would be the start of a profound reorientation in the life of Columbus eventually fell into well-established channels. Apparently it was impossible to sustain the effort on the part of ordinary pastors and lay leaders to keep the sense of Christian social responsibility alive.[81]

The personal outcome for B. Fay Mills was no more encouraging. In the summer of 1895, he again participated in the School of the Kingdom held at Iowa College, discussing the topic "The Evangelism of the Kingdom." By April 1896, he must have heard criticism of his methods because a statement by him appeared in *The Kingdom*, explaining his position with regard to the traditional task of the evangelist. "I shall not cease calling individuals to repentance and faith in the Lord Jesus Christ. I have no conception that does not enhance rather than depreciate the value of the individual."[82] However, Mills went on to explain that he saw his role to be "more of a seedsower than a harvester" and he had some doubts about inviting great multitudes to demonstrate their purpose to lead lives of unselfishness. "My present idea," he said, "is that we are approaching a time of the sifting rather than the great enlargement of the Church." This approach was not likely to be very popular.

Mills soon found himself criticized by conservatives like J. M. Buckley, editor of the Methodist *Christian Advocate*. In a series of articles in 1896 and 1897, Buckley accused Mills of overemphasizing ethics and departing from orthodoxy, and deprecated his attacks on the churches.[83] The controversy finally called forth a statement from Gladden, in which he suggested that "an evangelist who could multiply converts and build up churches was in demand; an evangelist who sought to purge the Church of selfishness, and make it the power of God in the community, was not hailed with enthusiasm."[84]

As the criticism continued, Mills gradually began drifting toward Unitarianism, a fact that Gladden profoundly regretted, and the blame for which he placed squarely on the evangelical churches.[85] Finally in 1899, Mills became pastor of the First Unitarian Church of Oakland, California. Following a course similar to Herron's, he became allied after 1899 with more radical social reform movements like the National Social Reform Union, under the presidency of W. D. P. Bliss. Although he finally returned to the church in 1915,[86] Mills's failure seemed to demonstrate the impossibility of using the traditional methods of revivalism to preach the message of social Christianity and, indeed, the difficulty of holding together both an individual and a social gospel at all. In that respect, it set the stage for the schism that would occur in the next decade and a half.

Religion at the World's Fair

Another interesting indication of the strength of the social gospel in this decade and the attitude of the evangelicals toward the problems posed by urban, industrialized society occurred in connection with the World's Columbian Exposition in Chicago in 1893. At the fair there were basically three important manifestations of American Christianity. The first and most famous of these was the World's Parliament of Religions, which was a milestone in the recognition by Christians of non-Christian religions. As such it was rightfully seen as evidence of new liberal currents in American Protestantism. Among its speakers were some of the country's outstanding social gospel leaders, including Peabody, Ely, Gladden, and Albion W. Small, professor of sociology at the University of Chicago. It was at the parliament that Mills gave his first address to reflect acceptance of social gospel views.

The second was the International Christian Conference held in connection with the World's Congress Auxiliary of the Columbian Exposition, under the auspices of the Evangelical Alliance for the United States. The third in the series of important conferences of the alliance organized by Josiah Strong to deal with religion and the social question, it concentrated on presenting "practical methods of Christian work by which the church might accomplish her social mission, and thus meet the great perils and needs of the times."[87] Of the four main divisions of the program, that devoted to the church and social problems received by far the most attention. There were twelve major addresses given by men like Graham Taylor, George Herron, George Gates, Charles Parkhurst (the anti-Tammany crusader), and Henry Drummond, a Scottish minister well known for his popular writings on evolution. In addition, there were smaller sectional conferences on several aspects of the church's work: evangelistic, reformatory, social, and educational, with a special conference on needs in theological education. In bringing greetings to the conference, Henry Drummond remarked on the amount of time allotted in the program to "the social side of Christianity" and saw this as marking "an entirely new departure" in the work of the Evangelical Alliance. Josiah Strong closed the conference and also gave an address on the aims of the Evangelical Alliance for the U.S. in which he described the supreme aim of the alliance as assisting the churches "to see and to accomplish their social mission."[88] This conference represented the high point of the alliance's efforts to promote social Christianity.

The third and probably least known manifestation of American Protestantism in Chicago in 1893 was the massive campaign organized by Dwight L. Moody to "beat" the fair. A biographer of Moody described it as the greatest single effort of Moody's evangelistic career.[89] The fair opened on May 1. That first Sunday, Moody opened his campaign with morning, afternoon, and evening services at his Chicago Avenue Church. Other services were held in different parts of the city by some of Moody's associates and students from the Bible Institute. By July, Moody had amassed an army of thirty-eight evangelistic preachers from around the world, mostly friends on whom he had prevailed to spend the summer in Chicago helping him. The biographies of men like R. A. Torrey, J. Wilbur Chapman, A. C. Dixon, and A. J. Gordon all mention proudly this SOS from the grand old man of evangelism. In addition there were hundreds of volunteers, including 250 students from Moody Bible Institute and various Chicago ministers.[90]

The first great goal of the campaign was to secure Sunday closing of the fair. Moody's idea was to "open so many preaching places and present so many attractions"[91] that people would come to hear the gospel instead of frequenting the fair. Apparently his plan was successful, because the management did eventually close the gates on Sunday due to low attendance.[92] In all, this attempt to counteract the effects of the "anti-Biblical" parliament and the fair itself cost about $100,000 and lasted until the fair closed at the end of October.[93]

The religious climate was changing in America in the 1890s, however, and Moody's successes in 1893 were not quite the same as they had been in the 1870s. As Moody's biographer James F. Findlay pointed out, even the World's Fair revival depended more on contrivances and relied to a greater extent on general public excitement (associated with the fair) than had his earlier revivals. There was also growing criticism of Moody's revival campaigns in the 1890s.

When Moody conducted a series of meetings at Coopers Union in New York in 1896, *The New York Times* bluntly asserted editorially that "we are unable to believe that these meetings, if conducted on the lines made familiar by Mr. Moody, will be of any permanent advantage to the cause of religion or will promote the happiness . . . of any large number of men and women of this city."[94] The following year, Moody conducted a revial elsewhere in the city, and the *Congregationalist* noted its ineffectiveness.[95]

Another indication of a shift in attitudes toward Moody came from the YMCA, which in the 1890s was placing greater emphasis on developing social services and recreational facilities. During the 1880s, the Chicago YMCA under L. Wilbur Messer launched such a program, at the same time largely dispensing with the old-time evangelism. During the 1890s, Reuben A. Torrey, superintendent of the Bible Institute, held weekday religious education classes under the auspices of the YMCA in their auditorium in the Loop, but suddenly in the fall of 1898 his services were canceled. Apparently the YMCA no longer wished to endorse Torrey's theological views. Moody sided with Torrey and refused to listen to the arguments of his opponents. "I am an old man," he said, "too old to change and positive in my convictions."[96]

This World a Wrecked Vessel

By the 1890s, the higher criticism, liberal theology, and the social gospel were making significant inroads on traditional evangelical Protestantism. At the same time, the conservative counterattack that had begun to take shape in the Bible and prophetic conferences, the Northfield conferences, and the Bible institutes of the 1880s was gathering momentum. Indeed, Ernest Sandeen referred to the 1890s as "the meridian of millenarianism."[97] During this period millenarians and conservatives following the Princeton position of the literally inspired Bible shared considerable common theological ground. Both believed in the inspiration of the "original autographs" of Scripture, in a Calvinistic view of human nature, and in the radical dichotomy between nature and the supernatural. They also shared a basically pessimistic worldview.[98] Especially within the Baptist and Presbyterian denominations, the two became increasingly cordial and cooperated in such efforts as the Northfield conferences and the Bible institutes. Many of the preachers who came to Chicago in 1893 to help Moody in his World's Fair campaign were well-known millenarians, like James M. Stifler, professor of New Testament at

Crozer Seminary, George C. Needham, William G. Moorehead, James H. Brookes, A. J. Gordon, and A. T. Pierson, all prominent leaders in the Bible and prophetic conferences and Northfield conferences in the 1880s, and C. I. Scofield, author of the *Scofield Reference Bible,* who was pastor of the Northfield Congregational Church in the 1890s.[99] As I noted earlier, these men had evangelical aims. Like Moody, they saw the world as a wrecked vessel and tried to work to save some souls by way of revivalism and foreign missions. They regarded the liberal tendencies in Protestantism as apostasy and although such degeneration fit in as part of the events predicted for the last days, they worked to try to arrest it as best they could.

Moody was undoubtedly influenced by his millenarian friends. He remained firm in his belief in the verbally inspired Bible, and his premillennial views were probably based on an increasingly pessimistic worldview as the 1890s deepened his perplexity and frustration. Yet he had an "open-mindedness"[100] that many of his friends lacked. He frequently invited liberal churchmen like Josiah Strong, Henry Drummond, and William Rainey Harper, New Testament scholar and later president of the University of Chicago, to his Northfield conferences. He was deeply distressed, however, by the changing religious scene and must have suffered from his own loss of prestige in the last decade of the century.

In 1899, Dwight L. Moody died. By the time of his death there were already signs that the old evangelical unity was beginning to pull apart. Perhaps Moody, with his great heart and generous spirit, had helped to keep the channels of communication open. And yet his own campaign at the Chicago World's Fair was symptomatic of the divergent ways Protestants were beginning to understand the role of the church in an industrialized, urbanized America.

FIVE

The New Evangelism

By the turn of the century, evangelicals of all stripes were becoming increasingly concerned about the need for some kind of religious awakening. Even the conservatives were beginning to have doubts about the effectiveness of mass revivalism in adding new church members, and they were also distressed by the sensationalism and commercialism of many evangelists who tried to fill Moody's shoes but lacked his good sense, sincerity, and integrity. Denominational journals between 1900 and 1906 were full of discussions about the need for some kind of new evangelism. Many felt that the appropriate center for evangelistic efforts was the local church, and that "pastoral evangelism" and "personal evangelism" by the church members ought to replace the mass revival meetings in priority and attention.[1]

Several denominations took steps to create evangelistic committees. The Presbyterians were first, with a Special Committee on Evangelistic Work appointed by the General Assembly in 1901. By 1905, Methodists, Congregationalists, and Disciples of Christ had also organized evangelistic committees.[2] These committees stressed soul winning in local churches and the training and oversight of professional evangelists by the denomination. While their principal supporters were the more conservative clergy and church members, even many of those who had begun to see the need for some kind of social service or social reform tended to think along older lines of evangelistic effort and hesitated to give up mass revivalism altogether.

The real challenge to modern revivalism came from the social gospelers. By 1900, it was apparent to them that mass evangelism was not only failing to meet the problems of the day, but it also was squandering the church's energies, which were desperately needed elsewhere. Perhaps the failure of B. Fay Mills helped to convince social gospel leaders that revivalism could not be coordinated with their aims. They felt that the old evangelism had become inadequate and therefore they called for something new. Yet they retained the traditional terminology; what they called for was a "new evangelism."

The fact that they chose to use this terminology was not a cover-up. These were religious people who were deeply concerned about individual salvation. Most of them had faced the problem of how to reconcile their concern for a just society with their inherited religious faith. They found their answer in the conception of the Kingdom of God, which allowed them to bring together personal religion and social salvation. This discovery they often described as a second conversion. As Rauschenbusch expressed it, "The triumphant return of the Kingdom idea has marked its line of march by thrice-born men."[3]

The Next Great Awakening

Since Josiah Strong was the first of the social gospelers to issue a call for a new religious awakening in the first years of the new century, it might be well to see that against the background of his efforts in the 1890s. In 1893, as secretary for the Evangelical Alliance, Strong had written *The New Era*. Although most of the book dealt with specific problems in the city and practical suggestions for mustering the resources of the community to deal with these problems, Strong took pains to clarify the relationship between social concern and evangelical Christianity.

His major criticism of socialism was that it attempted to regenerate society by dealing only with the social environment. Strong insisted that the fundamental consideration was the human personality; because human nature was basically selfish, individuals needed a new heart as well as a new environment. Then, because society was organized on a selfish basis, it too needed to be reformed so that human relations might be governed by love, cooperation, and mutuality in the public realm as well as the private. Strong summed up his position.

> Protestant churches have laid none too much stress on the relations of the individual to God. . . . The mistake of the churches has been, not in emphasizing the first great command, but in neglecting the second. If the pendulum should now swing to the other extreme and the churches should emphasize the second command to the neglect of the first, that would be a mistake greater than the other. . . . There can be no substitute for right relations with God.[4]

This statement is certainly clear enough, and Strong acted in accord with these principles. He saw no reason to offend the evangelical churches unnecessarily, and consequently avoided theological controversy wherever possible. Two examples are indicative of his approach and concerns. During the late 1880s and early 1890s, Strong was deeply involved in the process of organizing local branches of the Evangelical Alliance in various parts of the country. Something of a controversy occurred in Brooklyn when liberal churches—Unitarians, Universalists, Swedenborgians—asked to be admitted to the local alliance being formed, along with the evangelical churches. Strong's attitude was that the constitution of the Evangelical Alliance and its very name settled the matter: liberal churches were not to be included. He hoped to keep the alliance program free from theological controversy.[5]

A few years later he took a similar stand. When the executive committee of the Evangelical Alliance objected to Strong's association with what they considered George Herron's radicalism,[6] Strong withdrew his name from the list of associate editors of *The Kingdom*. In a letter to the editors he explained that his major interest was in having the orthodox evangelical churches and clergy awaken to their social mission and seek its application by way of interdenominational cooperation.[7] He felt the doctrine of the Kingdom of God on earth could be preached "without throwing down the theological gage of battle," and that any identification of the movement for an applied Christianity with a strange theology would "postpone the needed movement for a generation."[8]

He was not far wrong in his instinctive caution here, but anxious as he was to avoid unnecessary offense to the evangelicals, he soon went too far in his own programs for the Evangelical Alliance to suit the rest of the leadership. From about 1895 on, he stressed house-to-house visitation less in conventional evangelistic terms and more as a means of educating the popular conscience for involvement in social reforms. This should be seen as a change of technique rather than of underlying goals and aims. Strong's hope was still to enlist the cooperation of the churches in improving the conditions of the community.[9] He believed that most people were indifferent to social reforms because they were ignorant of social needs and what was being done to meet them. His plan was to have leaflets on various reform subjects distributed monthly to all the families in a community by the various young people's organizations (all evangelical in theology) like Christian Endeavor, the Epworth League, and so on. Through these leaflets, prepared by the local alliances, public opinion could be educated on matters of needed social reforms, and then brought to bear on appropriate legislation by petition or referendum.[10]

The Evangelical Alliance did not really approve of the leaflet plan from the beginning. In December 1897, it was resolved that writers of these pamphlets had to be approved first by the Executive Committee, and soon after, the budget for printing was restricted.[11] Finally, in 1898, the Executive Committee decided that Strong's plans for religious and social betterment could be carried out more effectively by an organization formed for that distinct purpose, and in May of that year, Strong resigned from the alliance. The official record stated that the alliance would henceforth "limit itself to the policy and scope of work in which it was engaged at the time of its incorporation under the laws of the State of New York in 1885."[12] The new general secretary, Dr. L. T. Chamberlain of Brooklyn, was apparently a conservative in his views. At any rate, this marked the end of the alliance's leadership in social Christianity. As he reflected on it later, Strong thought that probably most of those who had taken part in the alliance programs were more interested in saving the church than in saving society.[13]

By August 1898, the organization of a League for Social Service was complete. Under the leadership of Strong, it was open to all those interested in social betterment, whether individuals, societies, public officials, or even business firms. Its primary purpose was to continue the effort begun under the auspices of the Evangelical Alliance, namely, to educate the popular conscience, to awaken public opinion, and to afford a medium for its expression.[14] For financial reasons, the league was reorganized in 1902 and incorporated under a charter from the University of the State of New York as an educational organization, the American Institute of Social Service. It is against the background of these activities in the first years of the new century that Strong's writings must be seen.

In 1902, Josiah Strong wrote *The Next Great Awakening*, in which he asserted the need for a new message and a new method if there were to be a religious awakening in the twentieth century. He charged the church with having preached only half of the gospel, and insisted that its message of individual salvation and personal morality was no longer adequate for the complex and solidaristic society brought about by the industrial revolution. The church had become respectable and conservative, giving inspiration to individual lives but providing little in the way of answers to the great social questions of the day. Consequently, it had alienated the workers and lost its own vitality.

What was needed, Strong felt, was a rediscovery of the social teachings of Jesus, the great theme of which was the Kingdom of God, and the laws of which were service, sacrifice, and love.[15] When Jesus talked about seeking the Kingdom, he did not mean either heaven or the visible church, but rather seeking to bring about on earth as in heaven the actualization of the social ideals of Christianity. When the church understood the Kingdom, Strong believed it would no longer concentrate primarily on saving souls or on building up the church, but would work for the redemption of the whole social order. Then, he said,

> she will seek to save *men* rather than *souls*, and she will endeavor to discharge her mission to society as well as to the individual. She will discover that it is much wiser to clean up the "mud puddle" so that the jewels will no longer get lost than it is to devote all of her time to recovering a small proportion of the lost jewels.[16]

Strong still hoped that the evangelical churches would awaken to their social task in time to lead and direct the social movement already under way. He was well aware of the evangelical longing for a religious awakening and himself felt that since the real ill of society was human sin, some kind of religious awakening was very much needed. But the message and methods could no longer be simply those of Moody. Only the preaching of a neglected Scriptural truth precisely adapted to the needs of the day would be sufficient to bring about a religious awakening. Since the needs of the day were clearly the great social questions, Strong believed the next great awakening might be expected when the doctrine of the Kingdom—which brought together the dual concerns for the salvation of the soul and the transformation of the social order—was faithfully preached, and when Christians began to live a life of love, service, and sacrifice.

Other social gospelers also contributed to the discussion on the new evangelism in these years. Thus far I have looked at Washington Gladden primarily in terms of his leadership on questions of labor and industry. He was also one of the principal supporters of the revival held by B. Fay Mills in Columbus in 1895, and deeply regretted Mills's treatment by the evangelical churches. Thanks to the Gladden biography by Jacob H. Dorn, we know even more about Gladden's attitude toward revivalism and individual salvation.[17] In 1878, Gladden had supported Moody's revival in Springfield and even participated in it himself. As late as 1905, and as moderator of the Congregational National Council, he endorsed Rev. William J. Dawson, an Englishman who wanted to conduct evangelistic services in the United States. Perhaps Dawson was, like Mills, an unusual revivalist. A footnote in William

McLoughlin's *Modern Revivalism* indicates that he preached a liberal theology but attempted to reach a wider audience through the popular appeal of revivalism.[18] However, when J. Wilbur Chapman, a conventional and fairly conservative evangelist, appealed to Gladden in 1910 for help in sounding "the social note"[19] of the day, Gladden agreed to speak at one of Chapman's services in Dayton and later defended him during his revival in Columbus.

There is no question about Gladden's evangelical concern for individual salvation. In 1905, he asked Lyman Abbott to come to First Church to preach for a week on topics that would involve "an appeal to the will, a definite acceptance of Christ, and a definite choice of the Christian life."[20] In his *Social Salvation* (1902), he alleged that the country needed a revival of religion, but insisted that it must be a religion "which is less concerned about getting men to heaven than about fitting them for their proper work on earth."[21] In Gladden's mind, this did not mean neglecting individual salvation. Appropriate revival preaching would proclaim that conversion is not simply a private matter between the individual and God, but also involves the second great commandment. Living the Christian life means living according to the law of love, not only in the private realm, but also in the public realm of business and politics.

In 1908, Gladden turned his attention specifically to the problem of evangelism; the eighth chapter of his book written that year, *The Church and Modern Life*, was entitled "The New Evangelism." As he had indicated in a sermon on the financial panic of 1907, Gladden felt very clearly the need of a great revival of religion. But he was certain that it could not come along the lines of the old, individualistic evangelism. In spite of his willingness on occasion to support mass revivals, Gladden considered the old evangelism a failure, and he set out in "The New Evangelism" to explain why.[22]

Not only was the old evangelism not the answer to the problem of the masses outside the church, but its results were often only temporary even for those it did touch. According to Gladden's figures, the growth of membership in some denominations seemed actually to have been retarded by the mass revivals. Gladden felt the old evangelism had failed because it had fixed its attention too much on an appeal to individual self-interest. The church would regain its hold on the people only when it spoke to the highest that was in them. The new evangelism therefore must bring home to individuals the truth that their personal redemption was bound up with the redemption of society. The central sin from which people needed to be saved was selfishness; they were to become saviors of others. The object of the new evangelism then was "the redemption of society."[23] The role of the church was to believe and to teach that the existing social order could be Christianized and to furnish the spiritual dynamic for the construction of the necessary social machinery.

Christianity and the Social Crisis

For none of the social gospelers was personal religion more central than it was for Walter Rauschenbusch. In the early years of his pastorate in New York City, he had founded the little newspaper *For the Right* for the express purpose of bringing together personal regeneration and social reform.[24] He saw it as the special task of his generation to wed evangelical Christianity and the social movement.[25] We have seen how crucial the rediscovery of the Kingdom of God was for him because it enabled him to bring together his concern for the social order and his commitment to the evangelical faith. He shared with the other Brothers of the Kingdom a deeply religious sense of the significance of social Christianity. Indeed, he understood his own public work "as a form of evangelism, which called for a deeper repentance and a new experience of God's salvation."[26] When his friend Dores Sharpe once told Rauschenbusch that he thought of him as an evangelist, the great social gospel leader threw his arms around Sharpe and said that he had "always wanted to be thought of in that way."[27] He regarded it, he later said, as his "deepest satisfaction to get evidence now and then that I have been able to help men to a new spiritual birth."[28]

In 1904, Rauschenbusch provided what was probably the most persuasive statement of the need for a new evangelism in an article in the *Independent* entitled "The New Evangelism." Unlike Strong, Rauschenbusch did not yet feel he knew what the new evangelism ought to be; he saw clearly only that the old evangelism was no longer sufficient. The younger and more thoughtful minds of his generation were not moved to seek salvation by the old motives of the fear of hell and hope of heaven; they were more concerned with the duties of Christian living in the present. The old evangelism no longer offered an ethical imperative sufficient to summon men and women to repentance. In private life its standard differed little from respectability as defined by the mores of society. In commerce and industry, where the real problems existed, the church had no clear message and usually claimed to be under no obligation to have one. The church had failed to keep pace with the rapid and profound changes that had taken place in society and it was not surprising that the world had ceased to be guided by "statements of truth that were adequate to obsolete conditions."[29] A new evangelism was urgently needed to "give an adequate definition of how a Christian man should live under modern conditions, and then summon men to live so."[30] Rauschenbusch saw no such evangelism on the American scene, nor did he expect it to appear quickly. "It will be," he said, "the slow product of the fearless thought of many honest men. It will have to retain all that was true and good in the old synthesis, but advance the human conception of salvation one stage closer to the divine conception."[31] As Robert Handy pointed out, "three years later Rauschenbusch was to find himself in the vanguard of this new evangelism when *Christianity and the Social Crisis* became a religious best-seller."[32]

In the final chapter of this famous book, Rauschenbusch drew out the implications of the new evangelism for the churches. Just as in personal religion the first requirement was to repent and believe, so social religion too demanded repentance and faith, "repentance for our social sins; faith in the possibility of a new social order."[33] Nor did this mean that personal regeneration was no longer necessary. Almost in the same breath Rauschenbusch declared that the greatest contribution a person could make to the social movement was that of a "regenerated personality"[34] dedicated to the purposes of the Kingdom of God. It was largely through the contagion of the experience of this new salvation that social evangelization would take place. Believers in social Christianity would win other believers consciously or unconsciously. Because the new evangel called for the Christianization of all of life, it would depend more on the testimony of the ordinary Christian and less on the clergy. And yet Rauschenbusch felt it would "immeasurably speed the spread of the new conceptions" if the clergy would preach on social questions.[35] Those who found the institutional church a departure from the church's spiritual mission were more than ever obligated, he thought, to teach plainly the causes and remedies of social misery.

Perhaps interest in the social question would result in the neglect of individual salvation. This would be a serious defect, Rauschenbusch admitted, but he blamed any such one-sidedness on the church's long neglect of social preaching and obviously believed that the imbalance would eventually right itself. His own view he expressed very simply: "There are two great entities in human life,—the human soul and the human race,—and religion is to save both. The soul is to seek righteousness and eternal life; the race is to seek righteousness and the kingdom of God."[36] Although most of the early social Christians were deeply evangelical, Rauschenbusch managed to hold the two emphases of personal salvation and the redemption of society together more successfully than any other social gospel figure. He returned again and again throughout his life to this great theme of the relationship between social Christianity and personal religion.

Evangelism Old and New

Meanwhile, these challenges to the old evangelism by the social gospelers were answered from a number of points along the evangelical spectrum. From the camp of the early Fundamentalists came *Evangelism Old and New*, published in 1905 and aimed particularly at Josiah Strong. Its author was Amzi Clarence Dixon, Southern Baptist pastor of the Ruggles Street Church in Roxbury, Massachusetts.

Dixon was born in Shelby, North Carolina, in 1854, and received his education at Wake Forest College in North Carolina and one year of seminary at the Baptist Theological Seminary in Greenville, South Carolina. Before coming to Roxbury, he had been pastor of the Immanuel Baptist Church in Baltimore, and from 1890-1901, pastor of the Hanson Place Baptist Church in Brooklyn. In 1885, he paid his first visit to Northfield, Massachusetts, where he established lasting friendships with Moody, A. J. Gordon, and A. T. Pierson. He attended the Chicago conference of Baptist ministers on the Second Coming in 1889, and from that time on, according to his biographer, millenarian belief played an important part in his ministry.[37] In 1893, at Moody's invitation, he took part in the Chicago World's Fair revival campaign. In all of his pastorates, Dixon was an evangelistic preacher. He always fought for free seats in the church and for a plain tabernacle-like preaching hall rather than an elaborate church building. He was a strong temperance crusader and deplored the growing trend away from biblical authority.

The Ruggles Street Church, where Dixon went in 1901, was located in a largely working-class suburb of Boston. The church there had been equipped along institutional lines. Apparently, Dixon went to Roxbury believing that the institutional activities of the church would be an ideal background for his evangelistic work, but he found them a hindrance rather than a help. "I went to Boston," he explained,

> because of the call from a church there that had an endowment of more than a million dollars, the interest of which was to be applied for social service. We

were told that if we would feed the hungry man, clothe him, pay his rent, and give him a good doctor and medicine, it would be good preparation for preaching the Gospel to him. That seemed like common sense. I thought that we could win the whole community for Christ in no time, but I found that it did not work. . . . I have learned—and it has been a genuine conversion—that it is immensely easier to reach a man's body through his soul than his soul through his body.[38]

At the time of his reply to Strong in 1905, Dixon was engaged in a controversy with the Boston Baptist Social Union over the disposition of a legacy of Daniel Sharp Ford for the improvement of the working people of the Boston area. The point at issue was whether priority should be given to philanthropic or evangelistic enterprises. In the midst of this controversy, Dixon was glad to have the chance to go as a delegate to the Baptist World Congress held in London in July. According to his wife and biographer, he was so impressed during this summer abroad with what he saw as stirrings of a revival in many parts of the world, that he was moved to write *Evangelism Old and New*.[39]

Although Dixon never mentioned Strong by name, he devoted an entire chapter (which he called "Evangelism True and False") to a refutation of the case Strong had made for a new evangelism in *The Next Great Awakening*. Dixon began by rejecting Strong's claim that every great awakening had resulted from the preaching of a message peculiarly adapted to the needs of the time. On the contrary, he insisted, the same "great facts" of "the love of God as manifested in the incarnation, death, resurrection and exaltation of Jesus Christ" have been the keynote of "every true revival from the day of Pentecost to the present day."[40] Obviously, then, there was no need for a new message.

Dixon turned to a criticism of the new evangelism in all its forms. In reply to Strong and others who seemed to be talking about a revival to be brought about by changing the social environment, he cited the example of a wealthy New York philanthropist who built a model tenement for the poor, only to find before a month had gone by that some of his tenants were "using his bathtubs for coal bins." It cost him something, said Dixon, "to learn that swine cannot be made into sheep by change of environment."[41]

Dixon went on to criticize the new "Socialistic Evangelism," which talked about saving society and considered it selfish to be too concerned for one's own salvation. " 'What shall it profit a man,' " he said, 'if he shall gain the whole world, and lose his own soul?' If a man does not consider his own salvation of great importance, he will not regard the salvation of others as of great importance. Indeed, he can do nothing toward saving others until he is himself saved."[42] It was clear to Dixon that the only way to save society was by saving individuals.

Finally, Dixon warned the social gospelers that their theological principles were not conducive to evangelism in its true sense. He could not conceive of an evangelism that denied the inspiration and infallible authority of the Bible and accepted evolution as God's way of doing things. He wanted to see more preaching on the awful reality of sin; "if there were more of hell in our pulpits," he insisted, "there would be less hell on our streets and behind the doors of our houses."[43] His own view was, in sum, "without the preaching of the doctrine of the atonement and individual conversion, there never was and never can be a revival worthy of the name."[44]

Dixon was not a professional evangelist. Although there was much criticism of mass revivalism in the early years of the twentieth century, there was still widespread longing for a genuine religious awakening. And there were plenty of professional revivalists who stepped forward to assume the mantle of leadership Moody relinquished in 1899. According to William McLoughlin, there were "hundreds" of successful evangelists in the first quarter of the twentieth century.[45] He singled out six as of greatest significance: Reuben A. Torrey, J. Wilbur Chapman, Milan B. Williams, Burke Culpepper, Rodney Smith, and William E. Biederwolf.[46] Of these, Williams, Culpepper, and Smith followed very much in the tradition of Sam Jones in terms of folksy, colorful preaching and stress on prohibition. For our purposes, Torrey, Chapman, and Biederwolf are more important, since they were all closely related to the developments I have been tracing and since Torrey and Chapman were both widely considered Moody's legitimate successors. All three were college graduates with formal theological training and all were members of the Interdenominational Association of Evangelists, an association of professional evangelists begun at the Winona Lake Bible Conference in Indiana in 1904.[47]

Reuben A. Torrey was born in New Jersey, the son of a New York City banker. He graduated from both Yale College and Yale Seminary and studied for a year in Leipzig and Erlangen, Germany. However, instead of adopting the higher criticism for which German universities were noted, he became passionately opposed to it and probably attacked science and biblical criticism more frequently and vituperously than any other revival preacher. From 1883 to 1889, he was in Minneapolis, as pastor of the Open Door Church and, after 1886, as superintendent of the Minneapolis City Missionary Society. In

1889, Moody asked him to become superintendent of his newly opened Bible Institute in Chicago, and he was also pastor of the Moody Church from 1894 to 1906. Torrey took up professional revivalism in 1906, when he and Charles M. Alexander, his soloist and chorister, began a round-the-world evangelistic tour, starting with six months of meetings in Australia and climaxed by a five-month campaign in London. Statistically the results of Torrey's meetings in British cities surpassed even those of Moody.[48]

However, the reception given Torrey on his return in 1905 was indicative of the passing of the old evangelical unity.[49] Some welcomed Torrey and Alexander as Moody and Sankey's successors. Most of the social gospelers were critical. In fact, several leading Congregationalist ministers, among them Charles S. Macfarland, soon to be a prominent figure in the Federal Council of Churches, and S. Parkes Cadman, issued a call through the *Congregationalist* urging members of their denomination to dissociate themselves from all Torrey revivals. They charged him with "clinging to obsolete traditions," preaching a literal, narrow-minded view of the gospel, and using evangelistic work as a means of promoting divisive views within the church.[50] The majority of evangelicals fell somewhere in between. While they had some reservations about Torrey, they hesitated to oppose a revivalist who could bring in new church members, and Torrey had had an impressive statistical record abroad. An editorial comment on Torrey's revival meetings in Chicago in 1906 was typical of this point of view. "Not many of our ministers could accept his theology or the fundamental principles of his interpretation of the Bible," this spokesman said, "but there is not one of them who would not rejoice to be as useful as he has been, and as successful as he is in leading men to Christ."[51]

Similar to A. C. Dixon in views, Torrey preached the familiar message of salvation through the blood of Christ, personal morality, and denunciation of evolution, biblical criticism, and theological liberalism. He was a millenarian and believed the Second Coming of Christ to be "the perfect solution, and the only solution, of the political and commercial problems that now vex us."[52] He was not personally a very likable individual and much of the success of his revivals has been attributed to the vivacity and winsomeness of his singing partner, Charles Alexander.[53] In 1908, Alexander and Torrey split up. Torrey became dean of the Los Angeles Bible Institute in 1911, and Alexander joined forces with another revivalist, John Wilbur Chapman.

Chapman perhaps best represented the state of professional revivalism between Moody and Billy Sunday. He was closer to the "mainstream" of conservative evangelicalism, both in the breadth of his associations and in terms of his institutional affiliations. He chose to work within the structure of the Presbyterian Church, although he had ties with the more militant conservatives through a number of Bible conferences and institutes. In fact, he was chosen moderator of the Presbyterian General Assembly in 1917. And he probably best represented the concern for individual evangelism that later became institutionalized in the Commission on Evangelism of the Federal Council, Biederwolf being his successor in this regard. Although his education and learning far exceeded Moody's, he resembled the great revivalist in spirit and aims far more than most who styled themselves Moody's heirs.

As a revivalist, he had been trained by both Moody and B. Fay Mills. Born in Richmond, Indiana, in 1859, he was educated at Oberlin, Lake Forest College in Illinois, and Lane Theological Seminary in Cincinnati. While at Lake Forest in 1878 he had attended a Moody revival meeting in Chicago, and was personally converted by Moody from a nominal to a "born-again" Christian in the inquiry room following the service.[54] Mills and Chapman were classmates at Lake Forest and served neighboring pastorates in New York State after graduation. From 1890 to 1892, Chapman served as pastor of John Wanamaker's church, Bethany Presbyterian, in Philadelphia. In 1892, he left the church to assist his friend B. Fay Mills in revival campaigns, the most successful of which was the Cincinnati revival in 1892. During the three years he was a professional revivalist, he aided Moody (Chicago, 1893) and also conducted some revivals of his own. According to McLoughlin, Moody referred to Chapman in 1895 as "the greatest evangelist in the country."[55] He helped to found the Winona Lake Bible Conference in 1896, and also became vice president of the Moody Bible Institute that same year.[56]

Chapman returned to Bethany Church as pastor from 1895 to 1899, and then moved to the Fourth Presbyterian Church in New York City. In 1901, he was appointed a member of the Committee on Evangelism by the Presbyterian General Assembly, and shortly after elected secretary. In 1903, he gave up the New York pastorate to devote full time to work with the committee. That same year he published *Present-Day Evangelism*. Written the year after Strong's *Next Great Awakening*, it indicated that Chapman had read Strong and was even willing to admit the truth of some of his charges. He acknowledged the need for a social ethic and agreed that evangelistic preaching had been too little concerned with the duties of Christian living. However, he criticized the social gospel for prescribing material remedies for what he regarded as spiritual maladies. He suggested that the great work of the church for the twentieth century should be personal evangelism, "the winning of the individual by the individual,"[57] and strongly urged the necessity for lay evangelism and the training and oversight of professional evangelists. Both these emphases were later stressed by the Federal Council's Commission on Evangelism.

After 1905, Chapman devoted most of his time to promoting a new method of urban mass evangelism that he called the Chapman Simultaneous Evangelistic Campaign. In many ways it resembled the District Combination plan Mills had developed in the early 1890s, except that each of the districts conducted a revival simultaneously with the other districts.[58] Chapman and Alexander conducted revival meetings in a large, centrally located church or tabernacle, while pairs of evangelists and choristers conducted meetings in the other districts. Chapman apparently held two successful revival campaigns in the largest cities using this method, one in Philadelphia in 1908, and another in Boston in 1909. The latter was, according to McLoughlin, the most successful campaign of Chapman's career. The city was divided into twenty-seven districts, and Chapman brought thirty evangelists and thirty choristers with him for the three-week campaign. Between January 26 and February 17, some 990 services were held in Boston and the total attendance was estimated at over 750,000. The slogan for the campaign was "The King's Business," and 166 churches cooperated in the revival.[59]

The weakness of the plan was that so much depended on the choristers and evangelists who carried on the meetings in the districts. Apparently, after 1909, Chapman himself gradually became disappointed with the results of the campaigns and turned more of his attention to pastoral evangelism as perhaps the best method. What was significant about Chapman's revivals was the degree of cooperation he received, in spite of the growing criticism of mass revivalism. There is no question about his own conservatism with regard to the higher criticism, theology, and all the rest, but because he urged interdenominational harmony and avoided controversial matters as much as possible in his revival campaigns, he received the support of men like S. Parkes Cadman, who had denounced Torrey. He was a mild-mannered, genial man, and many evangelicals must have felt his "safe and sane" campaigns[60] were an answer to some of the problems of city evangelization. After 1912, the new chief of the revivalists was a very different kind of figure, though a former assistant of Chapman, Billy Sunday.

William E. Biederwolf was important largely because he was a central figure in the early years of the Commission on Evangelism of the Federal Council of

Churches. He received three degrees from Princeton University, bachelor's, master's, and bachelor of divinity, and like Torrey, studied for a year in Europe. Becoming an evangelist in 1900, he assisted Chapman for several years, both in the work of the evangelistic committee of the Presbyterian Church and in his simultaneous campaigns. In 1906, he began conducting revivals on his own, first in small towns and cities and, after 1910, city-wide campaigns in cities of moderate size. In 1910, he was elected president of the Interdenominational Association of Evangelicals, and in 1913 began his work with the Federal Council.[61]

Thus in spite of the social gospelers' call for a new evangelism in the early years of the twentieth century, there were still evangelists who believed in mass revival meetings, and thousands of evangelical Christians in the nation's cities and towns who were still willing to go hear them preach, and perhaps return night after night while the campaign continued. Large cities like Boston, Chicago, and Philadelphia sometimes saw two or more city-wide revival campaigns conducted by different evangelists within just a few years.[62] The great body of evangelicals, clergy and lay alike, still saw saving souls as the main purpose of the ministry and the best way to address problems like intemperance and the Americanization of the masses of immigrants. Most of them probably also felt the need for some kind of social reform and a sense of nostalgia for the old traditions and authority breaking down.

Great Revivals and the Great Republic

A good example of this moderate evangelical position was *Great Revivals and the Great Republic* by a Southern Methodist bishop, Warren A. Candler. Bishop Candler was the brother of Asa G. Candler, the Coca-Cola magnate, a friend of Sam Jones and an ardent prohibitionist. He was also a former president of Emory College in Atlanta, and a former editor of the *Nashville Christian Advocate*. His book, published in 1904, was an interesting combination of conservative and liberal ideas. William McLoughlin devoted ten pages in his *Modern Revivalism* to an analysis of it because he felt it was representative in so many ways of the prevailing evangelical outlook underlying the revivalism of this period.[63]

Like the conservatives, Candler believed that revivalistic religion had always been and would always be the way to solve the nation's problems. He insisted that the next great awakening would be a "revival of religion—not a political

117

reform nor a philanthropic scheme of social amelioration."[64] Nor would it bring forth any new doctrine. But Candler's book actually relied heavily on some of the concepts basic to the liberal, social gospel position. He shared their optimism and, like Strong, he believed in the supremacy of the Anglo-Saxon race and in America's manifest destiny as leader of that race. For him, evangelical Christianity was "the security of the Great Republic and the hope of the world."[65] He therefore wanted to see a massive campaign of Christian warfare against the enemies of evangelical religion. Perhaps this kind of appeal was responsible for keeping the evangelical forces together as long as they were.

In the first decade of the twentieth century then, the old evangelical unity—already strained in the 1890s—was beginning to give way. Two parties were developing out of evangelical Protestantism, each with its own understanding of the relation between the Christian and society, and between the church and the world. Social gospelers were drawing on the church's longer heritage and what they regarded as the best of the immediate evangelical past in an attempt to meet the new and pressing social needs brought about by the country's rapid industrialization and urbanization. And conservative evangelicals were insisting on remaining where individualistic evangelical Protestantism had stood in the 1850s (or 1870s), rejecting evolutionary science, defending biblical authority with a new and narrow view of inspiration, and maintaining a private role for the church. Some of them also held a pessimistic, and not typically American, belief in the premillennial Second Coming of Christ.

Both parties did, in fact, share some basic concerns. Both wanted to keep America a Christian nation, and both wanted to preserve the old evangelical Protestant dominance over the culture. Both were alarmed by the perils they saw facing the nation—the unchurched masses, millions of unassimilated immigrants with foreign, Roman Catholic, or Jewish, and often socialistic views; alcoholism, political corruption, and all the rest. But they had vastly different understandings of how these problems were to be solved.[66] The social gospelers called for a new evangelism that would make social as well as individual redemption its object. The individual evangelists continued to see soul winning as the primary responsibility of the church and to look to personal and pastoral evangelism to supplement the effectiveness of mass revival meetings.

To be sure, the ranks were not yet clearly defined. Particularly on the conservative side there were some who would form para-denominational organizations in order to fight the liberals (social and theological), and others who would remain within the denominational structures. Many of the ultraconservative clergy became leaders in the Fundamentalist movement. Probably most of the younger clergy in the mainline evangelical denominations became converts to the liberal, social gospel view. But after 1905, the lines between the two sides became more and more firmly drawn, until by 1912, the split had been institutionalized in the Federal Council and was fully evident in the polemics between the two parties.

This divergence of views was clearly manifested in the practical cooperative work of the churches. With the formation of the Federal Council of Churches in 1908, social Christianity was officially recognized and the member denominations had a vehicle for united social action. However, there were many within the council who opposed the social gospel position and favored cooperative efforts along older lines. It is important to try to understand why the council was able to hold together in spite of the presence of representatives of the two rapidly cohering sides. What goals were in the minds of its founders, and who were its leaders?

Making Social Christianity Official

The Federal Council grew out of two organizations begun in the 1890s, the Open and Institutional Church League, organized in 1894, and the New York City Federation of Churches and Christian Workers, founded the following year. The moving spirit behind the first was Dr. Charles L. Thompson, a Presbyterian minister whom I discuss in more detail in a later chapter. In 1888, Thompson was called from his church in Kansas City to the Madison Avenue Presbyterian Church in New York City. Like so many other city churches in these years, the Madison Avenue Church was faced with the problem of change in population around the church, most of the congregation having moved uptown to more desirable neighborhoods. Thompson quickly resolved that if the church were to stay in that neighborhood, it must change its program drastically to suit local needs. Consequently, he proposed to his congregation that the church abolish pew rents and adopt an "institutional" program of daily activities, on the principle that "the church was founded as a great missionary enterprise for the saving of men, for time and eternity; of body, mind and spirit; the remedy not only for personal ills, but the ills of the family, of the City and of the State."[67]

119

Thompson's church was neither the first nor the only institutional church. However, it was a success, and as such inspired Thompson to look for an organization to promote the free church ideal. In 1894, Elias B. Sanford, a Congregational pastor from Connecticut, visited Thompson to discuss the operation of an institutional church. Thompson asked Sanford if he would be willing to devote his time to such an organization and when Sanford replied affirmatively, the two issued an invitation to a small group of men active in city ministries to meet at the Madison Avenue Church. At this preliminary conference on March 27, 1894, the Open and Institutional Church League was organized and its first officers elected. They were Charles A. Dickinson, pastor of the (Congregationalist) Berkeley Temple in Boston, president; Thompson, vice president; and Frank Mason North, executive secretary of the New York City Extension and Missionary Society of the Methodist Episcopal Church, secretary-treasurer. Josiah Strong was also a central figure in the league.

The platform that grew out of that preliminary conference called on this fellowship to take a "leading part in every movement having for its end the alleviation of human suffering, the elevation of man, and the betterment of the world." The aim of the Open and Institutional Church League was declared to be the salvation of "all men and all of the man by all means, abolishing so far as possible the distinction between the religious and secular, and sanctifying all days and all means to the great end of saving the world for Christ." The league stood for:

> Open church doors for every day and all the day, free seats, a plurality of
> Christian workers, the personal activity of all church members, a ministry to all
> the community through educational, reformatory, and philanthropic channels,
> to the end that men may be won to Christ and his service, that the Church may
> be brought back to the simplicity and comprehensiveness of its primitive life,
> until it can be said of every community, 'The Kingdom of Heaven is within you'
> and 'Christ is all and in all.'[68]

At its fall meeting in Philadelphia in November 1895, Sanford was called to be corresponding secretary and Thompson elected president. Sanford gave an address on "the Institutional Church and Christian Unity," which he closed by affirming his belief that Christian unity though "federative relations" of the denominations was coming, and that the Open Church League was destined to play an important part in it.[69] From this time on, Sanford's aggressive leadership was prominent in the organization. He also served as editor of the journal of the league, *The Open Church: A Magazine of Applied Christianity.* His associate editors represented five denominations: Charles L. Thompson (Presbyterian), Frank Mason North (Methodist), Leighton Williams (Baptist), John P. Peters (Episcopal), and Sylvanus Stall (Lutheran). The journal was an effective means of spreading what Robert Handy referred to as "its double gospel of the institutional church and federation for Christian service."[70]

In 1895, the second of these two forerunners of the Federal Council was formed. In the fall of 1894, at a meeting of the Alumni Club of Union Theological Seminary, Rev. J. Winthrop Hegeman presented a resolution calling for a committee to consider organizing a federal council of the churches of New York City for the purpose of "applying the Gospel to every human need."[71] In 1895, the organization of the Federation of Churches and Christian Workers of New York City was completed, and in the fall of 1896, Dr. Walter Laidlaw became its executive secretary.

As a result of action taken by joint meetings of the executive committees of the New York City Federation and the Open Church League, steps were taken for the formation of a National Federation of Churches and Christian Workers. A conference was called in New York on February 12, 1900, which was composed of "men actively identified with nearly all the state and local church federation work then in existence."[72]

A National Committee on the Federation of Churches was created, composed of twenty-five men, representing most of the principal denominations. A letter prepared by the committee and explaining the purposes of the proposed federation was widely distributed to pastors throughout the country. As a consequence of these preparations, the organizing conference of the National Federation of Churches and Christian Workers was held in Philadelphia on February 5-6, 1901.[73] Papers were presented by Frank Mason North on "Federation in City Evangelization," Charles L. Thompson on "Cooperation in Home and Missionary Work," and Josiah Strong on "The Next Great Revival." A constitution was adopted, and officers were elected, including J. Cleveland Cady, a Presbyterian layman from New York City as president; Sanford as general secretary; and a large number of prominent leaders as vice presidents.

A committee of correspondence, appointed by a conference of this organization the following year, was empowered to call An Inter-Church Conference on Federation for 1905. Thus the National Federation was the immediate predecessor of the Federal Council of Churches. It is important to understand what the members of the National Federation saw as its aims. The principal object of this organization was stated in its constitution to be securing "cooperation among Churches and Christian Workers throughout the United States for the more effective promotion of the interests of the Kingdom of God."[74] Membership could be by individuals or local churches, or as representatives of church federations. Obviously such an aim could be variously interpreted. As John A. Hutchison pointed out in his history of the Federal Council, some people seem to have thought of these objectives of cooperation and service "largely in terms of union revival services and evangelistic efforts for workingmen." Others saw them along the lines of humanitarian service and even social and political reform.[75] We have seen that the conceptions behind the Open Church League embraced a broad sense of responsibility for the community, and the men active in the league constituted an important element in the National Federation.

On the other hand, a message of the Executive Board of the federation to the churches, adopted at its third annual meeting in 1903, while expressing the desire of federations to save their communities and the necessity of a thorough canvass for this purpose, stressed that moral and spiritual needs of the community were to have supreme consideration and strongly recommended personal evangelism and union evangelistic services.[76] At this same meeting, Rev. J. Wilbur Chapman and Dr. Charles L. Goodell presented "The Evangelistic Side of Our Work."

At the Washington conference of the National Federation in 1902, a resolution was unanimously adopted recommending the appointment of a committee of correspondence to call the Inter-Church Conference of 1905. As leader of that committee (responsible for all the arrangements for the proposed conference), Sanford suggested the name of Dr. William H. Roberts of Philadelphia, stated clerk of the Presbyterian General Assembly. It was generally agreed that "no one in the United States had had larger experience in arranging the details of church assemblies or was more familiar with church parliamentary procedure."[77] Roberts was to chair both the conference of 1905 and the first meeting of the Federal Council in 1908, and he carried the leadership of the Executive Committee all that time. The first denominational body to respond to the letter of invitation to send delegates to the conference of 1905 was the Methodist Episcopal Church, South, which heard a message by Elias Sanford and then took action to appoint its delegation at its General Conference in May of 1902. When the Inter-Church Conference on Federation assembled in New York's Carnegie Hall on November 15, 1905, delegates were present from twenty-nine denominations.[78]

In the course of the week-long conference, a plan of federation was adopted with but one dissenting vote. Charles L. Thompson gave a moving address on the Federated Church as a "mighty force for the salvation of people and the reconstruction of society,"[79] and addresses were presented on a United Church and religious education, the social order, home and foreign missions, the fellowship in faith, evangelization, the national life, and Christian progress.[80]

Two decisions made at this conference were of particular importance—the object of the Federal Council and the basis for its membership. As stated in the Plan of Federation, the object of the council was:

I.   To express the fellowship and catholic unity of the Christian Church.
II.   To bring the Christian bodies of America into united service for Christ and the world.
III.   To encourage devotional fellowship and mutual counsel concerning the spiritual life and religious activities of the Churches.
IV.   To secure a larger combined influence for the Churches of Christ in all matters affecting the moral and social condition of the people, so as to promote the application of the law of Christ in every relation of human life.
V.   To assist in the organization of local branches of the Federal Council to promote its aims in their communities.[81]

Thus the aims of social Christianity were from the first written into the basic purpose of the council, while concern was also expressed for the spiritual life of the churches.

At this conference it was decided that the Federal Council of Churches was to be a definitely evangelical body. On this issue there was more heated discussion than at any other point. The question was whether Christian bodies other than those admitted to membership in 1905 could be admitted at a later date, and on what basis. The primary concern seems to have been for those state and local federations that included members who would not be able to subscribe to an evangelical basis for membership. On an appeal presented by Rev. Samuel J. Niccolls, pastor of the Second Presbyterian Church, St. Louis, an amendment to the preamble of the plan was adopted that inserted before the words "Lord and Saviour" the word "Divine," so as to read: "it seems fitting more fully to manifest the essential oneness of the Christian Churches in America, in Jesus Christ as their Divine Lord and Saviour. . . ."[82] Further, it was decided that the question of representation of local councils should be deferred, and that membership at present applied to the twenty-nine Christian denominations represented at the conference. The Unitarians were thus precluded by the preamble from becoming members of the council, although Unitarian congregations were included in a few state and local federations.

On December 2, 1908, all these efforts were brought to fruition with the assembling in Philadelphia of the Federal Council of the Churches of Christ in America. William H. Roberts, permanent chairman of the Inter-Church Conference of 1905, and chairman of the Executive Committee in charge of the Philadelphia meeting, presided. The Plan of Federation of 1905 had been adopted by national assemblies of the constituent bodies and was ratified at the 1908 meeting. There were thirty-three denominations represented in the council of 1908.[83] Of the twenty-nine denominations sending delegates to the 1905 conference, all but one had adopted the plan. The Protestant Episcopal Church did not, but it did authorize its Commission on Christian Unity to appoint delegates to the 1908 council. Elected as officers for the next four years were Bishop Eugene R. Hendrix of the Methodist Episcopal Church, South, president; E. B. Sanford, corresponding secretary; Rivington Lord, pastor of the First Free Baptist Church of Brooklyn, New York, recording secretary; and Alfred Kimball of New York, treasurer.[84] Bishop Hendrix, of Kansas City, Missouri, had gained wide recognition as leader of the Business Committee of Forty, which handled all the important business details of the conference of 1905, and he was unanimously elected. It is interesting that of the three great southern denominational bodies, the Methodists alone were firm and consistent in their support of the council and its work. The southern Baptists did not join the Council, and the southern Presbyterians later withdrew.[85]

The most significant achievement of this 1908 meeting was the council's adoption of the committee report on the Church and Modern Industry, which included the famous Social Creed of the Churches. The memorable eighteen-page report was presented and largely prepared by the chairman of the committee, Frank Mason North. Beginning with an assertion of the church's task as the representative of Christ to establish the Kingdom, the report deplored the present estrangement between the church and both the workers and the rich. It recognized the natural right of laborers to organize for social and industrial betterment, welcomed it, and claimed trades unionism as the church's ally rather than its enemy. It expressed the profound belief of the council "that the complex problems of modern industry can be interpreted and solved only by the teachings of the New Testament, and that Jesus Christ is final authority in the social as in the individual life."[86]

The statement of the council's beliefs on the industrial situation, the so-called Social Creed of the Churches, was taken almost verbatim from the Methodist Social Creed written largely by Frank Mason North and Harry F. Ward, and adopted earlier in the year by the General Conference of the Methodist Episcopal Church. It was a magnificent statement of the church's commitment to the cause of working people and their struggle for justice. It concluded with a greeting of human brotherhood and a pledge of sympathy and help "to the toilers of America and to those who by organized effort are seeking to lift the crushing burdens of the poor, and to reduce the hardships and uphold the dignity of labor."[87]

Finally, the committee recommended the organization within the council of a Commission on the Church and Social Service, and strongly urged its constituent denominations to supply the spiritual motive for all movements aiming to fulfill the second great commandment and to socialize both their message and their activity.

The report as a whole was an unprecedented attempt to voice the convictions of the Protestant churches of America, speaking with one voice, on the industrial crisis. As Charles Macfarland later pointed out, it was "almost amazing" that the report should have been adopted with no opposition and providential that it was so adopted "before criticism and antagonism became seriously vocal."[88]

When the report had been presented, Charles Stelzle, invited to address the assembly because of his wide experience in work with laboring people, rose to express his hope that the resolutions of the report would be adopted. He praised the statement presented by Dr. North as "the greatest paper on this subject that I have ever heard or read," and went on to exclaim, "if I can say to the workmen of America that the Federal Council really means it, it will be the biggest thing that I can say or that I have ever yet said."[89] The resolutions having been adopted, the Executive Committee was instructed to publish the report "in the widest possible manner."[90]

Some members of the council were not as enthusiastic about the report as Stelzle was, however. Speaking before a popular meeting held that evening on the subject of "United Home Missions and Evangelistic Work," J. Wilbur Chapman referred to the afternoon's proceedings.

> The resolution passed this afternoon was simply great. . . . I was in fullest sympathy with Mr. Stelzle when he said that the resolutions were superb. But, you know, I can think of a resolution that would stir the country more than

that would stir it. What is that resolution? That you men . . . should meet together and send out an appeal to the whole Church of Christ in America, saying the time has come to pray.[91]

The memorable session of the Federal Council of Churches adjourned on Tuesday morning, December 8. By the time the proceedings were published in 1909, the Commission on the Church and Social Service had been duly organized, with Frank Mason North as chairman. Members of the commission included many of the most prominent leaders in social Christianity, including Walter Rauschenbusch, Washington Gladden, Charles Stelzle, Josiah Strong, and Graham Taylor. On the work of this commission was to depend the very life of the council in the critical years of 1908-12.

A Party with Opponents in All Denominations

At the opposite extreme there were some conservatives who not only remained outside the cooperative ventures of the mainline evangelical Protestant denominations, but also attempted to rally their own forces. In 1906, A. C. Dixon left the Ruggles Street Church in Roxbury to accept the pastorate of the Moody Church in Chicago. In doing so, he put denominational allegiance below the opportunity "to stand as a leader of a religious party not divided by denominational lines, but with opponents in all denominations."[92] He was replacing R. A. Torrey, who had left to do full-time evangelistic work. His wife and biographer described his state of mind on assuming his new position: "Of one thing he felt sure as he looked out upon his future task—no mere social reform could meet the deep needs of the people. Only the Gospel of Christ in its pure appeal to the spirit could touch the core of hungry hearts and lead men and women to the source of true satisfaction."[93]

In 1908, Dixon began paying for a weekly column in the Saturday edition of the *Chicago Daily News*, by means of which he hoped to reach "the man in the street" with the Gospel. During these years in Chicago, he apparently became deeply troubled by what he regarded as a "movement of growing hostility to the true Gospel of Christ" within the churches.[94] This "spreading apostasy" he saw as a sure sign of the end-time, heralding Christ's return "as the one hope of the world." Almost every Saturday night for two-and-a-half years, he met for prayer with a group of about ten men, to confront "modern infidelity."[95]

On a trip to the West Coast in 1908, he met Milton and Lyman Stewart, two wealthy laymen (brothers) who were generous in supporting various conservative religious enterprises. Lyman Stewart heard Dixon preach and, convinced that he was just the man for the job, got him to agree to assume responsibility for the publication of a multivolume work presenting the essential truths of the Christian faith. It would be called *The Fundamentals*. The work was a monument to the cooperative efforts of millenarians and biblical literalists of the Princeton school whom Ernest Sandeen has shown to be the early Fundamentalists.[96] Dixon edited the first five volumes, the first of which appeared in 1910.

Thus, by the end of the decade, both social gospelers and militant conservatives had the organizational structures with which to propagate their own version of the Gospel, and both sides had already begun to muster their forces.

PART THREE

Two Types of Christianity: The Individualistic and the Social

SIX

Full-Blown Polemic

Finally in 1912, the split between social Christianity and individualistic evangelicalism was institutionalized within the Federal Council itself, with the creation of a Commission on Evangelism to balance the Commission on the Church and Social Service. The first four years of the council's history had not been rosy. Apparently, it was a continuous struggle "against obscurity and bankruptcy."[1] Cooperation had been accepted in principle, but churches were too absorbed in established denominational activities to give it priority. Contributions had to be solicited from individuals because the member denominations failed to meet their obligations. The major historians of the council agree that in its early years it was the Commission on the Church and Social Service that kept the council alive.[2]

A Commission on Evangelism

Immediately after the council adjourned in 1908, the Executive Committee met and elected William H. Roberts, chairman; Frank Mason North vice chairman, and Rivington Lord recording secretary. On the assumption that the organization of state and local federations was to be the primary work of the council, the country had been divided administratively into eastern, western, and central districts. There was as yet no executive secretary. Elias Sanford, who had carried the secretarial burden of the Open and Institutional Church League and the National Federation of Churches and Christian Workers, was corresponding secretary of the Federal Council and its "main guiding spirit"[3] in its first years.

At both the 1909 and 1910 meetings of the Executive Committee, the only report of any significance was that of the Commission on the Church and Social Service. Charles Stelzle had been elected acting secretary for such part-time voluntary service as he could give, but there were no funds available to meet the commission's request for a paid executive secretary. In 1910, the

Social Service Commission reported considerable progress, particularly in terms of the important investigation of the steel industry at Bethlehem, Pennsylvania, by Josiah Strong, Charles Stelzle, and Paul U. Kellogg.[4]

With only $5,000 as its total budget, the commission took a bold step in May 1911 in securing Charles S. Macfarland as its first employed executive secretary. A Congregational minister, Macfarland had served two New England pastorates, in Malden, Massachusetts (1900-1906), and South Norwalk, Connecticut (1906-1911). He had already displayed considerable interest in the relation of the churches to social and industrial problems and had been a member of the Social Service Commission since 1910.[5]

By this time, five denominations had established departments of social service with full-time, paid secretaries. They were Rev. Henry A. Atkinson, secretary of the Congregational Brotherhood; Dr. Samuel Zane Batten, secretary of the Baptist Department of Social Service and Brotherhood; Rev. Frank M. Crouch, field secretary of the Protestant Episcopal Joint Commission on Social Service; Rev. Charles Stelzle, superintendent of the Presbyterian Bureau of Social Service; and Rev. Harry F. Ward, secretary of the Methodist Federation for Social Service.[6] At a conference in Chicago in November 1911, these five secretaries agreed to coordinate their efforts by organizing a Secretarial Council under Macfarland's chairmanship to carry out the work of the Commission on the Church and Social Service.

Two other significant steps were taken by the council in 1911. A Commission on Peace and Arbitration was organized with Frederick Lynch as secretary. With the work of state and local federations, there were now three fields of interdenominational cooperation open. Also, Dr. Sanford's failing health made it necessary for Macfarland to assume responsibility not only for the Social Service Commission but for the entire council as well. At the Executive Committee meeting of 1911, he was elected executive secretary of the council. In his autobiography, Macfarland described what it was like that first year.

> Administratively speaking, the institution consisted of little more than a constitution, a small office and a typist. . . . I even discovered that, outside the prophetic group responsible for the initiation of the movement, few church leaders were taking it seriously.
>
> The emphasis on the social gospel did not kindle the hearts and minds of some denominational leaders. But we had a few men of great faith. It was fortunate that, in days of experimentation, the Council was not tied so closely as now to the denominational machinery and that members of the several

departments were selected because of their capacity for service and their commitment to an ideal.[7]

Soon after assuming the burden of the executive leadership of the council, Macfarland decided that a drastic change was needed if the council were to survive. Thus far it had been based on state and local units. Macfarland's idea was to bring the denominations into cooperation in several basic areas where the churches needed creative leadership. He hoped that such a step would increase denominational interest and support, as well as enlist financial contributions from individuals and groups concerned about enabling certain objectives they supported to be successfully carried out. Furthermore, it would solve the problem of the relation of state and local federations to the council since they could now be left to determine their own constitutions and programs.[8] Macfarland wisely determined to meet privately with the committee members to convince them of the soundness of his plan rather than to approach the Executive Committee as a whole.

There is no record of the response of the committee members to Macfarland's plan. It was finally determined that the three areas in which the denominations particularly needed cooperative leadership were social service, peace and arbitration, and evangelism. It is difficult to know who was responsible for urging the need for a commission on evangelism. As chairman of the Executive Committee, William H. Roberts was undoubtedly one of the first men with whom Macfarland must have conferred. A member of the Evangelistic Committee in the Presbyterian Church and a well-known conservative, he was very likely the committee member who suggested to Macfarland that "a special effort" be made to develop a commission on evangelism.[9] At the Executive Committee meeting in December 1911, an Evangelistic Committee was created and Roberts was made its chairman.[10]

In March 1912, the Executive Committee resolved to recommend to the Federal Council the advisability of discontinuing the district system authorized by the 1908 session.[11] The district secretaries were to be retired, the assistant to the executive secretary was released as of October 1, and Elias Sanford was forced by ill health to retire from his position as corresponding secretary, so that by 1912, Macfarland was carrying the responsibilities that were to have been shared by six secretaries. By the end of 1912, more than half the total income of the council was provided by individuals ($18,500, as opposed to $14,500 from denominational appropriations). Central administrative expenses tended to be met by denominational contributions while specialized programs were largely sustained by interested individuals or foundations.[12] In general, the council's first four years were "so beset with difficulties" that when Shailer Mathews, dean of the Divinity School of the University of Chicago, was invited to become president in 1912, he hesitated to accept the office, thinking the council might already be moribund.[13]

About 400 delegates were present when the Federal Council met for its second quadrennial session in Chicago from December 4-9, 1912. Bishop Hendrix presided. At this meeting a Commission on Evangelism was created within the council to balance the Commission on the Church and Social Service; "tradition has it that the overture came first from the Presbyterian delegation to the Council."[14] In the report of the Committee on Evangelism, in which he asked for support for the projected commission, Dr. William H. Roberts declared evangelism to be the supreme mission of the church. By further defining evangelism as "the proclamation of Christ, the author of that new life which beginning with a new heart, shall make all things new,"[15] Roberts made it clear that he had in mind not the social evangelism of the social gospelers, but the salvation of souls according to the traditional pattern. "The fundamental error to be overcome is sin," he insisted, "and external need can best be relieved by beginning with the internal necessity."[16] He went on to stress the urgency of evangelistic work by referring (much in the style of Candler) to "the vast masses of unregenerate men" in the United States who constituted "a great barrier in the way of spiritual advance, moral progress, and true material welfare for the Republic."[17] He urged the need for revivals, and asked for the establishment of evangelistic committees in each denomination.

In order to present a united front at the 1912 meeting, Charles Macfarland had arranged that Frank Mason North should preside when Roberts gave the report on evangelism, and that Roberts should take the chair when North presented the report for the Social Service Commission. Macfarland had prepared the social service report and he later recalled that before the quadrennial session he went over it with Roberts, "who was not in entire sympathy with our social program," and asked him to "urge its acceptance with an approving speech."[18]

Macfarland's report recounted the major developments of the quadrennium and reaffirmed the Social Creed of 1908, with the addition of articles on divorce and prohibition. Much of the rest of it attempted to gain the support of conservatives for the commission's social program. "The Church," he said, "is not turning aside from her task, neither is she creating new forces. Still further than this, we are happily discovering that the conservation of the evangelistic note is essential to an effective social gospel, and are no longer disposed to rend asunder what Christ has joined together."[19] He went on to speak of God, sin, judgment, and redemption as "words belonging to a vocabulary that can interpret the whole universe of right and wrong, both individual and social."[20]

Looking to the future, the report concluded with a number of recommendations. Asserting the council's need for both spiritual vision and social service, Macfarland called on the conservatives to add the social note of the new evangelism to their message.

> We ask that the great army of our evangelists, both professional and pastoral, recognize that intelligent Christian discipleship involves a recognition of the justice, the sympathy, and the good will that are due to their fellow men, and we ask our evangelists to add the social note to the individual note of their message, that together we may infuse the religious spirit into social movements and the social spirit into religious movements.[21]

The reports of both the Evangelistic Committee and the Social Service Commission were accepted by the council, and the Evangelistic Committee was made into a permanent Commission on Evangelism, with William H. Roberts as its chairman. Thus, it is clear that by 1912 a strong voice was making itself heard in the council that insisted that, whatever the justification for social service, the primary task of the church had been and always would be the salvation of individuals. It was the proponents of this view who were responsible for the creation of the Commission on Evangelism in 1912. The report of the Social Service Commission of that same year is further evidence that by 1912 it was necessary to take this party seriously if the unity of the council were to be preserved.

Although it is always difficult to date the existence of a full-blown polemic by a single year, 1912 would seem to be an appropriate symbolic date to indicate the existence of a very real split within American Protestantism. For a number of reasons, by 1912, conservatives felt it necessary to assert their opposition to what they regarded as the replacing of the traditional tasks of the church by the newer emphases of social Christianity. After 1912, a new note of opposition and polemic characterized the encounters between these two parties.

It is certain that from the days of William Roberts on, the council's work in evangelism was a conservative influence. And yet the council was able to preserve a remarkable degree of unity. To be sure, there were some denominations that withdrew from the council. As early as 1912, the Presbyterian Church in the U.S. (Southern) objected to the theology and social program of the council and began to debate the issue of withdrawal from its membership. By 1913, the Primitive Methodist Church, the Congregational Methodist Church, the Reformed Presbyterian, and the Swedish Lutheran Augustana Synod had dropped out of the council's membership.[22]

However, that such withdrawals were few, and that the council was able to preserve unity of action in spite of genuine and profound differences of conviction over the church's task and the council's role in fulfilling that task, was primarily due to the wise statesmanship of its early leaders. Men like Macfarland were above all committed to preserving unity in the council, even if it meant "restraining the radicals in international affairs and in the realm of social service and industry."[23] And, as we have seen, without exception the men who provided the leadership for the Commission on the Church and Social Service in its early years—North, Stelzle, Macfarland, Strong—were evangelical liberals who plainly stressed the need for both personal religion and social service, and sought the cooperation of the conservatives.

Gladden versus Sunday in Columbus

The encounter that most dramatically revealed the extent of the split in American Protestantism was the confrontation that took place in 1912-13 between Washington Gladden and the evangelist Billy Sunday, who dominated the revival scene as much after 1912 as Moody had in the 1870s. Sunday had worked with two professional evangelists, J. Wilbur Chapman, whom he assisted from 1893 to 1895, and Milan B. Williams. Although the former was really his mentor, he had more in common with the "folk tradition"[24] of the latter and it was this style that he followed after 1900. In his folksy humor, his use of slang, his aggressiveness, and his stress on civic reform and prohibition, he much resembled Sam Jones.

Born near Ames, Iowa, in 1862, Billy Sunday had a strange preparation for an evangelistic career. From 1883 until 1891, when he went into full-time religious work, Sunday had been a professional baseball player. He had very little theological training of any kind. Converted by members of the Pacific Garden Mission in Chicago in 1886, he took Bible lessons for two winters at the Chicago YMCA and worked for three years (1891-1893) as a YMCA secretary in Chicago. He was not ordained until 1903, when the Chicago Presbytery passed him in spite of his lack of theological knowledge. Thus, like Moody, he preached a simple evangelical message, although he concentrated less on preaching the love of God, and more on calling people "to be decent."[25] He made conversion so simple that there was no longer any need for the inquiry rooms; all a person had to do was "hit the sawdust trail"[26] down to the front of the tabernacle, shake hands with the evangelist, and sign a decision card.

Sunday began conducting revival campaigns on his own in 1896. From 1896 to 1906, he conducted 100 separate crusades, 90 percent of them in cities of less than 10,000, and mostly in the Midwest. Besides producing results in terms of antisaloon petitions and Law and Order Leagues, Sunday had an amazing record as a soul winner in these years. According to McLoughlin, extant figures from thirty of these cities indicate that his converts averaged 20 percent of the population, and a high percentage of these joined a church.[27]

After 1906, he moved on to larger cities. Although the proportion of converts to the population steadily decreased in larger cities, Sunday nevertheless averaged 4 percent of the population in cities of 500,000 or more—a figure that "far outdistanced the totals attained by Chapman, Torrey, Moody, Jones, or Finney."[28] Sunday claimed to have converted one million persons during his career. Part of the reason for his success was the efficiency of his campaigns. He carried the techniques of urban mass evangelism to the peak of refinement with his large staff of more than twenty experts, including always an advance man to schedule and prepare for the revivals and Homer Rodeheaver as his "choir leader, soloist, trombonist, and expert master of ceremonies."[29] To assure continuous crowds, Sunday stipulated that all cooperating churches must remain closed for the duration of the campaign. The drama and excitement of his meetings and his use of the delegation system of bringing various groups in the city to the tabernacle also helped to keep the people coming. He received far more support from prominent businessmen than any revivalist since Moody and, except for the social gospelers, he also had the support of almost all the evangelical ministers in the cities where he held his campaigns.

When a group of his fellow ministers in Columbus began in 1911 to organize support for a Billy Sunday revival campaign there, Washington Gladden at once assumed the leadership of the opposition. As we have seen, he was not unwilling on occasion to support mass revivalism and there can be no question about his concern for individual salvation. But to his mind, Sunday embodied all the worst features of the old evangelism. At Gladden's instigation, nineteen ministers, including five Congregationalists, sent a remonstrance to the Columbus Ministerial Association, and eighteen Lutheran pastors signed their own protest. But Gladden's efforts were not enough to prevent a majority of sixty-three clergy from voting to call Sunday.[30]

The revival began on December 26, 1912, and ran until February 16, 1913. Both Gladden and Sunday recognized the importance to Sunday's career of a successful revival in Columbus since it was the largest city he had visited thus far. At the opening service Gladden heard his friend Ernest B. Allen, a Congregational minister in Toledo, testify to the way Sunday had won his wholehearted support. Throughout the campaign Sunday was praised by the press and clergy of Columbus, including many of Gladden's friends. And yet the evangelist condemned liberal theology, the social gospel, evolution, the Parliament of Religions—virtually everything with which Gladden had been identified. He referred to the universal fatherhood of God and brotherhood of man as "all rot," denounced "bastard evolution," referred to the Parliament of Religions as "one of the biggest curses that ever came to America," and said of biblical criticism, "When the latest scholarship says one thing and the Word of God another, the latest scholarship can go plumb to hell."[31] Although he never mentioned Gladden by name, some of his accusations were only thinly disguised. Near the close of the revival he said, "The trouble with a lot of you people in Columbus is you have had a lot of mutts here, professing to be preachers, who have been preaching a lot of tommy rot, and it's no wonder you have lost your idea of what is truth."[32]

During the revival, Gladden carefully refrained from replying directly to Sunday. However, from January to Easter, he gave a series of midweek lectures, later published as *Present Day Theology* (1913), which was intended to be a summary of the theology he had been developing since the 1870s.

The results of the revival were remarkable. The official count of "conversions" was 18,149, a full 10 percent of the population. Apparently the campaign also hurt somewhat the liquor interests of the city, partly because the chief of police, converted by Sunday, determined to enforce the city's blue laws. For some time after the revival ended, many of the city's businesses closed on Saturday night so that their employees could be in church on Sunday.

The real showdown occurred after the close of the revival. In May 1913, the *Congregationalist* published an article by Gladden entitled "The Trouble

138

with Mr. Sunday," in which he held that the results of Sunday's revivals were not all they were said to be. He further criticized Sunday for his intolerance, his commercialism (Sunday took home with him a free-will offering of $21,000), and his theology, which Gladden described as "the most hopeless form of medieval substitutionism."[33]

The response to Gladden's article was revealing. In spite of the fact that Gladden had been a prominent and respected pastor in Columbus for over thirty years, the clergy "rose almost en masse to Sunday's defense."[34] At the monthly meeting of Columbus ministers in June, Rev. Dr. John W. Day of the First Presbyterian Church, head of the Columbus Evangelistic Association, introduced a resolution deprecating the published attack on Sunday; it was passed by a vote of 23-5. Rev. W. C. Stevenson of the Russell Street Baptist Church organized a mass meeting to rebuke Gladden. Advertising the meeting with a sign outside his church reading "Billy Sunday or Dr. Gladden, Which?" Stevenson preached on "The Real Trouble with Dr. Gladden" and brought in eight of Sunday's converts to testify. Gladden's theology was attacked with the suggestion that it led to spiritual deadness. John B. Koehne, a Congregationalist from New Hampshire, was brought to Columbus twice by the conservative ministers of the city, the second time for a series of nine lectures on "Fundamentals of Christianity," which were later published in a pamphlet entitled *Future Punishment: An Examination of Dr. Washington Gladden's 'Present Day Theology' Theory of Hell*. Throughout these lectures it was insinuated that Gladden was a Unitarian and an infidel and that he was guilty of elevating "social consciousness" above the Bible.

After 1913, Billy Sunday was overwhelmingly accepted by the evangelical churches, while for Gladden this episode represented the low point of his influence and prestige. As Gladden's biographer pointed out, the whole experience was a startling indication that "the social gospel and liberal theology had permeated the thought of the average church-goer to a far lesser extent" than Gladden had realized.[35] He might have added that this applied to the clergy as well. It is certainly further evidence that after 1912, those who insisted on the primacy of individual salvation took on the characteristics of a party in opposition to the liberal social gospelers. By 1912, the polemic in American Protestantism was full-blown.

Two Types of Christianity

This polemic was also reflected in the works of the major social gospelers after 1912. In the writings of both Josiah Strong and Walter Rauschenbusch, for example, there is a new note of awareness of conservative opposition and a corresponding effort to refute and persuade the conservatives. In 1913, Josiah Strong wrote a special introduction for the tenth edition of *The Next Great Awakening*, first published in 1902. It began as follows:

> There are two types of Christianity, the old and the older. The one is traditional, familiar, and dominant. The other, though as old as the Gospel of Christ, is so rare that it is suspected of being new, or is overlooked altogether.
> They are not to be distinguished by any of the old lines of doctrinal or denominational cleavage. Their difference is one of spirit, aim, point of view, comprehensiveness. The one is individualistic; the other is social.[36]

Because Strong felt the social type of Christianity was misunderstood, he went on to discuss the differences between the two types. "The one seeks to save individuals," he said, "the other aims at the salvation of individuals, plus the organization of society on a Christian basis."[37] In all that he said about social Christianity, Strong took pains to point out that it was the more inclusive of the two types, that it did not minimize the importance of the first great commandment, right relations with God, or the spiritual; but also recognized the necessity for the second commandment, right relations with other human beings, and the physical.

There had been a religious revival in Wales in the closing years of the previous decade, and since it seemed to be of the "individualistic type," Strong had been asked why such a revival could not also take place in the United States. The rest of the introduction was devoted to answering that question. Revivals of the individualistic type, he explained, were appropriate for the nineteenth century, with its individualistic civilization, but they were no longer adequate for the needs of modern society.

> There are communities, churches, and classes, both in England and America, which are still living in the first half of the nineteenth century. Their lives have been outwardly affected by the new civilization, but they have not yet caught its spirit, are not yet perplexed by its problems; their theology is not yet influenced by the results of modern scholarship. Such classes, churches and communities may have a revival of the old individualistic type of religion. But that type of revival can never again move an enlightened people as a whole,

lifting a civilization to a higher plane, because it is not adapted to the peculiar needs of modern civilization, does not solve its fundamental problems.[38]

Strong criticized the prevalent, individualistic type of Christianity on three grounds: (1) it was not solving the social problems of the day; (2) even in terms of its avowed aim of saving individuals it was unsatisfactory, as shown by the decreasing growth rate of church membership and the increasing number of persons outside the churches; and (3) it had become "sadly superficial."[39] The last charge Strong felt was the most serious.

> We hear of so many thousand converts [Sunday revivals], I would like to know to what they are converted before I rejoice. Are they converted to Jesus Christ, or only to the church? If they are not converted from a life of selfishness to a life of service, they are not converted to Christ; and the larger the number of converts of that sort added to the church, the weaker will the church be.[40]

Two years later, Josiah Strong wrote *The New World-Religion*, which was intended to be the second volume in a four-volume work dealing with problems of modern civilization on a world scale. Here the tone of his writing was even more polemical than in 1913. Basically the book was divided in two parts. The first, called "The Christianity of Christ," dealt with the modern conception of the world and God's relation to it, and especially with the nature and laws of the Kingdom of God. The second part, "The Christianity of the Church," asserted that the individualistic interpretation of Christianity was passing, and called on the church to be converted to Christ and to an unselfish, social conception of Christianity.

Strong's case against individualistic Christianity was based on several major premises. For one thing, he questioned the adequacy of the individualistic understanding of conversion and regeneration. He felt it missed the basic insight that the nature of sin was selfishness and that the essence of new birth was the crucifixion of self-will and the birth of a new benevolent will, without which it was impossible to enter the Kingdom of God.[41] Furthermore, the individualistic interpretation was based on an outmoded worldview and philosophy of life that could neither square itself with the accepted facts of science and the highest scholarship nor satisfy the demands of the new social spirit. He insisted that institutional Christianity must adapt itself to the radically different intellectual atmosphere and social environment in which it found itself, or it would perish.[42]

Strong addressed himself to several kinds of conservatives. He told the revivalists that the nation could no longer be aroused by preaching a truth that was everywhere accepted and disregarded. Therefore, the preaching of the love of God would not do what it did in Moody's day. He also criticized the tendency to measure spiritual power by numbers rather than character. It would be better for the church, he said, if its membership were purged. If it had only one-fifth of its present membership, but these were Christians who had been crucified with Christ, it would have five times the spiritual power.[43]

He also criticized the millenarians, describing their views as "diametrically and irreconcilably opposed to the social interpretation of Christianity." They were hostile to the scientific spirit, antagonistic to biblical criticism, out of sympathy with modern culture, and skeptical of all progress.[44]

Again he stressed that social Christianity had been much misunderstood. He reminded the defenders of the individualistic interpretation that social Christianity did not substitute the salvation of society for the salvation of the individual. "All that the individualistic interpretation offers of individual salvation, consciousness of God and communion with him, peace here and blessed life after death—all this and much more is offered by the social interpretation of Christianity."[45] He devoted a good deal of space, he said, to the salvation of the individual because "there has been a widespread impression that the social interpretation of Christianity aims at the salvation of society instead of that of the individual."[46]

Referring to those who say that the business of the ministry is to save souls, Strong replied:

> The preacher who says that his business is not the regeneration of society but the regeneration of the individual is sure to misunderstand those who preach the social gospel. Because they stand for the regeneration of society, they are supposed to be indifferent to the regeneration of the individual. If I had to choose between them, I would work for the regeneration of the individual as the more fundamental, but why not *both*? Have political corruption, gambling dens, saloons and brothels no relation to individual character?[47]

Strong then quoted a letter from a minister who asked whether the increasing social service of the churches didn't involve the danger of diverting them from their proper work. Strong replied that the new conception of Christianity made social service not a program, but "the essential spirit of the Christian life."[48] As far as Strong was concerned, this change—which was surely coming—could not come too quickly.

He once again asked the churches to look at themselves. In order to have a great spiritual awakening, the church must first have new life. It must repent and believe the gospel of the Kingdom. He criticized the church for its acceptance of the existing social system, and asked whether those church members who did not want Christ's teachings applied to "the things of this world" were afraid that such application would interfere with their "comfortable selfishness."[49]

Finally, he more than once pleaded with those who defended the individualistic interpretation. "Let me say to those who still cling to this interpretation as Cromwell said to the framers of the Westminster Confession: 'Brethren, I beseech you in the bowels of the Lord, believe it possible that you may be mistaken.' " He rejoiced in the progress of the Federal Council and said that though its constituency included "thousands who accept social Christianity and millions who do not," nevertheless the thousands included most of the religious leaders; "and those who refuse to follow are as certain to be left behind as is the wake of a moving ship."[50]

He recognized that those who were opposing the new conception were good people who believed they were doing God's service in "stoning the prophets of the new order."[51] But he had no doubt that the individualistic conception was passing and a worthier understanding taking its place. If the visible church refused to adjust itself to changed conditions, it would perish. His hope was that, like Lyman Beecher, who mourned the disestablishment of the Congregational churches in Connecticut and later rejoiced that it was the "best thing that ever happened to the churches of Connecticut," those who opposed social Christianity would live to see that they were wrong. "This is certain—when men have against them the Scriptures, science, scholarship, and human experience, they are certainly mistaken, no matter how saintly; and, if they are not too old, they will live to rejoice over time's demonstration that they were in the wrong."[52]

Wanted: A Faith for a Task

Walter Rauschenbusch's *Christianizing the Social Order* (1912) has usually been described as his "most 'secular' book."[53] It is true that the section on "Our Semi-Christian Social Order" (the part of the book that is most often quoted) was largely an indictment of the American capitalistic system and a call to Christianize it by moving in the direction of socialism. However,

Rauschenbusch himself considered it "a religious book from beginning to end."[54] Looked at from our perspective, there can be little doubt about that. Most of Part Two was devoted to a discussion of social Christianity as a religious faith, what it was, why it was needed, and how it related to what Rauschenbusch called "personal religion." The whole section might well have taken the title of one of the chapters, "Wanted: A Faith for a Task," for that was the essence of the situation as Rauschenbusch saw it.

> We need a great faith to serve as a spiritual basis for the tremendous social task before us, and the working creed of our religion, in the form in which it has come down to us, has none. Its theology is silent or stammers where we most need a ringing and dogmatic message. It has no adequate answer to the fundamental moral questions of our day. . . . Its hymns, its ritual, its prayers, its books of devotion, are so devoid of social thought that the most thrilling passions of our generation lie in us half stifled for lack of religious utterance. . . . We need a new foundation for Christian thought.[55]

Rauschenbusch went on to review the heritage of social Christianity. Finally he turned to a lengthy consideration of the relation between social Christianity and personal religion. The whole section was obviously written in response to conservative opposition and attempted to answer the charges against social Christianity.

The basic question raised by conservative opponents was whether personal religion would not be sapped by devotion to social work. Or, as Rauschenbusch put it, "A hot breakfast is an event devoutly to be desired, but is it wise to chop up your precious old set of colonial furniture to cook the breakfast? Would the reenforcement of the social spirit be worth while if we lost our personal religion in the process?" He admitted that if that were the alternative—being compelled to choose between social righteousness and communion with God—it would be a tragic situation. He acknowledged that "spiritual regeneration is the most important fact in any life history." But he did not think it likely that striving to create a "free, just, and brotherly" social order would cause men and women to lose their contact with God.[56]

He then considered some of the examples conservatives had given of figures for whom progressive social interest had meant the receding of personal religion. Some of them, Rauschenbusch suggested, had little personal religion to lose. Others were simply discarding old religious forms. Rauschenbusch saw that as a healthy thing, and was convinced that those who temporarily lost sight of personal religious questions because of their new enthusiasm for the

144

social awakening would be restored to equilibrium by experience. The blame for their temporary one-sidedness would have to be shared, he thought, by the generations of "religious individualists" whose own one-sidedness had caused the present reaction.[57] With regard to the alienation of entire classes from religion, he blamed much of it on the anticlericalism and materialistic philosophy of continental socialism, but gave that as all the more convincing reason why the new social spirit needed to be combined with the inherited Christian faith.

As Rauschenbusch understood social Christianity, it was not in conflict with personal religion but rather was a new type of personal religion, preferable in many ways to the familiar, individualistic type. It involved the possibility of a purer, because unselfish and social, spirituality, and a keener recognition of sin. Rauschenbusch criticized traditional evangelicalism for defining sin solely in terms of one's relations with God, or one's personal morality. "Evangelicalism prides itself on its emphasis on sin and the need of conversion," he asserted,

> yet some of the men trained in its teachings do not seem to know the devil when they meet him in the street. The most devastating sins of our age do not look like sins to them. . . . Social Christianity involves a more trenchant kind of conversion and more effective means of grace. It may teach a more lenient theory of sin, but it gives a far keener eye for the lurking places of concrete and profitable sins. A man who gets the spiritual ideals of social Christianity is really set at odds with "the world" and enlisted in a lifelong fight with organized evil. But no man who casts out devils is against Christ.[58]

Social Christianity was superior to the older, individualistic conception because it involved more durable powers of growth. People whose principal concern was not for their souls but for the Kingdom of God had a task that was never completed, but always expanding and demanding more of them. Social Christianity would also offer a more personal evangelism. It would seek to bring salvation to people in their particular social locations and human relationships. It would do away with the "wholesale regimentation of souls," the mechanical and superficial methods that had characterized the old evangelism. It would offer every person a full salvation by demanding "a Christian social order which would serve as the spiritual environment of the individual."[59]

Finally, social Christianity was "the great highway by which this present generation can come to God." It put an end to most of the conflicts between science and religion. It demonstrated the sympathy of the religion of Christ for "the people." It provided the proper balance between the quest for freedom, and social solidarity and service. It was adjusted to the modern worldview as other-worldly religion had been appropriate for an ancient and medieval worldview now "melted away irretrievably." Rauschenbusch was not afraid that religion was dying. Although it was true that social enthusiasm was an unsettling force, Rauschenbusch urged his readers to let the new social spirit fuse with the old religious faith, to create "a new total that will be completer and more Christian than the old religious individualism at its best."[60]

Rauschenbusch summed up the entire "religious" discussion in the book.

> We do not want to substitute social activities for religion. If the Church comes to lean on social preachings and doings as a crutch because its religion has become paralytic, may the Lord have mercy on us all! We do not want less religion; we want more; but it must be a religion that gets its orientation from the Kingdom of God. To concentrate our efforts on personal salvation, as orthodoxy has done, or on soul culture, as liberalism has done, comes close to refined selfishness. . . . Seek ye first the Kingdom of God and God's righteousness and the salvation of your souls will be added to you.[61]

There seems to be little question that the social gospelers were aware of two distinct parties within American Protestantism after 1912. Strong described the two types of Christianity as individualistic and social; Rauschenbusch used the terms "personal religion" and "social Christianity." At least three groups were obviously among the conservatives to whom they addressed themselves: the revivalists, ordinary ministers and the church members who supported them, and the millenarians. The opposition to the social gospel by those who defended traditional, individualistic evangelicalism was apparently so strong and vocal by 1912 that the social gospelers felt it necessary to acknowledge it and attempt to refute the conservative charges.

Social Evangelism

As we have seen, the split within the Federal Council took the form of two commissions, that of social service and that of evangelism. Still further evidence of the existence of this polemic was Harry F. Ward's *Social Evangelism*, published in 1915. Ward was head of the Methodist Federation for Social Service, and consequently a member of the Federal Council Commission on the Church and Social Service. He was also one of the authors of the Social Creed of the Churches, adopted in 1908. He described the split that had occasioned the writing of *Social Evangelism*:

> The activities and propaganda which have recently been organized in the churches under the head of "Social Service" are often contrasted with the evangelistic function of the Church as though they were inherently antagonistic or mutually exclusive. This is largely because the terms social service and evangelism are both overworked. One has long been and the other is fast becoming a house of refuge for the crowd that cry "Lord, Lord, but do not the things that I say." The shibboleth is shouted but the deed remains undone, the fact unaccomplished.[62]

In contrast with this, Ward insisted that when the church actually labored at the tasks of evangelism and social service, they were found to be interdependent. "In fact," Ward concluded, "a social evangelism appears."[63]

Most of the book was an attempt to describe what Ward thought the new—or social—evangelism should be like and why it was necessary. But he first made it clear how much mutual misunderstanding there was in both parties to the polemic. "The social service movement," he said,

> does not propose to make the Church a mere agent for social reform. Its purpose is the regeneration of the social order, and it promotes reforms only as they are the working out of social salvation. It has never sought to substitute a "soup and soap salvation" for "spiritual regeneration," but it does believe that regeneration must affect the whole of life.[64]

Ward believed that the social awakening in the church was the culmination of evangelical Christianity because its aim was to put the "very dynamic of God" into all human movements.

He objected to the way evangelism had come to be understood. Where formerly it meant "the aggressive promulgation of the gospel," in its recent manifestations it meant the "aggressive attempt to secure individual adherents to organized Christianity." This he felt was a grievous mistake; evangelism must be both individual and social. Modern sociology had revealed a world in which the individual did not exist apart from his or her interrelationships. Society was seen as an organism, and the individual and community were recognized to be interdependent. Those who still insisted on "social salvation by addition" failed to understand that the collective mind or conscience was something more than that of the sum of individuals. Ward discerned the imperative for a social evangel in the historic purpose of Christianity, the

147

present emergency in the churches, and the call of urgent need from without. Religion must wrestle with this "thing which men jointly are" as well as with their individual existence.[65]

The conservative charge that social evangelism tended to overlook the individual was dismissed by Ward as "a total misunderstanding."

> Their favorite antithesis is whether the Church is to save the social order or to save souls from hell, whether we need the arousing of a new social conscience or a revival of religion, whether the world is to be saved by perfect laws or by redemption, by a new industrial system or by individual regeneration. The answer of course is "*By both*." These things are not in antithesis but are inseparable complements.[66]

People must be evangelized as "social beings"; they must be saved in all their group relationships, not as individuals abstracted from the world, who somehow are set apart in their relationship with God. Ward referred rather impatiently to the polemics involved in the "futile question" of which must come first, individual or social salvation. This question was based on the same kind of misconception, he thought. Its effect was that "each group works for the bit of good that it sees and hurls recriminations at the other for not quitting its job and coming over to work with them. Both fail to see that each of their desired and necessary ends depends upon the other, and that they can only be realized as they are realized together."[67]

However, the appeal to the individual must also be a social appeal. To appeal to individuals simply to seek their own salvation was to enforce human selfishness and obstruct the progress of the kingdom of God. A sound personal salvation would be accomplished by appealing to individuals to lose their lives, to join in the saving of the world, "not to attempt to appropriate the benefits of Calvary for personal ends, but to share in Calvary in order that the world might be redeemed."[68]

Practically speaking, social evangelism would entail new methods, a new message, and a different view regarding results. While Ward still allowed a place for mass revivals, he believed they must face the concrete social sins of the community and call on people to dedicate themselves to concrete service. This would seem to be similar to the social gospel revivalism of B. Fay Mills. But Ward realized the ineffectiveness of this type of approach. Probably the bulk of the real work of social evangelism would be done by carrying the gospel to people where they are. Laborers might have to be reached by going to their halls; poor and immigrant groups must be reached in their homes and natural meeting places. Social evangelism would be primarily a lay movement, and social service would be a crucial part of it.

The first task of social evangelism must be to arouse repentance for social sins by making the "so-called good people" aware of their responsibility for the vast corporate wrongs of the time. It must also indicate the proper fruits of repentance, that is, the fundamental principles of social morality. Ward cautioned against regarding the business of social evangelism as a "mealy-mouthed cant about love."[69] He warned that modern civilization would be destroyed if it continued in its social sins.

Finally, Ward had some strong words to say about the results to be expected from social evangelism. He insisted that the whole question of results was secondary—the important thing was to sow the seed. With obvious reference to the kind of evangelism then being promoted by Billy Sunday, Ward criticized this overemphasis on results.

> Religion has become commercialized until it is content with small profits if only it can get quick returns, until it reckons the cost per head of its converts [Sunday estimated his at $2 per soul], until it compares campaigns as to the number obtained the most quickly and the least expensively. By such a test the ministry of Jesus in his lifetime would be counted a monumental failure.[70]

Ward insisted that the value of the church's social ministries could never be determined by their success in bringing people into the church. The task of the modern evangelist was to go wherever people are gathered "to speak the word of life." While there might be noticeable improvement of community life, the responsibility of social evangelism was to put "the leaven of new life into the social organism"[71] without expecting immediate results.

It is not difficult to see why social evangelism of this type was not popular with church leaders for whom practical, often financial considerations made it hard to be careless of results. Ward was moving in the direction of an understanding of evangelism that would later revolutionize the self-conceptualization of the Department of Evangelism in the National Council of Churches. But in 1915, his view was vastly different from that of the Federal Council's Commission on Evangelism, which still defined "the real business of the Church" as "bringing men to Christ" in the old way. In 1916, it envisioned as its principal objectives the supervision of professional evangelists, the encouragement of evangelism in the local churches by means of the Sunday school and systematic personal visitation of the congregation, and, in general, a renewed emphasis on the *"fundamentals of the gospel."*[72]

Although a full-time secretary for the Commission on the Church and Social Service was not secured until Rev. Worth M. Tippy accepted the post in 1917, the Federal Council continued to move ahead in cooperative social action ventures of the denominations. For a time it seemed as if social Christianity had "become official."[73] The five largest old-line Protestant denominations had appointed official social service commissions or agencies. Older agencies of the Protestant churches like the Student Christian Movement and the Young Men's Christian Association were developing a strong social emphasis and program. Even in foreign missions there was a very real shift of motive and appeal from an individualistic to a social conception.

Both the social gospel and the middle-class reforming movement known as Progressivism, with which it was so closely associated, reached their zenith in 1912. In that year Theodore Roosevelt headed the ticket of the Progressive Party. Although he lost the election to his Democratic rival Woodrow Wilson, all the presidential candidates that year, even the Republican Taft, had been greatly influenced by the progressive reforming spirit. Moreover, the Socialist candidate, Eugene Debs, polled close to a million votes, or nearly 6 percent of the popular vote.

The Progressive movement united many middle-class groups that were protesting against the maldistribution of wealth and power resulting from the nation's rapid transformation to an industrial civilization. The progressives wanted to remove special, minority, and corrupt influence in the government on national, state, and local levels; to change the machinery of government to make it easier for the many rather than the few to control; and to extend the functions of government to secure social justice and relieve social and economic distress. Consequently, businessmen, farmers, women, clergy, social workers, lawyers, journalists, and others supported a wide variety of reforms, including government regulation of interstate commerce, revision of banking and currency laws, antitrust legislation, women's suffrage, the initiative, referendum, and recall, and various measures dealing with industry, such as the eight-hour day, a minimum wage, prohibition of child labor, safeguards against industrial accidents, and workmen's compensation.[74] Between 1912 and 1915, many of the progressive reforms were enacted into law.

The enthusiastic reception of the Men and Religion Forward Movement of 1911-12 seemed to demonstrate the popular interest in social reform. A lay movement aimed particularly at the men and boys of the nation, it combined evangelism, Bible study, and boys' work with social service. Charles Stelzle was asked to be dean of the social service team, and the conferences and mass meetings held to discuss social problems drew the largest attendance in practically all of the seventy or more cities visited.[75] On the basis of surveys made of each of the cities, the team of "social service experts" recommended specific programs to the churches, the social workers, the city, and the state. The popularity of the movement was widely held to be proof of the acceptance of social Christianity by the churches.[76] Walter Rauschenbusch claimed that it had "probably done more than any other single agency to lodge the social gospel in the common mind of the Church," and that it had "made social Christianity orthodox."[77] Yet the movement produced few permanent results and its failure to bring the masses into the churches may actually have added impetus to the reaction against the social gospel after 1912.[78] Billy Sunday voiced this opinion: "Some people are trying to make a religion out of social service with Jesus Christ left out. That is why your Men and Religion Forward Movement was a lamentable failure. They made the Christian religion a side issue."[79]

Almost as soon as progressivism and the social gospel had reached their zenith, they went into a gradual decline. The outbreak of war in Europe and the general feeling that the major evils had been conquered and reform had gone far enough in changing the old system contributed to the decline. Businesspeople also played an important role. Under the leadership of Theodore Roosevelt they had supported economic reform and regulation. However, they drew back when political power passed out of their hands in 1912. Many of them also found their interests threatened by the prying of social gospelers into the affairs of industry, as when Charles Stelzle protested in the name of the church against the "unnecessary slaughter of working men in the Pittsburgh steel mills." We have seen that the Federal Council had to yield to conservative pressure in 1912 and create a Commission on Evangelism. After 1912, conservatives and moderates seemed to be agreed that saving souls and not society was still the chief business of the churches.

This Godless Social Service Nonsense

The astounding success and acclaim of Billy Sunday from 1906 to 1917 reveals a great deal about the mind of evangelical Protestantism in these years. In 1914, he was ranked eighth in a nationwide poll conducted by *American Magazine* on the question, "Who is the greatest man in the United States?"[80] He seemed to be all things to all people. By the nation's leading businesspeople he was hailed as a social reformer. To the host of Protestant ministers for whom the decreasing growth in church attendance, particularly in the downtown areas, was a source of considerable anxiety, he was primarily an amazingly successful soul winner. And to the "forgotten men" (W. G. Sumner) of the middle class who saw themselves caught between the forces of big business and big labor, he seemed a spokesman for "the people."

In 1912, Charles Stelzle compiled figures to show that although Protestant church membership in the United States had grown almost twice as fast as the population from 1880 to 1890, it had barely kept up with the population growth in the decade from 1900 to 1910.[81] In the cities the situation was even worse. Many downtown churches were moving uptown or into the suburbs, and where they still existed they were struggling to find the necessary funds to stay alive. Churches that tried to reach the masses by supporting a downtown mission or institutional church found the cost of maintaining two establishments prohibitive. Ministers who were open to social gospel ideas often feared offending wealthy businessmen whose financial support was essential to the work of their congregations. Consequently, moderate evangelicals continued to hope that the old system of mass evangelism could be made to work, and they supported men like Sunday who seemed to produce results, although they deplored his theology, his sensationalism, and his use of invective. For example, Rev. Pearse Pinch gave a reporter for the *American Magazine* the following explanation for his support of Sunday:

> Why, my dear sir, the man has trampled all over me and my theology. He has kicked my teachings up and down that platform like a football. He has outraged every ideal I have had regarding my sacred profession. But what does that count against the results he has accomplished? My congregation will be increased by hundreds.[82]

Yet in spite of the impressive statistics, Sunday's revivals did not seriously affect the overall situation; the results in terms of church membership were negligible. Many of the nation's successful businesspeople liked the image of Billy Sunday as an efficiency expert for the churches. Several well-publicized aspects of his preaching appealed to them: his call for civic righteousness, his support of prohibition, and his supposed appeal to the masses. Many prominent businessmen, like John Wanamaker and John D. Rockefeller, Jr., sincerely desired to help the poor, but they thought this could best be done by converting them so that they might become respectable American citizens. Consequently, they paid the bills for the great mass revivals from the days of

Moody to those of Sunday. Fairly tolerant of the moral prescriptions of early social Christianity, they drew back as the social gospel analysis of society grew increasingly radical and its representatives began to move in the direction of socialism and an alliance with the workers. It was one thing to listen to talk about brotherhood; it was another to permit threats to the American free enterprise system or to have social gospel preachers meddling in one's industrial affairs.[83]

Finally, the views expressed by Billy Sunday in his urban revivals from 1906 to 1917 were probably shared by the great mass of middle-class American churchgoers, many of whom were simply ignorant of the social gospel. It is easy to forget while reading a history like that of C. H. Hopkins, that the social Christian movement was very much a movement of the elite; its spokespersons were educators and preachers, and its promotional channels largely books, lectures, and the pulpit. When it became institutionalized in the Federal Council, it represented a movement far in advance of all but the vanguard of its denominational constituencies.

The more militant conservatives like A. C. Dixon had long since ceased to support social service enterprises and had been mustering their forces to fight the widespread apostasy in the churches. Holding to the pietistic evangelical view that the church's principal business is saving souls, they opposed the social gospel because it was allied with liberal theology, Biblical criticism, and the doctrine of evolution, all of which seemed to threaten the very foundations of the Christian faith.

In the Federal Council of Churches, conservatives and liberals worked together, but from 1912 on, conservatives began to form a party of opposition to the social program of the liberals. Thus reforming sentiment in America waned, and by the time World War I was over, interest in social Christianity was largely confined to progressive clerical circles. Billy Sunday seemed to express the majority opinion when he said, "We've had enough of this godless social service nonsense."[84]

SEVEN

The Presbyterian Conflict

By 1912, there were two parties in American Protestantism, one asserting that the church must seek to transform the social order, the other claiming that the church's principal task is saving individuals. In order to observe the dynamics of this polemic at closer range, I present a case study of the development of the schism within a single denomination. Of the mainline Protestant denominations I have been considering, the Presbyterian Church in the U.S.A. was an obvious choice because of its clearly delineated polity and doctrine. It seemed likely that disputes over theology or social program would show up in its official records.

Furthermore, the Presbyterian story is interesting precisely because the Presbyterian Church in this period was one of the more conservative denominations. It contributed theologically to Fundamentalism both the biblical literalism of the Princeton school and a greater degree of leadership and participation in the millenarian movement than any other denomination.[1] The Presbyterian General Assembly in 1910 established as the definitive standard of belief a five-point doctrinal statement that lacked only an article on the Second Coming of Christ to make it the sum of Fundamentalist teaching in the 1920s. Where encounters took place within the denomination between representatives of the two parties, they did not involve major leaders of either side like Walter Rauschenbusch or A. C. Dixon. The key figures were all closer to a moderate position than in most other denominations; thus it is revealing to pinpoint the places where they disagreed.[2]

Any student of the Presbyterian Church in this period is indebted to the work of Lefferts A. Loetscher. His *The Broadening Church* is a history of the important theological issues in that church from the reunion of the Old and New School factions in 1869 to the 1930s. Loetscher makes it clear that from 1889 to 1903, the conservatives maintained a firm hold on the seminaries, the confessions, and the governing bodies of the church. However, the liberals were victorious in the Fundamentalist-Modernist struggle among the Presbyterians in the 1920s.[3] This chapter deals with the intervening years.

155

A succession of heresy trials, beginning with that of David Swing in 1874 and continuing almost to the turn of the century with the charges made against A. C. McGiffert in 1899, served to identify the conservative and liberal parties in terms of theology. The most famous and important of these trials was that of Rev. Dr. Charles A. Briggs, who was transferred to the Chair of Biblical Theology at Union Theological Seminary, New York City, in 1890. Charged with heresy in 1891 because of his acceptance of biblical criticism, Briggs was acquitted by the Presbytery of New York but finally found guilty and suspended from the ministry by action of the Presbyterian General Assembly in 1893. From that time on, lines within the church were rather clearly drawn. Those who supported Briggs were marked as dangerous liberals to be watched, even if their defense of him was primarily on the basis of their belief in a broader church. There were also those who resolved to transcend their theological differences in united action.[4]

The account of the developing polemic in the Presbyterian Church can best be told in terms of three aspects of the General Assembly's work: evangelism, home missions/social service, and church cooperation. The outstanding figures in the Presbyterian departments of evangelism and home missions were prominent men in the respective commissions of evangelism and social service within the Federal Council. Thus the Presbyterian story is intimately related at every point to that of the history of the dual emphases in the council. My account has to do with four principal figures: William H. Roberts and J. Wilbur Chapman, who were connected with evangelistic work, and Charles L. Thompson and Charles Stelzle, who represented Presbyterian social ministry.

J. Wilbur Chapman and the Special Evangelistic Committee

In April 1899, Dwight L. Moody addressed a meeting of the Presbyterian Social Union in Philadelphia and urged upon that influential group of laity the need for evangelistic work in their city. He suggested that they might raise the funds, provide the workers, and undertake the work, "systematically, year after year." Moody's plea did not go unheeded. By the summer of 1899, a Summer Evangelistic Committee of twelve laymen had been formed, and the two presbyteries in the Philadelphia area, Philadelphia and Philadelphia North, had been invited to cooperate officially by sending five ministerial representatives each, making a combined committee of twenty-two. Elected the first chairman of the new committee was John H. Converse, an elder in the Presbyterian

Church at Bryn Mawr, and a partner in (later president of) the Baldwin Locomotive Works. Much of the early success of the committee was due to his enthusiasm and generosity.[5]

In 1900, Converse was vice moderator of the Presbyterian General Assembly, meeting in St. Louis. At that time, a Forward Movement for the Twentieth Century was initiated. The following year, a resolution was passed by the assembly, appointing a Special Committee on Evangelistic Work with John Converse as chairman, the purpose of which was "to stimulate the churches in evangelistic work"[6] as part of that Forward Movement. The evangelist J. Wilbur Chapman was among the six ministers and six elders appointed by the moderator to that committee. William H. Roberts, stated clerk of the General Assembly, was at first the acting secretary for the committee, but at his request in the meeting of the Committee in October, 1901, he was made recording secretary and J. Wilbur Chapman became corresponding secretary.[7]

At the 1902 General Assembly, the committee urged that committees on evangelistic work be appointed in all presbyteries. It reported that field representatives had been appointed to speak in the interest of evangelistic work, and requested that the coming year be distinguished by "aggressive work for the winning of souls."[8] The following year, at its insistence, Chapman resigned his pastorate at the Fourth Presbyterian Church, New York City, to devote himself to full-time work for the committee.

During the first eighteen months, most of the meetings conducted by the committee were in the West and home mission territory. However, calls from larger cities were becoming increasingly insistent. In 1903, the committee reported that it had employed fifty-one evangelists during the previous year, its expenses totaling $66,641, of which only $11,457 was received from offerings, the balance—over $55,000—being contributed by fourteen individuals. The 1903 General Assembly increased the membership of the Special Evangelistic Committee to twenty, and in a resolution of thanks to the members, assured the committee of its "sympathy, prayers, and cooperation."[9]

Charles L. Thompson and the Board of Home Missions

Meanwhile, during precisely these years, the Board of Home Missions of the Presbyterian Church was launching into few fields of activity. In 1898, it called to its head Rev. Charles L. Thompson, pastor of the Madison Avenue

Presbyterian Church in New York City. Thompson was admirably suited for the executive leadership of the board. He knew home missions work well, having been a home missions pastor in his first charge at Juneau, Wisconsin, and having kept in touch with home missions work during a series of pastorates in the West and Midwest since that time. He had also served on the Board of Home Missions in New York since his coming there in 1888.

In addition, Thompson was qualified to lead the board into new fields of service because of his acquaintance with the problems of the city. When he came to the Madison Avenue Church, he soon discovered that it must change its methods or resign itself to a slow death. He therefore resolved that it should be both a free church—that is, no pew rents—and an institutional church, offering a variety of services suited to the needs of the community. In 1894, Thompson and Elias Sanford called the meeting in Thompson's study that led to the formation of the Open and Institutional Church League. Thus, Thompson was one of the founders of a direct predecessor of the Federal Council of Churches.

When Thompson was called to the secretaryship of the board, there was some opposition from the conservatives in the church. The Briggs trial had "drawn lines which had not been obliterated,"[10] and Thompson, while not in full sympathy with Briggs, had definitely opposed his trial for heresy. He had long since grown away from the conservative theology he learned at Princeton Seminary under the tutelage of Charles Hodge. There was some concern that a few of the conservatives would oppose Thompson's confirmation as secretary at the 1898 General Assembly. However, Thompson's first address was well suited to gain the support of conservatives and liberals alike: "The work is definite and easily stated. Our country for Christ! It appeals at once to our patriotism and our religion. If ever divine Providence set a land apart for high uses and a noble destiny, this land has been so set apart."[11]

In *The Soul of America*, Thompson explained the need for new departures in the field of home missions. In past generations, the evangelization of America had been thought of chiefly in terms of following the moving western frontier. Now that the frontier had essentially disappeared, home missions were confronted with two very different kinds of tasks. The one was to swing back over fields already occupied but not intensively covered. The other was to deal with the "new fields emerging with startling rapidity out of changed conditions."[12] Thus home missions must go both West and East. They must deal with changed conditions among rural populations as well as with the challenges of immigration and the city.

It was to Thompson's great credit that he quickly recognized the need for specialization in home missions work, for new departments to enable it to meet these new challenges. Recognizing, as he put it, "the new occasions which teach the new duties," Thompson took the bold step in 1903 of calling Rev. Charles Stelzle, of the Markham Memorial Church, St. Louis, to a special mission to working people.[13] On April 1, Stelzle was to begin a campaign of western cities, meeting with churches and working people's associations, and giving addresses on the relations of workers to the church.

Charles Stelzle and the Bureau of Social Service

It would have been difficult to find a man better suited than Stelzle for such a mission. Born on New York's East Side in 1869, Stelzle was a machinist's apprentice from age sixteen until, in 1890, he decided to become a preacher. After trying unsuccessfully to get into Princeton, Union, McCormick, and Drew seminaries, he was finally admitted to Moody Bible Institute, and ordained by the St. Louis Presbytery. Stelzle was therefore uniquely qualified for his task of bringing the churches and working people closer together.[14]

In its first two years, Stelzle's mission consisted largely of studying conditions throughout the country, preaching to workers and making suggestions to the churches. However, by 1906, the work had expanded in a number of directions and the mission had been made into a Department of Church and Labor, the first official denominational agency to pursue a social service program through a paid secretary. The headquarters for the department had become a clearinghouse for information, available to ministers and Christian workers, on "every phase of the workingman's problem, as it concerns the Church."[15] Leaflets were published to answer the misapprehensions of working people and to outline practical methods of reaching the working class with the Christian message. In addition, Stelzle had a weekly syndicated column in over 300 labor papers. Other special features of the work were noon-hour shop meetings and the appointment of ministers as fraternal delegates to labor unions. By 1906, this plan of ministerial representation at labor meetings was already in operation in over seventy-five cities. Stelzle was invited to address the annual meeting of the American Federation of Labor in 1905, at which the department's work was endorsed by the central labor body. Subcommittees were appointed within the presbyteries to cooperate with the department, and labor unions were urged by the A. F. of L. to give the department's work their support.[16]

By 1906, the Special Committee for Evangelistic Work had developed a strong program of city evangelism, under the leadership of J. Wilbur Chapman. In 1905, Chapman was already spending almost the entire season conducting interdenominational city campaigns along the lines of his simultaneous plan. Specialized work was also going on in lumber camps, colleges and seminaries, saloons, and special geographic areas like the South and Southwest. Desiring to concentrate primarily on city work, the Evangelistic Committee requested in 1906 that its responsibility for evangelistic work in home missionary territory be turned over to the Board of Home Missions.[17] The requested reorganization was made effective by the following year.

According to the new arrangement, the missionary field of the Home Missions Board had been divided into four districts, each with a field secretary appointed by the board: South and Southwest, Northwest, Mountain States, and Pacific Coast. At the request of the Evangelistic Committee, provision was made for the appointment of pastor-evangelists in all presbyteries and a synodical evangelist in each synod so desiring. However, Thompson and the other members of the board did not conceive their task—even in the missionary districts—to be solely the salvation of individuals. The 1907 annual report made clear the board's understanding of the evangelistic work it would undertake.

> [It shall be] constructive and permanent, looking toward the strengthening of the pastoral relation, and making the Church an aggressive spiritual agency in the community. To this end its methods shall have reference to the saving of men from sin and its consequences; to the purification of society and the improving of the social order; to the lifting of higher moral standards; as well as to seeking a deeper devotion to the Church's ministry of grace, to personal work for the spiritual quickening of individuals and the community, and growth in the sense of stewardship.[18]

Meanwhile, the Department of Church and Labor continued to make important progress, adding to its list of activities labor mass meetings on Sunday afternoons during the winter months, a correspondence course in applied Christianity designed primarily for ministers in industrial centers, temperance work with the laboring classes, and conferences on social problems in colleges and universities. Stelzle emphasized Labor Sunday and attempted to secure attendance of labor groups at the Labor Sunday services in the churches. The department reported being increasingly called upon to suggest solutions for various problems regarding capital and labor, and to preside over conferences representing both employers and unions. In 1909, Rev. Warren H. Wilson became Stelzle's assistant.

By 1908, the Federal Council of Churches had been organized and the Commission on the Church and Social Service had begun to move forward under the leadership of a few dedicated men. In all of the commission's early activities, Charles Stelzle played a prominent part. In 1909, he was elected acting secretary for such part-time voluntary service as he could give. In 1910, he pioneered with Josiah Strong and Paul U. Kellogg in the commission's investigation of the steel industry at South Bethlehem, Pennsylvania. In his report on the Social Service Commission to the second quadrennial meeting of the Federal Council in 1912, Charles S. Macfarland acknowledged the commission's debt to the Presbyterian Board of Home Missions: "This Board has largely led the way, has always done a largely unsectarian work and many of the general matters now committed to this Commission and in which other denominational bodies have shared, were initiated by it."[19]

The board's secretary, Charles L. Thompson, was of course an active participant in both the Inter-Church Conference on Federation in 1905, and the Federal Council of Churches in 1908. In addition, he was primarily responsible for the organization in the spring of 1908 of a Home Missions Council, to be composed of representatives of the national home missions boards and societies of the denominations. The aim of the council was "the evangelization of America" by counsel, cooperation, and—where possible—federation of home missions work. Thompson served as president of the Home Missions Council from its inception until his death in 1924.

William H. Roberts: Church Cooperation and Evangelism

The man who united the two concerns of church cooperation and evangelism was Dr. William H. Roberts, stated clerk of the General Assembly and recording secretary of the Special Evangelistic Committee of the Presbyterian Church. Born in Wales in 1844, Roberts came to this country with his family at the age of eleven. His father was a famous preacher in the Welsh Presbyterian Church. After serving four years as a statistician in the Treasury Department in Washington, D.C., and five as an assistant librarian at the Library of Congress, Roberts graduated from Princeton Seminary in 1873 and was ordained by the Presbytery of Elizabeth, New Jersey, the same year. Becoming a permanent clerk of the Presbyterian General Assembly in 1880, he was made stated clerk in 1884, an office he held for thirty-six years, until his death in 1920. From 1880 until he moved permanently to Philadelphia in 1893, he was professor of practical theology at Lane Seminary in Cincinnati. According to Lefferts Loetscher, Roberts was brought to Lane to help win the support of the Old School constituency surrounding the seminary, since his conservative views were well known. Roberts was at Lane when Henry Preserved Smith was suspended from the ministry in December 1893, for his critical views of the Bible.[20]

As an administrator and advocate of church unity, Roberts was indefatigable. He was ardent and effective in promoting unity among Presbyterians. The reunion of the Presbyterian Church in the U.S.A. with the Cumberland Presbyterian Church and the Welsh Presbyterian Church was largely the result of his efforts. For forty-two years he was the American secretary of the Alliance of Reformed Churches Holding the Presbyterian System. As chairman of the Committee of Church Cooperation and Reunion of the Presbyterian General Assembly, he was one of the architects of the Federal Council of Churches. In recognition of his administrative skill and vast knowledge of church polity, he was made chairman of the Executive Committee of the Inter-Church Conference on Federation in 1905, and acting president of the first meeting of the new Federal Council of Churches in 1908. At the 1907 General Assembly, his denomination elected him moderator of the Assembly for 1908, "by acclamation and unanimously," and a message of congratulation came from the Executive Committee of the Inter-Church Conference on Federation praising his "splendid service in the cause of Christian unity."[21] He was a man to be reckoned with.

It was clear from the beginning that Roberts saw the Federal Council as an agency for united evangelistic work. In 1907, the Report of the Special Evangelistic Committee noted that the Inter-Church Federation Movement offered "a splendid opportunity for aggressive and united evangelistic work among all the people."[22] When, as chairman of the Committee on Church Cooperation and Reunion, Roberts reported on the summoning of the Federal Council to meet in 1908, he spoke of its value as "an instrument for bringing to bear the resources of the Churches along spiritual lines for the thorough evangelization not only of the United States, but of the world."[23] In 1911, Roberts's report for the Committee of Church Cooperation and Union recommended, and the Presbyterian General Assembly adopted, a resolution urging "that earnest effort be made to secure more complete cooperation between the denominational agencies engaged in Social Service and Evangelization."[24] It was the first hint of trouble to come.

At the 1911 meeting of the Executive Committee of the Federal Council, a Committee on Evangelism was formed within the council and Roberts made its chairman. Roberts's report to the 1912 General Assembly indicated his satisfaction with the committee's action. "Realizing that Social Service is only one branch of general church work," he reported, "the Executive Committee has established a Commission on Evangelistic Work, composed of members from every denomination in the Federal Council." Through this new committee, Roberts expected, "much good can be accomplished."[25] The General Assembly passed a resolution expressing its pleasure at the organization of the general Evangelistic Committee, with Roberts as its head.[26]

By 1911, the scope of Stelzle's program within the Presbyterian Church had been enlarged to include "consideration of all moral and social problems." Now called the Bureau of Social Service, its principal function as defined by the Home Missions Board was "to study social conditions as they are related to the progress of the Kingdom of God and to suggest to the Church practical ways of realizing the social ideals of the gospel."[27]

In 1911, the bureau devoted special attention to the problems of the city. In February, conferences on the "Downtown Church" were held in eight different cities, including Chicago, Louisville, and Pittsburgh. The most significant venture, however, was the establishment of a Labor Temple on New York's Lower East Side, at Second Avenue and Fourteenth Street, made possible by a gift of some $2 million to the New York Presbytery by John S. Kennedy. The Labor Temple was inaugurated and supervised by the Home Missions Board from 1911-13, and then continued by the Church Extension Committee of the New York Presbytery. The aims of the temple as Thompson described them were "to bring the gospel message to the people of every class and language and with a wide social work to imbue a non-Christian community with the spirit of Christ in all life's relations."[28] The dominant ethnic groups in the community were Russians, Hungarians, and Italians. Special services for immigrants were begun.

In addition, the Labor Temple had several unique features. Stelzle felt there was a great need for open forum discussions on subjects of special interest to workers. The attendance at these meetings was "95 percent men," of whom, according to Stelzle, 75 percent were Socialists and radicals. About 50 percent of those who attended were Jews.[29] Sunday evenings were devoted to religious services, at which Stelzle preached "thoroughly evangelical" sermons, and later in the evening, from nine to ten, a motion picture hour. Stelzle used pledge cards at the Labor Temple, particularly during Holy Week. The statement on the cards was simple and brief; the signer pledged: "I accept the purpose of Jesus—I will help bring in the Kingdom of God."[30] Those who wished could become members of the Labor Temple Fellowship. At the end of its two-year period of responsibility for the temple, the board reported that the experiment had proved that "by an adaptation of its work, and without sacrificing any of the fundamental principles of Christianity, the Church may win the masses."[31]

The Presbyterian Department of Church and Labor had pioneered in the use of surveys to ascertain the religious and social needs of a community. When provision was made for social service as part of the Men and Religion Forward Movement in 1911-12. Stelzle was asked to be dean of the Social Service Department of the campaign. Stelzle recalled that early plans for the movement, made by Fred B. Smith and his associates, had provided for evangelism, missions, Bible study, boys' work, and the like, but had ignored social service. Finally, conceding that interest in social service was so high throughout the church that it must be included, Smith called upon Stelzle to set up a suitable program.[32]

During the winter of 1911, seventy principal American cities were studied. Stelzle prepared the survey blanks, designed the charts, and systematized statistical material for these campaigns. He also led a survey team assigned to a chain of southern cities. In May 1912, Governor Hooper of Tennessee called a Southern Sociological Congress to meet in Nashville to consider the results of Stelzle's findings.[33]

Both the Board of Home Missions and Stelzle were optimistic about the results to be derived from the Men and Religion Forward Movement. The board referred to the movement as "unquestionably the greatest religious movement of the year—if not of this generation," and Stelzle regarded it as "one of the most stirring social movements that ever swept this country."[34] Its practical consequences did not fulfill these high hopes.

The very next year Stelzle was called on to promote a publicity campaign for the Home Missions Council, culminating in Home Mission Week, to present to the churches the "outstanding social and religious problems" facing them. Campaigns were held in 1,000 cities across the nation, local committees arranging and carrying them out in correspondence with the central office. Study classes, conferences, and meetings of "every description and for all kinds of people" were held, presenting what had been the conception of the home missions task held by the Presbyterian Board since Thompson assumed its secretaryship in 1898—namely, that the new frontiers of American life were sociological, not only geographical, and that the resources of the church were desperately needed, both as a "social agency" and as a "great religious force."[35]

That there was a split in the Federal Council by 1912 is confirmed by events within the Presbyterian Church at its next General Assembly in May 1913. First, the assembly adopted two interesting resolutions recommended by the chairman of the Committee on Church Cooperation and Union, William Roberts. At the 1912 session of the Federal Council, an enlarged version of the 1908 Social Creed had been unanimously accepted by the delegates. The 1913 Presbyterian General Assembly passed the following resolution with regard to that Social Creed: "The Assembly, while heartily approving the recognition by the Council of some of those social needs which the Christian Church has so long pointed out, and called on men, in the name of God, to supply, at the same time expresses its conviction, that the power of the Gospel as the source of all true social progress, should be increasingly recognized by the Council in its advocacy of social service." Having given this word of caution to those involved in social service, the assembly went on to praise the council's action with regard to evangelism. "The Assembly also rejoices that the Council recognized Evangelism as the Supreme Mission of the Church, and commends its appointment of a Commission on Evangelism."[36] There is no indication that there was any discussion of the implications of these motions. Very likely they expressed the sentiments of most of the assembly.

The Special Committee on Evangelistic Work then presented its report. The assembly was reminded that Moody himself had once expressed the hope "that the Presbyterian Churches of the world would be federated in a world movement for the revival of spiritual religion and for the salvation of souls." Taking stock of the committee's accomplishments since its inception in 1901, it reported that the emphasis on personal and pastoral evangelism promoted by the committee was now generally accepted by the church at large.[37] It is an indication of the popular feeling within the Presbyterian Church that in 1913, this committee, begun in 1901 as a special committee to meet a peculiar need and reappointed every year by the assembly, was made a Permanent Committee on Evangelism.

A Modification of Methods

The real proof of the split within the Presbyterian Church, however, was the assembly's action with regard to its own social service wing in the Board of Home Missions. By 1912, the direction of this work and the conception of its task on the part of the leadership of the various departments within the board were unmistakable. At its meeting in February 1913, the Executive Commission of the General Assembly received an unidentified paper calling in question the policies and administration of the Board of Home Missions. The paper was referred to a committee of three, who were charged with a full investigation of the board and asked to report back to the Executive Commission on May 14, 1913, just before the opening of the 1913 Assembly. The Executive Commission had received a number of overtures, some asking for an endorsement of the board and its methods, others criticizing the board and asking for certain changes. The report of the investigation was intended as a reply to these overtures.[38]

The questions raised by the Home Board's critics can be gathered from the nature of the report presented by the Executive Commission, which was printed in full in the minutes. Every aspect of the board's work was considered in an attempt to determine whether the expenses incurred by the board were justified by the value of the results. The necessity of some of the expenditures—salaries for the 1,637 home missionaries, 75 pastor-evangelists, and 8 synodical missionaries, for example—was quickly established. It soon became apparent that the real questions concerned the work and value of the board's five special departments, costing the church in 1912, $42,000. These special departments were the Mexican, Indian, Church and Country Life, and Immigration Departments, and the Bureau of Social Service.

As a result of the investigation, the Executive Commission made a number of recommendations to the General Assembly about these special departments, all of which were accepted. The Mexican and Indian Departments were recognized as valuable for the present, but to be discontinued as soon as their work could be taken over by the presbyteries within whose bounds it was located. The Immigration Department was to be continued, its efficiency commended, and its work "encouraged and pushed vigorously." The Department of the Church and Country Life was to be disbanded, country churches to be looked after by home missions committees of the presbyteries, and any necessary surveys or investigations to be made henceforth by the Bureau of Social Service.[39]

Of greatest interest for our purposes were the Commission's recommendations concerning Stelzle's Bureau of the Church and Social Service. The much-criticized Labor Temple was to be transferred to the supervision and support of the Presbytery of New York. The other recommendations were as follows:

> That, although considerable criticism is made of the Bureau of Social Service, these criticisms seem to relate to methods rather than functions; that a Bureau of Social Service "to study social conditions as they are related to the progress of the Kingdom of God, and to suggest to the Church practical ways of realizing the social ideals of the Gospel" is needed and should be continued, but with such modification in methods as will more fully exalt and magnify the Church as the Body of Christ, and with such enlargement of its scope as to include Social Service in Country Life.[40]

In closing, the Executive Commission acknowledged the magnitude of the home missions problem, the wise policies generally adopted by the board in meeting difficult conditions, and the board's readiness to receive "counsel as to supervision and methods of administration." The commission further desired to place on record its commendation of the board and its officers and its recognition of their faithfulness and "successful achievements."[41] Nevertheless, it is clear that the Executive Commission had been under considerable pressure from the critics of the board's policies, and that its recommended changes were an attempt to satisfy them.

Unfortunately, the paper received by the Executive Commission and responsible for the initiation of this investigation had somehow been made public before the commission completed its report. The publicity given to the paper had apparently aroused much feeling against the board, and the Executive Commission expressed its regret for this occurrence and its assurance to the church at large that no doubt was being raised as to the integrity of the officers of the board.[42]

The extent of the opposition was more clearly revealed by the report of the Standing Committee on Home Missions to the 1913 General Assembly. With reference to the Executive Commission's report, the Standing Committee had this to say:

> Your Committee feels that the recommendations of the Executive Commission, adopted by the Assembly, regarding the work of the Board of Home Missions, indicate the Assembly's earnest desire for a new departure in

the methods of the Board *in the direction of an increase in evangelistic emphasis* [emphasis mine]. This will be a matter of approval by the whole Church.

Your Committee has learned with satisfaction that the Social Service Department has been directed by the Assembly to make its methods more definitely religious in their character. It earnestly urges the Board that this should be done, and points out that the salvation of men is through the Gospel of Christ, and that this is the vital and essential work committed to it by the Church, not in its evangelistic department alone, but in all its departments and through all of its officers.[43]

The report of the Standing Committee showed a decrease of some $71,000 from the previous year in contributions to the Home Board. Without qualification, the committee attributed this decrease to the criticism of the board, but urged that with the action of this assembly and the "cheerful acquiescence of the Board," ministers might be expected to renew their "interest, confidence and gifts" for the board's work. Finally, the assembly passed a resolution on the committee's recommendation, expressing its confidence in the board and its secretaries and commending them "to the liberality and confidence of the whole Church."[44]

Thus the proceedings of the 1913 General Assembly offer clear evidence of a widespread suspicion and disapproval of the social service wing within the Presbyterian Church. Furthermore, the opposition does not seem to have decreased by the 1914 Assembly, in spite of the assembly's extensive changes in the board's structure and methods.

In 1914, the Committee on Church Cooperation and Union once again approved the Federal Council's recognition of social needs, but cautioned it to remember that the source of all true social progress remains the power of the Gospel. It further advised its representatives to the council to be careful of action on subjects bordering on "the two independent jurisdictions of the Church and the State."[45]

With regard to its own Home Board, the General Assembly suggested still more extensive reorganization. The special departments were to be abolished and the board's organization vastly simplified by dividing all the work into four general departments: Executive or Administration, Church Extension (with its headquarters in the West), Immigration and Social Service, and Finance. The extent of the criticism of the board within the church appears to have become an embarrassment to the Executive Commission. After the report of the Standing Committee on Home Missions advocating these further changes had been read and accepted, the chairman of the Executive Commission requested permission to present a statement to the assembly and ordered it printed in the minutes.

The statement affirmed that the Executive Commission was in no way responsible for the "detrimental reports" printed in the public press and otherwise circulated as to the Home Board and its work. It regretted any inconvenience or embarrassment the Home Board might have suffered as a result and expressed emphatically its disapproval of such publicity. "As a Commission," it insisted, "we have confidence in the Board and appreciate the sincere efforts they have made to meet the increasing needs and varied interests of their great work. We have had differences in interpretation and definition as to methods of work; . . . [but we] here affirm our mutual confidence and hearty good will."[46] In closing, the commission urged united effort for the advancement of the Kingdom and an end to "prejudices and littlenesses."

The Superintendent's Resignation

However, in some respects the damage had already been done; the report of the Board of Home Missions for 1914 noted with sincere regret the resignation of the superintendent of the Bureau of Social Service, Rev. Charles Stelzle, in order that he might take up "a broader social ministry."[47] Stelzle's account of what happened, as he recalled it in his autobiography, casts light on the events of 1913-14. He attributed the opposition to the board's work to several factors within the Presbyterian Church: the question of reunion with other, more conservative Presbyterian groups like the Southern Presbyterian Church, the United Presbyterian Church, and the Reformed Presbyterian Church; the growing feeling within the church that there were too many special departments, headed by "experts"; and increased resistance from the conservatives as the social service wing of the church grew larger and more powerful.[48]

Stelzle did not refer to the paper that first attracted the attention of the Executive Commission and resulted in the reorganization of the board, but he did attribute the changes to the opposition of "a small coterie of Conservatives living mainly in and about Pittsburgh." According to him, this opposition was "so determined and so bitter" that the board gradually became timid about the newer features of its work under criticism. As a result of the investigation, the budget for Stelzle's department was drastically cut. Recognizing that the chief function of the board was, after all, to raise the necessary funds to carry on its work, Stelzle offered to resign. He stated specifically that he would be willing to return after the reorganization if the board wished him to, providing he could approve the way the program was organized. He felt he could not work under the new plan and so he resigned in the fall of 1913.[49]

In his autobiography, Stelzle took care to explain what he saw as the implications of the reorganization. "It had been decided in substance," he said,

> that instead of promoting a special social service program, an attempt would be made to "socialize" every Department of the Board's work, which, it later developed, was an exceedingly vague term and meant substantially that the Presbyterian Church, through the only Board which could express its convictions, determined to have nothing further to do with outstanding industrial problems, but rather to limit its activity to "social welfare work" in the local church. In other words, the comprehensive program in the field of industry became thoroughly emasculated and finally was dropped altogether.[50]

Stelzle acknowledged that there had never been any "unkind personal feeling" between his superiors in the board and himself, and that the officials of the board generally stood loyally for his program "even though at times they did not understand it nor approve it in its entirety." Much of the opposition to Stelzle's work seems to have been on financial grounds. Thus when he protested in the name of the church against the "unnecessary slaughter of workingmen in the Pittsburgh rolling mills," he was reminded by a former moderator of the General Assembly that he was " 'killing the goose that lays the golden egg.' " One prominent member of the board said he was "unalterably opposed" to what Stelzle was doing because his various enterprises (particularly the Labor Temple) were merely "sink holes" into which the board had for years been pouring its money. Such men felt that board money should be used only to organize churches that could later give a generous return on the investment.[51] This whole experience apparently convinced Stelzle that work done as the representative of a particular denomination was bound to be restricted, and that he wished to be free to engage in larger forms of social service for any groups desiring his services.

Charles Stelzle's resignation caused widespread comment in the religious press. An editorial in the Presbyterian *Continent* stated that the members of the board had put forth every possible effort to induce Stelzle to change his mind, and further urged the board on behalf of the church "to give him all [the] liberty he asks."[52] The conservative *Presbyterian*, however, approved of Stelzle's decision to withdraw from the board, saying that his drift from "the service of the Gospel" into sociology had long been coming and that Stelzle would surely "pass on into Socialism" if he continued in his present course.[53] Commendatory editorials appeared in journals like the *Christian Evangelist* and the *Baptist Examiner*. An official publication of the Home Missions Board, issued about a year after Stelzle's resignation, gave him due credit for the "definitive influence" he had exerted on the form in which social service was adopted by the churches.[54]

After resigning from the board, Stelzle began a speaking campaign throughout the country. At the Executive Committee meeting of the Federal Council in Columbus, Ohio, in 1915, Stelzle expressed his disappointment at the church's failure to make operative the Social Creed it had adopted in 1908. Taking up Stelzle's challenge, Charles S. Macfarland promptly offered him the position of field secretary for special service. This work Stelzle pursued from June 1916 until the United States entered the war in 1918, when he took charge of publicity for the American Red Cross in Washington in the field of industry and the church.[55]

The Larger Terms of the Kingdom

In 1914, the Presbyterian Board of Home Missions lost another of its outstanding men. In March 1914, Charles L. Thompson, now seventy-five years old, announced his intention to resign the secretaryship. It is difficult to know how large a part the criticisms of the board in 1913 and 1914 played in this decision. Thompson said he felt he should give his place to a younger man and devote his remaining strength to the interdenominational work of the Home Missions Council.[56] This work he was to continue until his death ten years later.

Thompson's work for the board had covered sixteen formative years. It was his vision that home missions work should consider "the denomination less and the common interests of the Kingdom more." Furthermore, he was largely responsible for recognizing that the task of home missions for the twentieth century involved not so much geographic extension as "getting a grasp on those problems of social and moral and educational conditions"[57] which were threatening the very foundations of American society. Thus new departments were organized to deal with the problems of modern rural populations, immigration, and the city.

Thompson referred to the criticism of these special departments. "The creation of these new departments in which educational, social and reformatory work was done, as well as that which is strictly evangelical, awakened a good deal of criticism among men of limited vision, who had not yet learned what the Church should do under the new conditions to christianize our nation."[58]

Thompson attributed the opposition of the conservatives in the Presbyterian Church to two major factors. First, many of them assumed "that somehow these lines of work antagonized personal salvation." To them, Thompson attempted to make it clear that what the board was doing was "quite in harmony with the most conservative views of the gospel, that we were not bringing in an innovation but only stating in modern terms what dated back to the days of the Apostles."[59] Second, Thompson felt that many Presbyterians were reluctant to think in the larger terms of the Kingdom if it meant (as it did) considering their own denomination less. Early efforts to eliminate competition on the home missions field met with considerable resistance, and such feeling was behind some of the opposition to Stelzle's work as well.

Referring once more to the situation at the time of his resignation, Thompson said that the criticisms of conservatives, together with the announcement of his intention to resign, "raised somewhat of a tempest in certain quarters."[60] However, the General Assembly in 1914 adopted a resolution expressing its profound appreciation of Thompson's sixteen years of service as general secretary of the Board of Home Missions, praising him for "his prophetic vision and utterance, his inspiring leadership, his indomitable courage, [and] his large-minded statesmanship. . . . We thank God," the resolution concluded, "that if he must lay down his task, it can be with the glad consciousness that he has served the Church of God as it is given to few men to serve her."[61]

Thus the conflict in the Presbyterian Church affords a microcosmic view of the way evangelical Protestants lined up on one or the other side of the polemic between social Christianity and individualistic evangelicalism. And it confirms that 1912 was the critical year for the split.

EIGHT

Innocent Bystanders

As I have traced the course of a developing polemic in American Protestantism, I have seen it as a family quarrel, in the sense that both sides grew out of the evangelical Protestantism that was dominant in American religious life by 1850. I have suggested that by the mid-nineteenth century, American Congregationalists, Presbyterians, Episcopalians, Baptists, and Methodists had become "assimilated to a common type"[1] that might be identified as Evangelicalism, and that they shared remarkably similar views about the church and its relation to society.

During the late nineteenth century, a social Christianity began to develop out of this evangelical Protestantism under the impact of new intellectual and social challenges. There were still those who held fast to the older individualism, although they often buttressed their views with a new biblical literalism and premillennialism. There were also American Protestants who did not participate in this polemic, although their own traditions might have ranged them on one side or the other in the long run. It is important to look at these "innocent bystanders" in order to gain perspective on the split I have been examining and in order to test the accuracy of the observations thus far.

In the introduction to his classic study, *Protestant Churches and Industrial America*, Henry May explained why he concentrated on the five major denominations I have described as evangelical. These churches, stemming from a common heritage and having undergone the same influences in early American religious history, represented by mid-century a "well-established Protestant bloc." Other groups differed from this bloc either in their European ties (Lutheran and Reformed), their largely rural constituencies that cut them off from the first shocks of industrial crisis (Disciples), or their basic religious outlook (e.g., Quakers, Christian Scientists). Thus, while they would be fitting objects for study, May felt they would require separate investigation and therefore chose to omit them.[2]

This chapter sketches out, with these rough categories in mind, where other Protestants stood in the years I have been examining. In no case can this be anything more than a brief survey. The point is, after all, simply to demonstrate how their experience differed from that of the dominant evangelical denominations, and why these differences were crucial with regard to the basic polemic I have been following. Since most of the history of social Christianity focused on the urban areas of the East and Midwest, it is also useful to look briefly at the situation in the South, to see whether comparable developments took place there at any time before 1912.

Lutherans

There were German and Scandinavian Lutherans in the Dutch Colony of New Netherland, the first Lutheran Church being organized in 1649.[3] However, most of the Lutherans in the American colonies were German refugees from the Palatinate who came—some by way of England—to Pennsylvania after 1720 and either settled there or moved to other colonies such as Virginia, Maryland, the Carolinas, and Georgia.[4] The organization of churches among these immigrants proceeded slowly until 1742, when the pietists at Halle answered the plea for help from Lutherans in Philadelphia and sent the young Henry Melchior Muhlenberg to aid in this work. By 1748, enough strong congregations had been organized to warrant the formation of the Ministerium of Pennsylvania, the first permanent Lutheran synod in America. By 1771, Muhlenberg reported eighty-one congregations under his care in Pennsylvania and adjacent colonies, and about thirty in other parts of the country.[5]

During the American Revolution, all correspondence with Halle was interrupted, and the Lutheran Church quietly obtained its independence. The synodical constitution was revised in terms of complete American control and democratic procedure, and a hymnbook, liturgy, and ministerial acts were printed. However, the Lutheran Church in America was still dependent on Europe for its ministry. A significant step forward was the organization in 1820 of the General Synod of the Lutheran Church in the United States. In this, as in the founding of the first official synodical Lutheran seminary in America at Gettysburg in 1826, Samuel S. Schmucker was the moving spirit.

Under Schmucker's leadership, American Lutheranism might well have become assimilated to the common evangelical type of American Protestantism. After 1820, Lutherans were organized locally for participation in the activities of various Protestant benevolent societies, particularly in congregations of synods belonging to the General Synod.[6] In 1838, Schmucker issued a *Fraternal Appeal* urging all branches of evangelical Protestantism in America to unite in a single Apostolic Protestant Church.[7] During the agitation over New Measures revivalism of the Finney type, Schmucker was on the side of the liberals who supported the New Measures. He was involved in the founding of the American branch of the Evangelical Alliance in 1846. He might have succeeded in Americanizing Lutheranism, had it not been for both a resurgence of confessionalism in the General Synod and a new wave of German immigration, which brought to America several groups of conservatives concerned with preserving the "pure and undefiled" faith of the historic Lutheran confessions.

In 1839, a group of immigrants from Saxony arrived in Missouri, having fled from the rationalism of the official church in their homeland. Leadership of the group soon fell to the young C. F. W. Walther, who became pastor of the congregation in St. Louis. In 1844, he began publication of *Der Lutheraner*, a polemical paper designed to expound confessional Lutheranism and to refute "those teachings that falsely call themselves Lutheran."[8] As immigration continued, steps were taken to form a new synod and in 1847 at Chicago, Walther became president of the German Evangelical Lutheran Synod of Missouri, Ohio, and other States. Other conservative synods were formed by immigrants from other parts of Germany, including the Buffalo Synod in 1845, the Wisconsin Synod in 1850, and the Iowa Synod in 1854. Although they engaged in doctrinal controversy among themselves and with the Missouri Synod, all of them were influenced by Walther, who after 1850 devoted full time to writing and teaching in the theological department of the Missouri Synod college (later Concordia Seminary) in St. Louis.[9]

As discussed in Chapter I, the period after 1837 saw the breakup of the old evangelical empire and renewed sectarian emphases. The Old and New School Presbyterians split in 1837, the Congregationalists and Presbyterians abrogated their Plan of Union, and Methodists and Baptists withdrew from the cooperative benevolent societies. The resurgence of more churchly Protestant traditions in the 1830s and 1840s had the immediate effect of stimulating denominationalism. Lutherans, Old School Presbyterians, High Church Anglicans, and the Mercersburg movement among the German Reformed challenged the dominant "Puritan-revivalistic-unionistic"[10] Protestantism by emphasizing the objective aspects of Christianity—creed, sacraments, or institutional features—as identifying the true church. Had the exponents of these churchly traditions been less scholastic in their creedal emphasis and less conservative in their social thinking, they might have offered a vital corrective to the dominant evangelicalism. However, they failed to win any appreciable following in terms of their central emphasis on the church, and on the Protestant religious scene as a whole, radical individualism continued to reign.

One form this renewed stress on ecclesiastical action took was the insistence that the church itself should conduct missionary and educational ventures (as opposed to groups of individuals, as in the benevolent societies). Thus in 1845, the Lutherans began to withdraw from cooperation with other churches in benevolence and organized the Home Missionary Society of the General Synod. After 1850, the Americanized Lutheranism of Schmucker was repudiated by the General Synod, and leaders and policies committed to a confessional program came into control. The foremost spokesmen for this new confessionalism were Charles Philip Krauth, professor at Gettysburg Seminary from 1850 to 1867, and his son, Charles Porterfield Krauth, who as a third-generation American was an especially effective advocate of this revived confessionalism in the English-speaking Lutheran churches.[11]

From 1830 to 1870, the membership of the Lutheran Church in America grew more than ninefold, largely as the result of the increased volume of German immigration after 1840. In 1870, the Lutherans were fourth in size among the Protestant churches, having a membership of about 400,000.[12] Although the great volume of Scandinavian immigration came later, Norwegian and Swedish immigrants also helped to strengthen the confessional reaction in this period. In 1860, the Scandinavian Evangelical Lutheran Augustana Synod of North America was organized, making clear by its very title its intention to preserve "the unaltered Augsburg Confession" as its doctrinal standard.[13]

With this background in mind, then, we are ready to look at the years from 1877 to 1912, which were crucial for the development of the polemic between individualistic and social Christianity in the mainline Protestant denominations, in order to see where the Lutheran Church stood in relation to this polemic. In general, the Lutherans were, as one Lutheran historian put it, "not among the first"[14] to develop a social gospel. They tended to conceive of the work of the church as mainly concerned with a spiritual ministry, and although Lutherans in urban areas were active in various relief and charitable organizations, their general attitude was that social reform must begin with individuals.[15]

There were many reasons for this general position. Actually, Lutheran influence on the whole was not really felt in the religious life of the nation until after World War I.[16] The reasons were much the same for both. The volume of immigration was a major factor. From 1870 to 1910, 3 million Germans entered the country, perhaps two-thirds of them of Protestant background, and about 1.75 million Scandinavians arrived, nearly all of them Lutheran by tradition. By 1910, the number of Lutheran communicants had increased to over 2,225,000, making the Lutherans the third largest Protestant denominational grouping.[17] The effort required simply to keep up with this tremendous influx of population was considerable, and the overwhelming majority of these Lutherans also tended to settle in self-sufficient rural communities. Many of them were further isolated because of the language barrier. Thus for social reasons they were considerably removed from the urban and industrial conditions that were perplexing the older evangelical denominations in this period. In addition, the whole Lutheran theological tradition, as opposed to the Calvinistic, tended to separate the spiritual and the temporal realms and to see the church's task as primarily concerned with the former. Finally, there was little organizational unity among the various Lutheran groups, representing different nationalities, conditions of settlement, and doctrinal emphases. Winthrop Hudson counted twenty-four different Lutheran groups in America in 1900.[18]

There was at least one notable exception to these generalizations, however, Lutheranism contributed a major figure to the social Christian movement in the person of Dr. J. H. W. Stuckenberg, whose *Christian Sociology*, published in 1880, was a "brilliant and pioneering outline"[19] of the social implications of the New Testament. Stuckenberg's background points up once again some of the reasons for the development of a social gospel. An immigrant in early childhood, Stuckenberg grew up in Pittsburgh and Cincinnati. He studied for the ministry at Wittenberg College in the 1850s, completing his theological education in Germany at the University of Halle in 1861 and at the Universities of Göttingen and Berlin after the close of the Civil War.

When in 1866-1867, the confessional party in the Lutheran General Synod withdrew to form the General Council, Stuckenberg was part of the minority party of the Pittsburgh Synod that insisted on remaining with the General Synod. Thus he chose to identify himself with the liberals, or "American Lutheran" party, rather than with those who demanded unreserved adherence to the Lutheran confessions. From 1868 to 1873, Stuckenberg served a largely working-class congregation in Pittsburgh. In 1873, he was called to Wittenberg College, in Springfield, Ohio, where he taught theology for seven years until poor health required rest and change. He and his wife left for

Berlin in 1880, little dreaming that their stay abroad would last fourteen years.[20]

In *Christian Sociology*, Stuckenberg insisted that the church must seek to build a Christian society in which the teachings of Christ are applied to human relationships. As C. H. Hopkins pointed out, it was another twenty years before the thought of the maturing social gospel began to be based on the social teachings of Jesus.[21] The social gospelers might have benefited considerably from Stuckenberg's training in both theology and sociology had they been aware of his work. Unfortunately *Christian Sociology* received little notice.

After returning to America in 1894, Stuckenberg settled in Cambridge, Massachusetts, where he was to remain the rest of his life, devoting his time to writing and occasional lecture tours. From 1895 until his death in 1903, he was editor of the Department of Sociology for the *Homiletic Review*. In 1894, he spoke at the Institute of Christian Sociology at Oberlin, of which Washington Gladden was president. His later writings dealt primarily with social and economic theory: *The Social Problem*, 1897; *Introduction to the Study of Sociology*, 1898; and *Sociology: The Science of Human Society*, published shortly after his death.[22]

Stuckenberg did not win many of his fellow Lutherans for the social gospel. When invited in 1902 to attend the meeting of his synod in Pennsylvania, Stuckenberg replied from Cambridge:

> I cherish no delusions respecting my position. My isolation is not due to location but to my specialty. I am trying to save Sociology from its materialistic and agnostic basis, and am told that I am not doing the work of the Church.
>
> I am trying to promote the Christian social movement in the spirit of Christ, and according to the teachings of the New Testament, and I am told that I am not doing the work of the Church. . . .
>
> Other denominations open their churches and institutions and heartily welcome me. One of my books will soon appear in Rome, in Italian. But my own Church is closed to me because I am not doing its work! Yet, I remain in that Church, as best I can, because outside of the great principles on which Luther based the Reformation, there is no place for me.[23]

Even John Evjen, Stuckenberg's biographer, felt he was wrong in thinking the church could reform the world or preach a social gospel. It is not surprising that the only official Lutheran body to appoint a standing committee on "The Church and Social Service" was Stuckenberg's Pittsburgh Synod, which did so in 1913.[24]

The following year, the Pittsburgh Synod cited statements of the Federal Council in protest against labor conditions and urged the need for general Christian social reform. The response of the General Synod was that the church could make its best contribution to the solution of social problems "by holding itself strictly to its 'churchly' duty of preaching the gospel, winning individual members of society to salvation, and using their consecrated lives in service for Christ's kingdom."[25] At its meeting in 1915, the General Synod repeated and emphasized the same conviction.

However, the impact of the social gospel had apparently been felt in some areas of the General Synod, which encompassed the most urban and industrialized regions served by the Lutheran Church. The General Synod was the only Lutheran body to participate from the outset in the formation of the Federal Council of Churches. When the newly organized National Federation of Churches and Christian Workers sent out a letter in 1901, announcing its intention to give way as soon as possible to an official federation of national denominations, the Lutheran General Synod was one of nine denominations represented by the signers.[26] George U. Wenner (Lutheran, General Synod) signed the letter sent out in 1903 calling an Inter-Church Conference on Federation to meet in 1905, and the General Synod of the Lutheran Church was the only Lutheran body to send delegates to the 1905 conference.[27] The Swedish Lutheran Augustana Synod sent representatives to the first session of the Federal Council of Churches in 1908, but it was one of four groups that had withdrawn from membership by 1913.[28]

Perhaps the General Synod might have been more fully involved in social action and interdenominational cooperation had it not been for negotiations leading to the reunion in 1918 of the General Synod, the General Council, and the United Synod in the South to form the United Lutheran Church. For the sake of harmony with these more conservative bodies, members of the General Synod apparently toned down their social involvement and cooperation in "general Christian enterprise."[29] The United Lutheran Church maintained what it preferred to call a "consultative" relationship to the Federal Council. However, it was not until the 1930s that most Lutheran groups began to move in the direction of a full social service program comparable to that of the mainline denominations in the Federal Council.

Largely because there was not a strong social gospel movement in Lutheranism, there was not a conservative movement comparable to that in the mainline Protestant denominations. Most Lutherans were opposed to the social gospel and liberalism and only within parts of the General Synod was

179

there anything like a genuine social Christianity in this period. With most of its constituency in the rural Midwest, the Missouri Synod was the stronghold of Lutheran conservatism. However, because its conservative character was shaped not only by its reliance on biblical authority, but also by its adherence to the historic Lutheran confessions and its loyalty to the writings of Martin Luther and the seventeenth-century dogmaticians of Lutheran orthodoxy, the Missouri Synod could not identify completely with the conservatives of other denominations. Missouri Synod members expressed sympathy with the Fundamentalists in their battle against biblical criticism and theological liberalism, but, as Milton L. Rudnick put it, their rejoicing was "always from the sidelines."[30] Missouri Synod Lutherans frequently called attention to the "sharp differences between Calvinistic Fundamentalism and confessional Lutheranism," even on issues like the interpretation of Scripture.[31]

With regard to social issues, the Missouri Synod held that the functions of the church were strictly spiritual, and while the church might testify against social wrongs, it was not its proper task to attempt to deal with economic or political problems. In an article by Theodore Graebner (editor) in the 1920 *Lutheran Witness* entitled "The Church and Industrial Disputes," this position was elaborated in terms of strict separation between the realms of the church and the state. In answer to the question, "has the Church the right and the duty . . . to raise her voice against low wages, poor housing conditions, unfair contracts, and other forms of social injustice?" Graebner replied:

> The Church has the right and duty to speak, wherever the Lord of the Church has commanded her to speak. Moreover, the Church has the right only to speak that which the Lord has commissioned her to speak. Because the Lord has not established that the eight-hour day is demanded by social justice, and that the twelve-hour day constitutes a case of social injustice, the Church has no right to speak for the one or against the other. For the settlement of all such questions, God has endowed men with reason, and has ordained another institution, the State. . . . [The Church's] commission is a spiritual one. It is, to call men to repentance and to point them to the Cross of Jesus Christ and His atonement. Jesus was more than once confronted with questions involving social justice, and in each case He refused to be arbiter.[32]

The author went on to explain that the church should testify against social wrongs when it knew them to exist, but that its aim in so doing must be only to convert individuals from their selfishness. The church's task must never be enforcement of what it saw as right, or it would be encroaching on the territory of the state. "Only the children of God can be instructed in righteousness."[33] Therefore, Christians as individual citizens should exert their influence for social justice, but in no sense were they to speak for the church. According to Graebner, the church could not exert herself for any "economic or social program without trespassing on a field in which she has no commission from her Lord."[34]

Missouri Synod Lutherans, then, for reasons of their own tradition, ended up on virtually the same side as the individualistic evangelicals although they did not participate in the polemic on the social question, particularly in the period from 1877 to 1917. The Missouri Synod, predominant in the federation of other conservative synods in The Evangelical Lutheran Synodical Conference of North America in 1872,[35] continued to maintain its aloofness from other Lutheran bodies and from all agencies of Protestant cooperation down to the 1960s. While it never became a member of either the Federal Council or its successor in 1950, the National Council of Churches, neither did it align itself with either of the two conservative agencies, the National Association of Evangelicals or the American Council of Christian Churches. It still remains outside any conciliar structure in order to preserve doctrinal purity.

The synod's convention in Cleveland in 1962 did seem to represent something of a turning point for the Missouri Synod, however. The convention decided that without compromising the Scriptures or Lutheran Confessions, there was room for a new spirit, particularly with regard to relations with other Lutherans and the recognition that the Gospel of Christ has social implications. Thus the convention urged representatives of the Missouri Synod to enter into conversations with fellow Christians with the synod's full approval. And in keeping with this new intention, the Lutheran Church-Missouri Synod (incorporating in 1964 the small National Lutheran Church) became on January 1, 1967, a member of the Lutheran Council in the U.S.A.[36] Finally, at the convention meeting in 1962, a Commission on Social Action was created "to initiate studies and secure 'position papers' on subjects of critical interest."[37] As the synod recognized, the convention's stress on the social implications of the Gospel was "a decisive move forward" in this church's attempt to relate itself to the needs of American society.[38]

Obviously it is not possible to survey as thoroughly as I have the Lutheran Church, each of the Protestant groups in America that differed because of European ties, rural constituency, or basic religious outlook from the mainline evangelical denominations. Because of having dealt at some length with the way European roots and continuing immigration were related to American developments in Lutheranism, however, it should now be possible simply to sketch out how these factors were related in the histories of a number of other Protestant groups.

German Reformed and Evangelical Synod

Two other German groups—the Reformed Church in the U.S. and the Evangelical Synod of North America—shared certain developments with the Lutherans but came out of significantly different theological and ecclesiastical traditions. I consider them together because in 1934 they united to become the Evangelical and Reformed Church.[39]

The German Reformed Church in the U.S. had its real beginnings in the same wave of immigration that brought so many German Lutherans to Pennsylvania after 1720. They came from the Palatinate and German-speaking Switzerland and, like the Lutherans, were often without pastors or adequate financial resources. John Philip Boehm, a farmer and son of a Reformed minister in Germany, informally assumed pastoral duties over three Pennsylvania congregations in 1725, although he was not ordained. After the arrival two years later of George Michael Weiss, a German Reformed minister, Boehm was ordained by the Dutch Reformed ministers of New York in 1729, and the two men worked together. The first real organization of German Reformed congregations took place after the arrival in 1746 of Michael Schlatter, a Swiss, educated and ordained in the Netherlands, who had been sent by the Synods of Holland to organize congregations into a *coetus*, or synod. This occurred in 1747 in Philadelphia, and the church continued to be responsible to and partly supported financially by the Dutch Synods until 1793. In that year, the *coetus* became the Synod of the Reformed German Church in the United States of America.

During the period from 1800 to 1837, when the American denominations were becoming assimilated to a common evangelicalism, the German Reformed Church was also influenced by the New Measures revivalism. As in Lutheranism, however, there was a churchly reaction among the Reformed in the 1840s, this one centered around John W. Nevin and Philip Schaff at Mercersburg Seminary in Pennsylvania. Nevin, the principal leader of the movement, had come to Mercersburg in 1840 after teaching at Western (Presbyterian) Seminary in Allegheny, now Pittsburgh, Pennsylvania. His *The Anxious Bench*, published in 1843, was an attack on the New Measures revivalism of Finney and others, and a plea to the German churches to cultivate a true spiritual revival, "centered in the life of the Church and nourished and guided through the catechetical system."[40] His major work, *The Mystical Presence* (1846), sought to substitute for the individualistic conception of Christianity central to revivalistic evangelicalism, an organic conception of the church in which "the mystical participation of the faithful in the life of Christ through the sacrament of the Lord's Supper" was central to the corporate life of the church.[41] Nevin's thought and work were much enriched by the presence of Philip Schaff, a native Swiss, educated in Germany, who came to Mercersburg to teach from 1843-1863.

As a number of historians[42] have pointed out, Nevin's *Mystical Presence* was one of the ablest American theological writings of this period. His work brought him into collision with both the scholasticism of the Princeton school and the defenders of New School doctrines and practices. His views were truer to the Reformed wing of the Reformation than those of his adversaries, particularly with regard to the doctrine of the church, but he was not to be appreciated until the issues he was addressing became of more general concern in the twentieth century. After the Civil War, the German Reformed Church was bitterly divided between those who supported Nevin and those who opposed him. Rival educational institutions were established and the denomination came near actual schism. Finally, in 1878, a peace commission was appointed and gradually the conflict subsided. However, most of the church's energies for a decade and a half had been absorbed by the controversy.

Another major responsibility was provision for the German Reformed immigrants who came in such numbers from 1840 to 1870 and then on into the twentieth century. Like the Lutherans, they formed a large rural constituency. Thus it was that the German Reformed Church in the period from 1877 to 1912 was largely occupied with benevolent work, foreign and home missions, and Christian education and publication. However, it not only became a charter member of the Federal Council by participating in the Inter-Church Conference on Federation in 1905, but it also followed the lead of the mainline denominations and appointed a Commission on Social Service in 1917.[43]

The other party to the 1934 merger, the Evangelical Synod of North America, was the American counterpart of the Evangelical Church of Prussia, which brought Lutherans and Reformed together in 1817. Its beginnings can be traced back to 1840, when groups of pietistic German immigrants of

Lutheran and Reformed backgrounds united in the Evangelical Union of the West. As the movement spread, other United Evangelical synods were formed—the Synods of the Northwest, and of the East. Finally, in 1872, these synods were united in the Evangelical Synod of North America. In 1871, a proseminary was opened at Elmhurst, Illinois (Elmhurst College), and in 1883, the building was completed for Eden Seminary in St. Louis. These schools played an important part in the growth of the denomination; in fact, the common need to train ministers for the German Evangelical people in the United States was one of the most effective motives in uniting the separate synods. It should be kept in mind that whereas the Lutherans and German Reformed each had a history in America dating back to colonial times, and thus a more "Americanized" wing to balance somewhat the European immigration that came flooding into the Midwest after 1840, the Evangelical Synod was entirely the product of this wave of immigration. In both rural areas and cities, the Germans tended to settle in compact communities where the use of German was perpetuated in the churches until past the turn of the century. Thus provision for the needs of its own people was the major concern of the Evangelical Synod until after 1900.

Nonetheless, the Evangelical Synod, like the German Reformed Church, was a charter member of the Federal Council. Probably stimulated by the council's work in the area of social service and by the concerns of the world war, the General Conference of 1917 approved the report of the newly created Commission for National Welfare and suggested that the name be changed to the Commission on Christianity and Social Problems. Among other things, the commission reported that it had brought Walter Rauschenbusch to Eden Seminary for a lecture on social issues. In 1925, the commission urged the adoption of a declaration in favor of outlawing war and of the "Social Ideals of the Churches" as enunciated by the Federal Council of Churches.[44] At one time, no less a figure than Reinhold Niebuhr served as a representative of the Evangelical Synod to the Federal Council. (He also served as chairman of the council's Commission on the Church and Social Service.) When the Evangelical and Reformed Church was formed in 1934, one of the four commissions provided for in its constitution was a commission on Christian Social Action.[45]

Among the factors that predisposed certain denominations to develop a social Christianity in the late nineteenth century would seem to have been: exposure to urban and industrial conditions, an educated ministry with large middle-class constituencies, availability of a tradition of responsibility for the social order, receptivity to new, solidaristic trends of thought, and a reaction against the excessive individualism of both American society and evangelical Protestant religion in the nineteenth century. All of these factors were present in the five denominations that developed a social gospel before the end of the nineteenth century.

The experience of these three European bodies—the Lutheran, German Reformed, and the Evangelical Synod—was very different from that of the mainline evangelical denominations on the American scene throughout the century. Not only were their European traditions reinforced by successive waves of immigration from the 1840s to the end of the century, but when once the immigrants reached this country, they tended to be isolated from American developments because of their rural conditions and language barriers, as well as differing theological views.

Where these denominations lacked exposure to urban and industrial conditions they tended to develop a social program later, often under the influence of the Federal Council's Social Creed and social service activities, and the concerns stimulated by the war. However, some were prevented by doctrinal concerns or a tradition of strict separation between the realms of the church and the state, as in Lutheranism, from moving in this direction. It would appear that only those denominations which shared to some extent the experiences of evangelical Protestantism—like the Lutheran General Synod—were interested in developing a social Christianity in the late nineteenth and early twentieth centuries.

Disciples of Christ

The simple fact of a predominantly rural constituency served to delay the development of a social gospel even in an indigenous American denomination like the Disciples of Christ. The Disciples grew out of two movements in the first decade of the nineteenth century which, as Disciples historian Winfred E. Garrison put it, "conceived of the restoration of simple New Testament Christianity not only as a duty in itself but also as a means for the promotion of unity among Christians."[46] The first of these began in 1803, when five Presbyterian ministers withdrew from the Synod of Kentucky and organized a separate presbytery. Nine months later, they left the Presbyterian Church altogether and organized the "Christian church." Under the leadership of Barton W. Stone, the movement was an outgrowth of the camp meeting revivalism that culminated in the Cane Ridge revival in 1801. Among the reasons for their separation were rejection of the Westminster Confession as the standard of doctrine and reliance on Scriptures only, objection in particular to the Presbyterian doctrine of election and the belief instead that all might believe and be saved, insistence on the independence of each local congregation, and the desire to put an end to sectarian divisions in Christendom.[47]

The second movement was that led by Thomas Campbell, who withdrew in 1809 from the Seceder branch of the Presbyterian Church after having been disciplined by his presbytery and synod in Pennsylvania. He immediately organized the Christian Association of Washington (Pennsylvania) and published a *Declaration and Address* setting forth the basic principles that were to guide the movement. Basically they were the rejection of both creeds and the authority of synods and presbyteries, the practice of biblical Christianity, and the objective of the reunion of Christians. Thomas Campbell was soon joined by his son Alexander, who had just arrived in America from studies in Glasgow, and who soon became the principal leader of the new movement. Because the Campbells' studies convinced them that baptism of believers by immersion was the New Testament practice, the Christian Association was connected with the Baptists from 1813 until 1830. Finally in 1830, the Campbells and their followers separated from the Baptists, calling themselves Disciples of Christ.[48]

Recognizing their common aims, the leaders of these two movements agreed in 1832 that they should unite. Actual unification took place by joining of local churches already in existence and the subsequent spread of the new united movement. Although the official name of the new body was the Disciples of Christ, the name Christian continued to be used in the area where it was already in use, and according to Garrison, has been the most common name for local churches throughout the country.[49] The first national convention of the new union, and the organization of the American Christian Missionary Society, took place in 1849. The Disciples spread rapidly on the American frontier. By 1850, the Disciples had grown to 118,000 members, and were sixth in size of the Protestant denominations.[50]

With the Methodists and Baptists on the southern frontier, the Disciples were one force in what Winthrop Hudson referred to as the "two-pronged counter-offensive of the churches,"[51] the other being the voluntary societies of the "benevolent empire." The Disciples closely resembled the Methodists in their emphasis on converting the nation as the means of reforming the nation.

Both Barton Stone and Alexander Campbell were highly individualistic and Wesleyan in their views. And in these early years, under Campbell's leadership, they were opposed to an educated ministry, voluntary societies, and even Sunday schools. Preachers saw themselves as evangelists and converts became part of locally organized churches affiliated loosely in this "brotherhood." They were especially concentrated in the Ohio Valley.[52] Because of their loose organization, and also because they considered the question of slavery a matter of opinion rather than of faith, the Disciples did not suffer schism on the slavery issue as did a number of denominations in the 1840s and 1850s. Both Stone and Campbell freed their own slaves, but slaveholders were not excluded from the church.[53]

After the Civil War, the Disciples expanded into the new western territories largely through individual initiative until a church extension board was formed in 1884. Where before the war they had concentrated largely on personal moral issues with regard to living a Christian life, after the war they were almost solidly behind the temperance crusade and efforts to secure legislation for prohibition.[54] However, they were considerably hampered by controversy over missionary methods and instrumental music, instigated by the more rigidly biblicistic wing, the Churches of Christ of the middle South, which by 1906 had become a separate body. With the new missionary endeavor after 1884, membership grew to over a million by 1900, and growth made possible an expansion of activities, including both lay and ministerial education, a new journalism, and in general, greater participation in the concerns of Protestantism as a whole.

The Disciples remained a largely rural and town people. They made little progress in the East and they generally retained their initial aversion to the cities. Therefore, while the predominantly northern denominations with large urban constituencies were much concerned after 1877 with trying to meet the problems of labor, poverty, and immigration that focused on the nation's cities, the Disciples on the whole did not share this concern. And they had virtually no contact with the immigrants.[55] However, by the 1890s, Chicago had become a real center of strength for the Disciples in the Midwest, and here they participated fully in the intellectual and social responses of the day.

In 1894, Disciples Divinity House was established in Chicago as a Disciples seminary to be connected with the newly opened University of Chicago (1892). Dr. Herbert L. Willett was dean. A colleague of William Rainey Harper in the department of Semitics at Chicago, he became the chief Disciples spokesman of the new higher critical views in biblical studies. The

187

Christian Evangelist, under the editorship of James H. Garrison, was hospitable to the new views and welcomed Willett's articles on biblical studies. The *Christian Standard*, on the other hand, ran a Biblical Criticism department that under Professor J. W. McGarvey was the outstanding opponent of the higher critics.

Two other Chicago men shared with Willett the liberal leadership of the Disciples. Edward Scribner Ames, one of the most prominent of the "modernistic" liberals in theology,[56] was for thirty-five years professor of philosophy at the University of Chicago and for forty years pastor of the University Church of the Disciples of Christ in Hyde Park. He also succeeded Willett as dean of Disciples Divinity House.

The Disciples in the early years of the twentieth century tended to divide between those who placed primary emphasis on the traditional Disciples' theme of "restoration" of primitive Christianity and those who stressed the equally traditional theme of Christian unity. Foremost of the advocates of the latter was Dr. Charles Clayton Morrison, who in 1908 bought the *Christian Century*, thus opening what Garrison called "a new era of frank commitment to liberalism"[57] within the Disciples. The *Christian Century* was begun in Des Moines in 1884 by Disciples who wanted a journal that might be the expression of interdenominational or nondenominational concerns. It moved to Chicago in 1888, and when Morrison took it over in 1908, announced its intention of opening its columns "to a discussion of the vital and acute problems now before our people and the religious world."[58] In 1918, the *Christian Century* assumed the subtitle, *An Undenominational Journal of Religion*. Since then it has become probably the most widely read weekly ecumenical journal of opinion in America.

In line with this stress on unity, the Disciples participated in the Inter-Church Conference on Federation of 1905, thus becoming charter members of the Federal Council of Churches. A special mass meeting was held in 1907 to appoint official delegates to the council's inaugural session in 1908. Finally, the Disciples also adopted a social service program. The convention of 1911 authorized a Commission on Social Service as a standing committee of the American Christian Missionary Society. Alva W. Taylor served for ten years as the unsalaried secretary of the commission.[59]

Thus the Disciples of Christ differed from the other mainline evangelical denominations largely in the strength and size of its rural constituency. It resembled in many ways the Baptists and Methodists in its frontier origins and characteristics, and like them tended to develop liberal leadership primarily where it spread to the cities, like Chicago. That what constituted a smaller minority among the Disciples than in some of the other denominations was permitted to move in such a liberal direction was probably due almost entirely to the Disciples' loose denominational organization. By 1912, there was a wing of the Disciples that had much in common with the five denominations I have been tracing. Largely in opposition to that liberal wing, the Disciples also had their fundamentalists in the 1920s, but they defined themselves in terms of the distinctive Disciples emphasis on the restoration of biblical Christianity.

From the mid-nineteenth century until well into the twentieth, the major old-line Protestant denominations remained overwhelmingly dominant in American Protestantism, and the basic adjustments they made to the new social and intellectual forces of the late nineteenth and early twentieth centuries were much the same.[60] However, after World War I, the denominational pattern of American Protestantism began to shift. Protestant groups of Continental background, like the Lutherans and the Evangelical and Reformed, began to assume a much more influential role in American Protestantism. And, as Winthrop Hudson pointed out, the most conspicuous new element in this changed configuration was the emergence of strong Fundamentalist, Holiness, and Adventist groups which, together with other conservative bodies like the Missouri Synod Lutherans and the Southern Baptists, amounted to a sizable grouping of Protestants not in sympathy with the tendencies exhibited by most of the old-line churches.[61] I have looked at both the Lutherans and the Evangelical and Reformed, and I have been tracing the roots of some of the Fundamentalist groups (and will do so at greater length in the concluding chapter). Now I look briefly at the origin of the Holiness groups, since they emerged in the period we have been covering.

The Holiness Churches

Although the Holiness groups did not come into being until the 1880s, they represented the continuing heritage of the Holiness movement, which was basically Methodist in background, but which swept through many denominations in the years just preceding and following the Civil War. Much of this concern for sanctification resulted from the widespread influence of Charles G. Finney and his colleagues at Oberlin after 1839. Within Methodism, it was promoted by the efforts of Phoebe Palmer and through the

189

organization of the National Association for the Promotion of Holiness, founded in 1867.[62] After the Civil War, Holiness groups arose in protest against the growing "worldliness" of the mainline denominations. I have observed that by the 1870s, most major Protestant churches regarded with approval the burgeoning middle-class acquisitive society. Methodists, for example, who had been a "plain people," were noting with some satisfaction in 1866 that they had risen as a body in the social scale and were no longer a church of the poor.[63] The Holiness groups, on the other hand, were "people's churches,"[64] appealing to those who were less privileged.

During the 1880s, numerous independent Holiness groups were formed. A few of the larger groups organized from these local fellowships continued to grow during the first half of the twentieth century. The Church of God (Anderson, Indiana) was founded in 1881 with a dual emphasis on holiness and Christian unity. From its beginnings in the rural Midwest, it spread into the South and to the West Coast. The Christian and Missionary Alliance was founded as an evangelistic and missionary movement in 1887 by Rev. A. B. Simpson, a Presbyterian minister in New York City. The most successful of these groups was the Church of the Nazarene, founded in 1895 in Los Angeles by a Methodist minister, Phineas Bresee. In 1907, it merged with an eastern holiness group, and the following year with a southern group, the Holiness Church of Christ. In 1910, the Church of the Nazarene had 10,000 members.[65]

From the beginning, the Church of the Nazarene was intended to be a church for the poor. Its aim was to win the lost "through the agency of city missions, evangelistic services, house-to-house visitation, caring for the poor, comforting the dying."[66] However, Bresee and the other leaders set the pattern of codes of behavior—the same codes that Baptist and Methodist preachers had taught to previous generations. Holiness leaders were staunch advocates of prohibition; teetotaling, strict Sabbath observance, plain dress, and abstinence from swearing were required of all members of the Church of the Nazarenes. Thus in the period when the mainline denominations were taking steps to meet the problem of the unchurched masses, these smaller Holiness bodies were attempting to win the poor by way of evangelistic missions and ministry to their human needs, meanwhile preaching traditional evangelical doctrine with a strong emphasis on holiness.[67]

Initially these groups were not involved in the polemic between social Christianity and individual evangelism. While primarily evangelistic, they did carry on a humanitarian ministry of relief for the poor. After 1915, however, some of them were caught up in the Fundamentalist movement. In 1917, for example, a Laymen's Holiness Association was formed in the Dakotas as the product of Methodist evangelistic crusades. Combining stress on sanctification with attacks on modernism, science, and social service, this movement reflected the increasing anxiety and pessimism of rural fundamentalism following World War I. In 1922-23, this association united with the Church of the Nazarene. From that time on, the Nazarenes shared much of the general Fundamentalist outlook, including a strong premillennialism. They became increasingly opposed to labor unions, neglected social work, and even restated their commitment to prohibition in terms of personal, rather than social, concerns. Although the Nazarenes made common cause with other Fundamentalists in the 1920s, they tended to become increasingly isolated after 1928 in order to protect their distinctive witness to the doctrine of entire sanctification.[68]

There was one group, however, that consistently attempted to bring together evangelical theology and social service, namely, the Salvation Army. Begun in England in 1865, when William Booth established a Christian Mission in the slums of East London, the new organization first referred to itself as the Salvation Army in 1878. The control of the army was from the outset invested in one person, the general superintendent. The deed poll filed in 1878 gave William Booth that office for life, with power to appoint his successor, and complete charge of all the property of the mission. As Booth's Christian Mission became the Salvation Army, military terminology was increasingly adopted, and Booth began to be referred to simply as "the General." In the deed poll, the organization specified as its theological basis what it regarded as generally accepted Protestant evangelical doctrines, including "a divinely inspired Bible, the Trinity, original sin, salvation for all who will it, and immortality of the soul." Abstinence from liquor was made a condition of membership in the army, and the use of tobacco was prohibited for officers. From the beginning, men and women served as equals in the army. Special techniques like brass bands, tambourines, and street parades were used to attract the hopeless and neglected, and meetings were held wherever the people were, in streets, in mission halls, or in taverns.[69]

By 1880, a detachment of the Salvation Army had been sent to America under the leadership of George S. Railton, who set up his headquarters in Philadelphia. After 1886, the Booth family itself assumed command of the American army, Ballington Booth and his wife Maud arriving in 1886, and F. L. Booth-Tucker, son-in-law of General Booth, ten years later. Public opinion in America was initially hostile to the Salvation Army. However, as the Protestant churches began in the 1880s to recognize the problem of the unchurched masses in the cities, they also began to acknowledge the worth of the army's evangelistic and humanitarian work among the urban poor. At a huge reception for visiting General William Booth in Carnegie Hall, New York, in 1894, Josiah Strong declared that he had been "converted to the brass drum and the cymbal."[70] Many Protestant leaders agreed that the army had succeeded in doing what the churches could not do. The army gradually won the liberty to hold its rather noisy outdoor services undisturbed in most of the nation's cities. By 1900 it had 700 corps in America with over 20,000 members, and its nearly 3,000 officers were holding over 11,000 weekly meetings attended by over 2 million people.[71]

Especially noteworthy was the Salvation Army's social service program. In 1900, it had 187 social institutions for the poor. Josiah Strong commended the army's combination of social service and evangelical religion, stating that "the Christianity of the Army is thoroughly philanthropic, and its philanthropy is thoroughly Christian."[72] Among its best-known agencies was the women's Slum Brigade, organized in New York City in 1889 to perform the threefold task of visitation and relief, the conducting of religious services in halls and saloons, and the creation of sentiment against vice.[73] From this work other forms of social service arose, including day nurseries, rescue work for prostitutes, orphanages, and slum maternity nursing programs. Food and shelter depots; labor bureaus; legal, first aid, and missing friends departments; and a life insurance scheme were all in operation soon after the turn of the century.[74]

The Salvation Army did not attempt to change the old evangelical theology to meet the challenge of the modern world, nor was it involved politically in attempts to transform the structures of American society. Although the army expressed itself on moral issues like lynching, Sabbath observance, and prohibition, its official policy was to avoid entering any public controversy on political, social, or economic matters. Yet during the labor strife of the 1880s and 1890s, the Salvation Army identified itself with the workers by its efforts to relieve the suffering of strikers and their families. For example, during the Pullman strike in 1894, the Salvation Army issued handbills calling on Chicagoans to donate food, clothing, fuel, or money to aid the people of Pullman. It collected the donations, held mass meetings to raise funds, and transported the supplies to Pullman, where army officers distributed them from house to house.[75] While progressive reformers investigated and exposed the deplorable conditions in the nation's slums, the Salvation Army went into them and attempted to bring about some improvements. Long before most Protestants had rid themselves of the view that poverty was the fault of the poor, the Salvation Army was at work in American cities offering to help the poor to their feet and supply them with shelter, food, and work. As Aaron Abell aptly put it, the army's "example of heroic self-sacrifice" was an inspiration to all of Protestant Christianity "to redouble its efforts for the social salvation of all men."[76]

Throughout this work I have been concerned almost exclusively with developments in the North. The social gospel figures have all been northerners, the revivalists have all been those who held campaigns in the North, and in the Baptist, Presbyterian, and Methodist Churches I have dealt primarily with the northern denominations. This is primarily because there was very little social Christianity to speak of in the period from 1877 to 1912 in the South. However, it is important to inquire into the nature of southern religion to ascertain the reasons for this.

Religion in the New South

In *Southern Churches in Crisis* (1966), Samuel S. Hill suggested that the distinctiveness of southern religion rests mainly in its remarkable homogeneity, being almost completely dominated by low-church Protestantism of the Baptist-Methodist type, and the degree to which this religious syndrome has been allied to regional life.[77] Hill characterized this "popular southern Protestantism" as revivalism-fundamentalism. That is, it focuses on the inauguration of the Christian life, conceives of ethics in individualist rather than social terms, and calls for assent to certain doctrines believed to contain the marrow of Christian truth, always around the central concern of saving souls.[78] What is important for my purposes is how this pattern of southern Protestantism has been related to that of the rest of the nation.

By 1830, this low-church Protestant orthodoxy (which I have called evangelicalism) had become dominant in the South *and also in the North.* Until about mid-century, popular religious life in America, with the partial exception of New England where the Puritan tradition held on longest, was more or less of a piece. I attempted to describe that characteristic American Protestantism in Chapter I. After 1850, however, changes began to come in the North. Or, as Hill phrased it, "the course of mainstream American religious life began to diverge from what had been common both to it and the

South."[79] Where the rest of the nation was subjected to various modifying factors—liberal dissenting traditions, new social concerns, new categories of thought, and an increasingly pluralistic culture—the South remained to an amazing degree insulated, introverted, and provincial, to a large extent because of the effects of the slavery controversy in creating a sectional and alien identity. Thus what was a transitional phase in the North remained the characteristic religious outlook in the South. Hill suggested that this isolation of southern religion from the national mainstream persisted from the 1830s to the 1950s, and only in the 1960s was in the process of breaking down.[80]

Where conversion of individuals is seen as the church's main task, the stress is on personal morality rather than social ethics. This was true of American Protestantism in the North until sometime in the 1870s. It was true of the South for three or four decades longer, and is still true of the popular Protestantism of many southern laypeople. From 1840 to 1870, three of the largest Protestant denominations, the Baptists, the Presbyterians, and the Methodists, experienced the bitterness and resentment engendered by division over the question of slavery, the fighting of a Civil War, and after the war, the phenomenon of missionaries from the northern branches working among blacks in the South. The result was to make the southern churches suspicious of anything that originated in the North, including social Christianity.[81]

With the rise of the New South after the end of Reconstruction, southern churchpeople welcomed industrialization, but they continued to fear urbanization and had little contact with immigrants. Although throughout the entire period from 1865 to 1900, the primary task of the church was seen as preaching the gospel and saving souls, in the late 1880s and 1890s, southern churches did concern themselves with personal moral issues. By the end of the 1880s, Methodists and Baptists were willing to resort to political action to secure prohibition. They opposed gambling, lynching, worldly amusements, and the Continental Sabbath. But in terms of economic and social issues, they had little as yet to say. Basically, like the northern Protestants before the widespread industrial conflicts that began in 1877, they approved of the society that was emerging and regarded poverty as the result either of sin or the schooling of Providence.[82] And because the South remained overwhelmingly rural throughout this period, they felt little need for anything beyond the individualistic gospel, which seemed to be adequate.

Between the turn of the century and World War I, however, the three major southern Protestant groups began to move in the direction of the kinds of social concerns already espoused by the principal northern denominations.

In 1890, the Southern Methodist General Conference designated a Standing Committee on Temperance, to which each annual conference sent a representative. This committee was reorganized in 1910 into a Standing Committee on Temperance and Other Moral and Social Questions. Southern Methodists became charter members of the Federal Council of Churches and in 1908, Southern Methodist bishop E. R. Hendrix served as its first president. By 1914, the Southern Methodist General Conference had incorporated the Social Creed of the Federal Council into its *Book of Discipline*.[83]

Largely because something of a social Christianity was beginning to develop in its denomination, Southern Methodists also had their conservative reaction. In 1914, Bishop Warren A. Candler, whom I discussed in Chapter V, was invited to give the Episcopal Address to the Southern Methodist General Conference. A well-known conservative and vigorous opponent of the social gospel (which he referred to as a "soap and soup religion"), he devoted most of his address to a discussion of the relation between individual and social salvation, decrying the present tendency to "leave the main line" of the church's life and purpose in order to "exchange the service of God" for " 'the service of humanity.' " Apparently he expressed the sentiments of a number of his listeners; the General Conference ordered 500,000 copies of the address printed.[84] Candler assumed the leadership of the party that fought reunion with the more liberal northern Methodists in the 1920s. More than any other single leader, he influenced the decision against unification in the southern annual conferences in 1925. The northern and southern branches of the Methodist Church were finally united in 1939.[85]

In 1908, the Southern Baptist Convention created a permanent Committee on Temperance. In 1913, it established a Social Service Commission "to deal with other such wrongs which curse society today, and call loudly for our help."[86] The following year these were merged into a Temperance and Social Service Commission. Southern Baptists did not affiliate with the Federal Council or adopt a social creed, but this newly formed commission did condemn social injustices and call on local churches to endeavor to influence legislation and create a Christian public opinion.[87]

Southern Presbyterians also participated in the Federal Council (although they later withdrew). In 1914, they adopted a milder social creed of their own devising entitled "United Declaration on Christian Faith and Social Service." This declaration affirmed the churches' responsibility for bettering social relations, and specifically denounced of child and female labor and insufficient wages.[88] Thus by World War I, all three major southern Protestant denominations had made some kind of pronouncement about the responsibility of the church for the social order. But as Kenneth Bailey pointed out, to proclaim is not to act, and on the local level the overwhelming concern of southern Protestants continued to be the salvation of souls, with ethical responsibility construed in a highly individual and personal, rather than social way.

We have seen that those religious groups most exposed to urbanization, industrialization, immigration, and new intellectual currents were most likely to develop some kind of social Christianity. Where denominations were part of the assimilation to a common evangelical Protestant type that took place in America by 1850, they tended to retain that revivalistic, individualistic pattern until it was changed by the stimulus of other modifying forces. Thus southern and rural areas were slow to develop a social gospel. But the social gospel itself bore witness to its origins in the evangelical tradition. There might be other, more "churchly" rationales for asserting Christian social responsibility, just as there might be other than evangelical grounds for taking a conservative position. But the polemic I have been describing took place among the old-line Protestant evangelical denominations as they faced the challenges of the modern world.

NINE

Two Protestantisms

Since 1912, the lines have hardened between the two Protestantisms I have been describing. While it is scarcely possible to indicate here all the changing religious moods of the American nation in the twentieth century, I will attempt simply to sketch the lines that lead from 1912 to the 1960s.

As many interpreters have pointed out, the end of World War I also marked the end of an era for American Protestantism. The moral idealism of the progressive era had begun to wane, the "age of crusades"[1] had ended, and President Harding's call for a "return to normalcy" mirrored the mood of the postwar generation. Robert T. Handy referred to the decline in religious interest and activity from 1925 to 1935 as America's "religious depression."[2] The waning of progressivism was accompanied by a declining interest in the social gospel. The three giants of the social gospel were dead. Josiah Strong passed away in 1916 and both Washington Gladden and Walter Rauschenbusch died in 1918. Although some of the clergy continued to be concerned about social problems—particularly labor, international relations, and civil liberties—the general mood of most Protestants did not favor any further meddling with the social order. Anti-Red, antilabor, and antiforeign sentiments were but the extreme form of a general reactionary temper in the 1920s. Billy Sunday's later career rode on the crest of this wave of reaction.[3]

The spirit of the 1920s was embodied in two struggles in which both Protestant parties participated, prohibition and the Fundamentalist controversy. Much has been made of the issue of prohibition as a conservative panacea and a tool of big business to divert attention from genuine reforms. However, with some significant differences, denominations that had been permeated by the social gospel were also committed to prohibition.

Legislating Prohibition

In its early days, the crusade against the liquor traffic had been closely allied with a wide range of social reforms, and it was the liberals who supported it. For example, Frances Willard of the Woman's Christian Temperance Union was also active in the fight for women's rights and the cause of labor. The formation of the Anti-Saloon League in 1896, however, marked the beginning of a new approach characterized by both a new singleness of purpose and a sense of opposition—as indicated by the very name of the league. In *Symbolic Crusade*, Joseph R. Gusfield described the prohibition crusade of 1900 to 1920 as a movement away from assimilative reform that relied primarily on education and persuasion, to coercive reform that sought legislative action. The former approach characterized the early temperance reformers, whose norms were still dominant in the society. The latter was the response of an essentially rural, native Protestant population to the challenge to the legitimacy of its norms by the rising forces of urbanism, immigration, and Roman Catholicism.[4] The old-stock Protestant middle classes in the cities also supported this drive for prohibition.[5]

Throughout his life Dwight L. Moody had opposed legislative prohibition, always insisting that conversion be kept primary. From Sam Jones on, however (with the exception of B. Fay Mills), every revivalist supported the prohibition movement. Sam Jones and Billy Sunday in particular played an important part in mobilizing public action for prohibition in towns and smaller cities in the South and Midwest. Many progressive reformers, including the social gospelers, also accepted prohibition as a step toward eliminating some of the problems of society. One of the provisions added to the amended Social Creed of the Churches in 1912 was a clause advocating "the protection of the individual and society from the social, economic, and moral waste of the liquor traffic."[6]

Thus the drive to end the liquor traffic had the support of both liberal and conservative Protestants. By the end of 1917, a constitutional amendment to bar the liquor traffic had been passed by Congress. With the approval of forty-five states, it went into effect on January 16, 1920, as the Eighteenth Amendment. Between 1916 and 1920, the Federal Council had spent $150,000 to help put prohibition across.[7] The chief difference between liberals and conservatives, however, was that the latter tended to substitute prohibition for all other social reforms, while the former did not allow their interest in controlling the liquor traffic to divert their attention from necessary reforms in the economic system. As Paul Carter has suggested, prohibition was for many conservatives a surrogate for the social gospel.[8]

Once the Eighteenth Amendment had been secured, interest within the Federal Council seems to have subsided. The council expressed concern over the widespread evasion of the law and felt the urgency of resuming the earlier educational work that had been such an important part of the temperance crusade. However, as the prohibitionist cause turned increasingly into a crusade against urbanism, immigration, and Catholicism, as it did especially in the Hoover-Smith presidential election campaign of 1928, the Federal Council and other moderate or liberal elements tended to leave the field to the conservatives. In a sense, the repeal of the Eighteenth Amendment in 1933 was symbolic of the end of rural Protestantism's dominance in the United States.[9]

The Fundamentalist Controversy

During the 1920s, the controversy that had been brewing in Protestantism before the war finally exploded in a struggle between conservatives and liberals for control of the denominations. The Fundamentalists[10] were opposed to Modernism (liberalism), evolution, and the social gospel. They included the millenarians and conservatives of the Princeton school who had participated in the Bible and prophetic conferences, the Bible institutes, and publishing ventures like the *Fundamentals* in the prewar years. (As Ernest Sandeen pointed out, both of these groups were not simply defending traditional, orthodox Protestantism. Both of them involved newly formulated, nineteenth-century theologies.) They also included some genuine conservatives like A. H. Strong, former president of Rochester Theological Seminary, who while chiefly concerned about the question of biblical authority did not wish to make an issue of evolution, biblical inerrancy, or premillennialism. However, these more moderate Fundamentalists were largely unheard among the protests of the more extreme and belligerent wing.

The Fundamentalists have usually been defined as those conservative Protestants who accepted the five points of doctrine first stated in a declaration by the Niagara Bible Conference of 1895, namely, the verbal inerrancy of Scripture, the deity and virgin birth of Christ, the substitutionary atonement, the physical resurrection of Christ, and his coming bodily return to earth. Actually, Ernest Sandeen has shown that the only creedal statement produced by the Niagara Bible Conference was a fourteen-point statement adopted in 1878. Apparently the error originated with Stewart G. Cole, who in his 1931 history of Fundamentalism stated that the Niagara group had adopted such a five-point declaration.[11] The General Assembly of the Presbyterian Church did adopt a five-point doctrinal statement in 1910, affirming as essential Christian doctrines the inerrancy of Scripture, the virgin birth, the substitutionary atonement, the physical resurrection, and the miracle-working power of Christ.[12] It did not include the premillennial Second Coming, which was, however, one of the doctrines in the fourteen-point Niagara statement.[13]

Although Fundamentalism was not just conservative Protestant orthodoxy, it is true that the Fundamentalist controversy arose in reaction to the liberals or modernists who were attempting to reconcile the tradition of Protestant evangelicalism with modern scientific, social, and theological thinking. In 1919, a World's Christian Fundamentals Association was founded at the instigation of William Bell Riley, pastor of the First Baptist Church of Minneapolis, and A. C. Dixon, for the purpose of organizing evangelicals into what they hoped would be a "world fellowship of conquest."[14] In May 1922, Harry Emerson Fosdick flung down the liberal gauntlet in a sermon at First Presbyterian Church of New York City entitled, "Shall the Fundamentalists Win?"

The three major denominations that suffered most from the Fundamentalist controversy were the Baptists, the Presbyterians, and the Disciples. Among the Disciples the question was that of restoration versus Christian unity—that is, which of the two distinctive Disciples emphases was to be more important. In 1924, a Christian Restoration Association was organized, and in the 1920s, the *Christian Standard*, the denominational journal favoring the restorationists, supported the Fundamentalists of other denominations.[15]

In both the Baptist and the Presbyterian churches, millenarianism was a significant issue and millenarians were well represented among those who withdrew.[16] Militant Fundamentalists in the Northern Baptist Convention organized the Baptist Bible Union of America in 1922 to fight against the Baptist Modernists. The leaders of the Union were John Roach Straton and William Bell Riley in the North, J. Frank Norris in the Southern Baptist Convention, and T. T. Shields among Canadian Baptists. So belligerent were the union's methods that even A. C. Dixon resigned in 1925, stating publicly that he thought the B.B.U. had served its purpose.[17] Two conservative Baptist seminaries were established to counteract the effect of liberal schools like the University of Chicago: the Northern Baptist Theological Seminary, founded in Chicago in 1913, and Eastern Baptist Theological Seminary, organized by dissidents from Crozer Seminary in 1925.[18]

Within Presbyterianism, the restrictive views of the Princeton theology had been established as the definitive standard of belief by the end of World War I. Again in 1923, the General Assembly passed a resolution making the five points of 1910 essential articles of faith, but it was to be the last victory for the conservatives. In 1926 and 1927, a Commission of Fifteen rejected the right of the General Assembly to make statements of necessary articles of faith. This settlement split the conservatives, the moderates abandoning their opposition to the liberals.[19] Under J. Gresham Machen, Princeton Theological Seminary became the site of the most vigorous Fundamentalist offensive among the Presbyterians. In 1929, the seminary was reorganized and Machen founded Westminster Theological Seminary in Philadelphia and, in 1936, what became known as the "Orthodox Presbyterian Church." A good example of the alliance of Princeton conservatives and millenarians, the church proved to be an unstable union and broke up when the millenarians, under Carl McIntire, formed the Bible Presbyterian Synod.[20]

The Fundamentalists opposed Modernism with its acceptance of the higher criticism. They also opposed the theory of evolution, which they felt contradicted the creation story in Genesis, made humans something less than children of God, and seemed to leave no room for the supernatural, including Christ's divinity. As George McCready Price summed up the threat of evolution to orthodox Christian beliefs, "No Adam, no fall, no fall, no atonement; no atonement, no Savior. Accepting Evolution, how can we believe in a fall?"[21] The great champion of the antievolution crusade was William Jennings Bryan, former Populist leader and Democratic candidate for president in 1896, who entered the struggle in 1920 and used his rhetorical skills to fight evolution as he had in the struggle to win free silver. He said of evolution, for example, "Christ has made of death a narrow, star-lit strip between the companionship of yesterday and the reunion of tomorrow; evolution strikes out the stars and deepens the gloom that enshrouds the tomb."[22] In 1925, the issue of whether or not evolution should be taught in the nation's public schools was fought out in the Scopes trial at Dayton, Tennessee; Bryan and Clarence Darrow as the chief prosecutor and counsel for the defense, respectively. Although the Fundamentalist forces were discredited by Bryan's performance in the cross-examination at Dayton, antievolution laws continued to be passed in a number of southern states.[23]

It has often been argued that Fundamentalism was part of the protest of a rural Protestant culture against the new urban, pluralistic society in America. It would probably be more accurate to say that the Fundamentalist controversy had both its more cultural and more theological aspects. Ernest Sandeen has shown that the theological strength of Fundamentalism was in the urban areas of the North, where cities like Minneapolis, Philadelphia, Chicago, and New York were bases of operation for the millenarians and conservatives of the Princeton school. However, it should be added that many of these Fundamentalist leaders, like their congregations, were old-stock middle-class Protestants who had moved to the cities from the more rural areas in the late nineteenth century, thus bringing with them traditional values and beliefs. In its more cultural aspects, Fundamentalism included the antievolution agitation, which found its strongest support in the rural South, under the leadership of the old spokesman for agrarian interests, William Jennings Bryan. It also included certain mores of personal behavior, and a tendency to see the free enterprise system and "one hundred percent Americanism" as corollaries of religious belief.

One of the best statements of the Fundamentalist case was J. Gresham Machen's *Christianity and Liberalism*, published in 1923. Referring to liberalism as "this modern non-redemptive religion," Machen accused its representatives of having relinquished everything distinctive of Christianity in their attempt to reconcile the Christian faith with modern science.[24] He also insinuated that the "materialistic paternalism"[25] of the social gospelers was responsible for the spiritual decline in the 1920s. Machen's self-appointed task was to make clear the differences between true Christianity and liberalism. These he discussed in terms of six basic areas: doctrine, God and humanity, the Bible, Christ, salvation, and the Church. On the basis of these differences, Machen concluded that liberalism was not Christianity but a different religion altogether, and that "separation between the two parties in the Church" was "the crying need of the hour."[26] He felt that liberals should be honest enough to withdraw from the evangelical churches. However, he insisted that evangelical Christians must be prepared to withdraw should the liberal party gain control of the church.[27]

Machen regarded the social gospel as "one of the most obvious lines of cleavage between Christianity and the liberal Church," but he preferred to define the difference not so much in terms of individual versus social evangelism, as in terms of otherworldly versus this-worldly concerns and aims.[28] Liberals and Fundamentalists alike recognized that they were dealing with understandings of Protestant Christianity so vastly different as to constitute two Protestantisms. Social gospelers continued to define the distinction in terms of individualistic versus social, while pointing out that the social gospel did not undermine personal religion. In *Social Work of the Churches*, F. Ernest Johnson, research secretary for the Federal Council's Commission on the Church and Social Service, described as "one of the most notable characteristics of modern Christianity" the existence of two schools of thought, the one preoccupied with the salvation of the individual by means that are essentially personal and private, the other interested chiefly in the redemption of the world as a whole and conceiving the destiny of the individual as inseparable from that.[29]

Most of the denominations continued to be disturbed by the Fundamentalist controversy throughout the 1930s.[30] However, the chief strength of Fundamentalism was in the smaller denominational bodies, the independent Bible churches and local congregations, with leadership supplied by the Bible institutes and conservative seminaries. The decade of the 1920s registered a decline in many ways for the mainline Protestant churches. For example, church attendance and missionary giving were down, and so were the prestige and authority of the churches. Both Liberalism and Fundamentalism seemed to have become culture religions. But the religious climate in America was soon to change significantly.

In 1929, the stock market crashed. Although there was no general religious revival during the Depression, the Holiness, Pentecostal, and Fundamentalist groups made significant gains, and at the other end of the social scale, many prominent people found individual guidance and inspiration in the Oxford Group Movement (later known as Moral Rearmament) led by Frank Buchman. Most of the parish clergy were overwhelmed by the social and personal needs of their parishioners during the Depression. However, by the 1930s, a theological revival was underway in the seminaries and by the late 1940s, it had affected local churchpeople as well.

From Liberalism to Neo-Orthodoxy

The commonly used terms to describe the change were that it marked a transition from liberalism to neo-orthodoxy. Borrowing heavily from both "neo-Reformation"[31] and existentialist emphases in European theology, American neo-orthodoxy was most influenced by the thought of Karl Barth and Emil Brunner, Paul Tillich, Rudolf Bultmann, and Dietrich Bonhoeffer. Some of the major themes of the theological revival included a reassertion of the sovereignty of God, a reaction against the optimistic view of human nature in liberalism, a more radical view of sin, a renewed appreciation of the centrality of biblical revelation, a revival of interest in Christology, and a new concern for the church. Finally, the leaders of the theological revival tended to move to the left politically. As Reinhold Niebuhr suggested in *Reflections on the End of an Era* (1934), "In my opinion, adequate spiritual guidance can come only through more radical political orientation and more conservative religious convictions than are [at present] comprehended in the culture of our era."[32]

It might be thought that the heirs of the Fundamentalists would welcome this transition as more closely approximating their theological definition of Christianity, but such was not the case. The Fundamentalists fought neo-orthodoxy as a new form of Modernism because the neo-orthodox accepted the methods of higher criticism and were interested in ecumenism. Fundamentalists also looked with displeasure on the social and political views of the leaders of the theological revival and attacked them as promoters of "socialism, communism, anti-capitalism, pacifism, internationalism, and a world church for the United Nations."[33]

During the 1930s and 1940s, conservatives concentrated their efforts on a number of enterprises, including education through the Bible institutes and conservative colleges and seminaries, foreign missions, mass evangelism and gospel radio broadcasting (e.g., Charles E. Fuller's Old Fashioned Revival Hour, begun in California in 1925), conservative publications issued from conservative presses like Eerdmans & Moody, evangelistic youth movements like Youth for Christ and Inter-Varsity Fellowships on college campuses, and various Christian businessmen's organizations like the Gideons. Finally, during the 1940s, the split evident in the Federal Council since 1912 was actualized when two groups of conservatives withdrew from the council and set up their own organizations for united action.

Cooperation without Compromise

The first of these, the American Council of Christian Churches, was the more militantly fundamentalist of the two. Organized in 1941 under the leadership of Carl McIntire, who became its first president, the American

Council was an "exclusivist"[34] organization, admitting to membership only those who renounced modernism and withdrew from the Federal Council. McIntire saw it as one of his principal duties as president of the new council to fight the Federal Council in every way possible.

The other group withdrew from the Federal Council in 1942 to form a National Association of Evangelicals for United Action because it was unwilling to be represented by an organization that had "departed from the faith of Jesus Christ." The official history of the association was, significantly, entitled *Cooperation Without Compromise*.[35] In this history, James DeForest Murch traced the origins of the cleavage in the Federal Council between evangelicals and liberals. He blamed the liberals in the old evangelical alliance for raising the first impediments to cooperative effort in America and saw the handwriting on the wall for conservatives with the organization of the Open Church League (1894) and the National Federation of Churches and Christian Workers (1900), both forerunners of the Federal Council. He noted, as I have done, that the split within the council was evident in its early days but that conservatives and liberals were still able to work together. "Whenever the Council met there was debate," he recalled, "but both parties were determined not to permit their differences to wreck this new attempt at Christian cooperation."[36] Murch admitted that initially evangelicals could feel somewhat at home in the council; as he put it, "while majoring in social programs it did not neglect evangelism."[37] But as the years passed, "the line between 'liberalism' and true Christianity in the F.C.C.C.A. became more and more distinct." Finally from the mid-1920s on, the liberals came into control of the "leadership, policy and program" of the council, and conservatives began to oppose the council's claim to represent American Protestantism.[38]

Evangelicals regretted the absence of a creedal test for membership in the council. They objected strenuously to some of the pronouncements made by liberal leaders of the council like Harry Emerson Fosdick, Francis J. McConnell, Henry Sloane Coffin, and G. Bromley Oxnam. They began to regard the council's approach to social problems as essentially humanistic, and particularly opposed the positions taken by the council in the 1930s with regard to a more socialized economic system, political action, and pacifism. They felt that the council was functioning increasingly as a "super-church," putting pressure on all Protestants. Consequently, to protect their own freedom, they concluded in 1942 that the Federal Council was "no longer a fit vehicle for evangelical cooperation at the national level" and formed a new organization on the basis of "scriptural ecumenicity," the National Association of Evangelicals.[39]

At the association's constitutional convention, meeting in Chicago in 1943, a Statement of Faith was adopted without dissent and it was agreed that membership should be open to all denominations, independent religious organizations, local churches, and groups of churches willing to subscribe to the doctrinal statement. While denominations affiliated with the Federal Council were ineligible for membership, individual churches or groups of churches belonging to those denominations but not in sympathy with the views and policies of their ecclesiastical superiors might become members. All members were required to sign the Statement of Faith not only on joining the association, but also annually when they renewed their membership. Various committees and departments were organized, and Dr. Harold J. Ockenga, pastor of the Park Street Congregational Church in Boston, was elected the association's first president.[40]

Representatives of McIntire's American Council of Churches were invited to give their proposals at this convention in the hope that one national fundamentalist organization might be formed. But the N.A.E. proposed to follow an inclusivist membership policy rather than the exclusivist policy advocated by the American Council, and it disapproved of the American Council's virulent attacks on the Federal Council, preferring to work by persuasion from within the major denominations. The attitude of these moderate fundamentalists was expressed in their desire to be known as "evangelicals, rather than fundamentalists—in order to avoid the connotations of obscurantism, bigotry, and intolerance associated with the discredited older label."[41] In this attitude they differed considerably from McIntire's group.

Much of the leadership of this new evangelicalism came from a group of young scholars with earned doctorates from reputable universities and seminaries, who were teaching at conservative schools like Fuller Theological Seminary in Pasadena, California; California Baptist Theological Seminary in Covina; Northern Baptist Theological Seminary in Chicago; Gordon Divinity School near Boston; Westminster Theological Seminary in Philadelphia; and Wheaton College in Illinois. These evangelical theologians were "endeavoring to disentangle the core of concern for unqualified theological orthodoxy from the more objectionable traits which heretofore seemed inseparable from fundamentalism."[42]

Protestants United for Church-State Separation

There was one organization in the 1940s that brought together liberals and fundamentalists. Called Protestants and Other Americans United for Separation of Church and State, it was formed in November 1947, to defend the principle of church-state separation by opposing government aid to parochial schools and the appointment of a United States envoy to the Vatican. Among the founders of Americans United, or POAU, were some distinguished Protestants, including Dr. Charles Clayton Morrison, editor of the *Christian Century*; Methodist Bishop G. Bromley Oxnam, a prominent liberal in the Federal Council; Dr. Edwin McNeill Poteat, president of Colgate-Rochester Divinity School; Dr. Joseph M. Dawson, executive director of the Baptist Joint Committee on Public Affairs; and Dr. Clyde W. Taylor, secretary of the National Association of Evangelicals. Charles Clayton Morrison prepared the *Manifesto* for the new organization and was elected in 1947 to serve as first vice president. Other officers were E. M. Poteat, president; John A. Mackay, president of Princeton Theological Seminary, second vice president; Louie D. Newton, president of the Southern Baptist Convention, third vice president; J. M. Dawson, secretary; and E. J. DeGroot, Jr., a Washington, D.C., attorney, treasurer. In 1948, Glenn L. Archer, dean of the Washburn University Law School in Topeka, Kansas, became executive director. The organization was another interesting example of the way the two parties in American Protestantism have worked together for the sake of defending America's nationalistic evangelical religion. As such it would be prominent in the 1960 election campaign when for the first time it appeared likely that the United States might have a non-Protestant president.[43]

In the early 1950s, it became evident that in terms of an increase in public interest in religion, the United States was in the midst of a religious revival. Unlike earlier revivals in America, this was unstructured, manifesting itself in many ways and places and among all religious faiths. Church attendance and giving soared, religious books—both scholarly and popular—had an unusually good market, religion was enshrined in national affairs, and 96 percent of the American people identified themselves according to specific religious affiliation in a 1957 survey by the U.S. Census Bureau.[44] World War II, the atom bomb, and atheistic communism all contributed to a climate of anxiety, insecurity, and the awareness of humanity's destructive powers. In such an atmosphere, religion was sought on many levels, from the "peace of mind," "positive thinking" faith of Norman Vincent Peale, Monsignor Fulton J.

Sheen, and Rabbi Joshua Liebman, to the wide audience given the sophisticated theological thinking of Paul Tillich and Reinhold Niebuhr.

Billy Graham's Evangelistic Crusades

The most important new personality to come on the scene was the evangelist Billy Graham. Under his leadership, mass evangelism of the Moody-Sunday type experienced a rebirth. Born near Charlotte, North Carolina, in 1918, Billy Graham was ordained a Southern Baptist minister in 1939, and received a bachelor of arts degree from Wheaton College in Illinois in 1943. Beginning as an itinerant evangelist for Youth for Christ rallies in 1945, Graham attracted public attention when three minor celebrities were converted during his Los Angeles Crusade in 1949. After the close of the eight-week campaign, Graham was invited by the Park Street Congregational Church in Boston (the church of Harold Ockenga, first President of the N.A.E.) to conduct meetings there. Because of the response, it was soon necessary to move to larger halls in the city, and this revival was followed in 1950 by a major city-wide revival in Portland, Oregon. In 1954, Graham conducted a three months' crusade in England, and finally in 1957, a New York Crusade that opened on May 15 in Madison Square Garden, filled Yankee Stadium on July 20 (in what was to have been the climax of the crusade), and was eventually extended three times until September 1.[45]

Graham was much influenced in his style and message by the neo-evangelicals. He turned down an invitation from the American Council to conduct a crusade in New York on a separatist basis, preferring to be sponsored by a majority of the clergy in the city, a condition that he insisted on in all revivals after 1950. He wanted to avoid the intolerance and sectarianism typical of the more militant fundamentalists and tried to emulate the irenic spirit of Dwight L. Moody.[46] For this reason he was supported by the National Association of Evangelicals and attacked by fundamentalists like Carl McIntire and Bob Jones, Sr., representatives of the American Council, who accused him of consorting with modernists and betraying the fundamentalist cause.

Billy Graham made full use of the mass media, including his weekly "Hour of Decision" radio broadcasts, television appearances, and films. During the anxious years of the Korean War and the McCarthy anti-Red hysteria, Graham's combination of personal religion and political and social conservatism had a wide appeal. Like his evangelistic predecessors, he saw revivalistic religion as an answer to the nation's perils, but this time the chief peril was that of communism. "The greatest and most effective weapon against Communism today is a born again Christian," Graham said.[47] Like Billy Sunday, Graham linked Christianity and patriotism. "If you would be a loyal American then become a loyal Christian."[48] Generally, liberal Protestants were disturbed by this resurgence of mass evangelism. Churchpeople in the National Council of Churches criticized Graham, but many Protestants (like the Protestant Council of New York, which sponsored Graham's New York crusade) once again thought that a man like Graham might reach the masses and were willing to cooperate with him in spite of their disapproval of his technique or his message.[49]

By 1956, the official membership of the National Association of Evangelicals exceeded 1.5 million. Some of the largest denominational bodies included the Assemblies of God, the National Association of Free Will Baptists, the Church of God (Cleveland, Tennessee), the Church of the Foursquare Gospel, the Pentecostal Holiness Church, and the Wesleyan Methodist Church. Many Pentecostal groups were represented in the N.A.E.,[50] whereas the American Council refused to grant them membership, regarding them as a disruptive force "not in the historic succession of the evangelical church."[51] Constituent membership figures for the American Council of Churches in the mid-1950s were approximately 200,000.[52] The sectarianism and intolerance typical of this "radical come-outer wing of Fundamentalism"[53] kept this group from making any appreciable gains in membership.

New Conciliar Bodies

Although vastly different in their methods, both of these conservative groups have been strongly opposed to the ecumenical movement. When the World Council of Churches was to convene for the first time in September 1948 in Amsterdam, Carl McIntire assembled a delegation of separatist fundamentalists in the same city in August and formed an International Council of Christian Churches as a counter organization. From that time on, he and his cohorts dogged the assemblies of the World Council whenever and wherever they met. McIntire was untiring in his attacks on the council, and although they did not adopt his tactics, James DeForest Murch and the

National Association of Evangelicals also condemned the World Council for what they saw as its pretensions to be a "super-church."[54]

When, in 1950, delegates from the Federal Council, eight interdenominational agencies, and four Eastern orthodox churches met to form a National Council of Churches, both fundamentalist bodies were vigorous in their criticism of the new organization. They looked on the inclusion of Eastern Orthodox churches as "an ominous departure from strict Protestantism"[55] and charged that the ultimate goal of the National Council, as of the World Council, was one Catholic Church. McIntire led the fundamentalists in a crusade charging the leaders of the National Council, particularly Methodist Bishop G. Bromley Oxnam, with "pro-Red leaning and communist-front connections."[56] On July 21, 1953, Bishop Oxnam appeared voluntarily before the House Un-American Activities Committee and after a grueling ten-hour session was cleared of any link with the Communist Party. McIntire's next move was to attempt to wreck the second plenary session of the World Council, scheduled to meet in Evanston, Illinois, in August 1954, by blocking the admission of delegates from Communist countries. However, this effort was also unsuccessful, as all of the disputed delegates were granted visas. Although small in numbers, the American Council has shown itself to be disruptive and troublesome. The N.A.E. refused to participate in most of these vindictive campaigns and at least one of their members, Donald Grey Barnhouse, editor of *Eternity*, was highly critical of McIntire's activities. However, the N.A.E. is equally opposed to the policies and work of these two conciliar bodies.

Religion in the 1960s

If the 1950s were characterized by a revival of interest in religion, particularly in a comfortable, nationalistic, peace-of-mind religion, the 1960s saw an attack on that kind of religion. From within the church, the ecumenical movement and a radical theological revolution that embraced the secular and talked about the "death of God" were part of the impetus toward change. The election of John F. Kennedy, the civil rights revolution after 1954 (which probably reached its peak, in terms of Protestant clergy participating, in the marches in Alabama in the spring of 1965), the continued pressures of urbanization and new kinds of Protestant involvement in the inner city, and the widespread sense of a new personal morality contributed to the change in American religion.[57]

This new social activist, civil-rights-oriented, radically experimenting religion of the 1960s evoked a variety of responses from the religious public. Because of extensive reporting through the mass media, few people were unaware of these developments. Probably most of the younger clergy, and a small minority of the laity, were attempting to "bring Protestantism into a new age." The majority of the people in the churches preferred to resist this kind of change and kept the more comfortable religion with which they were familiar, and they were not without clerical allies.[58]

The Uneasy Conscience of Modern Fundamentalism

Although it is difficult to gain proper perspective on the recent past, it is important to attempt to take stock of the situation in contemporary Protestantism in terms of the way both parties have been related to these changes. One of the most important consequences of the new evangelical scholarship has been the awakening of concern among evangelicals for the social application of the Gospel. Carl F. H. Henry's *The Uneasy Conscience of Modern Fundamentalism*, published in 1947, broke new ground in this regard and reflected a growing sense of guilt among evangelicals for Fundamentalism's long silence on serious social problems. Fundamentalism had reacted so strongly against the social gospel, Henry admitted, that it had lost all humanitarian concern and become indifferent to the social implications of its own religious message. Consequently it was widely regarded by non-evangelicals as "the modern priest and Levite, by-passing suffering humanity,"[59] lacking in social passion, and having too pessimistic a view of human nature to undertake a social program. Henry viewed with dismay the divorce between evangelical Christianity and the great social reform movements. But he saw "a rising tide of reaction in Fundamentalism today—a reaction born of an uneasy conscience and determined no longer to becloud the challenge of the Gospel to modern times."[60] He urged evangelicals to apply the Gospel in the more constructive spheres of social welfare and to preach it so that divine redemption would be recognized as the best solution to individual and social problems.[61]

In 1951, a Forum on Social Action was included in the program of the national convention of the N.A.E., and as a result of the interest generated in these sessions a permanent Commission on Social Action was set up with Henry as chairman. Among the issues discussed at that convention were "the Politico-Economic Problem, Labor Relations and Race Relations." James D. Murch's view in 1956 was that "while there is still much to be accomplished before evangelicals' 'uneasy conscience' is assuaged in the field of Social Action, nevertheless their critics cannot justifiably accuse them of quiescence in this field."[62] In more recent years there have been several books on social ethics written by conservatives, especially Carl F. H. Henry's *Aspects of Christian Social Ethics* (1964) and *The Social Conscience of the Evangelical* (1963) by Sherwood Eliot Wirt, a member of the Billy Graham team.[63] Again both these men admitted the failure of conservative evangelical Christianity to be articulate about the social dimension of the Gospel, but their views on social action remained poles apart from those of the liberals in the National Council of Churches. Essentially they insisted on holding to the contract made in the mid-nineteenth century when America was becoming an industrialized nation. Their concerns were still basically private, they insisted on maintaining a nonpolitical role for the church, and they stressed that society can be transformed only by the spiritual regeneration of individuals. As Carl F. H. Henry put it, "Christian social action condones no social solutions in which personal acceptance of Jesus Christ as Saviour and Lord is an optional consideration."[64]

According to the results of the 1965 Gallup poll on American religious belief, the majority of American churchgoers agreed with this insistence on a nonpolitical role for the church. Three-fourths of American Protestants still did not expect either the clergy or the churches as such to be involved critically in social-political issues. Because of the upheavals of the 1960's, this failure of the majority of American Protestant churchgoers to understand the social involvements of the clergy had become one of the most perplexing problems for contemporary Protestantism.[65]

As I have demonstrated throughout this book, the differences between the two parties in American Protestantism are nowhere more clearly revealed than in their understandings of evangelism. In 1966, evangelicals summoned a World Congress on Evangelism (meeting in Berlin), to express corporate concern for the task of world evangelism and to offer an alternative to what they regarded an "the unhappy distortion" of evangelism by conciliar ecumenists. The evangelicals were responding to the views of evangelism expressed in the National Council of Churches and at the World Council of Churches' Conference on the Church and Society earlier that summer.

212

New Structures for Mission

The Central Department of Evangelism of the National Council had begun by the early 1960s to conceive of its task more and more broadly as including all those matters related to the proclamation of the Gospel to the world. The staff report for the department in 1964 summed up some of these concerns:

> We are taking more seriously than ever before the world and its structures and needs. How these structures affect individual and family and community and leisure and work existence, and how they are affected by individuals and groups. How real decision-making takes place and how the Gospel may be able to penetrate it. The places where the world is open to the Gospel. The nature of genuine communication of the Gospel there. The sharing of the Gospel with the individual—its relevance to his privatized life and all his wider relationships. We are increasingly concerned with helping the churches to study the world in which the Gospel must be communicated, and to study the nature of the Gospel itself, the means by which it may be communicated—embodied and spoken—without dilution and in its fulness in our present age.[66]

In line with this understanding, studies were in process on leisure time, the church and the Jews, and new structures for mission, and the department was working with other commissions and task forces in the council on desegregation of the churches and the elimination of poverty. It had held an Ecumenical Evangelism Conference for "study and dialogue, inspiration and planning at the creative growing edge of evangelism."[67]

One of the foremost leaders in the reexamination of the church's structure for mission was Dr. Colin W. Williams, executive director of the Central Department of Evangelism of the National Council, and chairman of the World Council's Department on Studies in Evangelism. At the third assembly of the World Council of Churches in New Delhi in December 1961, this department was authorized to undertake a long-range study on "The Missionary Structure of the Congregation," arising out of the persistent question facing those involved in evangelism, "Is the present form of church life a major hindrance to the work of evangelism?" Two study books were written by Williams for use in this continuing study on the local church level, *Where in the World?*, published in 1963, and *What in the World?*, published the following year. Basically these two small books attempted to make clear why the church, in order to affect the public realm, must develop new structures for mission.[68]

When the National Council of Churches was reorganized in 1965, the former Central Department of Evangelism was lodged as a commission in the Department of Parish and Community Life of the Division of Christian Life and Mission, and Williams was given the leadership of the whole Department of Parish and Community Life. This restructuring was an accurate reflection of the Council's broad understanding of evangelism. The staff report to the commission for 1965 underlined the fact that the task of evangelism was not to seek conversions in a vacuum, "but in the context of our everyday existence—conversion with social consequences, relationship to Jesus Christ that brings into judgment our sin, our prejudice, our acquiescence to injustice and oppression."[69] The World Council of Churches' Conference on the Church and Society in 1966 also underlined the church's mission in the revolutionizing of social structures.

The evangelicals responded to all of this with dismay, regarding it as deplorable when the very leaders entrusted with the formulation of evangelistic policies and the implementation of evangelistic practices for the major churches were guilty of operating with a secularized concept of evangelism from which the New Testament evangel had been left out.[70] The World Congress on Evangelism drew up a definition of evangelism that stressed the substitutionary death and resurrection of Christ for sinners and the eschatological hope of the church.

> Evangelism is the proclamation of the Gospel of the crucified and risen Christ, the only Redeemer of men, according to the Scriptures, with the purpose of persuading condemned and lost sinners to put their trust in God by receiving and accepting Christ as Saviour through the power of the Holy Spirit, and to serve Christ as Lord in every calling of life and in the fellowship of His Church, looking toward the day of His coming in glory.[71]

Unlike the conciliar Protestants who were developing a much more widely conceived evangelism, World Congress participants found new opportunities for evangelism among the illiterate and newly literate masses, through secular journalism and other mass media, in the world's cities and among its student population, but neither in definition nor in method was there any significant change. For these evangelicals, the crucial concern was one of commitment: were evangelicals to be guilty of failing to fulfill the Great Commission? Were they to abandon evangelism to "communism and the cults" and thus deprive their generation of "the good news of the mediator"?[72]

Radically Different Ways to Change the World

As a special correspondent for the London *Times* recognized, Christian forces were divided over two radically different views of changing the world. He compared Billy Graham and Martin Luther King, Jr., as representatives of the opposing views—the one seeking to rescue individuals through personal faith in Christ as Redeemer, the other espousing a theology and program of "Christian revolution" that functions through political involvement. These, he said, are "two utterly different attitudes toward the hell that men have made of the world. Both claim to be Christian. . . . They reflect a division in the Church that probably goes deeper than any historic denominational dispute. The very nature of faith is at issue. This dispute runs right through every denomination."[73]

Speaking for the evangelicals, Carl F. H. Henry was well aware of the depth of the conflict between what he liked to refer to as "neo-Protestant liberalism" and evangelical Christianity. He described the difference between the two parties:

> A generation ago the clash between champions of miraculous theism and of secular modernism was especially evident in the area of theology. . . . But by the 1960's the center of controversy had further shifted from theology to social ethics; the stance of non-evangelical Protestantism had now become so anti-metaphysical and anti-intellectual that truth was subordinated to unity, theology was widely viewed as a matter of subjective preference, and in place of an absolute dogma stood an approved program of social action which—as the liberals saw it—was now the real test of genuine Christian commitment. Instead of personal evangelism and the spiritual regeneration of individuals, they advocated changing the social structures by the Church's direct engagement in political controversy.[74]

Evangelicals also objected vigorously to the sympathy for socialism and hostility to capitalism evident at the Church and Society conference sponsored by the World Council of Churches, insisting that evangelical Christians reject this attempt to "confer Christian sanction on secular and often anti-biblical ends" and also reject revolution as an approved means of social change. Yet although they maintained that the Christian challenge to the existing orders of society was too "thoroughgoing and radical" to permit the endorsement of any particular economic system, in practice they tended to give just that kind of endorsement to the individualist free enterprise system. For example, in almost the next breath, Henry could claim that "the Bible is clearly on the side

215

of private property held as a stewardship under God."[75] Evangelicals at the World Congress on Evangelism did generally assert the need for social concern, but their understanding of what this entailed was, as we have seen, vastly different from that of the liberals. (And indeed, conservatives could not generally agree among themselves how this Christian social concern ought to be expressed.)[76]

Two Protestant Parties

The result of this deep division in the 1960s was that two ecumenical coalitions were emerging—the conciliar ecumenism of Protestant and Eastern Orthodox churches, with increasing dialogue and cooperation with Roman Catholicism, and "an evangelical ecumenical vanguard," which seemed to be emerging at the World Congress on evangelism in 1966.[77] Although it was not clear just what form such an evangelical ecumenism would take, Henry felt it was inevitable unless the conciliar movement made some real efforts to engage evangelical support. "Who knows," he said, "but that the next decade will see the emergence of two world frameworks—a commonwealth of neo-Protestant, Orthodox, and Roman Catholic churches, and a global fellowship of evangelical churches."[78]

The numbers of Christians who might be involved in such an evangelical fellowship were far from negligible. In the United States in 1960, the dominant Protestant group was composed of those moderately liberal or progressive denominations affiliated with the National Council of Churches. These bodies belonging to "ecumenical" or "cooperative" Protestantism represented a constituency of some 37 million members. The Fundamentalist-Adventist-Holiness-Pentecostal coalition represented almost 8.5 million members in 1960. In addition, there were more than 19 million other Protestants—10 million Southern Baptists and almost 5 million members each of the American Lutheran Church and the Lutheran Church, Missouri Synod—who while not belonging to any coalition were considered part of the constituency served by the commissions and affiliated agencies of the N.A.E. Thus in 1960, there were some 27.5 million members in groups outside the sphere of cooperative Protestantism, as opposed to 37 million members within.[79] When allowance is made for the number of Protestants belonging to denominations affiliated with the National Council who were not themselves in sympathy with the Council's social-political and theological views, the evangelical faction probably represented the majority of American Protestants.[80]

Recognizing this situation, both National Council and World Council leaders tried to improve communication between the two parties. Evangelical representatives were invited to address conciliar gatherings; Billy Graham was invited to address a luncheon meeting during the General Assembly sessions of the National Council at Miami Beach in December 1956 and also to address the fourth World Assembly of the World Council of Churches in Uppsala, Sweden, in 1968. Carl F. H. Henry (until the mid-1960s editor of *Christianity Today*, the major periodical voice of the evangelicals) was invited to speak on a number of occasions, including the U.S. Conference for the World Council of Churches, at Buck Hill Falls, Pennsylvania, in May 1966. However, the results of such exchanges were not hopeful. When Billy Graham spoke at the Miami meetings of the W.C.C., Colin Williams at a later meeting criticized his approach, stressing the view that evangelism that emphasized personal conversion without relating it to the whole of life was no longer adequate. Although some at the meeting interpreted Graham's combination of personal regeneration and social compassion as a conciliatory synthesis, it was clear that crucial differences remained. Colin Williams warned that the conflict between the two parties was serious and could not be glossed over.[81]

As the social gospelers had begun to do in the early years of the new century, Williams and much of the conciliar leadership were calling for a new evangelism, while the evangelicals were insisting, as their predecessors like A. C. Dixon had done, that the old ways were still sufficient. Thus the schism between social Christianity and individualistic evangelicalism, evident as early as 1912, had now widened and deepened. It had taken on ecumenical implications and the lines between the two parties had hardened so that there was very little genuine cooperation or communication between them. There were now two Protestantisms in America, and the schism between them showed few signs of being speedily overcome.

Conclusion

From the 1880s on, there were basically three strands in American Protestantism. Both social Christianity and an aggressive, millenarian conservatism had by degrees developed out of the older evangelicalism under the impact of the challenges of modern science and industrialization. What was left was a moderate evangelicalism to a high degree amalgamated with "Americanism," defined in terms of nineteenth-century individualism, democracy, and the free enterprise system. Social Christianity and millenarian conservatism also had their cultural aspects. Central to the social gospel movement was reaction against the identification of Protestant Christianity with economic laissez-faire and individualism, but the social gospelers did not exercise the same critical judgment of themselves and their theology. They too were guilty of adopting cultural values, although they were different values from those enshrined by the older evangelicalism. The militant conservatives—fundamentalists in the broadest sense—were more theologically minded than the liberals, but because they resisted all encroachments of modern thought and society, they operated with an archaic theology and accepted the older prevailing views of American society.

Professional evangelists played a complex part in this picture. From Sam Jones in the 1890s to Billy Sunday in the Progressive Era, they spoke for and appealed to both the conservatives and the moderates. As the atmosphere of American society grew more congenial toward some kind of reform by the closing years of the century, they tended to lend their support to prohibition and civic reform, while adhering to the older individualistic views on religion.

After 1912, the majority of American Protestants seemed to agree with Billy Sunday that saving souls and not society was still the chief task of the churches. In the early years of the Federal Council, conservatives and liberals worked together to make America Christian, but by the 1940s, some evangelicals felt they could no longer remain within the same national organization without compromising their view of the faith.

The social gospel had tried to relate to the complex forces of the modern world. Yet its concern for the public realm was not new. It stood in direct continuity with a long Christian tradition of responsibility for the social order, including colonial Puritanism. The conservatives regarded social Christianity as something new on the American scene because they thought of the immediate evangelical Protestant past in America as normative. They did not recognize that it represented a very brief period in the long history of the Christian, even the Protestant, churches. Walter Rauschenbusch and other social gospelers tried to demonstrate their continuity with the older Christian tradition by pointing to those neglected elements in the Christian heritage which provided the basis for a social understanding of Christianity. In the end, however, they simply insisted that in view of the vast changes brought about by the industrial revolution, the burden of proof rested on those who thought the old ways still sufficient.

Over half a century later, there were many who still insisted on the old ways. While Colin Williams and the National Council of Churches were calling for new structures for mission and an evangelism more and more broadly conceived, conservative evangelicals like those in the N.A.E. still defined evangelism in terms of personal conversion and the proclamation of traditional doctrines. Probably the majority of Protestant churchgoers still believed that the main business of the church was with individuals, and that only as private citizens should Christians be involved in social-political issues. However, in a political world, to insist on a nonpolitical role for the church is to lend political support to the status quo. Thus conservative evangelicalism in America had become identified with one kind of political force and had attracted to itself those who had an interest in maintaining the status quo.

Predictions are not the task of the historian. But it is difficult not to be profoundly concerned about the outcome of this schism, which may well be the most crucial problem still facing the Protestant churches. The dispute over social versus individual, public versus private Protestantism runs through every denomination. It has occasioned deep division between clergy and laity, and, as this study shows, among the clergy themselves. Those who insist on the social involvement of the church are committed to change for the sake of a more just and more Christian social order. Those who want to maintain a privatized religion resist this kind of change, some in an attempt to defend what they see as the central doctrines of the faith; others for the sake of preserving the familiar religion that offers them comfort and meaning in a troubled and unstable world.

The question is, what are the "possibilities for accommodation and reconciliation"[1] between these two parties within the institutional structures of American Protestantism? Both parties still share common symbols and a heritage based on the Protestant principle of perpetual re-evaluation and self-criticism. One can only hope that they engage in meaningful dialogue and the common struggle for a new future, in obedience to the judging and transforming Word of God that calls in question every existing order of society.

Notes

INTRODUCTION: A Twenty Years' Retrospective

1. "On Seeing and Not Seeing: A Case of Historical Invisibility," *Journal of American History* 71 (June 1984): 7-21.
2. Robert McAfee Brown, *Creative Dislocation: The Movement of Grace* (Nashville: Abingdon Press, 1980).
3. See Kathryn Kish Sklar, "The Last Fifteen Years," *Women in New Worlds*, eds. Hilah F. Thomas and Rosemary Skinner Keller (Nashville: Abingdon Press, 1981), pp. 48-65. Two important works appeared in the late 1960s: Barbara Welter's influential article, "The Cult of True Womanhood, 1820-1860," *American Quarterly* 18/2 (Summer 1966), and Gerda Lerner's *The Grimké Sisters of South Carolina: Pioneers for Woman's Rights and Abolition* (Boston: Houghton Mifflin Co., 1967).
4. Published in 1985 with a slightly revised title: "Reexamining the Public/Private Split: Reforming the Continent and Spreading Scriptural Holiness," in Russell E. Richey and Kenneth E. Rowe, eds., *Rethinking Methodist History* (Nashville: Kingswood Books, 1985), pp. 75-88.
5. The major study of Haven is William B. Gravely, *Gilbert Haven, Methodist Abolitionist: A Study in Race, Religion, and Reform, 1850-1880* (New York: Abingdon Press, 1973).
6. David Wood Wills, "Aspects of Social Thought in the African Methodist Episcopal Church, 1884-1910" (Ph.D. dissertation, Harvard University, 1975), chap. 6, "The Vision of Reverdy C. Ransom." See also Wills, "Reverdy C. Ransom: The Making of an A.M.E. Bishop," in *Black Apostles: Afro-American Clergy Confront the Twentieth Century*, eds. Randall K. Burkett and Richard Newman (Boston: G. K. Hall, 1978), pp. 181-212.
7. The works of Timothy L. Smith, Donald W. Dayton, Melvin E. Dieter, and Charles E. Jones were especially helpful. Much of what I learned found later expression in Jean Miller Schmidt, "Holiness and Perfection," in *Encyclopedia of the American Religious Experience*, ed. Charles H. Lippy and Peter W. Williams (New York: Charles Scribner's Sons, 1988), vol. 2, 813-29.
8. Vincent Harding, *The Other American Revolution* (Los Angeles: Center for Afro-American Studies, UCLA, and Atlanta: Institute of the Black World, 1980). See p. 79: "For a brief time, Reconstruction had provided the nineteenth century's most complete opportunity for the nation to forge a

binding chain between the best possibilities of the white American revolution
and the deep and pulsing movement of the black struggle for freedom. It was
a magnificent chance for the two to become one in the creation of a new
society. . . . Instead, America chose a 'New South.' "

9. Among the first to write about evangelical religion as empowering for women
were Nancy Hardesty, Lucille Sider Dayton, and Donald W. Dayton. See, for
example, "Women in the Holiness Movement: Feminism in the Evangelical
Tradition," in *Women of Spirit: Female Leadership in the Jewish and Christian
Traditions*, eds. Rosemary Ruether and Eleanor McLaughlin (New York: Simon
and Schuster, 1979), pp. 226-54.

10. See Barbara Hargrove, Jean Miller Schmidt, and Sheila Greeve Davaney,
"Religion and the Changing Role of Women," *Annals of the American Academy
of Political and Social Science* 480 (July 1985): 117-31.

11. Jean Miller Schmidt, "Beyond Separate Spheres: Women, Religion, and Social
Change," *The Drew Gateway* 57/3 (Fall 1987): 80-94.

12. Donald G. Mathews, *Religion in the Old South* (Chicago: University of Chicago
Press, 1977), pp. 104-5; Nancy F. Cott, *The Bonds of Womanhood* (New
Haven: Yale University Press, 1977), p. 140.

13. Scott, "On Seeing and Not Seeing," p. 9.

14. See Leonard I. Sweet, " 'A Nation Born Again': The Union Prayer Meeting
Revival and Cultural Revitalization," *In the Great Tradition: In Honor of
Winthrop S. Hudson*, ed. Joseph D. Ban and Paul R. Dekar (Valley Forge, Pa.:
Judson Press, 1982), pp. 193-221. There may still be justification for the older
term "businessmen's revival," in spite of the participation of lay evangelists like
Phoebe and Walter Palmer and other husband and wife teams. According to
Sweet, women's participation in the noonday prayer meetings was resented by
businessmen with the result that women stayed away from the meetings. Two
major works on Phoebe Palmer are Charles Edward White, *The Beauty of
Holiness: Phoebe Palmer as Theologian, Revivalist, Feminist, and Humanitarian*
(Grand Rapids, Mich.: Francis Asbury Press, 1986) and Thomas C. Oden, ed.,
Phoebe Palmer: Selected Writings (New York: Paulist Press, 1988).

15. *See* Gerda Lerner, *The Majority Finds Its Past: Placing Women in History*
(Oxford University Press, 1979), pp. 94-128, and Bettina Aptheker, *Woman's
Legacy: Essays on Race, Sex, and Class in American History* (Amherst: University
of Massachusetts Press, 1982), pp. 9-52.

16. McLoughlin, *Modern Revivalism*, p. 153.

17. See, for example, Mary Agnes Dougherty, "The Social Gospel According to
Phoebe," *Women in New Worlds*, ed. Thomas and Keller, pp. 200-216; John
Patrick McDowell, *The Social Gospel in the South: The Woman's Home Mission
Movement in the Methodist Episcopal Church, South, 1886-1939* (Baton Rouge:
Louisiana State University Press, 1982); Alice G. Knotts, "Bound by the Spirit,
Found on the Journey: The Methodist Women's Campaign for Southern Civil
Rights, 1940-1968" (Ph.D. dissertation, Iliff School of Theology and the
University of Denver, 1989).

18. Beverly Wildung Harrison, "Sexism and the Contemporary Church: When Evasion Becomes Complicity," in Alice L. Hageman, ed., *Sexist Religion and Women in the Church* (New York: Association Press, 1974), p. 202. This relates to Barbara Hargrove's insights about gender and modernization: even middle-class women were "outsiders" to the modern social order men were creating. Or, as Anne Firor Scott explained, "women had not been invited to the Great Barbecue except as cheap labor or as status symbols." ("On Seeing and Not Seeing," p. 17).

19. Betty A. DeBerg, *Ungodly Women: Gender and the First Wave of American Fundamentalism* (Minneapolis: Fortress Press, 1990), pp. 13-41.

20. Ibid., pp. 75-98. She refers to Janette Hassey, *No Time for Silence: Evangelical Women in Ministry Around the Turn of the Century* (Grand Rapids, Mich.: Zondervan, 1986), which documents growing opposition to evangelical women's public ministry after World War I. (E.g., she traces the conservative Protestant backlash in *Moody Monthly* magazines in the 1930s, p. 141.) See also Virginia Lieson Brereton, *Training God's Army: The American Bible School, 1880-1940* (Bloomington: Indiana University Press, 1990).

21. Janet Forsythe Fishburn, *The Fatherhood of God and the Victorian Family: The Social Gospel in America* (Philadelphia: Fortress Press, 1981). On Victorian domestic ideology, see also Colleen McDannell, *The Christian Home in Victorian America, 1840-1900* (Bloomington: Indiana University Press, 1986).

22. Ronald C. White, Jr. and C. Howard Hopkins, eds., *The Social Gospel: Religion and Reform in Changing America* (Philadelphia: Temple University Press, 1976).

23. Ronald C. White, Jr., *Liberty and Justice for All: Racial Reform and the Social Gospel* (San Francisco: Harper & Row, 1990).

24. William McGuire King, "The Emergence of Social Gospel Radicalism in American Methodism" (Ph.D. dissertation, Harvard University, 1977); see also King, "The Emergence of Social Gospel Radicalism: The Methodist Case," *Church History* 50 (December 1981): 436-49.

25. Ibid., 448. My doctoral student Jeanne Knepper's forthcoming dissertation on the Methodist Federation for Social Service/Action and human rights from 1907 to 1960, focuses on the intersection of a number of these issues, particularly race and gender, in the context of the radical social gospel. Although there is not room to address them here, issues of the relation of both Protestant parties to missions, treatment of Native Americans, Roman Catholic and Jewish immigrants, and colonialism would all be important to any adequate treatment of my subject today.

26. Martin E. Marty, *Righteous Empire: The Protestant Experience in America* (New York: Dial Press, 1970). It won the 1972 National Book Award in Philosophy and Religion.

27. Marty, *Righteous Empire*, p. 268.

28. Ibid., p. 270.

29. Henry Warner Bowden, "The Historiography of American Religion," in *Encyclopedia of the American Religious Experience*, ed. Charles H. Lippy and Peter W. Williams (New York: Charles Scribner's Sons, 1988), vol. 1, p. 10.

30. Martin E. Marty, *A Nation of Behavers* (Chicago: University of Chicago Press, 1976).

31. Dean M. Kelley, *Why Conservative Churches Are Growing* (New York: Harper & Row, 1972).

32. Marty traced the earlier roots of the Evangelical-Fundamentalist cluster to the nineteenth-century Evangelical Protestant mainstream and described the development in the second half of the century of a liberal/ conservative or public/private split, institutionalized with the founding of the Federal Council of Churches in 1908. After 1940, a New Evangelical, or Neo-Evangelical, party had emerged out of Fundamentalism.

33. Marty, *Nation of Behavers*, pp. 95-105. This behavioral approach was also used very successfully by Timothy P. Weber, in his study of American premillennialism. In *Living in the Shadow of the Second Coming: American Premillennialism, 1875-1982* (Chicago: University of Chicago Press, 1987, enl. ed.), Weber explained that from the late 1870s premillennialism was a haven for those who had given up on history, whose world seemed to be falling apart. Premillennialism was the "perfect solution" for those who had become disillusioned with *human* efforts to bring about the perfect social order, but still believed it would be brought about by the personal intervention of Christ. (See Weber's helpful exploration of the implications of premillennialism for social action and reform, pp. 82-104.)

34. Martin E. Marty, *The Public Church: Mainline-Evangelical-Catholic* (New York: Crossroad, 1981). See pp. ix, 43. Important for this work was Marty's distinction between fundamentalism and the side of evangelicalism that "always had the mien and openness of the public church." (p. 12) See also his updated summary of the two-party system, or public/private split, pp. 96-98, using the interpretive literature dealing with religion and modernization.

35. Martin E. Marty, "Religion in America Since Mid-Century," *Daedalus* 111 (Winter 1982): 149-63, see esp. p. 157. Cf. James Davison Hunter, *American Evangelicalism: Conservative Religion and the Quandary of Modernity* (New Brunswick, N.J.: Rutgers University Press, 1983).

36. Martin E. Marty, *Modern American Religion, Volume 1: The Irony of It All: 1839-1919* (Chicago: University of Chicago Press, 1986), pp. 13-14. Two volumes are now available of what will be Marty's monumental four-volume history. In volume 2, *The Noise of Conflict, 1919-1941* (1991), Marty's focus is on public religious conflicts.

37. Marty, *Irony*, pp. 208-18, 283-97.

38. Marty, *Protestantism in the United States* (Chicago: University of Chicago Press, 1986), pp. 260-66. Marty also referred here to fundamentalism's countermodern reaction as a worldwide phenomenon. Since 1987 he has been director of the Fundamentalism Project, a five-year program of interdisciplinary comparative study of fundamentalism.

39. No single interpreter of American religion has been called on more frequently in the last two decades to make sense of the surprising twists and turns related to these issues. In numerous articles, as well as in his regular forums in *Context* and the *Christian Century*, Marty has helped readers keep up with the complex developments in evangelicalism.

40. Sociologist Dean R. Hoge tested the public/private split thesis by building indices around several theological doctrines that Marty identified as key to his two-party characterizations. On the basis of his research Hoge concluded in *Division in the Protestant House* (Philadelphia: Westminster Press, 1976) that Marty was right in identifying these two basic parties in Protestantism. Neill Q. Hamilton in *Recovery of the Protestant Adventure* (New York: Seabury Press, 1981) explored ways to overcome the split.

41. See George M. Marsden, *Fundamentalism and American Culture: The Shaping of Twentieth Century Evangelicalism, 1870-1925* (New York: Oxford University Press, 1980); Donald W. Dayton, *Discovering An Evangelical Heritage* (New York: Harper & Row, 1976); also David O. Moberg, *The Great Reversal: Evangelism and Social Concern* (Philadelphia: J. B. Lippincott, 1972).

42. Hannah Arendt discussed the meaning of "public" in *The Human Condition* (Chicago: University of Chicago Press, 1958), especially in chapter two, pp. 22-78. She emphasized the public realm as a common meeting ground and suggested that healthy public life depends on discourse about the common good that transcends private interest. Also helpful are Parker J. Palmer, *The Company of Strangers: Christians and the Renewal of America's Public Life* (New York: Crossroad, 1981), and the older, but still useful work by John Dewey, *The Public and Its Problems* (New York: Henry Holt & Co., 1927). A good recent illustration of interdisciplinary inquiry into the meaning of "public" was the Project on Religion and American Public Life coordinated through the University of Chicago Divinity School. Some of the essays resulting from this Project were published in a special issue of *The Journal of Law and Religion* 2/2 (1984), guest ed. Robin W. Lovin.

43. Ferenc Morton Szasz, *The Divided Mind of Protestant America, 1880-1930* (University of Alabama Press, 1982). With the publication of William R. Hutchison, *The Modernist Impulse in American Protestantism* (Cambridge: Harvard University Press, 1976), there were major scholarly works on both sides of the Fundamentalist/Modernist split.

44. Marsden, *Fundamentalism and American Culture*, p. 4.

45. Ibid., pp. 85-93. Marsden was right: more careful distinctions were needed. I would still claim there is an important difference between social concern and social *action*, which moves beyond amelioration of conditions within the system to attempt to change social structures themselves. It might be wise to allow for a spectrum of positions within these two poles.

46. Szasz, *Divided Mind*, p. xi.

47. Ibid., p. 56.

48. Ibid., p. 67.

49. "The Evangelical Tradition in America," in Leonard I. Sweet, ed., *The Evangelical Tradition in America* (Macon, Ga.: Mercer University Press, 1984), pp. 1-86. The section to which I refer is on pp. 70ff. (This essay is a helpful survey of the literature on the Evangelical tradition since 1970.)

50. Ibid., p. 71, citing Marty's *Righteous Empire*.

51. Robert S. Michaelsen and Wade Clark Roof, eds., *Liberal Protestantism: Realities and Possibilities* (New York: Pilgrim Press, 1986). See Intro., p. 5, where the split is characterized as between those who "continued to seek to shape the society of which they were a part" and those who "understood the Christian call to entail escape from this corrupt world into the kingdom that is not of this world." An article by Michael Burdick in the same volume ("Overseas Mission: Failure of Nerve or Change in Strategy?," pp. 102-14) accepts the reality of the "two-party system" and elaborates two competing paradigms based on that division, an evangelical mission paradigm and an ecumenical mission paradigm.

52. Wade Clark Roof and William McKinney, *American Mainline Religion: Its Changing Shape and Future* (New Brunswick, N.J.: Rutgers University Press, 1987). Chap. 3 is entitled "The Fragmented Mainline."

53. See Robert Wuthnow, *The Restructuring of American Religion: Society and Faith Since World War II* (Princeton: Princeton University Press, 1988), and Wuthnow, *The Struggle for America's Soul: Evangelicals, Liberals, and Secularism* (Grand Rapids, Mich.: William B. Eerdmans, 1989).

54. Wuthnow, *The Struggle for America's Soul*, pp. 17, xii. Wuthnow cites a number of surveys to show that, although further distinctions could be made on each side, this binary way of thinking has reality in the popular mind. He found a high level of awareness of this division and a great deal of hostility between the two sides. The public was almost equally divided between self-styled religious liberals and religious conservatives, and only one person in six was reluctant to use these labels. Ibid., p. 23.

55. Ibid., pp. 8-18, 177-86.

56. Ibid., p. 22.

57. Wuthnow, *The Restructuring of American Religion*, pp. 148-49, 225-35, 244-57.

58. Ibid., pp. 135ff.

59. Wuthnow, *Struggle*, p. 32. This is part of a chapter entitled "Old Fissures, New Fractures." The Herberg reference is to Will Herberg, *Protestant-Catholic-Jew* (Garden City, N.Y.: Doubleday-Anchor, 1955). There is no citation for the "two-party system."

60. Jeffrey K. Hadden's *The Gathering Storm in the Churches: The Widening Gap Between Clergy and Laymen* (Garden City, N.Y.: Doubleday, 1969) was a sociological study of the growing conflict between clergy and laity in their attitudes toward and involvement in civil rights activity in the 1960s.

INTRODUCTION, 1969

1. Winthrop S. Hudson, *American Protestantism* (Chicago: University of Chicago Press, 1961), p. 60.
2. Gilbert Hobbs Barnes, *The Antislavery Impulse, 1830-1844* (New York: Appleton-Century-Crofts, 1933), p. 23.
3. Charles Worcester Clark, "Applied Christianity: Who Shall Apply It First?" *Andover Review* 19 (1893): 24-25.
4. I have used this term throughout to refer in a shorthand way to the spokespeople for the social gospel. Although it is not a proper dictionary term, its use seemed to commend itself for purposes of convenience and style.
5. Henry F. May, *Protestant Churches and Industrial America* (New York: Harper & Bros., 1949); Charles H. Hopkins, *The Rise of the Social Gospel in American Protestantism, 1865-1915* (New Haven: Yale University Press, 1940); Aaron I. Abell, *The Urban Impact on Americana Protestantism, 1865-1900* (Cambridge: Harvard University Press, 1943).

CHAPTER ONE

1. Philip Schaff, *America: A Sketch of Its Political, Social, and Religious Character*, ed. Perry Miller (Cambridge: Harvard University Press, 1961), p. 11. For Smith's statistics, see Timothy L. Smith, *Revivalism and Social Reform: American Protestantism on the Eve of the Civil War* (New York: Abingdon Press, 1957), chap. 1, pp. 15-33. On "shaping a Protestant America," see Hudson, *American Protestantism*, pp. 60, 96-99, 109.
2. Sidney E. Mead, *The Lively Experiment: The Shaping of Christianity in America* (New York: Harper & Row, Publishers, 1963), pp. 16-54.
3. Ibid., p. 57.
4. *The Autobiography of Lyman Beecher*, ed. Barbara M. Cross, 2 vols. (Cambridge: Belknap Press of Harvard University Press, 1961), 1: 252.
5. William G. McLoughlin, Jr., *Modern Revivalism: Charles Grandison Finney to Billy Graham* (New York: Ronald Press Company, 1959), p. 9; Mead, *Lively Experiment*, p. 55. See also Winthrop S. Hudson, "The Methodist Age in America," *Methodist History* 12 (April 1974): 3-15.
6. William McLoughlin defined the second great awakening—used as a more general term—in these three phases. The dates are his. See *Modern Revivalism*, pp. 12-13. In *Revivals, Awakenings, and Reform: An Essay on Religion and Social Change in America, 1607-1977* (Chicago: University of Chicago Press, 1978), McLoughlin described America's great awakenings as periods of cultural revitalization. (For the Second Great Awakening, see chap. 4, pp. 98-140.) Cf. Donald G. Mathews, "The Second Great Awakening as an Organizing Process," *American Quarterly* 21 (1969): 23-43.

7. Sidney E. Mead, *Nathaniel William Taylor, 1786-1858: A Connecticut Liberal* (Chicago: University of Chicago Press, 1942), p. 62.
8. For a more detailed examination of the "New Divinity" of Taylor and Beecher, see ibid. Mead points out Dwight's influence on Taylor, pp. 25-35.
9. Ibid., p. 111.
10. Ibid., p. 189.
11. Beecher, *Autobiography*, 2: 75. On new measures and the New Lebanon convention, see Mead, *Nathaniel W. Taylor*, pp. 200-210, and McLoughlin, *Modern Revivalism*, pp. 30-37.
12. Mead, *Nathaniel W. Taylor*, p. 200. See also George M. Marsden's major study, *The Evangelical Mind and the New School Presbyterian Experience* (New Haven: Yale University Press, 1970).
13. Ibid., p. 233.
14. McLoughlin, *Modern Revivalism*, pp. 12-13.
15. Ibid. See Leonard Sweet's discussion of evangelicalism and social reform in *The Evangelical Tradition in America*, ed. Leonard I. Sweet (Macon, Ga.: Mercer University Press, 1984), pp. 34-41, and in the same volume, Garth M. Rosell, "Charles G. Finney: His Place in the Stream," pp. 131-47. Also important for Finney's views on social reform is James M. Moorhead, "Social Reform and the Divided Conscience of Antebellum Protestantism," *Church History* 48 (December 1979): 416-30.
16. Ibid., p. 27.
17. Beecher, *Autobiography*, 2: 75.
18. McLoughlin, *Modern Revivalism*, p. 66.
19. Charles G. Finney, *Sermons on Various Subjects* (New York, 1835), pp. 3-28, discussed ibid., pp. 68-73.
20. For a discussion of Finney's lectures on revivals, see McLoughlin, *Modern Revivalism*, pp. 83-99.
21. McLoughlin, *Modern Revivalism*, pp. 101-106. Mead's study on Taylor also includes some helpful references to Hopkins and his followers. On disinterested benevolence, for example, see *Nathaniel W. Taylor*, p. 104 n.
22. McLoughlin, *Modern Revivalism*, p. 106. Important for understanding American premillennialism is Timothy P. Weber, *Living in the Shadow of the Second Coming: American Premillennialism, 1875-1982* (Chicago: University of Chicago Press, 1987).
23. Charles G. Finney, *Lectures on Systematic Theology* (London, 1851), p. 450, cited in ibid.
24. May, *Protestant Churches and Industrial America*, pp. 29-36.
25. Charles I. Foster, *An Errand of Mercy: The Evangelical United Front, 1790-1837* (Chapel Hill: University of North Carolina Press, 1960), p. 117.
26. Smith, *Revivalism and Social Reform*, p. 8.
27. Sidney E. Mead, "The Rise of the Evangelical Conception of the Ministry in America, 1607-1850," in *The Ministry in Historical Perspectives*, ed. H. Richard Niebuhr and Daniel Day Williams (New York: Harper & Bros., 1956), p. 225.

28. Clifford S. Griffin, *Their Brothers' Keepers: Moral Stewardship in the United States, 1800-1865* (New Brunswick, N.J.: Rutgers University Press, 1960), pp. 6-7, 99.
29. From the beginnings of the Society for the Promotion of Temperance in 1826, there was a strong trend toward defining temperance in terms of abstinence. Lyman Beecher's *Six Sermons on the Nature, Occasions, Signs, Evils, and Remedy of Intemperance* (Boston, 1826) reinforced that trend. Although initially a distinction was made between "ardent spirits" (distilled liquor) and fermented drinks like beer and wine, by 1833 many temperance leaders denounced tippling of any kind. See Griffin, *Their Brothers' Keepers*, pp. 38-39, 70-72; Foster, *Errand of Mercy*, pp. 167-77.
30. Griffin, *Their Brothers' Keepers*, pp. xii-xiii, 22, 44-45.
31. Foster, *Errand of Mercy*, p. 183.
32. An earlier society, which tried to deal on somewhat different premises with the problem of slavery, was the American Colonization Society, founded in 1817. Its object was to send free blacks to Africa. On the American Female Moral Reform Society, see Carroll Smith-Rosenberg, "Beauty, the Beast and the Militant Woman: Sex Roles and Social Stress in Jacksonian America," *American Quarterly* 23 (October 1971): 562-84. For a brief account of women's voluntary associations in America, see Anne Firor Scott's important article "On Seeing and Not Seeing: A Case of Historical Invisibility," *Journal of American History* 71/1 (June 1984): 7-21.
33. Barnes, *Antislavery Impulse*, pp. 17-18; Foster, *Errand of Mercy*, pp. 125, 148.
34. Griffin, *Their Brothers' Keepers*, p. 83.
35. May, *Protestant Churches and Industrial America*, p. 7.
36. Martin E. Marty, *The Infidel: Freethought and American Religion* (Cleveland: World Publishing Company, 1961), p. 108.
37. May, *Protestant Churches and Industrial America*, p. 7.
38. Marty, *Infidel*, p. 75, paraphrased from Emerson.
39. Beecher, *Works*, 1: 159-60, cited ibid., p. 111.
40. Marty, *Infidel*, p. 108.
41. Ely, *The Duty of Christian Freemen to Elect Christian Rulers*, pp. 4, 6, 8, 11, cited in Charles C. Cole, Jr., *The Social Ideas of the Northern Evangelists, 1826-1860* (New York: Columbia University Press, 1954), p. 139.
42. May, *Protestant Churches and Industrial America*, p. 25.
43. Griffin, *Their Brothers' Keepers*, p. 121.
44. Beecher, *Autobiography*, 1: 337.
45. Mead, *Lively Experiment*, p. 53.
46. Marty, *Infidel*, p. 119. On the popular denominations, see Nathan O. Hatch, *The Democratization of American Christianity* (New Haven: Yale University Press, 1989).
47. Wade Crawford Barclay, *Early American Methodism, 1769-1844* (New York: The Board of Missions and Church Extension of the Methodist Church, 1950), 2: 2, 8. See the reference to my changing views on this in the new Introduction.

For a fuller discussion see Jean Miller Schmidt, "Reexamining the Public/Private Split: Reforming the Continent and Spreading Scriptural Holiness," in *Rethinking Methodist History*, ed. Russell E. Richey and Kenneth E. Rowe (Nashville: Kingswood Books, 1985), pp. 75-88. Donald G. Mathews, *Religion in the Old South* (Chicago: University of Chicago Press, 1977), is a compelling account of the role of evangelical religion as a liberating force in the experience of black slaves and women.

48. Mead, "Evangelical Conception of the Ministry," p. 226.
49. Marty, *Infidel*, p. 119.
50. Cole, *Social Ideas*, p. 33. The basic work is Peter Cartwright, *Autobiography* (Nashville: Abingdon, 1986. Reprint of the 1956 ed.).
51. McLoughlin, *Modern Revivalism*, p. 100.
52. Ibid., p. 132.
53. Hudson, *American Protestantism*, p. 99.
54. May, *Protestant Churches and Industrial America*, p. 27. Among the important literature on abolitionism since 1969 is James M. McPherson, *The Abolitionist Legacy* (Princeton: Princeton University Press, 1975); Lawrence J. Friedman, *Gregarious Saints: Self and Community in American Abolitionism, 1830-1870* (Cambridge: Cambridge University Press, 1982); James D. Essig, *The Bonds of Wickedness: American Evangelicals Against Slavery, 1770-1808* (Philadelphia: Temple University Press, 1982); and John R. McKivigan, *The War Against Proslavery Religion: Abolitionism and the Northern Churches, 1830-1865* (Ithaca: Cornell University Press, 1984).
55. McLoughlin, *Modern Revivalism*, pp. 79-80.
56. Ibid., pp. 108-9; Barnes, *Antislavery Impulse*, pp. 35, 43-44, 48-49, 55.
57. Finney, *Lectures on Revivals*, pp. 275-76, cited by McLoughlin, *Modern Revivalism*, p. 109.
58. Barnes, *Antislavery Impulse*, pp. 66-68.
59. McLoughlin, *Modern Revivalism*, p. 82.
60. Ibid., p. 83.
61. Ibid., p. 111.
62. Barnes, *Antislavery Impulse*, p. 103.
63. Ibid., pp. 104-7.
64. Foster, *Errand of Mercy*, p. 251. As Foster indicates, among Methodists this involved the republican reform agitation leading to the 1828 schism and resulting organization of the Methodist Protestant Church in 1830.
65. McLoughlin, *Modern Revivalism*, p. 122.
66. Ibid.
67. Calvin Colton, *History and Character of American Revivals of Religion*, 3d ed.; (London, 1832), pp. 4-5, cited in Mead, "Evangelical Conception of Ministry," p. 227.
68. The term was used by a disgruntled Theodore Parker; see Mead, "Evangelical Conception of Ministry," p. 228.
69. McLoughlin, *Modern Revivalism*, pp. 137-44, 153-60.

70. Griffin, *Their Brothers' Keepers*, p. 119.
71. Ibid., p. 140.
72. Ibid., p. 159. Two basic sources on Methodism and slavery are: Donald G. Mathews, *Slavery and Methodism: A Chapter in American Morality, 1780-1845* (Princeton: Princeton University Press, 1965) and William B. Gravely, "Methodist Preachers, Slavery and Caste: Types of Social Concern in Antebellum America," *Duke Divinity School Review* 34 (Autumn 1969): 209-29.
73. Griffin, *Their Brothers' Keepers*, pp. 178-79.
74. McLoughlin, *Modern Revivalism*, p. 114.
75. Joseph Dorfman, *The Economic Mind in American Civilization, 1606-1865*, 2 vols. (New York: Viking Press, 1946), Vol. 2, especially chaps. 19 and 25.
76. May, *Protestant Churches and Industrial America*, pp. 14-15.
77. Ibid., p. 14.
78. Ernest Gellner, *Thought and Change* (Chicago: University of Chicago Press, 1965), p. 123.
79. Sidney Fine, *Laissez Faire and the General Welfare State: A Study of Conflict in American Thought, 1865-1901* (Ann Arbor: University of Michigan Press, 1956), pp. 3-25, passim.
80. Stephen Colwell, *New Themes for the Protestant Clergy: Creeds without Charity, Theology without Humanity, and Protestantism without Christianity*, 2d ed., rev. (Philadelphia: Lippincott, Grambo & Co., 1853), p. 361. See also Bruce Morgan, "Stephen Colwell: Social Prophet Before the Social Gospel," in T. Hugh Kerr, ed., *Sons of the Prophets: Leaders in Protestantism from Princeton Seminary* (Princeton: Princeton University Press, 1963), pp. 123-47.
81. Hopkins, *Rise of the Social Gospel*, p. 6.
82. Colwell, *New Themes*, p. 131.
83. Ibid., pp. 238, 361.

CHAPTER TWO

1. Leo Marx, *The Machine in the Garden: Technology and the Pastoral Ideal in America* (New York: Oxford University Press, 1967), pp. 26-27.
2. For example, Thoreau's *Walden*, Mark Twain's *Huckleberry Finn*, etc. On the "Sleepy Hollow" episode, see Marx, *Machine in the Garden*, pp. 11-16.
3. Thomas C. Cochran and William Miller, *The Age of Enterprise: A Social History of Industrial America*, rev. ed. (New York: Harper & Row, 1961), p. 74.
4. Ibid., p. 83.
5. Grover C. Loud, *Evangelized America* (New York: Dial Press, 1928), p. 224. On the name historians have given this revival, as well as women's role in it, see Leonard I. Sweet, " 'A Nation Born Again': The Union Prayer Meeting Revival and Cultural Revitalization," *In the Great Tradition: In Honor of Winthrop S. Hudson*, ed. Joseph D. Ban and Paul R. Dekar (Valley Forge, Pa.: Judson Press, 1982), pp. 193-221.

6. Smith, *Revivalism and Social Reform*, p. 64.
7. McLoughlin, *Modern Revivalism*, p. 163.
8. Smith, *Revivalism and Social Reform*, p. 63.
9. Ibid.
10. Loud, *Evangelized America*, p. 221.
11. Ibid.
12. James F. Findlay, Jr., *Dwight L. Moody: American Evangelist, 1837-1899* (Chicago: University of Chicago Press, 1969), p. 63.
13. Smith, *Revivalism and Social Reform*, pp. 67, 68.
14. Charles H. Hopkins, *History of the Y.M.C.A. in North America* (New York: Association Press, 1951), pp. 43-44.
15. Theodore Parker in Boston, who resented the "revival machinery" and questioned its effects on morality, was one outstanding exception. See his sermon on April 4, 1858, from Boston Music Hall, in Loud, *Evangelized America*, pp. 225-31.
16. Griffin, *Their Brothers' Keepers*, p. 241. On abolitionism and the benevolent empire, see John R. McKivigan, *The War Against Proslavery Religion*, pp. 111-27.
17. Ibid., p. 249.
18. Ibid.
19. Findlay, *Dwight L. Moody*, pp. 103-4.
20. Smith, *Revivalism and Social Reform*, p. 76. For a discussion of women's role in soldier's aid societies during the Civil War, see Anne Firor Scott, "On Seeing and Not Seeing," p. 12.
21. Griffin, *Their Brothers' Keepers*, p. 258.
22. William E. Dodge, lecture delivered in Baltimore, Md., March 13, 1865, quoted in Griffin, *Their Brothers' Keepers*, p. 261.
23. Henry Ward Beecher, "Home Missions and Our Country's Future," *Home Missionary* 36 (September 1863): 112, quoted in Mead, *Lively Experiment*, pp. 143-44.
24. *Congregationalist*, April 28, 1866, p. 2, cited by May, *Protestant Churches and Industrial America*, p. 41.
25. May, *Protestant Churches and Industrial America*, p. 44.
26. For example, see H. Wayne Morgan, ed., *The Gilded Age: A Reappraisal* (Syracuse: Syracuse University Press, 1963); also Paul A. Carter, *The Spiritual Crisis of the Gilded Age* (DeKalb: Northern Illinois University Press, 1971).
27. William Jewett Tucker, *My Generation* (Boston: Houghton, Mifflin Co., 1919), pp. 1-18.
28. Ibid., p. 17.
29. Henry Ward Beecher, *Evolution and Religion* (New York, 1885), p. 115, quoted in Richard Hofstadter, *Social Darwinism in American Thought*, rev. ed. (Boston: Beacon Press, 1955), p. 29. Ferenc Morton Szasz's important book, *The Divided Mind of Protestant America, 1880-1930* (University of Alabama

Press, 1982) deals at some length with the role of evolution in the liberal-conservative polarization.

30. This whole section is much indebted to Hofstadter's *Social Darwinism*. For Parrington, see Vernon Louis Parrington, *Main Currents in American Thought* (New York: Harcourt, Brace & World, Inc., 1930), 3: 198.

31. Hofstadter, *Social Darwinism*, p. 39.

32. Ibid., p. 44.

33. Quoted in ibid., p. 45.

34. *Autobiography of Andrew Carnegie* (Boston, 1920), p. 327, cited in ibid.

35. Hofstadter, *Social Darwinism*, p. 51.

36. Ibid., p. 76.

37. Fine, *Laissez Faire*, p. 82.

38. See "The Absurd Effort to Make the World Over," in *Essays of William Graham Sumner*, ed. Albert G. Keller and Maurice R. Davie (New Haven: Yale University Press, 1934), 1: 105.

39. Ibid., p. 109.

40. Hofstadter, *Social Darwinism*, p.66.

41. Fine, *Laissez Faire*, p. 126.

42. Eric F. Goldman, *Rendezvous with Destiny: A History of Modern American Reform*, rev. ed. (New York: Random House, 1956), p. 66.

43. Said by Spencer's American disciple and popularizer Edward L. Youmans, when asked by Henry George what he proposed to do about the political corruption of New York. See ibid., p.66; Hofstadter, *Social Darwinism*, p. 47.

44. Fine, *Laissez Faire*, pp. 117-25. Also Ralph Henry Gabriel, *The Course of American Democratic Thought*, 2d ed. (New York: Ronald Press Company, 1956), pp. 151-69.

45. See Roy H. Johnson, "American Baptists in the Age of Big Business," *Journal of Religion* 11 (January, 1931): 63-85. On the age of Methodist affluence, see Walter W. Benjamin, "The Methodist Episcopal Church in the Postwar Era," in Emory Stevens Bucke, ed., *The History of American Methodism* (Nashville: Abingdon Press, 1964), vol. 2, pp. 315-60.

46. Mead, *Lively Experiment*, p. 143. William G. McLoughlin, *The Meaning of Henry Ward Beecher: An Essay on the Shifting Values of Mid-Victorian America, 1840-1870* (New York: Alfred A. Knopf, 1970), pp. 99-100, argues that Beecher was not a child of the Gilded Age but of the Age of Jackson.

47. May, *Protestant Churches and Industrial America*, p. 72.

48. Henry Ward Beecher, *The Original Plymouth Pulpit: Sermons in Plymouth Church, Brooklyn*, from stenographic reports by T. J. Ellinwood, 10 vols. (Boston: Pilgrim Press, 1873), 9: 100-101.

49. Ibid., p. 192.

50. Ibid., pp. 195-96.

51. Henry Ward Beecher, *Plymouth Pulpit: Sermons Preached in Plymouth Church, Brooklyn*, from Ellinwood's stenographic reports, 4 vols. (New York: Fords, Howard & Hulbert, 1892), 4: 463-64.

52. Beecher, *Original Plymouth Pulpit*, 10: 366.
53. Herbert G. Gutman, "The Worker's Search for Power: Labor in the Gilded Age," in Morgan, *The Gilded Age*, p. 44.
54. Gutman's work seems to indicate that laborers were somewhat better off in the smaller industrial towns, ibid., pp. 41-68, passim.
55. May, *Protestant Churches and Industrial America*, p. 59.
56. *Watchman and Reflector*, November 20, 1873, p. 6, cited in ibid., p. 60. See also *New York Tribune*, December 12, 1873 quoted in Gutman, "Worker's Search for Power," p. 62.
57. See Abell, *Urban Impact on American Protestantism*.
58. Herbert G. Gutman, "Protestantism and the American Labor Movement," *American Historical Review* 72 (October 1966): 74-101.
59. Abell, *Urban Impact*, pp. 21-26.
60. May, *Protestant Churches and Industrial America*, p. 91.
61. Bernard A. Weisberger, *They Gathered at the River: The Story of the Great Revivalists and Their Impact upon Religion in America* (Boston: Little, Brown and Company, 1958); McLoughlin, *Modern Revivalism*; Findlay, *Dwight L. Moody*.
62. By 1860, he had already saved $7,000. See Findlay, *Dwight L. Moody*, p. 61.
63. Weisberger, *They Gathered at the River*, p. 196; but see Findlay, *Dwight L. Moody*, p. 126.
64. McLoughlin, *Modern Revivalism*, p. 221.
65. The depot, its location well known, later became Wanamaker's main downtown department store in Philadelphia. McLoughlin, *Modern Revivalism*, pp. 223-27.
66. From Arthur P. Fitt, *The Shorter Life of D. L. Moody* (Chicago, 1900), p. 80, quoted in Weisberger, *They Gathered at the River*, p. 210.
67. McLoughlin, *Modern Revivalism*, p. 241.
68. From A. W. Williams, *D. L. Moody* (Philadelphia, 1900), p. 324, cited in ibid., p. 253.
69. Dwight L. Moody, "To All People," pp. 489-90, quoted in McLoughlin, *Modern Revivalism*, p. 255.
70. Findlay, *Dwight L. Moody*, p. 284.
71. Ibid., pp. 249-50.
72. W. H. Daniels, *Moody, His Words* (New York, 1877), pp. 475-76, cited in McLoughlin, *Modern Revivalism*, p. 257.
73. Ernest R. Sandeen, *The Roots of Fundamentalism: British and American Millenarianism, 1800-1930* (Chicago: University of Chicago Press, 1970), pp. 88-89, 71-73. See also Phyllis D. Airhart, " 'What Must I Do To Be Saved?' Two Paths to Evangelical Conversion in Late Victorian Canada," *Church History* 59 (September 1990): 372-85.
74. Sandeen, *Roots of Fundamentalism*, p. 173.
75. Findlay, *Dwight L. Moody*, p. 253.
76. Ibid.

77. McLoughlin, *Modern Revivalism*, pp. 167-68; also McLoughlin, *Revivals, Awakenings, and Reform*.
78. Findlay, *Dwight L. Moody*, p. 302.
79. McLoughlin, *Modern Revivalism*, pp. 219-20.

CHAPTER THREE

1. Shailer Mathews, "Social Gospel," in Shailer Mathews and Gerald Birney Smith, *Dictionary of Religion and Ethics* (New York: Macmillan Company, 1921), pp. 416-17.
2. May, *Protestant Churches and Industrial America*, p. 170.
3. Hopkins, *Rise of the Social Gospel*, p. 12.
4. May, *Protestant Churches and Industrial America*, p. 91.
5. Ibid., p. 111.
6. Foster Rhea Dulles, *Labor in America*, 3d ed. (New York: T. Y. Crowell & Company, 1966), pp. 106-8. Also Arthur Mann, *Yankee Reformers in the Urban Age: Social Reform in Boston, 1880-1900* (Cambridge: Belknap Press of Harvard University Press, 1954), pp. 178-80.
7. Mann, *Yankee Reformers*, p. 176.
8. May, *Protestant Churches and Industrial America*, p. 92.
9. *Independent*, August 2, 1877, p. 16; *Congregationalist*, July 25, 1877, p. 236, quoted in ibid., pp. 92-93.
10. July 25, 1877, p. 62, cited in ibid., p. 93.
11. From the *Christian Union*, August 1, 1877, p. 93, quoted in ibid., p. 94.
12. May, *Protestant Churches and Industrial America*, p. 95.
13. Dulles, *Labor in America*, p. 141.
14. May, *Protestant Churches and Industrial America*, p. 100.
15. Dulles, *Labor in America*, p. 124.
16. Arthur Meier Schlesinger, *The Rise of the City, 1828-1898* (New York: Macmillan Company, 1933), pp. 68, 76.
17. Ibid., pp. 64, 68, and chap. 4.
18. Josiah Strong, *Our Country: Its Possible Future and Its Present Crisis*, rev. ed., based on census of 1890 (New York: Baker & Taylor Co., 1891), p. 218.
19. Ibid., p. 172.
20. Ibid., pp. 143-44.
21. May, *Protestant Churches and Industrial America*, p. 116.
22. From Ida M. Tarbell, *The Nationalizing of Business, 1878-1898* (New York, 1936), p. 89, cited by Hopkins, *Rise of the Social Gospel*, p. 99.
23. Hopkins, *Rise of the Social Gospel*, p. 79.
24. From Henry George, Jr., *The Life of Henry George*, 25th anniv. ed. (New York, 1905), pp. 191-93, cited by Fine, *Laissez Faire*, p. 290.

25. Henry George, Jr., "How the Book Came to Be Written," in Henry George, *Progress and Poverty* (New York, 1879), p. xii, cited by Fine, *Laissez Faire*, p. 290.
26. Quoted in Goldman, *Rendezvous with Destiny*, p. 35.
27. Walter Rauschenbusch, *Christianizing the Social Order* (New York: Macmillan Company, 1912), p. 394.
28. Edward Bellamy, *Looking Backward: 2000-1887* (New York: New American Library, 1960), p. 73.
29. Fine, *Laissez Faire*, p. 300.
30. Ibid., p. 301.
31. Robert T. Handy included him with Washington Gladden and Walter Rauschenbusch as representative of the theology, ethics, and social program of the social gospel movement in America. See Robert T. Handy, ed., *The Social Gospel in America, 1870-1920: Gladden, Ely, Rauschenbusch* (New York: Oxford University Press, 1966), pp. 16, 173-250. On the new reforming radicalism in economics and sociology, see also Dorothy Ross, *The Origins of American Social Science* (Cambridge: Cambridge University Press, 1991), pp. 98-140.
32. From *Social Aspects of Christianity*, quoted in ibid., p. 205.
33. Handy, *Social Gospel*, p. 177.
34. Fine, *Laissez Faire*, p. 255.
35. Hofstadter, *Social Darwinism*, p. 123.
36. On this basis, Kenneth Cauthen distinguished between "evangelical" and "modernistic" liberalism; see *The Impact of American Religious Liberalism* (New York: Harper & Row, 1962), pp. 27-30. Lloyd J. Averill made the same point in a slightly different way by defining late-nineteenth-century American liberalism as the convergence of two movements, evangelicalism and the "rising tide of secular, scientific, intellectual, and social reform." See Lloyd J. Averill, *American Theology in the Liberal Tradition* (Philadelphia: Westminster Press, 1967), p. 69. On liberalism, the "New Theology," and the social gospel, see also: Theodore T. Munger, *The Freedom of Faith* (Boston: Houghton, Mifflin Company, 1883), prefatory essay on the "New Theology"; H. Shelton Smith, *Changing Conceptions of Original Sin: A Study in American Theology Since 1750* (New York: Charles Scribner's Sons, 1955); and Sydney E. Ahlstrom, "Theology in America: A Historical Survey," in James Ward Smith and A. Leland Jamison, eds., *The Shaping of American Religion* (Princeton: Princeton University Press, 1961), 1: 285-98. William McGuire King explored the relationship between the Boston Personalist school of liberal theology and the social reconstructionist views of Methodist social gospel radicals in "The Emergence of Social Gospel Radicalism in American Methodism," (Ph.D. dissertation, Harvard University, 1977).
37. Handy, *Social Gospel*, p. 7.
38. There is a brief biographical sketch of Gladden by Handy in ibid., pp. 19-32. For a full-length biography, see Jacob Henry Dorn, *Washington Gladden: Prophet of the Social Gospel* (Columbus: Ohio State University Press, 1967).

39. Washington Gladden, *Working People and Their Employers* (Boston, 1876), cited by Handy, *Social Gospel*, p. 38.
40. Washington Gladden, *Applied Christianity: Moral Aspects of Social Questions* (Boston: Houghton, Mifflin Company, 1886), p. 125.
41. Handy, *Social Gospel*, p. 49.
42. Hopkins, *Rise of the Social Gospel*, pp. 113-14. The reports of the meetings were published; see Evangelical Alliance for the U.S., *National Perils and Opportunities* (New York: Baker & Taylor Co., 1887) and *National Needs and Remedies* (New York: Baker & Taylor Co., 1890). On the Evangelical Alliance, see Philip D. Jordan, *The Evangelical Alliance for the United States of America, 1847-1900: Ecumenism, Identity, and the Religion of the Republic* (New York: Edwin Mellen Press, 1982).
43. Dorothea R. Muller, "Josiah Strong and the Social Gospel: A Christian's Response to the Challenge of the City," *Journal of the Presbyterian Historical Society* 39 (September 1961): 151. See also Dorothea R. Muller, "Josiah Strong and the Challenge of the City" (unpublished Ph.D. dissertation, New York University, 1955) and "The Social Philosophy of Josiah Strong: Social Christianity and American Progressivism," *Church History* 28 (June 1959): 183-201.
44. Josiah Strong, *Religious Movements for Social Betterment* (New York: Baker & Taylor Co., 1900), p. 42.
45. See W. S. Rainsford, *The Story of a Varied Life: An Autobiography* (New York: Doubleday, Page & Co., 1924).
46. It should be added that other social Christians were also indebted to British literature and sociological investigation. Works like those of Maurice, Kingsley, and John Ruskin; Sir John Seeley's *Ecce Homo* (1866), William H. Fremantle's *The World as the Subject of Redemption* (1885), and William Booth's *In Darkest England* (1890) were widely read. The relationship was reciprocal, however. See Winthrop S. Hudson, "How American Is Religion in America?" in *Reinterpretations in American Church History*, ed. Jerald C. Brauer (Chicago: University of Chicago Press, 1968), pp. 163-66.
47. May, *Protestant Churches and Industrial America*, p. 186.
48. Ibid., p. 184.
49. See Christopher L. Webber, "William Dwight Porter Bliss: Priest and Socialist," *Historical Magazine of the Protestant Episcopal Church* 28 (1959): 11-39.
50. William Dwight Porter Bliss, *The Dawn*, Vol. 1, No. 1 (May 15, 1889), quoted in Hopkins, *Rise of the Social Gospel*, p. 175.
51. Dores Robinson Sharpe, *Walter Rauschenbusch* (New York: Macmillan Company, 1942), p. 61. See also Paul M. Minus, *Walter Rauschenbusch: American Reformer* (New York: Macmillan Publishing Company, 1988).
52. May, *Protestant Churches and Industrial America*, p. 136.
53. Fine, *Laissez Faire*, pp. 113-16.
54. Winthrop S. Hudson, *The Great Tradition of the American Churches* (New York: Harper & Bros., 1953), pp. 161-62.

55. Ibid., p. 157.
56. Russell H. Conwell, *Acres of Diamonds* (New York: Harper & Brothers, 1915), p. 19.
57. Findlay, *Dwight L. Moody*, pp. 308-21.
58. Ibid., p. 306.
59. Dwight L. Moody, *Record of Christian Work*, 5 (April 1886): 3, quoted in ibid., p. 327.
60. The phrase was actually used by a friend of Moody's, T. W. Harvey of Chicago. See Findlay, *Dwight L. Moody*, p. 327.
61. Ibid., p. 328.
62. Ibid., pp. 339-40.
63. Sandeen, *Roots of Fundamentalism*, pp. 174-75; Findlay, *Dwight L. Moody*, pp. 351-52.
64. Findlay, *Dwight L. Moody*, pp. 351-52; Sandeen, *Roots of Fundamentalism*, pp. 183-85.
65. Sandeen, *Roots of Fundamentalism*, p. 132.
66. Ibid.
67. Ibid., p. 134.
68. Ibid., pp. 140-41.
69. Ibid., p. 159.
70. Ibid., p. 155.
71. Ibid., pp. 114-31.
72. Arthur M. Schlesinger, Sr., "A Critical Period in American Religion," *Massachusetts Historical Society Proceedings*, 64 (October 1930-June 1932): 523-46.

CHAPTER FOUR

1. Hopkins, *Rise of the Social Gospel*, p. 122.
2. Although Andrew Carnegie was in Scotland at the time, his acquiescence in Frick's policies and actions indicated his general approval of Frick's plan. Yet it is probably true that had Carnegie himself been at the plant he would have avoided bringing in outside labor to enforce his terms. See Robert Green McCloskey, *American Conservatism in the Age of Enterprise, 1865-1910* (Cambridge: Harvard University Press, 1951), pp. 149-52; Dulles, *Labor in America*, pp. 166-71.
3. "Omaha Platform," July 1892, in John D. Hicks, *The Populist Revolt* (Minneapolis: University of Minnesota Press, 1931), p. 441.
4. Goldman, *Rendezvous with Destiny*, pp. 42-43.
5. May, *Protestant Churches and Industrial America*. p. 107.
6. Dulles, *Labor in America*, p. 172.
7. Ibid., pp. 171-80.
8. May, *Protestant Churches and Industrial America*, p. 110.

9. Goldman, *Rendezvous with Destiny*, p. 54.
10. Josiah Strong, *The New Era: or the Coming Kingdom* (New York: Baker & Taylor Co., 1893), pp. 261-62, 334, 313-14.
11. May, *Protestant Churches and Industrial America*, p. 110.
12. Fine, *Laissez Faire*, p. 264.
13. Hofstadter, *Social Darwinism*, p. 104. Hofstadter thought it significant that these three very different writers all saw the group as the unit of survival and regarded solidarity as a thoroughly natural phenomenon.
14. Hopkins, *Rise of the Social Gospel*, p. 123.
15. May, *Protestant Churches and Industrial America*. p. 202.
16. Walter Rauschenbusch, "The Genesis of 'Christianity and the Social Crisis,' " *Rochester Theological Seminary Bulletin* (November 1918), pp. 51-52.
17. Rauschenbusch, *Christianizing the Social Order*, p. 93.
18. From the pamphlet "Spirit and Aims of the Brotherhood of the Kingdom," 1893, in Sharpe, *Walter Rauschenbusch*, p. 116.
19. Sharpe, *Walter Rauschenbusch*, p. 116.
20. "Spirit and Aims of the Brotherhood of the Kingdom," in ibid., p. 122.
21. Ibid.
22. Ibid., p. 124.
23. Hopkins, *Rise of the Social Gospel*, p. 131. Cf. Paul Minus, *Walter Rauschenbusch*, pp. 85-93. Minus indicates that after 1894 the circle of members widened to include women and non-Baptists (p. 87).
24. Sharpe, *Walter Rauschenbusch*, p. 128.
25. Robert Theodore Handy, "George D. Herron and the Social Gospel in American Protestantism, 1890-1901" (Ph.D. dissertation, University of Chicago, 1949), p. iii.
26. Ibid., p. 90.
27. Hopkins, *Rise of the Social Gospel*, pp. 184-85.
28. Handy, "George D. Herron," p. 20.
29. Hopkins, *Rise of the Social Gospel*, p. 187.
30. *The Kingdom*, April 20, 1894, p. 9.
31. Ibid., April 20, 1894, p. 9; June 7, 1895, p. 12.
32. Ibid., April 20, 1894, pp. 3-4.
33. Handy, "George D. Herron," p. 65.
34. George D. Herron, *The New Redemption: A Call to the Church to Reconstruct Society According to the Gospel of Christ* (New York: Thomas Y. Crowell & Company, 1893), pp. 14-15.
35. Ibid., pp. 17-18.
36. Ibid., p. 60.
37. Ibid., p. 143.
38. George D. Herron, *A Plea for the Gospel* (New York, 1892), preface, quoted in Hopkins, *Rise of the Social Gospel*, p, 193.
39. George D. Herron, *The Christian State: A Political Vision of Christ* (New York: Thomas Y. Crowell & Company, 1895), p. 62.

NOTES TO PAGES 86-93

40. Herron, *A Plea for the Gospel*, pp. 145-46, quoted in May, *Protestant Churches and Industrial America*, p. 253.
41. Herron, *The Christian State*, pp. 179, 183.
42. *The Kingdom*, April 27, 1894, p. 24.
43. May, *Protestant Churches and Industrial America*, p. 253.
44. "Forward Movements in Theological Training," in *Congregationalist*, April 19, 1894, pp. 557-58. A similar article also appeared in *The Kingdom*, April 27, 1894, pp. 25-26.
45. Handy, "George D. Herron," p. 54.
46. David R. Breed, "Christian Beneficence and Some Theories Affecting Property," *Presbyterian and Reformed Review* 5 (1894): 287, quoted in Handy, "George D. Herron," p. 51.
47. May, *Protestant Churches and Industrial America*, p. 255.
48. Handy, "George D. Herron," p. 90.
49. Ibid., pp. 115-16.
50. Hopkins, *Rise of the Social Gospel*, p. 200. Studies on later periods of Herron's life include Phyllis Ann Nelson, "George D. Herron and the Socialist Clergy, 1890-1914" (Ann Arbor, Mich.: University Microfilms, 1953); Herbert Kieterich, "Patterns of Dissent: The Reform Ideas and Activities of George D. Herron" (University of New Mexico: microfilm, 1957); and Mitchell Pirie Briggs, *George D. Herron and the European Settlement* (Stanford University Press, 1932).
51. Union Settlement Association, *Seventh Report*, 1902, pp. 9-10, cited in Hopkins, *Rise of the Social Gospel*, p. 157.
52. "The Ethics of Some Publishers," *Christian Century* 50 (1933), 1206-8, cited by Hopkins, *Rise of the Social Gospel*, p. 143. See also Charles M. Sheldon, *His Life Story* (New York: George H. Doran Company, 1925), pp. 99, 102. For a recent study of Sheldon, see Timothy Miller, *Following In His Steps: A Biography of Charles M. Sheldon* (Knoxville: University of Tennessee Press, 1987).
53. Laura M. Jones, *The Life and Sayings of Sam P. Jones, a Minister of the Gospel*, 2d and rev. ed. (Atlanta, Ga.: Franklin-Turner Company, 1907).
54. In a sense this represented for the South a first step in the direction of social Christianity, although a social gospel comparable to that of the North did not exist in the South until after the turn of the century.
55. Laura M. Jones, *Life of Sam Jones*, p. 189.
56. Ibid., p. 147.
57. Ibid., p. 211.
58. Herron, *The New Redemption*, p. 61.
59. See McLoughlin, *Modern Revivalism*, p. 316.
60. Ibid., pp. 317-18.
61. Headlines in the Democratic Toledo *Bee*, quoted in ibid., p. 321.
62. Brand Whitlock, *Forty Years of It* (New York, 1916), p. 114, quoted in McLoughlin, *Modern Revivalism*, p. 324.
63. Jones, *Life of Sam Jones*, p. 284.

64. McLoughlin, *Modern Revivalism*, p. 326.
65. Biographical sketch of Mills in John Junkin Francis and Charles B. Morrell, eds., *Mills' Meetings Memorial Volume* (Cincinnati: The Standard Publishing Company, 1892), pp. 88-95. Also McLoughlin, *Modern Revivalism*, p. 330.
66. Francis and Morrell, *Mills' Meetings Memorial Volume*, pp. i, 215-16.
67. Ibid. p. 94.
68. Ibid., p. 112.
69. *The Kingdom*, April 20, 1894, p. 9.
70. Handy, "George D. Herron," p. 61.
71. *The Kingdom*, June 1, 1894, p. 109.
72. McLoughlin, *Modern Revivalism*, p. 345.
73. Dorn, *Washington Gladden*, p. 113.
74. B. Fay Mills, *God's World and Other Sermons* (New York: Fleming H. Revell Company, 1894), p. 279.
75. Three of these sermons are contained in Henry Stauffer, ed., *The Great Awakening in Columbus, Ohio, under the labors of Rev. B. Fay Mills and His Associates* (Columbus, Ohio: Rev. W. L. Lemon, 1895), pp. 43-49, 50-61, 61-69; the quotation is on p. 46.
76. Ibid., pp. 51, 58-59, 60, 55, 62.
77. Ibid., p. 74.
78. Ibid., pastors' testimonies, pp. 143-45.
79. Washington Gladden, "The New Evangelism," December 4, 1895, Preface to Stauffer, *Great Awakening*, p. 5. On social evangelism as an early strategy of social reform, compared with social engineering and social reconstructionism, see William McGuire King, "The Emergence of Social Gospel Radicalism: The Methodist Case," *Church History* 50 (December 1981), pp. 436-49.
80. Stauffer, *Great Awakening*, p. 147.
81. McLoughlin, *Modern Revivalism*, pp. 341-42.
82. *The Kingdom*, April 10, 1890, pp. 127-28.
83. *Christian Advocate*, April 23, 1896, p. 265; July 23, p. 490; September 23, 1897, p. 618.
84. Washington Gladden, "The New Departure of Mr. Mills," *The Kingdom*, October 14, 1897, pp. 23-24.
85. Ibid.
86. See "Why I Return to the Church," *Advance*, June 24, 1915, pp. 1251-52.
87. Evangelical Alliance for the U.S.A., *Christianity Practically Applied* (New York: Baker & Taylor Company, 1894), 1: iv. Cf. Philip Jordan, *The Evangelical Alliance* (1982), pp. 177-78.
88. Ibid., p. 250.
89. Richard K. Curtis, *They Called Him Mister Moody* (Grand Rapids, Mich. Wm. B. Eerdmans Publishing Company, 1967), p. 274.
90. A complete account of this campaign is given in H. B. Hartzler, *Moody in Chicago: The World's Fair Gospel Campaign* (New York: Fleming H. Revell Company, 1894).

91. Ibid., p. 70.
92. Ibid., pp. 64, 69-70. See also Schlesinger, "A Critical Period in American Religion," p. 19; and Rufus B. Spain, *At Ease in Zion: A Social History of Southern Baptists, 1865-1900* (Nashville, Tenn.: Vanderbilt University Press, 1967), pp. 150-51.
93. Hartzler, *Moody in Chicago*, p. 232.
94. *The New York Times*, October 11, 1896, quoted in Findlay, *Dwight L. Moody*, p. 403.
95. *Congregationalist*, April 21, 1897, pp. 598-99.
96. Findlay, *Dwight L. Moody*, pp. 403-5.
97. Sandeen, *Roots of Fundamentalism*, p. 173.
98. Ibid., pp. 168-69.
99. Hartzler, *Moody in Chicago*, p. 37.
100. Findlay, *Dwight L. Moody*, p. 410.

CHAPTER FIVE

1. For example, *Congregationalist*, February 3, 1906, p. 145. See also the *Watchman*, September 6, 1900, p. 9, quoted in McLoughlin, *Modern Revivalism*, p. 348.
2. The report of the Presbyterian Evangelistic Committee to the General Assembly in 1905 noted the formation of the Methodist and Congregational committees; see Presbyterian Church in the U.S.A., *Minutes of the General Assembly* (Philadelphia: by the Stated Clerk, 1905), p. 34. The report of the organization of a National Board of Evangelism of the Disciples appeared in the *Congregationalist*, January 6, 1906, p. 34. The Disciples Board was established in 1904.
3. Rauschenbusch, *Christianizing the Social Order*, p. 94.
4. Strong, *The New Era*, p. 118.
5. Ibid., p. 126. See also Philip Jordan, *Evangelical Alliance*, p. 164.
6. Muller, "Josiah Strong and the Challenge of the City," pp. 54-55. Philip Jordan, *Evangelical Alliance*, pp. 164-65.
7. May, *Protestant Churches and Industrial America*, p. 255, from the now lost manuscript biography of Strong by E. and M. Strong.
8. Letter to the editors of *The Kingdom*, n.d., in Scrapbook, vol. 4, cited by Muller, "Josiah Strong and the Challenge of the City," p. 57.
9. Ibid., p. 86.
10. Ibid., pp. 88-102.
11. Ibid., p. 105.
12. *Minutes*, 5, May 6, 1898, p. 9, quoted in ibid., p. 103.
13. Josiah Strong, *Our World: The New World-Life* (Garden City, N.Y.: Doubleday, Page & Company, 1913), pp. 462-63. Strong's resignation from the leadership

of the Alliance in 1898 may well have been evidence of his moving into a new strategy of social reform, what William McGuire King calls social engineering.

14. Muller, "Josiah Strong and the Challenge of the City," p. 122.
15. Josiah Strong, *The Next Great Awakening* (New York; Baker & Taylor Co., 1902), pp. 53, 120, 127, 139.
16. Ibid., p. 109.
17. Dorn, *Washington Gladden*, pp. 379-81.
18. McLoughlin, *Modern Revivalism*, p. 393 n.
19. Dorn, *Washington Gladden*, p. 381.
20. Letter, January 16, 1905, Gladden Papers, cited in ibid.
21. Washington Gladden, *Social Salvation* (Boston: Houghton, Mifflin Company, 1902), p. 30.
22. Indeed, he had said in his remarks at Chapman's revival in Dayton, that this form of evangelism made only a slight impression on the unchurched masses and that only re-establishment of the social role of the churches would bring them the influence they were seeking. See Dorn, *Washington Gladden*, p. 382.
23. Washington Gladden, *The Church and Modern Life* (Boston: Houghton, Mifflin Company, 1908), pp. 180-85.
24. Sharpe, *Walter Rauschenbusch*, p. 92.
25. Walter Rauschenbusch, "The Ideals of Social Reformers," *American Journal of Sociology* 2 (July 1896-May 1897): 202-19, reprinted in Handy, *Social Gospel*, pp. 274-75.
26. Letter to L. C. Barnes, 1918, quoted in Sharpe, *Walter Rauschenbusch*, p. 435.
27. Sharpe, *Walter Rauschenbusch*, p. 393.
28. Ibid., p. 435.
29. Walter Rauschenbusch, "The New Evangelism," *Independent* 56 (January-June 1904): 1054-59, in Handy, *Social Gospel*, p. 325.
30. Ibid., p. 329.
31. Ibid.
32. Handy, *Social Gospel*, p. 323.
33. Walter Rauschenbusch, *Christianity and the Social Crisis* (New York: Macmillan Company, 1907), p. 349.
34. Ibid., p. 351
35. Ibid., p. 357.
36. Ibid., p. 367.
37. Helen A. C. Dixon, *A. C. Dixon: A Romance of Preaching* (New York: n.p., 1931), p. 23.
38. Ibid., pp. 145-46.
39. Ibid., pp. 162-63.
40. Amzi Clarence Dixon, *Evangelism Old and New: God's Search for Man in All Ages* (New York: American Tract Society, 1905), pp. 38, 43.
41. Ibid., p. 43.
42. Ibid., p. 44.
43. Ibid., p. 46.

44. Ibid., p. 39.
45. McLoughlin, *Modern Revivalism*, p. 393.
46. Ibid., p. 364.
47. Ibid., p. 365.
48. Ibid., p. 367.
49. Ibid., p. 368.
50. *Congregationalist*, December 9, 1905, p. 882; January 27, 1906, p. 134.
51. Ibid., January 6, 1906, p. 26.
52. McLoughlin, *Modern Revivalism*, p. 374.
53. Ibid.
54. Ford Cyrinde Ottman, *J. Wilbur Chapman, A Biography* (Garden City, N.Y.: Doubleday, Page & Company, 1920), pp. 29-30.
55. McLoughlin, *Modern Revivalism*, p. 377.
56. Ottman, *J. Wilbur Chapman*, p. 28.
57. J. Wilbur Chapman, *Present-Day Evangelism* (New York: Baker & Taylor Co., 1903), p. 17.
58. McLoughlin gives a full description of the plan, *Modern Revivalism*, pp. 378-79.
59. Ibid., pp. 380-81. See also Ottman, *J. Wilbur Chapman*, p. 131.
60. McLoughlin, *Modern Revivalism*, p. 382.
61. Ibid.
62. For example, "Gypsy" Smith held what was reputed to be a very popular series of revival meetings in Boston just three years before Chapman's city-wide campaign in 1909. See ibid., p. 392.
63. Ibid., pp. 354-63.
64. Warren A. Candler, *Great Revivals and the Great Republic* (Nashville, Tenn.: Publishing House of the Methodist Episcopal Church, South, 1904), pp. 276, 271.
65. Ibid., p. 271.
66. See Robert T. Handy, "The Protestant Quest for a Christian America, 1830-1930," *Church History* 22 (March 1952): 8-20, reprinted in *Facet Books* (Philadelphia: Fortress Press, 1967). Handy makes it clear that both sides "were one in their effort to Christianize a nation," but I think he underestimated their different understandings as to how this should be done. See especially pp. 15-17 in the Fortress Press edition. In *A Christian America: Protestant Hopes and Historical Realities* (New York: Oxford University Press, 1971), Handy rightly emphasized the dynamic, culture-shaping power of religious traditions as a corrective to the stimulus-response interpretation of the rise of the social gospel (formulated by Arthur Schlesinger, Henry May, and others).
67. Robert T. Handy, "Charles L. Thompson—Presbyterian Architect of Cooperative Protestantism," *Journal of the Presbyterian Historical Society* 33 (December 1955): 214.
68. "Platform of the Open and Institutional Church League," in Elias B. Sanford, *Origin and History of the Federal Council of the Churches of Christ in America* (Hartford, Conn.: S. S. Scranton Company, 1916), pp. 397-98.
69. Sanford, *Origin and History of the F. C. C.*, p. 38.

70. Handy, "Charles L. Thompson," p. 216.
71. Sanford, *Origin and History of the F. C. C.* p. 108.
72. Ibid., p. 112.
73. Ibid., p. 146.
74. Ibid., p. 449.
75. John A. Hutchison, *We Are Not Divided: A Critical and Historical Study of the Federal Council of the Churches of Christ in America* (New York: Round Table Press, Inc., 1941), p. 30.
76. Sanford, *Origin and History of the F. C. C.*, pp. 188-89.
77. Ibid., p. 176.
78. Charles S. Macfarland, *Christian Unity in the Making: The First Twenty-Five Years of the Federal Council of the Churches of Christ in America, 1905-1930* (New York: Federal Council of the Churches of Christ in America, 1948), p. 15. See also Samuel McCrea Cavert, *The American Churches in the Ecumenical Movement: 1900-1968* (New York: Association Press, 1968), p. 43.
79. Elias B. Sanford, ed., *Church Federation: Inter-Church Conference on Federation* (New York: Fleming H. Revell Company, 1905), pp. 133-39.
80. Ibid., pp. 173-585.
81. Ibid., p. 34.
82. Ibid., pp. 87, 33.
83. Cavert, *American Churches in the Ecumenical Movement*, p. 52.
84. Elias B. Sanford, ed., *Federal Council of the Churches of Christ in America: Report of the First Meeting of the Federal Council, Philadelphia, 1908* (New York: Revell Press, 1909), p. 20 (hereafter referred to as *Federal Council Proceedings, 1908*).
85. Sanford, *Origin and History of the F. C. C.*, pp. 248, 324; Cavert, *American Churches in the Ecumenical Movement*, p. 70.
86. *Federal Council Proceedings*, 1908, pp. 235-36.
87. Ibid., p. 239. Two paragraphs regarding the rights of workers were added to the Methodist statement; Charles Stelzle probably suggested these. See Hopkins, *Rise of the Social Gospel*, pp. 310-11; Macfarland, *Christian Unity in the Making*, p. 46. On the Methodist Social Creed and the Social Creed of the Churches, see Donald K. Gorrell, "The Methodist Federation for Social Service and the Social Creed," *Methodist History* 13 (January 1975): 16-22. Gorrell identified Harry F. Ward as the principal author of the Methodist Social Creed.
88. Macfarland, *Christian Unity in the Making*, p. 46.
89. *Federal Council Proceedings*, 1908, p. 69.
90. Ibid., p. 76.
91. Ibid., p. 395.
92. *Congregationalist*, September 29, 1906, p. 396.
93. Helen Dixon, *A. C. Dixon*, p. 170.
94. Ibid., p. 181.
95. Ibid.
96. Sandeen, *The Roots of Fundamentalism*, p. 172.

CHAPTER SIX

1. Hutchinson, *We Are Not Divided*, p. 59.
2. See especially Macfarland, *Christian Unity in the Making*, pp. 51-60; Cavert, *American Churches in the Ecumenical Movement*, p. 54.
3. Cavert, *American Churches in the Ecumenical Movement*, p. 66.
4. Macfarland, *Christian Unity in the Making*, pp. 53-54.
5. Cavert, *American Churches in the Ecumenical Movement*, p. 66.
6. Charles S. Macfarland, ed., *Christian Unity at Work: The Federal Council of the Churches of Christ in America in Quadrennial Session at Chicago, Illinois, 1912*, 2d ed. (New York: F.C.C.C.A., 1913), p. 165 (hereafter referred to as *Federal Council Proceedings*, 1912). On the institutionalization of the social gospel in mainstream Protestant denominations and in the Federal Council of Churches, see Donald K. Gorrell, *The Age of Social Responsibility: The Social Gospel in the Progressive Era, 1900-1920* (Macon, Ga.: Mercer University Press, 1988).
7. Excerpts from *Across the Years* (New York: Macmillan Company, 1936), quoted in Macfarland, *Christian Unity in the Making* pp. 63-64.
8. Macfarland, *Christian Unity in the Making* pp. 66-67.
9. Ibid., p. 68.
10. Elias B. Sanford, ed., *Third Annual Report of the Executive Committee of the Federal Council of the Churches of Christ in America* (New York: National Office, 1911), p. 9.
11. Macfarland, *Christian Unity in the Making*, p. 68.
12. Cavert, *American Churches in the Ecumenical Movement*, p. 68.
13. Ibid., p. 67.
14. Jesse Bader, "Data regarding the Department of Evangelism of the Federal Council of Churches and the National Council of Churches," mimeographed (New York, 1950), p. 1.
15. *Federal Council Proceedings*, 1912, p. 149.
16. Ibid., p. 153.
17. Ibid., p. 151.
18. Macfarland, *Across the Years*, p. 298.
19. *Federal Council Proceedings*, 1912, p. 188.
20. Ibid., pp. 188-89.
21. Ibid., p. 191.
22. Cavert, *American Churches in the Ecumenical Movement*, p. 70.
23. Macfarland, *Christian Unity in The Making*, p. 350.
24. McLoughlin, *Modern Revivalism*, p. 405. See also William G. McLoughlin, Jr., *Billy Sunday Was His Real Name* (Chicago: University of Chicago Press, 1955).
25. McLoughlin, *Modern Revivalism*, p. 409.
26. Ibid., p. 410.
27. Ibid., pp. 387-88.
28. Ibid., p. 388.
29. Ibid., p. 421.

30. A full account of Sunday's Columbus revival and the confrontation with Gladden is given in Dorn, *Washington Gladden*, pp. 378-401.
31. Ibid., pp. 387-88.
32. Ibid., p. 388.
33. Ibid., p. 393.
34. Ibid., p. 394.
35. Ibid., p. 401.
36. Josiah Strong, *The Next Great Awakening*, 10th ed. (New York: Baker & Taylor Co., 1913), p. iii.
37. Ibid., p. iv.
38. Ibid., pp. ix-x.
39. Ibid., pp. xi-xv, xix.
40. Ibid., pp. xx-xxi.
41. Josiah Strong, *The New World-Religion* (Garden City, N.Y.: Doubleday, Page & Co., 1915), p. 248.
42. Ibid., pp. 229-30.
43. Ibid., pp. 342-43, 264-65.
44. Ibid., p. 285.
45. Ibid., pp. 121-22.
46. Ibid., p. 151.
47. Ibid., p. 412.
48. Ibid., pp. 414-15.
49. Ibid., p. 480.
50. Ibid., pp. 437, 465.
51. Ibid., p. 505.
52. Ibid., p. 466.
53. Handy, *Social Gospel*, p. 338.
54. Rauschenbusch, *Christianizing the Social Order*, p. 458.
55. Ibid., p. 42. In 1917, Rauschenbusch himself supplied the needed theology for the social awakening in his famous *A Theology for the Social Gospel* (New York: Macmillan Company, 1917). He also attempted to give voice to the social passions of his generation in a book of prayers published in 1910, *For God and the People: Prayers of the Social Awakening* (Boston: Pilgrim Press, 1910).
56. Rauschenbusch, *Christianizing the Social Order*, pp. 103-4.
57. Ibid., pp. 107-8.
58. Ibid., p. 142.
59. Ibid., pp. 114, 116.
60. Ibid., pp. 118, 120, 122.
61. Ibid., pp. 464-65.
62. Harry F. Ward, *Social Evangelism* (New York: Missionary Education Movement of the United States and Canada, 1915), pp. 1-2.
63. Ibid., p. 2.
64. Ibid., pp. 2-3.
65. Ibid., pp. 4, 52, 39, 53.
66. Ibid., pp. 54-55.

67. Ibid., pp. 59-60.
68. Ibid., p. 64.
69. Ibid., pp. 98, 108.
70. Ibid., pp. 131-32.
71. Ibid., pp. 137, 142.
72. Charles S. Macfarland, ed., *Library of Christian Cooperation: Reports of the Federal Council and its Commissions and Committees to the Third Quadrennial Meeting at St. Louis, Mo., December, 1916* (New York: Missionary Education Movement, 1917), 5: 1-31.
73. Hopkins, *Rise of the Social Gospel*, p. 280. Gorrell, *Age of Social Responsibility*, pp. 152-53.
74. Later historians have not succeeded in defining the aims of the Progressive movement any more clearly or precisely than did a contemporary, Benjamin Parke DeWitt, in *The Progressive Movement: a Non-Partisan, Comprehensive Discussion of Current Tendencies in American Politics* (New York: Macmillan Company, 1915), pp. 4-5; reprinted, with an introduction by Arthur Mann (Seattle: University of Washington Press, 1968). See also George E. Mowry, "The Progressive Movement, 1900-1920: Recent Ideas and New Literature," pamphlet (Washington, D.C., 1958); and Arthur Mann, "The Progressive Tradition," in John Higham, ed., *The Reconstruction of American History* (New York: Harper & Row, Publishers, 1962), pp. 157-79.
75. Hopkins, *Rise of the Social Gospel*, p. 297. On the Men and Religion Forward Movement, see also Gorrell, *Age of Social Responsibility*, pp. 155-79.
76. Hopkins, *Rise of the Social Gospel*, pp. 296, 298.
77. Rauschenbusch, *Christianizing the Social Order*, p. 20.
78. McLoughlin, *Billy Sunday*, p. 226.
79. Quoted in ibid., pp. 226-27.
80. McLoughlin, *Modern Revivalism*, p. 401.
81. Charles Stelzle, *American Social and Religious Conditions* (New York, 1912), p. 192, cited in ibid., p. 417.
82. Lindsay Denison, "The Rev. Billy Sunday and His War on the Devil," *American Magazine* 64 (September 1907): 454-55, quoted in McLoughlin, *Modern Revivalism*, pp. 419-20.
83. William McGuire King distinguished three different models of social reform in the social gospel movement: social evangelism, social engineering, and social reconstructionism. According to him, it was the last of these, explicit by 1912, that provided the basis for social gospel radicalism after World War I. See King, "The Emergence of Social Gospel Radicalism," *Church History* 50 (December 1981): 436-49.
84. *Watchman-Examiner*, August 13, 1914, p. 1066, quoted in McLoughlin, *Modern Revivalism*, p. 399.

CHAPTER SEVEN

1. Sandeen, *The Roots of Fundamentalism*, pp. 166-67.
2. Robert Hastings Nichols, "Fundamentalism in the Presbyterian Church," *Journal of Religion* 5 (January 1925): 18. Donald Gorrell, *Age of Social Responsibility*, pp. 219-41, sheds helpful light on the Presbyterian episode in 1912-13. For the later Fundamentalist/Modernist controversy among the Presbyterians, see Bradley James Longfield, "The Presbyterian Controversy, 1922-1936: Christianity, Culture, and Ecclesiastical Conflict" (Ph.D. dissertation, Duke University, 1988).
3. Lefferts A. Loetscher, *The Broadening Church: A Study of Theological Issues in the Presbyterian Church Since 1869* (Philadelphia: University of Pennsylvania Press, 1954), pp. 94-95.
4. Ibid., p. 59.
5. Lefferts A. Loetscher, "Presbyterianism in Philadelphia since 1870," pamphlet (essential portion of Ph.D. dissertation, University of Pennsylvania, 1944), pp. 19-20.
6. Presbyterian Church, *Minutes of the General Assembly*, 1901, p. 119.
7. Ibid., 1902, p. 34.
8. Ibid., pp. 35-36, 38.
9. Ibid., 1903, pp. 36-37, 146.
10. Elizabeth Osborn Thompson, ed., *Charles Lemuel Thompson: An Autobiography* (New York: Fleming H. Revell Company, 1924), p. 128.
11. Ibid., p. 130.
12. Charles Lemuel Thompson, *The Soul of America: The Contribution of Presbyterian Home Missions* (New York: Fleming H. Revell Company, 1919), p. 150.
13. Ibid., p. 152; Board of Home Missions of the Presbyterian Church in the U.S.A., *Annual Report*, Presented to the General Assembly (New York Presbyterian Building, 1903), p. 6.
14. Charles Stelzle, *A Son of the Bowery: The Life Story of an East Side American* (New York: George H. Doran Company, 1926), p. 65.
15. Board of Home Missions, *Report*, 1906, p. 5.
16. Ibid., pp. 5-7.
17. Presbyterian Church, *Minutes of the General Assembly*, 1906, pp. 22-24.
18. Board of Home Missions, *Report*, 1907, pp. 14, 25.
19. *Federal Council Proceedings*, 1912, p. 167.
20. Loetscher, *Broadening Church*, pp. 63-65.
21. Presbyterian Church, *Minutes of the General Assembly*, 1907, pp. 14, 25.
22. Ibid., p. 32.
23. Ibid., 1909, p. 77.
24. Ibid., 1911, p. 229.
25. Ibid., 1912, p. 121.
26. Ibid., p. 123.

27. Board of Home Missions, *Report*, 1912, pp. 4, 10.
28. Charles L. Thompson, *Soul of America*, p. 157.
29. Stelzle, *Son of the Bowery*, p. 123.
30. Ibid., pp. 125, 130.
31. Board of Home Missions, *Report*. 1912, p. 12. The temple was the occasion for much criticism of the board. Two years after the Church Extension Committee of the New York Presbytery had assumed full responsibility for the temple, it was organized as "the American International Presbyterian Church," with a pastor, plus one deacon and one elder from each of the ethnic groups in the community. The church membership in 1918 was 596.
32. Stelzle, *Son of the Bowery*, p. 154.
33. Ibid., p. 111; Board of Home Missions, *Report*, 1912, p. 11.
34. Board of Home Missions, *Report*, 1912, p. 11; Stelzle, *Son of the Bowery*, p. 113.
35. Stelzle, *Son of the Bowery*, pp. 154-55.
36. Presbyterian Church, *Minutes of the General Assembly*, 1913, p. 72.
37. Ibid., pp. 30, 32.
38. Ibid., pp. 178-79.
39. Ibid., p. 189.
40. Ibid.
41. Ibid., pp. 187-88.
42. Ibid., p. 179.
43. Ibid., p. 117.
44. Ibid., pp. 118, 121.
45. Ibid., 1914, p. 28.
46. Ibid., p. 128.
47. Board of Home Missions, *Report*, 1914, p. 9.
48. Stelzle, *Son of the Bowery*, p. 157.
49. Ibid., pp. 168-69.
50. Ibid., p. 169.
51. Ibid., pp. 169-70.
52. Cited in ibid., p. 171.
53. Cited in ibid.
54. Cited in ibid., p. 173.
55. Stelzle, *Son of the Bowery*, pp. 174-75.
56. Thompson, *Charles L. Thompson*, p. 168.
57. Ibid.
58. Ibid., p. 159.
59. Ibid., pp. 159-60.
60. Ibid., p. 119.
61. Ibid., pp. 169-70.

CHAPTER EIGHT

1. James Hastings Nichols, *History of Christianity, 1650-1950: Secularization of the West* (New York: Ronald Press Company, 1956), p. 269.
2. May, *Protestant Churches and Industrial America*, p. x. From the larger perspective of religious traditions and modernity in America, there are no "innocent bystanders," in the sense that no tradition has been immune to modernity. There are only differences in response. Leonard Sweet calls attention to Richard J. Mouw's protest against the Anglo-American bias in studies of American evangelicalism, slighting evangelical groups like the Christian Reformed Church and Missouri Synod Lutherans. See Mouw's review essay in *Calvin Theological Journal* 11 (November 1976): 260-64.
3. Abdel Ross Wentz, *A Basic History of Lutheranism in America*, rev. ed. (Philadelphia: Fortress Press, 1964), p. 6.
4. Ibid., pp. 14-21.
5. Ibid., p. 42.
6. Ibid., p. 89.
7. Hudson, *Religion in America*, p. 167.
8. Cited in Wentz, *Lutheranism in America*, p. 112.
9. Wentz, *Lutheranism in America*, p. 115.
10. H. Shelton Smith, Robert T. Handy, and Lefferts A. Loetscher, *American Christianity: An Historical Interpretation with Representative Documents* (New York: Charles Scribner's Sons, 1963), 2: 68.
11. Wentz, *Lutheranism in America*, p. 99; Smith, Handy, and Loetscher, *American Christianity*, 2: 101; Hudson, *Religion in America*, p. 168.
12. Wentz, *Lutheranism in America*, p. 109.
13. Ibid., p. 125.
14. Ibid., p. 316.
15. Ibid., p. 321. The man who was responsible, either directly or indirectly, for nearly all the early Lutheran charities was William Alfred Passavant, a former student of Schmucker's at Gettysburg Seminary and pioneer in Lutheran charities designed to meet the problems of the cities. After serving parishes in Baltimore and Pittsburgh, he devoted himself full time to organizing hospitals, orphanages, and other institutions, and through Theodore Fliedner, founder of the Kaiserswerth deaconesses in Germany, helped introduce deaconesses into the American churches. On Passavant, see Abell, *Urban Impact on American Protestantism*, pp. 52-53; Wentz, *Lutheranism in America*, p. 319. Methodist deaconesses in the 1880s initiated a whole range of activities that constituted a pragmatic social gospel. See Mary Agnes Dougherty, "The Social Gospel According to Phoebe," in Hilah F. Thomas and Rosemary Skinner Keller, eds., *Women in New Worlds* (Nashville: Abingdon Press, 1981), pp. 200-216; also Catherine M. Prelinger and Rosemary S. Keller, "The Function of Female Bonding: The Restored Diaconessate of the Nineteenth Century," Rosemary S.

Keller, Louise L. Queen, and Hilah F. Thomas, eds., *Women in New Worlds*, vol. 2 (Abingdon, 1982), pp. 318-37.

16. Hudson makes this point, among others. See *Religion in America*, p. 260.
17. Ibid.
18. Ibid.
19. Hopkins, *Rise of the Social Gospel*, p. iii.
20. John O. Evjen, *The Life of J. H. W. Stuckenberg: Theologian-Philosopher-Sociologist* (Minneapolis: Lutheran Free Church Publishing Company, 1938), pp. 43-48, 62-70, 82-90, 146-61. On the schism in the Lutheran General Synod, see pp. 169-73; on the Pittsburgh pastorate, pp. 183-220; on Wittenberg, pp. 221-41.
21. Hopkins, *Rise of the Social Gospel*, p. 112.
22. Evjen, *Life of Stuckenberg*, pp. 394-402, 409, 413, 477; Wentz, *Lutheranism in America*, p. 320.
23. Evjen, *Life of Stuckenberg*, p. 456.
24. Ibid., p. 246; Wentz, *Lutheranism in America*. p. 322.
25. Wentz, *Lutheranism in America*, pp. 322-23.
26. Cavert, *American Churches in the Ecumenical Movement*, p. 41.
27. Ibid., p. 44.
28. Ibid., p. 70.
29. Wentz, *Lutheranism in America*, p. 323.
30. Milton L. Rudnick, *Fundamentalism and the Missouri Synod: A Historical Study of their Interaction and Mutual Influence* (St. Louis: Concordia Publishing House, 1966), p. 75.
31. Ibid., p. 79. See also John H. C. Fritz, "Will the Fundamentalists Win Out in Their Fight Against the Modern Liberalists?" *Theological Monthly* 4 (1924): 234, 237-40, in Smith, Handy, and Loetscher, *American Christianity*, 2: 351-54.
32. [Theodore] G[raebaer], ed., "The Church and Industrial Disputes," *Lutheran Witness* 39 (September 14, 1920): 292, in Carl S. Meyer, ed., *Moving Frontiers: Readings in the History of the Lutheran Church-Missouri Synod* (St. Louis: Concordia Publishing House, 1964), 376-77.
33. Ibid.
34. Ibid.
35. Wentz, *Lutheranism in America*, p. 217.
36. Cavert, *American Churches in the Ecumenical Movement*, p. 262.
37. [Martin W. Mueller], editorial, *Lutheran Witness*, August 1962, pp. 406-7, 415, in Meyer, *Moving Frontiers*, p. 434.
38. Ibid., p. 435.
39. In 1957, this Evangelical and Reformed Church merged with the Congregational Christian Churches (also the product of an earlier union, that of the Congregational Churches and the Christian Churches in 1931) to become the United Church of Christ. The 1957 merger was remarkable for representing the blending of more diverse denominational heritages than in any other union in American Protestantism.

40. David Dunn, et al., *A History of the Evangelical and Reformed Church* (Philadelphia: Christian Education Press, 1961), p. 73. It should be noted that Nevin was converted to this position. His own earlier background was evangelical; he graduated from Princeton Seminary, and only entered the German Reformed Church (after leaving the Presbyterian Church) in 1840. See Sydney E. Ahlstrom, ed., *Theology in America: The Major Protestant Voices from Puritanism to Neo-Orthodoxy* (New York: Bobbs-Merrill Company, Inc., 1967), pp. 371-73.

41. Hudson, *Religion in America*, p. 170.

42. Smith, Handy, and Loetscher, *American Christianity* 2: 94; Ahlstrom, *Theology in America*, p. 373. See also James Hastings Nichols, *Romanticism in American Theology: Nevin and Schaff at Mercersburg* (Chicago: University of Chicago Press, 1961).

43. Dunn, *History of the Evangelical and Reformed Church*, p. 110.

44. Ibid., p. 273.

45. Cavert, *American Churches in the Ecumenical Movement*, p. 144; Dunn, *History of the Evangelical and Reformed Church*, p. 311.

46. Winfred Ernest Garrison and Alfred T. DeGroot, *The Disciples of Christ: A History* (St. Louis: Christian Board of Publication, 1948), p. 12.

47. Ibid.

48. Ibid., p. 13.

49. Ibid., p. 15.

50. Hudson, *American Protestantism*, p. 97.

51. Ibid., p. 95.

52. Ibid., p. 94.

53. Garrison and DeGroot, *Disciples of Christ*, p. 331.

54. Ibid., pp. 422-23.

55. Ibid., p. 411.

56. See Hudson, *Religion in America*, pp. 274-77.

57. Garrison and DeGroot, *Disciples of Christ*, p. 431.

58. Ibid.

59. Ibid., p. 424.

60. Hudson, *American Protestantism*. pp. 153-54.

61. Ibid., pp. 159, 161.

62. Ibid., p. 160; Hudson, *Religion in America*, pp. 342-43; Timothy L. Smith, *Revivalism and Social Reform*, pp. 103-38. For a brief summary see Jean Miller Schmidt, "Holiness and Perfection," *Encyclopedia of the American Religious Experience*, ed. Charles H. Lippy and Peter W. Williams (New York: Charles Scribner's Sons, 1988), 2: 813-29. Not all Holiness groups originated after 1880. On the Wesleyan Methodists and others, see Donald W. Dayton, *Discovering An Evangelical Heritage* (New York: Harper & Row, 1976). A good study of holiness social work is Norris Magnuson, *Salvation in the Slums: Evangelical Social Work, 1865-1920* (Metuchen, N.J.: Scarecrow Press, 1977).

63. *Christian Advocate*, 1866, quoted in Hudson, *Religion in America*, p. 343.

64. Hudson, *American Protestantism*, p. 160.
65. Hudson, *Religion in America*, p. 345.
66. Nazarene Manual, 1898, p. 2, quoted in Timothy L. Smith, *Called Unto Holiness: The Story of the Nazarenes, The Formative Years* (Kansas City, Mo.: Nazarene Publishing House, 1962), p. 114.
67. Timothy L. Smith, *Called Unto Holiness*, pp. 201, 115.
68. Ibid., pp. 315-19.
69. Herbert A. Wisbey, Jr., *Soldiers Without Swords: A History of the Salvation Army in the United States* (New York: Macmillan Company, 1955), pp. 18-20.
70. Abell, *Urban Impact on American Protestantism*, p. 123.
71. Ibid., p. 125.
72. Ibid.
73. Ibid., p. 126.
74. Ibid., p. 133.
75. Wisbey, *Soldiers Without Swords*, p. 89.
76. Abell, *Urban Impact on American Protestantism*, p. 136.
77. Samuel S. Hill, Jr., *Southern Churches in Crisis* (Boston: Beacon Press, 1968), pp. 33, 39.
78. Ibid., pp. 25-26.
79. Ibid., p. 14.
80. Ibid., pp. 15, 7, 16.
81. Hunter Dickinson Farish, *The Circuit Rider Dismounts: A Social History of Southern Methodism, 1865-1900* (Richmond, Va.: Dietz Press, 1938), p. 161; Spain, *At Ease in Zion*, p. 211.
82. Spain, *At Ease in Zion*, p. 146.
83. Kenneth Kyle Bailey, *Southern White Protestantism in the Twentieth Century* (New York: Harper & Row, 1964), pp. 40-41.
84. Alfred M. Pierce, *Giant Against the Sky: The Life of Bishop Warren Akin Candler* (New York: Abingdon-Cokesbury Press, 1948), pp. 245-50.
85. Ibid., pp. 199-210.
86. Southern Baptist Convention *Annual*, 1913, p. 76, quoted in Bailey, *Southern White Protestantism*, p. 40.
87. Bailey, *Southern White Protestantism*, pp. 41-42. Spain lists a number of prominent Baptists who seemed to lean toward social Christianity, including Arthur J. Barton, Clinton C. Brown, Charles S. Gardner, Victor I. Masters, Sr., Edwin McN. Poteat, Sr., William L. Poteat, and Arthur Yager; see Spain, *At Ease in Zion*, p. 211 n.
88. Bailey, *Southern White Protestantism*, p. 41.

CHAPTER NINE

1. Gaius Glenn Atkins, *Religion in Our Times* (New York, 1932), p. 156, cited in Handy, *Social Gospel*, p. 3.

2. Robert T. Handy, "The American Religious Depression, 1925-1935," *Church History* 29 (1960): 2-16.

3. On the later social gospel, see Paul A. Carter, *The Decline and Revival of the Social Gospel: Social and Political Liberalism in American Protestant Churches, 1920-1940* (Ithaca, N.Y.: Cornell University Press, 1954); Donald B. Meyer, *The Protestant Search for Political Realism, 1919-1941* (Berkeley: University of California Press, 1960); and Robert Moats Miller, *American Protestantism and Social Issues, 1919-1932* (Chapel Hill: University of North Carolina Press, 1958). But see William McGuire King's work on social gospel radicalism after World War I: "Emergence of Social Gospel Radicalism" (Ph.D. dissertation, Harvard, 1977), and *Church History* 50 (December 1981): 436-49.

4. Joseph R. Gusfield, *Symbolic Crusade: Status Politics and the American Temperance Movement* (Urbana, Ill.: University of Illinois Press, 1963), p. 99.

5. Hudson, *Religion in America*, p. 317.

6. *Federal Council Proceedings*, 1912, p. 182.

7. Carter, *Decline and Revival of the Social Gospel*, p. 34.

8. Ibid., p. 42.

9. Hutchison, *We Are Not Divided*, pp. 148-51; Gusfield, *Symbolic Crusade*, pp. 125-27.

10. The name was coined by Curtis Lee Laws, Baptist editor of the *Watchman-Examiner*, in 1920 to designate those prepared to battle for the "fundamentals" of the faith. See Hudson, *Religion in America*, p. 368. To Sandeen's work must now be added George M. Marsden, *Fundamentalism and American Culture: The Shaping of Twentieth-Century Evangelicalism, 1870-1925* (New York: Oxford University Press, 1980). Leonard Sweet summarizes some of the major developments in Fundamentalist studies since 1970 in Sweet, ed., *The Evangelical Tradition in America*, pp. 75-76.

11. Stewart G. Cole, *The History of Fundamentalism* (New York: Richard R. Smith, Inc., 1931), p. 34.

12. Loetscher, *Broadening Church*, p. 98.

13. Sandeen, *The Roots of Fundamentalism*, p. xv.

14. Cole, *History of Fundamentalism*, p. 299.

15. Ibid., p. 154.

16. Sandeen, *The Roots of Fundamentalism*, pp. 265-66.

17. Cole, *History of Fundamentalism*. p. 286.

18. One of the central figures in the Crozer controversy was Henry C. Vedder, professor of church history, who between 1910 and 1913 had become converted to the social gospel and who much resembled Walter Rauschenbusch in his thinking. He wrote two social gospel works, *Socialism and the Ethics of Jesus* (New York: Macmillan Company, 1912) and *The Gospel of Jesus and the Problem of Democracy* (New York: Macmillan Company, 1914).

19. Sandeen, *The Roots of Fundamentalism*, pp. 253-56.

20. Ibid., pp. 256-60. Cf. Marsden, *Fundamentalism and American Culture*, p. 192.

21. George McCready Price, *Back to the Bible, or the New Protestantism*, 3d. ed. (Washington: Review and Herald Publishing Company, 1920), p. 124, cited in Norman F. Furniss, *The Fundamentalist Controversy, 1918-1931* (New Haven: Yale University Press, 1954), p. 16.

22. *The Last Message of William Jennings Bryan* (New York: Revell, 1925), p. 28, quoted in Furniss, *Fundamentalist Controversy*, p. 17.

23. See Furniss, *Fundamentalist Controversy*, pp. 76-100.

24. J. Gresham Machen, *Christianity and Liberalism* (New York: Macmillan Company, 1923), pp. 2, 7.

25. Ibid. p. 14.

26. Ibid., p. 160.

27. Ibid., pp. 160, 166.

28. Ibid., pp. 152, 148-49.

29. F. Ernest Johnson, ed., *The Social Work of the Churches: A Handbook of Information* (New York: Department of Research and Education, Federal Council of the Churches of Christ in America, 1930), p. 8.

30. Hudson, *Religion in America*, p. 371.

31. Ibid., p. 380.

32. Ibid., pp. 381-82.

33. Louis Gasper, *The Fundamentalist Movement* (The Hague: Mouton & Co,, 1963), p. vi.

34. Ibid., p. 24.

35. James DeForest Murch, *Cooperation Without Compromise: A History of the National Association of Evangelicals* (Grand Rapids, Mich.: Eerdmans, 1956), p. 59.

36. Ibid., p. 40.

37. Ibid.

38. Ibid., p. 41.

39. Ibid., pp. 46, v.

40. Ibid., pp. 66-67.

41. Gasper, *Fundamentalist Movement*, p. 115. From this point on, it is necessary to distinguish two senses of *evangelical*. When used as *new evangelical*, *neo-evangelical*, or *conservative evangelical*, it is intended to designate this group of moderate fundamentalists whose leadership is centered in the N.A.E. When used in the broader sense, without any qualifying adjectives and usually as *evangelicalism*, it refers to the general type of Protestantism dominant in America by 1850, out of which the two parties I have been tracing developed.

42. Arnold W. Hearn, "Fundamentalist Renascence," *Christian Century* (April 30, 1958), p. 523, cited in ibid. See also George M. Marsden, *Reforming Fundamentalism: Fuller Seminary and the New Evangelicalism* (Grand Rapids, Mich.: Eerdmans, 1987).

43. C. Stanley Lowell, *Embattled Wall: Americans United, an Idea and a Man* (Washington: Americans United, 1966), pp. 18, 27-30.

44. Hudson, *Religion in America*, pp. 382-83.

45. Gasper, *Fundamentalist Movement*, pp. 139-41. See also William G. McLoughlin, Jr., *Billy Graham: Revivalist in a Secular Age* (New York: Ronald Press Company, 1960).
46. Gasper, *Fundamentalist Movement*, p. 143.
47. McLoughlin, *Modern Revivalism*, p. 511.
48. Ibid.
49. Gasper, *Fundamentalist Movement*, p. 145.
50. Growing out of the Holiness movement in the late nineteenth and early twentieth centuries, Pentecostal churches emphasize the baptism of the Holy Spirit, as evidenced by speaking in tongues. They also frequently stress faith healing and the imminent return of Christ.
51. Carl McIntire, *The Testimony of Separation* (Collingswood, N.J.: Christian Beacon Press, 1946), p. 61, cited in Gasper, *Fundamentalist Movement*, p. 30.
52. Gasper, *Fundamentalist Movement*, pp. 34-35.
53. Hudson, *Religion in America*, p. 384.
54. Gasper, *Fundamentalist Movement*, pp. 44, 50.
55. Ibid., p. 58.
56. Carl McIntire, "Methodist Church Blasts ACCC at Meeting in Pittsburgh," *Beacon* (February 21, 1952), pp. 1, 8, cited in ibid., p. 65.
57. See Martin E. Marty's analysis in Martin E. Marty, Andrew M. Greeley, and Stuart E. Rosenberg, *What Do We Believe? The Stance of Religion in America* (New York: Meredith Press, 1968), pp. 3-49.
58. Ibid., pp. 22-25.
59. Carl F. H. Henry, *The Uneasy Conscience of Modern Fundamentalism* (Grand Rapids, Mich.: Wm. B. Eerdmans Publ. Co., 1947), p. 17.
60. Ibid., p. 34.
61. Ibid., p. 88.
62. Murch, *Cooperation Without Compromise*, pp. 161, 166.
63. Carl F. H. Henry, *Aspects of Christian Social Ethics* (Grand Rapids, Mich.: Wm. B. Eerdmans Publ. Co., 1964); Sherwood Eliot Wirt, *The Social Conscience of the Evangelical* (New York: Harper & Row, 1968).
64. Henry, *Christian Social Ethics*, p. 25.
65. Marty, Greeley, and Rosenberg, *What Do We Believe?*, pp. 24-25, 28-29, based on q. 19 of 1965 Gallup poll. An important study of the disparity between clergy and lay attitudes toward social-political issues and involvement is Jeffrey K. Hadden, *The Gathering Storm in the Churches* (Garden City, N.Y.: Doubleday & Company, Inc., 1969). The study is based on a national survey of almost 10,000 clergy, initiated under the auspices of the Danforth Foundation's Study of Campus Ministries, and also on a national survey of the public's attitudes toward clergy involvement in civil rights, undertaken by Case Western Reserve University.
66. Central Department of Evangelism, National Council of Churches, "Staff Report," 1964, p. 1.
67. Ibid., p. 4.

68. Colin W. Williams, *Where in the World? Changing Forms of the Church's Witness* (Central Department of Evangelism, National Council of the Churches of Christ in America, 1963); and *What in the World?* (Central Department of Evangelism, National Council of the Churches of Christ in America, 1964).
69. Commission on Evangelism, "Staff Report to the Board of Managers," Atlanta, Georgia, May 4, 1965, p. 1.
70. Carl F. H. Henry, *Evangelicals At the Brink of Crisis: Significance of the World Congress on Evangelism* (Waco, Texas: Word Books, 1967), pp. 34-35.
71. Ibid., p. 37.
72. Ibid., p. 52.
73. "Are Religion and Politics the Same?" *The Times* (London), November 5, 1966, cited in ibid., pp. 56-57.
74. Henry, *Evangelicals At the Brink of Crisis*, pp. 56-57.
75. Ibid., pp. 58-59, 61.
76. Ibid., p. 55.
77. Ibid., p. 87.
78. Ibid., p. 108.
79. Hudson, *Religion in America*, pp. 355-56. On the service constituency of the N.A.E., see Murch, *Cooperation Without Compromise*, p. 203.
80. In 1966, John A. Mackay, former president of Princeton Theological Seminary, estimated that one-fourth to one-third of the conciliar constituency in the United States was theologically conservative. Henry estimated that there might have been 40 million Protestants involved in such an evangelical fellowship. See Henry, *Evangelicals At the Brink of Crisis*, p. 90.
81. Colin Williams presented this position at the second annual National Faith and Order Colloquium, meeting at the University of Notre Dame, South Bend, Indiana, from June 11-16, 1967. For a report on that colloquium, the theme of which was "Evangelism in A Pluralistic Society," see *Unity Trends*, edited by Department of Faith and Order, National Council of Churches, November 15, 1967, pp. 4-5. On Billy Graham and Colin Williams at Miami, see Henry, *Evangelicals At the Brink of Crisis*, pp. 95-96; *Christian Century*, December 21, 1966, p. 1564. (There was no actual confrontation between Graham and Williams because Graham had to leave the meetings soon after giving his statement; letter from Ralph M. Holdeman, director for evangelism, Department of Church Renewal, National Council of Churches, July 23, 1969).

CONCLUSION

1. Hadden, *Gathering Storm*, p. 207.

Bibliography

PRIMARY SOURCES

A. Denominational and Interdenominational Organizations, Official Records

Barrows, John Henry, ed. *The World's Parliament of Religions.* 2 vols. Chicago: Parliament Publishing Company, 1893.

Board of Home Missions of the Presbyterian Church in the U.S.A. *Annual Reports, Presented to the General Assembly.* New York: Presbyterian Building, 1903-14.

Central Department of Evangelism, National Council of the Churches of Christ in America. *Staff Report,* 1964.

Commission on Evangelism, National Council of the Churches of Christ in America. *Staff Report to the Board of Managers,* meeting at Atlanta, Georgia, May 4, 1965.

Evangelical Alliance for the U.S. *Christianity Practically Applied.* 2 vols. New York: Baker & Taylor Co., 1894. (Records of meeting of 1893.)

_____. *National Needs and Remedies.* New York: Baker & Taylor Co., 1890. (Records of meeting of 1889.)

_____. *National Perils and Opportunities.* New York: Baker & Taylor Co., 1887. (Records of meeting of 1887.)

Macfarland, Charles S., ed. *Christian Unity at Work: The Federal Council of the Churches of Christ in America in Quadrennial Session at Chicago, Illinois, 1912.* 2d ed. New York: F.C.C.C.A., 1913.

_____. *Library of Christian Cooperation: Reports of the Federal Council and its Commissions and Committees to the Third Quadrennial Meeting at St. Louis, Mo., December, 1916.* New York: Missionary Education Movement, 1917.

Presbyterian Church in the U.S.A. *Minutes of the General Assembly.* Philadelphia: by the stated clerk, 1900-14.

Sanford, Elias B., ed. *Church Federation: Inter-Church Conference on Federation*. New York: Fleming H. Revell Co., 1906.

_____. *Federal Council of the Churches of Christ in America: Report of the First Meeting of the Federal Council, Philadelphia, 1908*. New York: Revell Press, 1909.

_____. *Third Annual Report of the Executive Committee of the Federal Council of the Churches of Christ in America*. New York: National Office, 1911.

B. Religious Press

Congregationalist (Boston). January 4-June 28, 1894; July 8-December 30, 1897; January 6-June 30, 1906.

The Kingdom (Minneapolis). April 20, 1894-April 20, 1899.

C. Christian Social Opinion

Batten, Samuel Zane. *The Social Task of Christianity: A Summons to the New Crusade*. New York: Fleming H. Revell Company, 1911.

Beecher, Henry Ward. *The Original Plymouth Pulpit: Sermons in Plymouth Church, Brooklyn*. From stenographic reports by T. J. Ellinwood. 10 Vols. Boston: Pilgrim Press, 1873.

_____. *Plymouth Pulpit: Sermons Preached in Plymouth Church, Brooklyn*. From Ellinwood's stenographic reports. 4 vols. New York: Fords, Howard & Hulbert, 1892.

Beecher, Lyman. *Lectures on Political Atheism*. London: Clarke, Beeton & Co., n.d.

_____. *Six Sermons on the Nature, Occasions, Signs, Evils, and Remedy of Intemperance*. 3d ed. Boston: T. R. Marvin, 1828.

Bellamy, Edward. *Looking Backward: 2000-1887*. New York: New American Library, 1960.

Buckley, James M. *Christian Advocate*. Editorials, April 23, 1896, p. 265; July 23, 1896, p. 490; September 23, 1897, p. 613.

Candler, Warren A. *Great Revivals and the Great Republic*. Nashville, Tenn.: Publishing House of the Methodist Episcopal Church, South, 1904.

Chapman, J. Wilbur. *Present-Day Evangelism.* New York: Baker & Taylor Co., 1903.

Clark, Charles Worcester. "Applied Christianity: Who Shall Apply It First?" *Andover Review* 19 (1893): 8-33.

Colwell, Stephen. *The Claims of Labor, and their Precedence to the Claims of Free Trade.* Philadelphia: C. Sherman & Son, 1861.

_____. *New Themes for the Protestant Clergy: Creeds without Charity, Theology without Humanity, and Protestantism without Christianity.* 2d ed., rev. Philadelphia: Lippincott, Grambo & Co., 1853.

Conwell, Russell H. *Acres of Diamonds.* New York: Harper & Bros., 1915.

Dixon, Amzi Clarence. *Evangelism Old and New: God's Search for Man in All Ages.* New York: American Tract Society, 1905.

Finney, Ross L. *Personal Religion and the Social Awakening.* Cincinnati: Jennings and Graham, 1913.

Francis, John Junkin, and Charles B. Morrell, eds. *Mills' Meetings Memorial Volume.* Cincinnati: Standard Publishing Company, 1892.

Fremantle, William H. *The World As the Subject of Redemption.* New York: E. & J. B. Young & Co., 1885.

Gladden, Washington. *Applied Christianity: Moral Aspects of Social Questions.* Boston: Houghton, Mifflin Co., 1886.

_____. *The Church and Modern Life.* Boston: Houghton, Mifflin Co., 1908.

_____. *Present Day Theology.* Columbus, Ohio: McClelland & Company, 1913.

_____. *Ruling Ideas of the Present Age.* Boston: Houghton, Mifflin Co., 1895.

_____. *Social Salvation.* Boston: Houghton, Mifflin Co., 1902.

Henry, Carl F. H. *Aspects of Christian Social Ethics.* Grand Rapids, Mich.: Wm. B. Eerdmans Publ. Co., 1964.

_____. *Evangelicals At the Brink of Crisis: Significance of the World Congress on Evangelism.* Waco, Texas: Word Books, 1967.

_____. *The Uneasy Conscience of Modern Fundamentalism.* Grand Rapids, Mich.: Wm. B. Eerdmans Publ. Co., 1947.

Herron, George D. *The Christian State: A Political Vision of Christ.* New York: Thomas Y. Crowell & Co., 1895.

_____. *The New Redemption: A Call to the Church to Reconstruct Society According to the Gospel of Christ.* New York: Thomas Y. Crowell & Co., 1893.

Johnson, F. Ernest. *The Social Gospel and Personal Religion: Are They in Conflict?* New York: Association Press, 1922.

Keller, Albert G., and Maurice R. Davie. *Essays of William Graham Sumner.* New Haven: Yale University Press, 1934.

Macfarland, Charles S. *Spiritual Culture and Social Service.* New York: Fleming H. Revell Co., 1912.

Machen, J. Gresham. *Christianity and Liberalism.* New York: Macmillan Company, 1923.

Mathews, Shailer. *The Individual and the Social Gospel.* New York: Laymen's Missionary Movement, 1914.

_____. *The Social Gospel.* Philadelphia: Griffith & Rowland Press, 1910.

Mills, B. Fay. *God's World and Other Sermons.* New York: Fleming H. Revell Co., 1894.

_____. "Why I Return to the Church." *Advance,* June 24, 1915, pp. 1251-52; July 1, 1915, p. 1281; July 3, 1915, p. 1321.

Munger, Theodore T. *The Freedom of Faith.* Boston: Houghton, Mifflin Co., 1883.

Peabody, Francis Greenwood. *Jesus Christ and the Social Question: An Examination of the Teaching of Jesus in its Relation to Some of the Problems of Modern Social Life.* New York: Macmillan Company, 1901.

Rauschenbusch, Walter. *Christianity and the Social Crisis.* New York: Macmillan Company, 1907.

_____. *Christianizing the Social Order.* New York: Macmillan Company, 1912.

_____. *For God and the People: Prayers of the Social Awakening.* Boston: Pilgrim Press, 1910.

_____. "The Genesis of 'Christianity and the Social Crisis.' " *Rochester Theological Seminary Bulletin* (November 1918), pp. 51-53.

_____. "The New Evangelism." *Independent* 56 (January-June 1904): 1054-59.

_____. *The Righteousness of the Kingdom.* Edited and introduced by Max L. Stackhouse. Nashville: Abingdon Press, 1968.

_____. *A Theology for the Social Gospel.* New York: Macmillan Company, 1917.

_____. *Unto Me.* Boston: Pilgrim Press, 1912.

Sheldon, Charles M. *In His Steps: What Would Jesus Do?* Philadelphia: American Baptist Publication Society, 1898.

Stauffer, Henry, ed. *The Great Awakening in Columbus, Ohio, under the Labors of Rev. B. Fay Mills and His Associates.* Introduction by Washington Gladden. Columbus, Ohio: Rev. W. L. Lemon, 1895.

Stelzle, Charles. *American Social and Religious Conditions.* New York: Fleming H. Revell Co., 1912.

Strong, Josiah. *My Religion in Everyday Life.* New York: Baker & Taylor Co., 1910.

_____. *The New Era: or the Coming Kingdom.* New York: Baker & Taylor Co., 1893.

_____. *The New World-Religion.* Garden City, N.Y.: Doubleday, Page & Co., 1915.

_____. *The Next Great Awakening.* New York: Baker & Taylor Co., 1902.

_____. *The Next Great Awakening.* 10th ed. New York: Baker & Taylor Co., 1913.

_____. *Our Country: Its Possible Future and Its Present Crisis.* Rev. ed., based on census of 1890. New York: Baker & Taylor Co., 1891.

_____. *Our World: The New World-Life.* Garden City, N.Y.: Doubleday, Page & Co., 1913.

_____. *Religious Movements for Social Betterment.* New York: Baker & Taylor Co., 1900.

Thompson, Charles Lemuel. *The Soul of America: The Contribution of Presbyterian Home Missions.* New York: Fleming H. Revell Co., 1919.

Vedder, Henry C. *The Gospel of Jesus and the Problems of Democracy.* New York: Macmillan Company, 1914.

_____. *Socialism and the Ethics of Jesus.* New York: Macmillan Company, 1912.

Ward, Harry F. *Social Evangelism.* New York: Missionary Education Movement of the U.S. and Canada, 1915.

Wirt, Sherwood Eliot. *The Social Conscience of the Evangelical.* New York: Harper & Row, 1968.

D. Biographies and Autobiographies

Abbott, Lyman. *Reminiscences.* Boston: Houghton, Mifflin Co., 1915.

Beecher, Lyman. *The Autobiography of Lyman Beecher.* Edited by Barbara M. Cross. 2 vols. Cambridge: Belknap Press of Harvard University Press, 1961.

Curtis, Richard K. *They Called Him Mister Moody.* Grand Rapids, Mich.: Wm. B. Eerdmans Publ. Co., 1967.

Dixon, Helen A. C. *A. C. Dixon: A Romance of Preaching.* New York, 1931.

Dorn, Jacob Henry. *Washington Gladden: Prophet of the Social Gospel.* Columbus: Ohio State University Press, 1967.

Evjen, John O. *The Life of J. H. W. Stuckenberg: Theologian-Philosopher-Sociologist.* Minneapolis, Minn.: Lutheran Free Church Publishing Company, 1938.

Findlay, James F., Jr. *Dwight L. Moody: American Evangelist, 1837-1899.* Chicago: University of Chicago Press, 1969.

Gladden, Washington. *Recollections.* Boston: Houghton, Mifflin Co., 1909.

Handy, Robert Theodore. "George D. Herron and the Social Gospel in American Protestantism, 1890-1901." Unpublished Ph.D. dissertation, University of Chicago, 1949.

Hartzler, H. B. *Moody in Chicago: The World's Fair Gospel Campaign.* New York: Fleming H. Revell Co., 1894.

Jones, Laura M. *The Life and Sayings of Sam P. Jones, a Minister of the Gospel.* 2d and rev. ed. Atlanta, Ga.: Franklin-Turner Company, 1907.

Macfarland, Charles S. *Across the Years.* New York: Macmillan Company, 1936.

McLoughlin, William G., Jr. *Billy Graham: Revivalist in a Secular Age.* New York: Ronald Press Company, 1960.

_____. *Billy Sunday Was His Real Name.* Chicago: University of Chicago Press, 1955.

Muller, Dorothea S. "Josiah Strong and the Challenge of the City." Unpublished Ph.D. dissertation, New York University, 1955.

Ottman, Ford Cyrinde. *J. Wilbur Chapman, a Biography.* Garden City, N.Y.: Doubleday, Page & Co., 1920.

Pierce, Alfred M. *Giant Against the Sky: The Life of Bishop Warren Akin Candler.* New York: Abingdon-Cokesbury Press, 1948.

Rainsford, W. S. *The Story of a Varied Life: An Autobiography.* Garden City, N.Y.: Doubleday, Page & Co., 1924.

Sharpe, Dores Robinson. *Walter Rauschenbusch.* New York: Macmillan Company, 1942.

Sheldon, Charles M. *His Life Story.* New York: George H. Doran Company, 1925.

Stelzle, Charles. *A Son of the Bowery: The Life Story of an East Side American.* New York: George H. Doran Company, 1926.

Thompson, Elizabeth Osborn, ed. *Charles Lemuel Thompson: An Autobiography.* New York: Fleming H. Revell Co., 1924.

Tucker, William Jewett. *My Generation.* Boston: Houghton, Mifflin Co., 1919.

Wade, Louise C. *Graham Taylor: Pioneer for Social Justice, 1851-1938.* Chicago: University of Chicago Press, 1964.

SECONDARY SOURCES

Abell, Aaron I. *The Urban Impact on American Protestantism, 1865-1900.* Cambridge: Harvard University Press, 1943.

Ahlstrom, Sydney E. "Theology in America: A Historical Survey." *The Shaping of American Religion*, edited by James Ward Smith and A. Leland Jamison. Princeton: Princeton University Press, 1961.

_____, ed. *Theology in America: The Major Protestant Voices from Puritanism to Neo-Orthodoxy.* New York: Bobbs-Merrill Company, Inc., 1967.

Averill, Lloyd J. *American Theology in the Liberal Tradition.* Philadelphia: Westminster Press, 1967.

Bader, Jesse. "Data Regarding the Department of Evangelism of the Federal Council of Churches and the National Council of Churches." New York, 1950.

Bailey, Kenneth Kyle. *Southern White Protestantism in the Twentieth Century.* New York: Harper & Row, 1964.

Barclay, Wade Crawford. *Early American Methodism, 1769-1844.* New York: Board of Missions and Church Extension of the Methodist Church, 1950.

Barnes, Gilbert Hobbs. *The Antislavery Impulse: 1830-1844.* New York: Appleton-Century-Crofts, 1933.

Bodo, John R. *The Protestant Clergy and Public Issues: 1812-1848.* Princeton, N.J.: Princeton University Press, 1954.

Brauer, Jerald C., ed. *Reinterpretations in American Church History.* Chicago: University of Chicago Press, 1968.

Carter, Paul A. *The Decline and Revival of the Social Gospel: Social and Political Liberalism in American Protestant Churches, 1920-1940.* Ithaca, N.Y.: Cornell University Press, 1954.

Cauthen, Kenneth, *The Impact of American Religious Liberalism.* New York: Harper & Row, 1962.

Cavert, Samuel McCrea. *The American Churches in the Ecumenical Movement: 1900-1968*. New York: Association Press, 1968.

Cochran, Thomas C., and William Miller. *The Age of Enterprise: A Social History of Industrial America*. Rev. ed. New York: Harper & Row, 1961.

Cole, Charles C., Jr. *The Social Ideas of the Northern Evangelists, 1826-1860*. New York: Columbia University Press, 1954.

Cole, Stewart G. *The History of Fundamentalism*. New York: Richard R. Smith, Inc., 1931.

DeWitt, Benjamin Parke. *The Progressive Movement: a Non-Partisan, Comprehensive Discussion of Current Tendencies in American Politics*. New York: Macmillan Company, 1915.

Dorfman, Joseph. *The Economic Mind in American Civilization, 1606-1865*. 2 vols. New York: Viking Press, 1946.

Dulles, Foster Rhea. *Labor in America*. 3d ed. New York: T. Y. Crowell & Company, 1966.

Dunn, David, Paul N. Crusius, Josias Friedli, Theophil W. Menzel, Carl E. Schneider, William Toth, and James E. Wagner. *A History of the Evangelical and Reformed Church*. Philadelphia: Christian Education Press, 1961.

Farish, Hunter Dickinson. *The Circuit Rider Dismounts: A Social History of Southern Methodism, 1865-1900*. Richmond, Va.: Dietz Press, 1938.

Fine, Sidney. *Laissez Faire and the General Welfare State: A Study of Conflict in American Thought, 1865-1901*. Ann Arbor, Mich.: University of Michigan Press, 1956.

Foster, Charles I. *An Errand of Mercy: The Evangelical United Front, 1790-1837*. Chapel Hill: University of North Carolina Press, 1960.

Furniss, Norman F. *The Fundamentalist Controversy, 1918-1931*. New Haven: Yale University Press, 1954.

Gabriel, Ralph Henry. *The Course of American Democratic Thought*. 2d ed. New York: Ronald Press Company, 1956.

Garrison, Winfred Ernest, and Alfred T. DeGroot. *The Disciples of Christ: A History*. St. Louis, Mo.: Christian Board of Publication, 1948.

Gasper, Louis. *The Fundamentalist Movement*. The Hague: Mouton & Co., 1963.

Gellner, Ernest. *Thought and Change*. Chicago: University of Chicago Press, 1965.

Goldman, Eric F. *Rendezvous with Destiny: A History of Modern American Reform*. Rev. ed. New York: Random House, 1956.

Griffin, Clifford S. *Their Brothers' Keepers: Moral Stewardship in the United States, 1800-1865.* New Brunswick, N.J.: Rutgers University Press, 1960.

Gusfield, Joseph R. *Symbolic Crusade: Status Politics and the American Temperance Movement.* Urbana, Ill.: University of Illinois Press, 1963.

Gutman, Herbert G. "Protestantism and the American Labor Movement." *American Historical Review* 72 (October 1966): 74-101.

Hadden, Jeffrey K. *The Gathering Storm in the Churches.* Garden City, N.Y.: Doubleday & Company, Inc., 1969.

Handy, Robert T. "Charles L. Thompson—Presbyterian Architect of Cooperative Protestantism." *Journal of the Presbyterian Historical Society* 33 (December 1955): 207-28.

_____. "The American Religious Depression, 1925-1935." *Church History* 29 (1960): 2-16.

_____. "The Protestant Quest for a Christian America, 1830-1930." *Church History* 22 (March 1952): 8-20.

_____, ed. *The Social Gospel in America, 1870-1920: Gladden, Ely, Rauschenbusch.* New York: Oxford University Press, 1966.

_____. *We Witness Together: A History of Cooperative Home Missions.* New York: Friendship Press, 1956.

Hicks, John D. *The Populist Revolt.* Minneapolis: University of Minnesota Press, 1931.

Hill, Samuel S., Jr. *Southern Churches in Crisis.* Boston: Beacon Press, 1968.

Hofstadter, Richard. *The Age of Reform: From Bryan to F.D.R.* New York: Random House, 1955.

_____. *Social Darwinism in American Thought.* Rev. ed. Boston: Beacon Press, 1955.

Hopkins, Charles H. *History of the Y.M.C.A. in North America.* New York: Association Press, 1951.

_____. *The Rise of the Social Gospel in American Protestantism, 1865-1915.* New Haven: Yale University Press, 1940.

_____. "Walter Rauschenbusch and the Brotherhood of the Kingdom." *Church History* 7 (June 1938): 138-56.

Hudson, Winthrop S. *American Protestantism.* Chicago: University of Chicago Press, 1961.

_____. *The Great Tradition of the American Churches.* New York: Harper & Bros., 1953.

_____. *Religion in America.* New York: Charles Scribner's Sons, 1965.

_____. "Walter Rauschenbusch and the New Evangelism." *Religion in Life*, 30 (Winter 1960-61): 412-30.

Hutchison, John A. *We Are Not Divided: A Critical and Historical Study of the Federal Council of the Churches of Christ in America*. New York: Round Table Press, Inc., 1941.

Johnson, F. Ernest, ed. *The Social Work of the Churches: A Handbook of Information*. New York: Department of Research and Education, Federal Council of the Churches of Christ in America, 1930.

Johnson, Roy H. "American Baptists in the Age of Big Business," *Journal of Religion* 11 (January 1931): 63-85.

Latta, Maurice C. "The Background for the Social Gospel in American Protestantism." *Church History* 5 (September 1936): 256-70.

Loetscher, Lefferts A. *The Broadening Church: A Study of Theological Issues in the Presbyterian Church since 1869*. Philadelphia: University of Pennsylvania Press, 1954.

_____. "Presbyterianism in Philadelphia since 1870." Pamphlet. Essential portion of Ph.D. dissertation, University of Pennsylvania, 1944.

_____. "Presbyterians and Political Reform in Philadelphia from 1870 to 1917." *Journal of the Presbyterian Historical Society* 23 (1945): 2-18, 119-36.

Loud, Grover C. *Evangelized America*. New York: Dial Press, 1928.

Lowell, C. Stanley. *Embattled Wall: Americans United, an Idea and a Man*. Washington: Americans United, 1966.

McCloskey, Robert Green. *American Conservatism in the Age of Enterprise, 1865-1910*. Cambridge: Harvard University Press, 1951.

Macfarland, Charles S. *Christian Unity in the Making: The First Twenty-Five Years of the Federal Council of the Churches of Christ in America, 1905-1930*. New York: F.C.C.C.A., 1948.

McGiffert, Arthur Cushman. *The Rise of Modern Religious Ideas*. New York: Macmillan Company, 1929.

McLoughlin, William G., Jr. *Modern Revivalism: Charles Grandison Finney to Billy Graham*. New York: Ronald Press Company, 1959.

Macoskey, Robert A. "Henry C. Vedder: Historian Ahead of his Hour." *The Voice*, 59, 60 (April 1967, April 1968): 18-31, 3-7, 15-23.

Mann, Arthur. "The Progressive Tradition." *The Reconstruction of American History*, edited by John Higham. New York: Harper & Row, Publishers, 1962.

_____. *Yankee Reformers in the Urban Age: Social Reform in Boston, 1880-1900*. Cambridge: Belknap Press of Harvard University Press, 1954.

Marty, Martin E. *The Infidel: Freethought and American Religion*. Cleveland: World Publishing Company, 1961.

_____, Andrew M. Greeley, and Stuart E. Rosenberg. *What Do We Believe? The Stance of Religion in America*. New York: Meredith Press, 1968.

Marx, Leo. *The Machine in the Garden: Technology and the Pastoral Ideal in America*. New York: Oxford University Press, 1967.

Mathews, Shailer, and Gerald Birney Smith. *Dictionary of Religion and Ethics*. New York: Macmillan Company, 1921.

May, Henry, F. *Protestant Churches and Industrial America*. New York: Harper & Bros., 1949.

Mead, Sidney E. *The Lively Experiment: The Shaping of Christianity in America*. New York: Harper & Row, 1963.

_____. *Nathaniel William Taylor, 1786-1858: A Connecticut Liberal*. Chicago: University of Chicago Press, 1942.

_____. "The Rise of the Evangelical Conception of the Ministry in America, 1607-1850." *The Ministry in Historical Perspectives*, edited by H. Richard Niebuhr and Daniel Day Williams. New York: Harper & Bros., 1956.

Meehan, Brenda M. "A. C. Dixon: An Early Fundamentalist." *Foundations* 10 (January-March 1967): 50-63.

Meyer, Carl S., ed. *Moving Frontiers: Readings in the History of the Lutheran Church-Missouri Synod*. St. Louis, Mo.: Concordia Publishing House, 1964.

Meyer, Donald B. *The Protestant Search for Political Realism, 1919-1941*. Berkeley: University of California Press, 1960.

Miller, Robert Moats. *American Protestantism and Social Issues, 1919-1939*. Chapel Hill: University of North Carolina Press, 1958.

Miller, Spencer, Jr., and Joseph F. Fletcher. *The Church and Industry*. New York: Longmans, Green and Co., 1930.

Morgan, H. Wayne, ed. *The Gilded Age: A Reappraisal*. Syracuse: Syracuse University Press, 1963.

Mowry, George E. "The Progressive Movement, 1900-1920: Recent Ideas and New Literature." Pamphlet. Washington, D.C., 1958.

Muller, Dorothea R. "Josiah Strong and the Social Gospel: A Christian's Response to the Challenge of the City." *Journal of the Presbyterian Historical Society* 39 (September 1961): 150-75.

_____. "The Social Philosophy of Josiah Strong: Social Christianity and American Progressivism." *Church History* 28 (June 1959): 183-201.

Murch, James DeForest. *Cooperation Without Compromise: A History of the National Association of Evangelicals.* Grand Rapids, Mich.: Wm. B. Eerdmans Publ. Co., 1956.

Nichols, James Hastings. *History of Christianity, 1650-1950: Secularization of the West.* New York: Ronald Press Company, 1956.

_____. *Romanticism in American Theology: Nevin and Schaff at Mercersburg.* Chicago: University of Chicago Press, 1961.

Nichols, Robert Hastings. "Fundamentalism in the Presbyterian Church." *Journal of Religion* 5 (January 1925): 14-36.

Niebuhr, H. Richard. *The Kingdom of God in America.* New York: Harper & Row, Publishers, Inc., 1937.

Nye, Russel B. *Midwestern Progressive Politics: A Historical Study of Its Origins and Development, 1870-1958.* East Lansing, Mich.: Michigan State University Press, 1959.

Parrington, Vernon Lewis. *Main Currents in American Thought.* New York: Harcourt, Brace & World, 1930.

Rudnick, Milton L. *Fundamentalism and the Missouri Synod: A Historical Study of their Interaction and Mutual Influence.* St. Louis, Mo.: Concordia Publishing House, 1966.

Sandeen, Ernest R. *The Roots of Fundamentalism: British and American Millenarianism, 1800-1930.* Chicago: University of Chicago Press, 1970.

Sanford, Elias B. *Origin and History of the Federal Council of the Churches of Christ in America.* Hartford, Conn.: S. S. Scranton Company, 1916.

Schlesinger, Arthur M., Sr. "A Critical Period in American Religion." *Massachusetts Historical Society Proceedings* 64 (October 1930-June 1932): 523-46.

_____. *The Rise of the City, 1828-1898.* New York: Macmillan Company, 1933.

Smith, H. Shelton. *Changing Conceptions of Original Sin: A Study in American Theology Since 1750.* New York: Charles Scribner's Sons, 1955.

Smith, H. Shelton, Robert T. Handy, and Lefferts A. Loetscher. *American Christianity: An Historical Interpretation with Representative Documents.* New York: Charles Scribner's Sons, 1963.

Smith, James Ward, and A. Leland Jamison, eds. *The Shaping of American Religion.* Princeton: Princeton University Press, 1961.

Smith, Timothy L. *Called Unto Holiness: The Story of the Nazarenes, The Formative Years*. Kansas City, Mo. Nazarene Publishing House, 1962.

_____. *Revivalism and Social Reform: American Protestantism on the Eve of the Civil War*. New York: Abingdon Press, 1957.

Spain, Rufus B. *At Ease in Zion: A Social History of Southern Baptists, 1865-1900*. Nashville, Tenn.: Vanderbilt University Press, 1967.

Webber, Christopher L. "William Dwight Porter Bliss: Priest and Socialist." *Historical Magazine of the Protestant Episcopal Church* 28 (1959): 11-39.

Weisberger, Bernard A. *They Gathered at the River: The Story of the Great Revivalists and Their Impact upon Religion in America*. Boston: Little, Brown and Company, 1958.

Wentz, Abdel Ross. *A Basic History of Lutheranism in American*. Rev. ed. Philadelphia: Fortress Press, 1964.

Williams, Colin W. *What in the World?* General Department of Evangelism, National Council of the Churches of Christ in America, 1964.

_____. *Where in the World? Changing Forms of the Church's Witness*. Central Department of Evangelism, National Council of the Churches of Christ in America, 1963.

Wisbey, Herbert A., Jr. *Soldiers Without Swords: A History of the Salvation Army in the United States*. New York: Macmillan Company, 1955.

ADDITIONAL BIBLIOGRAPHY, 1991

Airhart, Phyllis D. " 'What Must I Do To Be Saved?' Two Paths to Evangelical Conversion in Late Victorian Canada." *Church History* 59 (September 1990): 372-85.

Aptheker, Bettina. *Woman's Legacy: Essays on Race, Sex, and Class in American History*. Amherst: University of Massachusetts Press, 1982.

Arendt, Hannah. *The Human Condition*. Chicago: University of Chicago Press, 1958.

Benjamin, Walter W. "The Methodist Episcopal Church in the Postwar Era," in Emory Stevens Bucke, ed., *The History of American Methodism* (Nashville: Abingdon Press, 1964), 2: 315-60.

Bowden, Henry Warner. "The Historiography of American Religion." In Charles H. Lippy and Peter W. Williams, eds., *Encyclopedia of the American Religious Experience*. New York: Charles Scribner's Sons, 1988. 1: 3-16.

Brereton, Virginia Lieson. *Training God's Army: The American Bible School, 1880-1940*. Bloomington: Indiana University Press, 1990.

Briggs, Mitchell Pirie. *George D. Herron and the European Settlement*. Stanford: Stanford University Press, 1932.

Brown, Robert McAfee. *Creative Dislocation: The Movement of Grace*. Nashville: Abingdon Press, 1980.

Burdick, Michael. "Overseas Mission: Failure of Nerve or Change in Strategy?" In Robert S. Michaelsen and Wade Clark Roof, eds., *Liberal Protestantism: Realities and Possibilities*. New York: Pilgrim Press, 1986, pp. 102-14.

Cartwright, Peter. *Autobiography*. Nashville: Abingdon, 1986.

Cott, Nancy F. *The Bonds of Womanhood*. New Haven: Yale University Press, 1977.

Dayton, Donald W. *Discovering an Evangelical Heritage*. New York: Harper & Row, 1976.

DeBerg, Betty A. *Ungodly Women: Gender and the First Wave of American Fundamentalism*. Minneapolis: Fortress Press, 1990.

Dewey, John. *The Public and Its Problems*. New York: Henry Holt & Co., 1927.

Dougherty, Mary Agnes. "The Social Gospel According to Phoebe." In Hilah F. Thomas and Rosemary Skinner Keller, eds., *Women in New Worlds*. Nashville: Abingdon Press, 1981, pp. 200-216.

Essig, James D. *The Bonds of Wickedness: American Evangelicals Against Slavery, 1770-1808*. Philadelphia: Temple University Press, 1982.

Fishburn, Janet Forsythe. *The Fatherhood of God and the Victorian Family: The Social Gospel in America*. Philadelphia: Fortress Press, 1981.

Friedman, Lawrence J. *Gregarious Saints: Self and Community in American Abolitionism, 1830-1870*. Cambridge: Cambridge University Press, 1982.

Gorrell, Donald K. *The Age of Social Responsibility: The Social Gospel in the Progressive Era, 1900-1920*. Macon, Ga.: Mercer University Press, 1988.

_____. "The Methodist Federation for Social Service and the Social Creed." *Methodist History* 13 (January 1975): 16-22.

Gravely, William B. *Gilbert Haven, Methodist Abolitionist: A Study in Race, Religion, and Reform, 1850-1880*. New York: Abingdon Press, 1973.

_____. "Methodist Preachers, Slavery and Caste: Types of Social Concern in Antebellum America." *Duke Divinity School Review* 34 (Autumn 1969): 209-29.

Hadden, Jeffrey K. *The Gathering Storm in the Churches: The Widening Gap Between Clergy and Laymen*. Garden City, N.Y.: Doubleday, 1969.

Hamilton, Neill Q. *Recovery of the Protestant Adventure*. New York: Seabury Press, 1981.

Handy, Robert Theodore. *A Christian America: Protestant Hopes and Historical Realities*. New York: Oxford University Press, 1971.

Hardesty, Nancy, Lucille Sider Dayton, and Donald W. Dayton. "Women in the Holiness Movement: Feminism in the Evangelical Tradition." In Ruether, Rosemary, and Eleanor McLaughlin, eds. *Women of Spirit: Female Leadership in the Jewish and Christian Traditions*. New York: Simon and Schuster, 1979.

Harding, Vincent. *The Other American Revolution*. Los Angeles: Center for Afro-American Studies, UCLA, and Atlanta: Institute of the Black World, 1980.

Hargrove, Barbara, Jean Miller Schmidt, and Sheila Greeve Davaney. "Religion and the Changing Role of Women." *Annals of the American Academy of Political and Social Science* 480 (July 1985): 117-31.

Harrison, Beverly Wildung. "Sexism and the Contemporary Church: When Evasion Becomes Complicity." In Alice L. Hageman, ed., *Sexist Religion and Women in the Church*. New York: Association Press, 1974.

Hassey, Janette. *No Time for Silence: Evangelical Women in Ministry Around the Turn of the Century*. Grand Rapids, Mich.: Zondervan, 1986.

Hatch, Nathan O. *The Democratization of American Christianity*. New Haven: Yale University Press, 1989.

Herberg, Will. *Protestant-Catholic-Jew*. Garden City, N.Y.: Doubleday-Anchor, 1955.

Hoge, Dean R. *Division in the Protestant House*. Philadelphia: Westminster Press, 1976.

Hudson, Winthrop S. "The Methodist Age in America." *Methodist History* 12 (April 1974): 3-15.

Hunter, James Davison. *American Evangelicalism: Conservative Religion and the Quandary of Modernity*. New Brunswick, N.J.: Rutgers University Press, 1983.

Hutchison, William R. *The Modernist Impulse in American Protestantism*. Cambridge: Harvard University Press, 1976.

Jordan, Philip D. *The Evangelical Alliance for the United States of America, 1847-1900: Ecumenism, Identity, and the Religion of the Republic*. New York: Edwin Mellen Press, 1982.

Kelley, Dean M. *Why Conservative Churches Are Growing*. New York: Harper & Row, 1972.

Kieterich, Herbert. "Patterns of Dissent: The Reform Ideas and Activities of George D. Herron." University of New Mexico: microfilm, 1957.

King, William McGuire. "The Emergence of Social Gospel Radicalism in American Methodism." Ph.D. dissertation, Harvard University, 1977.

_____. "The Emergence of Social Gospel Radicalism: The Methodist Case." *Church History* 50 (December 1981): 436-49.

Knotts, Alice G. "Bound by the Spirit, Found on the Journey: The Methodist Women's Campaign for Southern Civil Rights, 1940-1968." Ph.D. dissertation, Iliff School of Theology and the University of Denver, 1989.

Lerner, Gerda. *The Grimké Sisters of South Carolina: Pioneers for Woman's Rights and Abolition.* Boston: Houghton Mifflin Co., 1967.

_____. *The Majority Finds Its Past: Placing Women in History.* New York: Oxford University Press, 1979.

Longfield, Bradley James. "The Presbyterian Controversy, 1922-1936: Christianity, Culture, and Ecclesiastical Conflict." Ph.D. dissertation, Duke University, 1988.

Magnuson, Norris. *Salvation in the Slums: Evangelical Social Work, 1865-1920.* Metuchen, N.J.: Scarecrow Press, 1977.

Marsden, George M. *Fundamentalism and American Culture: The Shaping of Twentieth-Century Evangelicalism, 1870-1925.* New York: Oxford University Press, 1980.

_____. *Reforming Fundamentalism: Fuller Seminary and the New Evangelicalism.* Grand Rapids, Mich.: Eerdmans, 1987.

Marty, Martin E. "Fundamentalism as a Social Phenomenon." In George Marsden, ed., *Evangelicalism and Modern America.* Grand Rapids, Mich.: William B. Eerdmans Co., 1984, pp. 56-68.

_____. *Modern American Religion.* Vol. 1, *The Irony of It All: 1893-1919.* Chicago: University of Chicago Press, 1986.

_____. *Modern American Religion.* Vol. 2, *The Noise of Conflict, 1919-1941.* Chicago: University of Chicago Press, 1991.

_____. *A Nation of Behavers.* Chicago: University of Chicago Press, 1976.

_____. *Protestantism in the United States: Righteous Empire.* Chicago: University of Chicago Press, 1986.

_____. *The Public Church: Mainline-Evangelical-Catholic.* New York: Crossroad, 1981.

_____. "Religion in America Since Mid-Century." *Daedalus* 111 (Winter 1982): 149-63.

_____. *Righteous Empire: The Protestant Experience in America*. New York: Dial Press, 1970.

_____. "Tensions Within Contemporary Evangelicalism: A Critical Appraisal." In David F. Wells and John D. Woodbridge, eds., *The Evangelicals*. Nashville: Abingdon Press, 1975, pp. 170-88.

Mathews, Donald G. "The Second Great Awakening as an Organizing Process." *American Quarterly* 21 (1969): 23-43.

_____. *Religion in the Old South*. Chicago: University of Chicago Press, 1977.

_____. *Slavery and Methodism: A Chapter in American Morality, 1780-1845*. Princeton: Princeton University Press, 1965.

McDannell, Colleen. *The Christian Home in Victorian America, 1840-1900*. Bloomington: Indiana University Press, 1986.

McDowell, John Patrick. *The Social Gospel in the South: The Woman's Home Mission Movement in the Methodist Episcopal Church, South, 1886-1939*. Baton Rouge: Louisiana State University Press, 1982.

McKivigan, John R. *The War Against Proslavery Religion: Abolitionism and the Northern Churches, 1830-1865*. Ithaca: Cornell University Press, 1984.

McLoughlin, William. *The Meaning of Henry Ward Beecher: An Essay on the Shifting Values of Mid-Victorian America, 1840-1870*. New York: Alfred A. Knopf, 1970.

_____. *Revivals, Awakenings, and Reform: An Essay on Religion and Social Change in America, 1607-1977*. Chicago: University of Chicago Press, 1978.

McPherson, James M. *The Abolitionist Legacy*. Princeton: Princeton University Press, 1975.

Michaelsen, Robert S., and Wade Clark Roof, eds. *Liberal Protestantism: Realities and Possibilities*. New York: Pilgrim Press, 1986.

Miller, Timothy. *Following in His Steps: A Biography of Charles M. Sheldon*. Knoxville: University of Tennessee Press, 1987.

Minus, Paul D. *Walter Rauschenbusch: American Reformer*. New York: Macmillan Publishing Co., 1988.

Moberg, David O. *The Great Reversal: Evangelism and Social Concern*. Philadelphia: J. B. Lippincott, 1972.

Moorehead, James M. "Social Reform and the Divided Conscience of Antebellum Protestantism." *Church History* 48 (December 1979): 416-30.

Morgan, Bruce. "Stephen Colwell: Social Prophet Before the Social Gospel." In Hugh T. Kerr, ed., *Sons of the Prophets: Leaders in Protestantism from*

Princeton Seminary. Princeton: Princeton University Press, 1963, pp. 123-47.

Mouw, Richard J. Review essay. *Calvin Theological Journal* 11 (November 1976): 260-64.

Nelson, Phyllis Ann. "George D. Herron and the Socialist Clergy, 1890-1914." Ann Arbor, Mich.: University Microfilms, 1953.

Oden, Thomas C., ed. *Phoebe Palmer: Selected Writings*. New York: Paulist Press, 1988.

Palmer, Parker J. *The Company of Strangers: Christians and the Renewal of America's Public Life*. New York: Crossroad, 1981.

Prelinger, Catherine M., and Rosemary S. Keller. "The Function of Female Bonding: The Restored Diaconessate of the Nineteenth Century." In Rosemary S. Keller, Louise L. Queen, and Hilah F. Thomas, eds., *Women in New Worlds*. Nashville: Abingdon Press, 1982. 2: 318-37.

Roof, Wade Clark, and William McKinney. *American Mainline Religion: Its Changing Shape and Future*. New Brunswick, N.J.: Rutgers University Press, 1987.

Rosell, Garth M. "Charles G. Finney: His Place in the Stream." In Leonard I. Sweet, ed., *The Evangelical Tradition in America*. Macon, Ga.: Mercer University Press, 1984, pp. 131-47.

Ross, Dorothy. *The Origins of American Social Science*. Cambridge: Cambridge University Press, 1991.

Sandeen, Ernest R. *The Roots of Fundamentalism: British and American Millenarianism, 1800-1930*. Chicago: University of Chicago Press, 1970.

Schmidt, Jean Miller. "Beyond Separate Spheres: Women, Religion, and Social Change." *The Drew Gateway* 57/3 (Fall 1987): 80-94.

_____. "Holiness and Perfection." In Charles H. Lippy and Peter W. Williams, eds., *Encyclopedia of the American Religious Experience*. New York: Charles Scribner's Sons, 1988. 2: 813-29.

_____. "Reexamining the Public/Private Split: Reforming the Continent and Spreading Scriptural Holiness." In Russell E. Richey and Kenneth E. Rowe, eds., *Rethinking Methodist History*. Nashville: Kingswood Books, 1985, pp. 75-88.

Scott, Anne Firor. "On Seeing and Not Seeing: A Case of Historical Invisibility." *Journal of American History* 71/1 (June 1984): 7-21.

Sklar, Kathryn Kish. "The Last Fifteen Years." In Hilah F. Thomas and Rosemary Skinner Keller, eds., *Women in New Worlds*. Nashville: Abingdon Press, 1981, pp. 48-65.

Smith-Rosenberg, Carroll. "Beauty, the Beast and the Militant Woman: Sex Roles and Social Stress in Jacksonian America." *American Quarterly* 23 (October 1971): 562-84.

Sweet, Leonard I. " 'A Nation Born Again': The Union Prayer Meeting Revival and Cultural Revitalization." In Joseph D. Ban and Paul R. Dekar, eds., *In the Great Tradition: In Honor of Winthrop S. Hudson*. Valley Forge, Pa.: Judson Press, 1982, pp. 193-221.

_____. "The Evangelical Tradition in America." In Leonard I. Sweet, ed., *The Evangelical Tradition in America*. Macon, Ga.: Mercer University Press, 1984, pp. 1-84.

Sweet, Leonard I., ed. *The Evangelical Tradition in America*. Macon, Ga.: Mercer University Press, 1984.

Szasz, Ferenc Morton. *The Divided Mind of Protestant America, 1880-1930*. University of Alabama Press, 1982.

Weber, Timothy P. *Living in the Shadow of the Second Coming: American Premillennialism, 1875-1982*. Chicago: University of Chicago Press, 1987.

Welter, Barbara. "The Cult of True Womanhood, 1820-1860." *American Quarterly* 18/2 (Summer 1966).

White, Charles Edward. *The Beauty of Holiness: Phoebe Palmer as Theologian, Revivalist, Feminist, and Humanitarian*. Grand Rapids, Mich.: Francis Asbury Press, 1986.

White, Ronald C., Jr. *Liberty and Justice for All: Racial Reform and the Social Gospel*. San Francisco: Harper & Row, 1990.

_____, and C. Howard Hopkins. *The Social Gospel: Religion and Reform in Changing America*. Philadelphia: Temple University Press, 1976.

Wills, David Wood. "Aspects of Social Thought in the African Methodist Episcopal Church, 1884-1910." Ph.D. dissertation, Harvard University, 1975. See chap. 6, "The Vision of Reverdy C. Ransom."

_____. "Reverdy C. Ransom: The Making of an A.M.E. Bishop," in Randall K. Burkett and Richard Newman, eds., *Black Apostles: Afro-American Clergy Confront the Twentieth Century* (Boston: G. K. Hall, 1978): 181-212.

Wuthnow, Robert. *The Restructuring of American Religion: Society and Faith Since World War II*. Princeton: Princeton University Press, 1988.

_____. *The Struggle for America's Soul: Evangelicals, Liberals, and Secularism*. Grand Rapids, Mich.: William B. Eerdmans Co., 1989.

Index

Chicago Studies in the History of American Religion

Editors

JERALD C. BRAUER & MARTIN E. MARTY

(continued, over)

11. Kountz, Peter. *Thomas Merton as Writer and Monk: A Cultural Study, 1915-1951*
12. Lagerquist, L. DeAne. *In America the Men Milk the Cows: Factors of Gender, Ethnicity, and Religion in the Americanization of Norwegian-American Women*
13. Markwell, Bernard Kent. *The Anglican Left: Radical Social Reformers in the Church of England and the Protestant Episcopal Church, 1846-1954*
14. Morris, William Sparkes. *The Young Jonathan Edwards: A Reconstruction*
15. Pellauer, Mary D. *Toward a Tradition of Feminist Theology: The Religious Social Thought of Elizabeth Cady Stanton, Susan B. Anthony, and Anna Howard Shaw*
16. Potash, P. Jeffrey. *Vermont's Burned-Over District: Patterns of Community Development and Religious Activity, 1761-1850*
17. Queen, Edward L., II. *In the South the Baptists are the Center of Gravity: Southern Baptists and Social Change, 1930-1980*
18. Schmidt, Jean Miller. *Souls or the Social Order: The Two-Party System in American Protestantism*
19. Shaw, Stephen J. *The Catholic Parish as a Way-Station of Ethnicity and Americanization: Chicago's Germans and Italians, 1903-1939*
20. Shepard, Robert S. *God's People in the Ivory Tower: Religion in the Early American University*
21. Snyder, Stephen H. *Lyman Beecher and his Children: The Transformation of a Religious Tradition*

DATE DUE

HIGHSMITH 45-220